Juvenile
Justice
& Youth
Violence

To my mom, Ethel, my dad, J. C.,
my sisters, Annette and Lynda,
my wife Karen, our daughter, Megan,
and adolescents who are victims of philosophical
changes in the administration of juvenile justice.

Juvenile Justice & Youth Violence

James C. Howell

SAGE Publications
International Educational and Professional Publisher
Thousand Oaks   London   New Delhi

For information:

SAGE Publications, Inc.
2455 Teller Road
Thousand Oaks, California 91320
E-mail: order@sagepub.com

SAGE Publications Ltd.
6 Bonhill Street
London EC2A 4PU
United Kingdom

SAGE Publications India Pvt. Ltd.
M-32 Market
Greater Kailash I
New Delhi 110 048 India

Printed in the United States of America

Library of Congress Cataloging-in-Publication Data

Howell, James C.
  Juvenile justice and youth violence/
author, James C. Howell.
    p. cm.
  Includes bibliographical references and index.
  ISBN 0-7619-0373-9 (cloth)
  1. Juvenile justice, Administration of—United States.
  2. Juvenile delinquency—United States. 3. Violent crimes—United
  States. I. Title.
  KF9779.H69 1997
  364.36'0973—dc21   97-4673

This book is printed on acid-free paper

97 98 99 00 01 02 03 10 9 8 7 6 5 4 3 2 1

Acquiring Editor:	C. Terry Hendrix
Editorial Assistant:	Dale Grenfell
Production Editor:	Sherrise M. Purdum
Production Assistant:	Denise Santoyo
Typesetter/Designer:	Danielle Dillahunt
Indexer:	Edwin Durbin
Cover Designer:	Ravi Balasuriya
Print Buyer:	Anna Chin

Contents

PART II

Preface

Part I of this book takes stock of juvenile justice and youth violence in the United States. The first chapter chronicles the origins and evolution of the juvenile justice system, a uniquely American invention. It would be presumptuous of me to expect that my recounting of that intellectual history improves on Finestone's (1976) masterful account in his classic book, *Victims of Change*. No such pretention exists. Rather, I thought it would be useful to put recent developments in the administration of juvenile justice in the United States into a historical context.

The contributions of the federal Juvenile Justice and Delinquency Prevention Act to juvenile justice are reviewed (Chapter 2) against the intellectual history backdrop of the uniquely American juvenile justice system. I hope that my brief summary of historical events aids understanding of the current state of juvenile justice. I also hope that future juvenile justice reformers will benefit in some way from knowledge of recent changes to the juvenile justice system in this country. As Santayana (1948, p. 284) admonished, "Those who can not remember the past are condemned to repeat it."

Chapter 3 is the first of three chapters that provide an analysis of youth violence and the responses of our society to this form of juvenile delinquency. Adult and juvenile contributions to the total volume of violent crime are examined in an attempt to answer the question, Who's to blame for violent crime? Juvenile delinquency trends are then reviewed (Chapter 4) to assess the extent and nature of violent behavior and juvenile justice system responses.

A key premise guiding this assessment is that care must be taken in selecting indicators of increasing juvenile violent behavior versus how society responds to juvenile delinquency. Chapter 5 reviews a major change in the administration of juvenile justice: transfer of adolescents to the criminal justice system and confinement in adult prisons. I assess research on the results of this development.

In Part II of the book, modifications in U.S. delinquency policies are proposed. Part II begins (Chapter 6) with a review of current knowledge of youth gang homicides and drug trafficking. This form of violent youth crime is chosen as a starting point in revising juvenile delinquency policies because gang violence represents a major proportion of juvenile violence. Surprisingly, few gang-related homicides are related to gang drug trafficking. I suggest, therefore, that a clearer understanding of risk factors for youth violence is needed (Chapter 7), and present a methodology for improving our understanding of violence: developmental criminology (Chapter 8). Part II concludes (Chapter 9) with a recommended strategy for dealing with serious, violent, and chronic delinquency.

The conclusions of this book are not suspenseful, though they may come as a surprise to many readers. Part I shows, through a detailed assessment, that the juvenile contributions to violence in the United States are small and that a significant increase has not occurred, except for homicides; most of that increase may be accounted for by youth gangs. Because of a philosophical shift in crime policy, reliance on the wrong information, and misguided perceptions, juvenile crime policies in the United States have taken an unfortunate turn—with deleterious outcomes. Part II demonstrates a major misunderstanding of the most violent delinquency, homicides. A way of achieving a more precise understanding of the evolution of serious and violent juvenile offender careers is offered. A comprehensive strategy is suggested for developing more effective prevention programs, achieving a better match between offender characteristics and treatment programs, and developing a more cost-effective juvenile justice system.

Acknowledgments

I owe a debt of gratitude to a number of good people who helped bring this book to life. At Sage, my Editor, Terry Hendrix, gave me the encouragement I sought to develop this volume. His able assistant, Dale Grenfell, sheparded it along. Sherrise Purdum expertly managed its production, A. J. Sobczak, copy editor for Sage, performed the feat of identifying and helping me resolve discrepancies in references and source material. My research of the literature on serious, violent, chronic juvenile offenders was greatly aided by Phyllis Schultze, Librarian of the Criminal Justice and National Council on Crime and Delinquency collection at Rutgers University. She generously facilitated my access to this wonderful library of juvenile and criminal justice literature. I am also indebted to Barry Krisberg, President, NCCD, for making this invaluable resource available to me. Many of my colleagues helped enormously to improve the manuscript. Discussions with Hunter Hurst, Director of the National Center for Juvenile Justice, gave me a number of ideas for Chapters three and four, which Melissa Sickmund at NCJJ later reviewed carefully and helped me correct a number of interpretative errors. Other NCJJ staff also facilitated access to and helped me understand the enormous collection of statistical information NCJJ has amassed in the National Juvenile Court Data Archive, and in other projects: Howard Snyder, Richard Gable, Melissa Sickmund, and Jeffrey Butts. I am especially indebted to Hunter Hurst, for permitting my extensive use of material NCJJ generated on juvenile delinquency and adult criminality, and juvenile and criminal justice system handling of offenders in the book, *Juvenile Offenders and Victims: A National Report* (Snyder & Sickmund, 1995), and the update of it, *Juvenile Offenders and Victims: 1996 Update on Violence* (Snyder, Sickmund, & Poe-Yamagata, 1996). Howard Snyder and Melissa Sickmund at the NCJJ not only encouraged my use of their outstanding compilation of data and statistical review, but also facilitated my access to data files. I also thank the Illinois Criminal Justice Information Authority, Developmental Research and Programs, Inc., Cambridge University Press, and the National Council on Crime and Delinquency for permission to reprint previously published material. An earlier version of chapter five was published in *Law and Policy* (1996, vol. 18, pp. 17-60, titled "Juvenile Transfers to the Criminal Justice System"). I am grateful to the editors of that volume, Barry Feld and Simon Singer for excellent ideas for improvements. Donna Hamparian, Barry Krisberg, and Elizabeth McNulty also reviewed early drafts and gave me helpful comments and suggestions. I am also indebted to Barry Krisberg and Dominic Del Rosario at NCCD for analyses on serious and violent juvenile offenders in juvenile and adult correctional systems they provided for this chapter. Chapter six is a compilation from two products developed under the support of the National Youth Gang Center in Tallahassee. Bruce Buckley and John Moore at the Center performed thorough reviews of draft products, greatly helping me to improve them. Carolyn Block, Lee Colwell, David Curry, Wes McBride, Cheryl Maxson, Joan Moore, Walter Miller, Jim Short, and Irving

Spergel also provided valuable reviews of my original products for the National Youth Gang Center. Richard Catalano reviewed chapters seven and eight, and was of enormous help with suggestions for their reorganization. He and David Hawkins kindly authorized extensive use of their written material on the Social Development Model (in chapter eight), for which I am grateful. Rolf Loeber also reviewed chapter eight and made many helpful suggestions for improvements. John Wilson, Deputy Administrator, Office of Juvenile Justice and Delinquency Prevention, co-authored with me the Comprehensive Strategy for Serious, Violent, and Chronic Juvenile Offenders. I am indebted to him for his Comprehensive Strategy vision, intellectual stimulation and the pleasure of working with him on it while I was at OJJDP. We enjoyed two decades of challenging work on juvenile justice at OJJDP. He and I are both indebted to Shay Bilchik, Administrator, OJJDP, for facilitating adoption of the Comprehensive Strategy in communities and states across the country. Finally, and most important, I am very grateful to my wife, Karen, and our daughter, Megan, for graciously tolerating extended periods of time I spent at my computer. Karen helped analyze a number of issues with which I wrestled. She also reviewed portions of the manuscript, and politely encouraged me to simplify the material. Despite all this valuable assistance, no doubt there are errors of omission and commission in this book. For these, I accept full responsibility.

JAMES C. HOWELL
Herndon, Virginia
April, 1997

Part I

The background of the juvenile justice system is summarized in the first chapter in this part. This discussion is followed in Chapter 2 by an intellectual history of federal legislation that created the Office of Juvenile Justice and Delinquency Prevention, the first major federal office charged with preventing and reducing juvenile delinquency. Chapter 3 focuses on the total volume of violent crime in the United States and recent increases, to assess who is to blame. Juvenile delinquency and violence trends are then discussed in Chapter 4. The final chapter in Part I reviews the main product of the current juvenile justice reform movement: transfer of juveniles to the criminal justice system.

Juvenile Reform Movements

Four major reform movements have given rise to and shaped the juvenile justice system in the United States. The first movement resulted in the establishment of institutions for juveniles, removing them from confinement in prisons with adults. Creation of the juvenile court at the end of the 19th century represents the second reform movement. The third flourished in the mid-20th century with the development of alternatives to both institutions and juvenile courts. The current and fourth reform movement replicates, in large part, the first one. Its advocates urge increased use of confinement and returning serious juvenile offenders to adult prisons.

The First Juvenile Justice Reform Movement: Moralists

Before the 1800s, the United States had no juvenile justice system. Criminal cases involving children and adolescents were handled in criminal courts. Three events led to the creation of correctional institutions specifically for wayward children and juvenile delinquents: the emergence of "pauperism," the development of prisons, and the work of "gentleman reformers."

Pauperism

In the opening decades of the 19th century, New England was suffering the unexpected social consequences of the Industrial Revolution. From 1790 to 1830, the New York state population increased fivefold (Rothman, 1971, p. 57).

Rapid immigration into the major eastern cities (particularly Boston, New York City, and Philadelphia) in the early 1800s disrupted the social order. Small, relatively self-contained communities and the agrarian way of life, in which the family was able to control its offspring, gave way to urbanization. The previous orderly society was no more. Ambitious strangers were everywhere, competing for wealth, status, and power. Urbanization was a destructive force that undermined sources of morality and left individuals rudderless (Finestone, 1976, pp. 3-7).

Arrival of Irish immigrants exacerbated social problems. Their sheer numbers and their impoverishment created stress in making the transition in the new country. Virtually destitute, rife with illnesses, and unemployed, many became homeless and resorted to begging and stealing. Family solidarity was destroyed. According to Finestone (1976, p. 4), "Juvenile delinquency slipped out of the hands of the family and the church and became a manifest public problem."

White Anglo-Saxon Protestants (WASPs) were offended by the arrival of non-Protestants. The large waves of Irish immigrants produced ethnic and religious tensions. Feeling that their way of life was threatened by increasing numbers of poor, destitute, and apparently idle people, these WASP moralists defined the enemy as "pauperism" and came to perceive pauperism and crime in terms of the Irish stereotype: "slatterns and drunken hell-raisers" (Pickett, 1969, p. 16). The upper- and upper-middle-class Protestants feared that paupers might be a source of violence and anarchy such as

3

France had seen during the French Revolution (Finestone, 1976, p. 19). Their fears were bolstered by the breakdown of colonial controls on society. As Pickett (1969) describes conditions,

> Young ruffians ran in gangs through the streets, and watchmen found hungry urchins asleep under doorsteps. Beggars and cutpurses jostled the wealthy on busy thoroughfares. It had been less than fifty years since the supposedly perfect nation had been devised, but the noble plans of the forefathers already seemed in jeopardy. (pp. xviii-xix)

Prisons

The use of prisons to punish juveniles and adults is an invention of the United States and France, a product of the French and American revolutions (Cressey, 1973, pp. 119-124; McKelvey, 1968). In both countries, revolutionaries who suffered from the tyranny of despots decided that loss of freedom was sufficient punishment. Quakers in New England had not forgotten the persecutions they suffered at the hands of English rule in the Massachusetts Bay Colony in the mid-1600s (Erikson, 1966) or the "Salem witchcraft outbreak" in 1692 (Starkley, 1949). In that era, Puritans were punished for questionable and minor offenses by the "burning ugly brands into their flesh, turning them out into the wilderness, shaming them in the stocks and pillory, flogging them with a heavy hand, severing their ears and mutilating their noses, and sometimes even hanging them from the gallows" (Erikson, 1966, pp. 187-188).

Thus, the Quakers and other reformers were quick to choose imprisonment over physical punishment for crime. The leading advocate of this new concept was William Penn, who developed a criminal code, adopted as the "Great Law of Pennsylvania" by the Colony in 1682 (Cressey, 1973, p. 120). Penn's code ended bloody tortures and decreed that crimes were to be punished by imprisonment, substituting confinement for public torture, as was common practice in the colonies. The colonies' leaders, however, were not sure that mere deprivation of liberty was sufficiently painful. Hard labor therefore was substituted for capital punishment in Pennsylvania's 1776 constitution. "The law was enforced by organizing convicts into chain gangs, tethering them on the streets like cattle. The result was degradation and misery"

(Cressey, 1973, p. 120). There was opposition to this practice, and it was soon abandoned. Rather, some inmates "were forced to perform tasks such as carrying a cannon ball back and forth along a corridor, walking treadmills, turning cranks, and smashing boulders with mauls and sledge hammers" (Cressey, 1973, p. 121).

Subsequent development of the prison innovation in the United States (Cressey, 1973, pp. 119-128; Erikson, 1966, pp. 199-205) centered on the essence of imprisonment. Two contrasting punishment philosophies emerged, one in Philadelphia and the other in Auburn, New York. Eastern State Penitentiary in Philadelphia, opened in 1829, was a product of Quaker thinking and planning. Its philosophy emphasized penitence and solitude. Reformation required separation of inmates from evil influences, putting them in positions where the "better nature could begin to assert itself" (Erikson, 1966, p. 201). Later, innovators decided the criminal's degree of freedom should be severely limited by pressing the prison walls against him. Each prisoner was locked alone in a tiny cell. Interaction with others was minimized. In the Western State Penitentiary at Pittsburgh, opened in 1836, a similar "separate and silent" system was adopted. Prisoners were not required to work and confinement was solitary, in almost complete isolation. "They went crazy" (Cressey, 1973, p. 19).

The alternative philosophy was implemented slowly in New York's Auburn prison, opened in 1820, and came to be called the "congregate system," under which cells were used only at night. During the day, prisoners worked in shops and tightly controlled groups, even outside the prison. Erikson (1966) describes conditions:

> The keynote was discipline: the men were assembled in long grey ranks, forbidden to speak to one another, forced to work as slaves, and subject to constant harassment from the guards—all of which mirrored the Puritan conviction that a reprobate spirit must be broken to the routines of a useful life because it cannot be truly redeemed. (pp. 201-202)

Prison labor, used to manufacture products and in farming, produced enough revenue to cover most prison expenses.

Competition developed between the two models as visitors came from all over the world to visit the respective prisons. Whereas the Philadelphia model claimed to be more humane, to be less costly, and to provide a setting "in which man's natural grace could emerge," the Auburn congregate system "offered a setting in which his inherent wickedness could at least be curbed and bent to the needs of society" (Erikson, 1966, p. 202). The results of the rivalry can be seen in prison systems throughout the world. Almost every maximum security system in the United States is patterned after the Auburn model. Europe adopted the Philadelphia model.

The Auburn congregate model was superseded in the late 1800s by the "Elmira system," developed in New York's Elmira Reformatory (1876). Educational programs were added in a prison school, administered in conjunction with indeterminate sentences. The latter was governed by a "mark system" under which inmates could earn release and parole by accumulating credits. Although this practice generally has been abandoned, the practice of requiring labor of inmates has not been discontinued. Labor for the generation of prison income became the goal. Cressey (1973, p. 123) concludes that "prisons have not changed much, really, in the hundred years since Elmira was conceived. . . . Various ineffective rehabilitation programs have been added, along with public relations departments that puff them up."

Europe adopted the Pennsylvania solitary confinement system. As late as the beginning of the 20th century, between 2,000 and 3,000 children under the age of 16 were imprisoned annually in England (Burt, 1925, p. 105). Burt also reported that "less than a century ago, they were not only forced to await their trial in the common jail, but were liable to be sentenced to death . . . for petty offenses that to-day would hardly be thought to warrant a fine" (p. 105). Although the Crown had become more civilized of late, Burt tells of one case "of a boy of eight, who . . . had set fire to a barn; and, being convicted of a felony, was duly hanged," and that "so late as 1833 a boy of nine was sentenced to death, though not executed, for stealing twopenny-worth of paint" (p. 105). Fortunately, in 1908 such measures were abolished by the Children Act, which prohibited imprisoning children under the age of 14. Burt suggested that "it would be well if, by future legislation, an age yet higher might be fixed" (p. 106). England's first reformatory school—a school for girls—was opened at Bristol in 1854, after enactment of the first Reformatory School Act (p. 111).

In 1909, the first English Borstal was created, at the prison near the village of Borstal, which was converted into a fresh type of penal institution, a halfway house between a prison and a reformatory. Key features of the Borstal were "segregation of the 'juvenile adult' from the adult fully grown," strong emphasis on "physical and industrial training, and upon after-care" (Burt, 1925, p. 235). Juvenile Colonies also were established, patterned after the American George Junior Republic. England had Bridewells since 1555. These were the first institutions specifically designed to control adolescent beggars and vagrants (Krisberg & Austin, 1993, pp. 9-10).

Krisberg and Austin (1993, pp. 10-15; see also Starkley, 1949) detail the treatment wayward children and adolescents received in the New World. Children previously held in the overcrowded Bridewells were brought to the Americas as indentured servants. In 1619, the Virginia Colony contracted for the shipment of orphans and destitute children from England. A large proportion of slaves were children, many of them African. Punishment was harsh. Children in the Massachusetts Bay Colony could be put to death for cursing or "smiting" their natural father or mother. Children of poor families could be "bound out" as indentured servants. Compulsory apprenticeships were used as a norm of social control for youths perceived as troublesome. Child labor in industries supplanted the apprenticeship system.

Prisons were first viewed as a humane alternative to barbaric public beating and torture of adult criminals and juvenile delinquents (Aichorn, 1939). Reformers in early 19th century America believed that the criminal class could be saved through the application of reason, equity, and humane treatment (Rothman, 1971, pp. 60-61). Thus, penitentiaries were erected for adults, along with Houses of Refuge and asylums for children. Presumably, jails and detention centers were created at about the same time, although the historical record is silent or vague in these areas (Mattick, 1974, p. 782). Institutions were seen as the panacea for treatment and control of deviants (Bremner, 1970, p. 104). Although reformers wanted to develop specialized correctional institutions for children and adolescents, it does not appear that they intended that prisons be used to warehouse juveniles. In choosing to use prisons and reformatories to punish and correct juvenile delinquents,

> Americans took a step that was to leave an indelible imprint on the future treatment of children and adults in trouble and to change irrevocably the search for community solutions to deviant behavior that had characterized the social order of colonial society. . . . It was a social invention of profound significance. (Empey, 1978, p. 81)

The precedent for institutions for children originated in 16th century European and French religious reform movements. These reformers changed the public perception of children from that of "miniature adults" to immature persons whose moral and mental capacities were not fully formed. The solution was provision of boarding schools in which rigid regimens would help develop the mental and moral capacities of the child (Aries, 1962).

There is no record of the numbers of youths confined in adult prisons in this country during either the colonial era or the period of the Industrial Revolution. In fact, a complete current count is not available to this day. As appalling as this is, the reality is that this country inherited from England and other European countries a disregard for children. "Childhood" was not discovered until much later (Empey, 1978). "Adolescence" was not yet understood. It was not until the next reform movement, in which the juvenile court was created near the beginning of the 20th century, that these terms were developed and used in delinquency prevention and control policies.

Gentleman Reformers

Eastern society in the early 1800s was led by a group of moralist advocates whom Finestone (1976, p. 18) calls "gentleman reformers." They were largely white Anglo-Saxon Protestants (although quite a few were Quakers), middle- and upper-class, cosmopolitan men who kept up with reforms elsewhere, including abroad. They were a very active group of amateur, but diligent and highly dedicated, individuals. Guided by the 18th century Enlightenment, they were imbued with humanitarian idealism, moralism, and rationalism. They

sought to turn back the clock, to deny urbanization.

Having concluded that pauperism (poverty) undermined their dream society, the gentleman reformers set out to eliminate its effects. Their initial efforts targeted wayward children. They grouped together in voluntary associations and promoted reforms that would neutralize urbanization's consequences. Something was needed in the large cities, because continuation of the colonial practice of placing unruly or neglected children in the home of a neighbor became impractical in expanding urban areas such as New York, Boston, and Philadelphia. A meeting was convened in 1817 to consider cures for pauperism and crime. This meeting led to formation of the Society for the Prevention of Pauperism in New York City. The society was appalled to find children confined with thieves, prostitutes, and lunatics in unsanitary quarters (Dean & Reppucci, 1974, p. 866). In 1822, it called public attention to the corruption of children by locking them up with adult criminals. The society called for the rescue of children from a future of crime and degradation. In 1823, it reconstituted itself as the Society for the Reformation of Juvenile Delinquents, as juveniles became its target for reform (Finestone, 1976, p. 22). No doubt, this decision was influenced by an 1822 report to the Society for the Prevention of Pauperism that said,

> It is with pain that we state that, in five or six years past, and until the last few months, the number of youth under fourteen years of age charged with offenses against the law has doubled; and that the same boys are again and again brought up for examination, some of whom are committed, and some tried; and that imprisonment by its frequency renders them hardened and fearless. (cited in Hawes, 1971, p. 29)

In the view of the gentleman reformers, wayward youth were a product of their bad environment and the failure of the family. Armed with the idealism of the Enlightenment, the gentleman reformers believed that delinquents and other deviants could be helped by exposing them to a good environment, provided that one could get to them early enough, before criminal influences got to them. They were influenced by Locke's *tabula rasa* doctrine that children's minds were shaped entirely by their early experiences, rather than being predetermined (Finestone, 1976, pp. 20-21).

Houses of Refuge

The gentleman reformers created the New York House of Refuge in 1825. Because an unstable environment was corrupting, they felt that children needed to be placed in a controlled environment, in a "refuge," a shelter, where they could be inculcated with the "appropriate morality" (Finestone, 1976, p. 5). "Their general purpose was to save children from lives of crime by inculcating them with middle-class values—neatness, diligence, punctuality, and thrift" (Mennel, 1973, p. 18). They offered food, clothing, shelter, and education to homeless and destitute children while removing juvenile offenders from prisons (Fox, 1970, pp. 1188-1189). Emphasis was placed on work, education, and morality. Reformation was encouraged by a complex system of rewards and punishments. The aim was to create small models for the reformers' ideal society. Rescuing children from the destructive forces in a rapidly changing society was considered a benevolent act. "So certain were its founders of the righteousness of their mission that they showed little concern with the niceties of the civil rights of the children they institutionalized; admissions included homeless children and convicted juvenile offenders indiscriminately" (Finestone, 1976, p. 6).

The reformers were aware of the failure of prisons to correct adults, which Finestone (1976) believes partly explains, ironically, their enthusiasm for juvenile institutions. "The hope was always there that measures that had failed with adults might prove to be effective with children" because children were believed to be more malleable (p. 24). There were other reasons reformers favored incarceration for juveniles. They were perturbed by the apparent leniency of criminal court judges toward deviant youth. They objected to housing juveniles with adult criminals. Perhaps more important, they were alarmed over a large increase in offenses among young offenders. Finally, they were enticed by the idea of specialized correctional institutions for young offenders because they had begun to erect an array of institutions: "penitentiaries for the criminal, asylums for the insane, almshouses for the poor, and orphan asylums for homeless children . . ." (Rothman, 1971, p. xiii).

The concept of reformatories for delinquents caught on. Houses of Refuge were built by private philanthropists in New York City in 1825, in Philadelphia in 1828, by the Boston City Council in 1825, and subsequently in other cities. They became family substitutes, "not only for the less serious juvenile, but for other children who were defined as a problem—the runaway, the disobedient or defiant child, or the vagrant who was in danger of falling prey to loose women, taverns, gambling halls, or theaters" (Empey, 1978, p. 82). Only those who could still be rescued could be sent to the House by the courts—children who were prematurely corrupted and corrupting. Major juvenile offenders were left in the adult criminal system (Fox, 1970, pp. 1190-1191). Dependent, neglected, and delinquent children were housed together, a practice that lingers in most juvenile detention facilities today (Krisberg & Austin, 1993, p. 17). These institutions were patterned after the Auburn congregate model and the Elmira Reformatory for adults. A congregate structure was implemented that mixed education and income-generating labor. Soon, the juvenile facilities were called reform schools. When this name became objectionable, the school idea was given prominence, and they came to be called industrial or training schools (Dean & Reppucci, 1974, p. 867).

It did not occur to reformers that they might infringe on the rights or best interests of the children they tried to save with the Houses of Refuge. For the most part, clients were predelinquents, guilty of little more than being poor and neglected. There were no notices of charges or jury trial. The Supreme Court (*Ex parte Crouse*, 4 Whart. 9, 1838) allowed state commitment of a juvenile to an institution without due process rights, upholding the House of Refuge practice. The *Crouse* court also elaborated the *parens patriae* concept, providing the legal basis for the extended powers of the future juvenile court.

Parens patriae (part of the country) originated in British doctrine, referring to the right of the king (state) to provide protection for any persons who did not possess full legal capacity, including insane and incompetent persons. The jurisdiction of English chancery courts was extended to abused, dependent, and neglected children. In the United States, the *parens patriae* concept was expanded to include delinquent children.

Institutionalization of Reform Schools

Despite an enormous amount of criticism (Finestone, 1976, pp. 29-30; Krisberg & Austin, 1993, pp. 17-21) and little evidence of success, Houses of Refuge survived; indeed, they thrived for a time. The New York City House of Refuge grew to consist of several massive buildings and housed 1,000 children by the mid-1800s (Fox, 1970, p. 1208). Practices inside the Houses of Refuge did not match the benevolence with which they were founded (Krisberg & Austin, pp. 18-21). First, children of immigrants made up the majority of inmates. Middle- and upper-class whites were hostile toward Irish immigrants and viewed their parents to be corrupt and unsuitable for parenting. Second, routines were enforced by corporal punishment, solitary confinement, whipping, and other physical punishments (Devoe, 1848). Third, the children were required to labor in large workshops, producing shoes, nails, and chairs. Fourth, they were committed to the refuge houses for indeterminate periods and could generally obtain release only by reaching age of majority, through an apprenticeship, or escaping. Few were declared to be "reformed" and released. Despite these problems, the enthusiasm of the gentleman reformers for Houses of Refuge was not dampened. They argued that the idea only needed further perfection. Public relations efforts helped lead to a rapid proliferation of similar institutions across the country (Rothman, 1971).

The House of Refuge concept "phased over into that of the reformatory as the 19th century progressed" (Finestone, 1976, p. 30). Sustaining support came from reformers who were highly critical of penitentiaries. This development renewed reformers' interest in correctional facilities for young offenders. They also saw a role for juvenile reform schools in the larger correctional apparatus, as a first resort within the evolving correctional system (Finestone, 1976, pp. 19-30).

Massachusetts built the first state-supported institutions for juveniles: the Lyman School for Boys in Westborough in 1847 and the School for Girls in Lancaster in 1854. These reform schools were modeled after the earlier Houses of Refuge, European boarding schools, and

Sunday schools that provided moral and academic instruction, as well as the adult prisons in Elmira, New York, and to a lesser extent, those in Pennsylvania and Massachusetts (Miller & Ohlin, 1985, pp. 13-14). The Chicago Reform School was established in 1856. It received boys convicted of any noncapital offense, including juveniles convicted in criminal courts. It differed from the House of Refuge, however, in other respects. Emphasis was placed on small facilities. Children were to be protected, not punished for their misdeeds. Emphasis was placed on creating a family life for children (Fox, 1970, pp. 1207-1213). By the middle of the 19th century, establishment of correctional institutions for poor, wayward, and delinquent youth was well entrenched.

Throughout the 19th century, juvenile reform schools witnessed repeated scandals, overcrowding, abusive discipline, subsequent reforms, and renewed regimentation (Bremner, 1970; Hawes, 1971; Holl, 1971; Mennel, 1973; Pickett, 1969; Platt, 1969; Schlossman, 1977). Variations emerged in the 1850s and 1860s, consisting of family-style cottages in rural settings that resembled school campuses, patterned after the Elmira, New York, reformatory for adults. These too were characterized by extreme disciplinary measures, excessive regimentation, and overcrowding. Although treatment was the professed goal, the custodial character of juvenile institutions prevailed, dominated by maintenance of order and discipline as preconditions for treatment (Miller & Ohlin, 1985, p. 14). In some instances, overcrowding was relieved by transferring older boys to reformatories in other states that provided vocational training (Mennel, 1973).

Juvenile reform schools did not become what the reformers envisaged (Finestone, 1976, pp. 29-32; Krisberg & Austin, 1993, pp. 23-26). Rather than an institution of first resort, juvenile reformatories became an institution of last resort. Their metamorphosis turned them into prisons, providing custody rather than treatment. Gradually, they became acceptable as the choice place for confinement of lower-class and minority youths. In about 1860, state and municipal governments began taking over their administration. By 1876, there were 51 refuges or reform schools in the United States. Problems persisted and grew. Repeated violence in the reformatories became public knowledge. A series of investigations was conducted (Wines,

1880/1970) that produced further efforts to improve juvenile reform schools. Boards of State Charity were established to inspect reform schools and recommend improvements (Krisberg & Austin, 1993, pp. 25-26). Several changes were attempted, including transferring youngsters to more decent facilities and selecting the more "hardened offenders" for specialized facilities such as the Elmira Reformatory.

Both large reform schools and cottage systems with centralized academic or vocational education facilities were relied on by the states to house delinquents, status offenders, and nonoffenders into the 20th century. After World War II, small group homes, housing from 12 to 20 youth, were used as a residential alternative for part of the reformatory population. These were followed by small forestry camps for youth, modeled after those created by the California Youth Authority (Breed, 1953). These developments did not do much to relieve overcrowding of juvenile reform schools or improve programming within them.

The Second Reform Movement: The Progressives

A new era of reformers critiqued juvenile reformatories and led the search for alternative ways of addressing the juvenile delinquency problem. Two groups of "progressives" dominated reform efforts during the period 1850-1920, one on the East Coast and the other in Chicago.

East Coast "Charity Workers"

The first group of "progressives" was led by a new group of East Coast reformers that Finestone (1976, p. 33) called "charity workers." Critics of the Houses of Refuge, they were a new breed of upper-class pragmatic philanthropists who made social reform their vocation. Despite having come from conservative backgrounds, once they became familiar with the poverty issue, they became liberal reformers. More optimistic than the gentleman reformers about the possibilities of reforming youth, they objected that these institutions did not reach enough children. Moreover, they preferred family life to institutions for generating moral reform (Krisberg & Austin, 1993). The East Coast charity workers felt challenged to overcome the deleterious effects of urbanization. Their main

target was the individual, and their strategic approach required getting to the individual early, before the harmful effects of the urban environment could take hold (Finestone, 1976, p. 35).

The charity workers, who later called themselves "social workers," created the Five Points Mission (1850), the New York Juvenile Asylum (1851), and the Children's Aid Society (1853). One of their leaders was Charles Loring Brace, founder of the New York Children's Aid Society. He initially sought to reform children by removing homeless youth from the poverty-ridden slums of New York City and relocating them with foster families out West (Brace, 1872/1967; Langsam, 1964). Brace called his remedy "placing out." In addition to alleviating the vagrancy problem, Brace expected to demonstrate the effectiveness of foster homes as an alternative to institutions. Good Christian homes in the country were advertised for dependent and neglected children. Labor was performed by the children in exchange for room, board, religious training, and education. They were visited by an official of the Society within a few months to determine whether or not the child should remain there. Subsequent contacts were made periodically by mail or personal visits. Over the next 40 years, nearly 100,000 children were placed across the country (Brace, 1872/1967; Langsam, 1964).

Out-of-state placement of children was called into question because of due process and equal protection issues associated with the involuntary nature of the practice, although many youths were placed by their relatives (often with other relatives). Concerns also were raised regarding abuse, indentured servitude, substandard facilities, undesirable foster homes, and the likelihood of higher rates of delinquency and vagrancy in the receiving states (Hall, Barker, Parkhill, Pilotta, & White, 1982, pp. 1-3). Once this practice drew strong criticism, Brace became reconciled to training children for life in the urban environment. To assist the children, he created a variety of schools, lodging houses, and other special programs, all emphasizing the role of the family, in sharp contrast to the distrust that gentleman reformers had of poor families. His mantra was "The family is God's reformatory" (quoted in Finestone, 1976, p. 33).

Brace became the first notable critic of the use of institutions to reform juvenile delinquents. He was convinced that large institutions, like the New York House of Refuge, "by virtue of their size, severe discipline, and inflexible routine, eliminated individuality and personal responsibility, converting the inmates into machinelike creatures who were unfit to do well outside the institution" (Finestone, 1976, p. 34). He was joined by another charity worker, Homer Folks, the head of the Children's Aid Society of Pennsylvania, who devoted his career to developing alternatives to institutions for impoverished families and their children (Mennel, 1973, p. 112). Folks "viewed the environment as primarily social, as composed of parents, peer groups, and the individual's view of himself" (Finestone, 1976, p. 34). His main concerns were the child's parents, protecting their relationship with their creations, and ensuring the integrity of the child. Thus, methods of working with the child in his or her own environment without diminishing parental responsibility were preferred over institutionalization. Folks even devised a program for supervision of children who had been convicted by criminal courts, providing an alternative to their imprisonment (Finestone, 1976, p. 35). Like Brace, Folks focused his efforts on saving the individual.

Chicago Progressive Reformers

In contrast to the East Coast charity workers, the Chicago progressive reformers of the late 19th and early 20th centuries accepted the reality of urbanization and its destructiveness. Instead of attempting to neutralize urbanization's effects by preparing individuals for it, they sought to humanize it "through a broadly conceived program of social engineering based upon empirical inquiry and the principles of the social and psychological sciences" (Finestone, 1976, p. 7). The Chicago progressive reformers saw social conditions, rather than the individual, as the target for change. Their strategy called for changing the neighborhood by improving social conditions. They were buoyed by the social optimism of the late 1800s, the growth of Chicago, and a new kind of social thought that humanitarian values could be incorporated into social institutions (Finestone, 1976, p. 41).

Jane Addams was one of the most influential leaders among the Chicago progressive reformers. She was one of several upper-middle-class advocates who had achieved success with the growth of Chicago. Addams and others (Julia Lathrop and Lucy Flower) formed a fellowship that was bound together by the same reform interests: the child and his or her family. They viewed juvenile delinquency and youth problems from a social-psychological perspective, and they saw aberrant youth behavior as a response to urban changes, poverty, culture conflict, and lower-class origin. They established settlement houses, therefore, that targeted the neighborhood for change. Unlike the gentleman reformers, workers in the settlement houses did not view the poor with disdain. Rather, they knew them as fellow human beings who were victims of dissolution of social institutions as a consequence of urbanization (Finestone, 1976, pp. 42-43).

In the meantime, efforts to make juvenile reform schools an effective instrument for dealing with juvenile delinquency did not appear to be succeeding, despite continuing optimism. Several innovations were introduced in the late 1800s (Krisberg & Austin, 1993, pp. 27-28), including physical exercise training, military-like drills, nutritional regimens, inmate self-government, and privately financed systems. Less socially acceptable innovations were attempted in the South. A convict lease system replaced the prisons destroyed by the Civil War. Convicts, including juveniles, were leased to private industry in a forced labor system. This system eventually was replaced by public chain gangs. None of these innovations served to increase acceptance of incarceration as an effective method for preventing or reducing delinquency.

Homer Folks's assessment of major problems with reformatories in the late 1800s seemed valid to the progressives: They tempted parents to throw off their sacred responsibilities, they provided a "contaminating influence of association, an enduring stigma resulted from having been committed, it was impossible to study and treat each child individually in the institutional environment, and the institution created a life greatly dissimilar from life outside" (Mennel, 1973, p. 111). Several court decisions questioned the lack of procedural safeguards and the quasi-penal character of juvenile institutions, including *The People v. Turner* (1870), *State v. Ray* (1886), and *Ex parte Becknell* (1897). See Empey and Stafford (1991) and Ketcham and Paulsen (1967) for these and other pertinent cases.

Creation of the Juvenile Court

By the end of the 19th century, public policy in response to the juvenile delinquency problem reached a turning point. Several reforms had been tried. Progressive reformers on the East Coast and in Chicago shared a common perspective, the importance of focusing on the environment as a means of combating delinquency. Despite the fact that the two groups chose different priorities (individual versus community change) to achieve their aims, it was their emphasis on the importance of taking into account the individual in his or her family and community setting that gave rise to the concept of the juvenile court. This ethos, or distinctive outlook, embodied in the work of the two progressive reform groups provided the foundation for the juvenile court (Finestone, 1976, pp. 39, 43).

Both East Coast and Chicago progressive reformers concluded that juvenile correctional institutions seemed inappropriate for remediation of delinquency because they did not take into account the environment, specifically its community locus. The Chicago progressive reformers in particular came to see adolescence as a cleavage between parents and children that was an inevitable development in the city. In the urban environment, parents were no longer able to exert traditional familial authority over their children. The Chicago progressives saw not only that poor families needed help in providing moral guidance to their children but also that other institutions needed to be structured in a way that would be beneficial, rather than harmful, to children and adolescents. They campaigned, therefore, for compulsory schooling and the abolition of child labor. Moreover, they saw that a different instrument of social change was needed for the task of dealing with juvenile delinquency.

There was yet another important basis for progressive reformers' views. They came to adopt a different view of children and of childhood, one that began to emerge following the Middle Ages (500 to 1400; Empey & Stafford, 1991, pp. 21-30). Until then, children were either discarded, ignored, or exploited. It was not uncommon in the ancient civilizations of the Middle East, and in Greece, Rome, and Europe, to "throw children away." Infanticide appears to have been practiced as late as the 17th century in France and England (Illick, 1974). DeMause (1974, p. 25) reports that the age-old practice of killing illegitimate children continued into the 19th century. Practices adopted by the wealthy, such as using wet nurses and swaddling, resulted in high infant mortality rates (Empey & Stafford, 1991, p. 23). Children were sometimes used as sex objects. Roman men preferred castrated boys (DeMause, 1974, p. 46). Apprenticeship rather than formal education was the main method of educating children, preparing them for adult roles, although it is not clear whether children were viewed primarily as apprentices or as servants (Gillis, 1974).

The modern view of childhood began to emerge during the colonial period, despite the fact that older traditions continued to carry weight (Empey & Stafford, 1991, p. 27). Children typically "were viewed as sources of labor and service, not as fragile, undeveloped beings requiring long periods of special care and freedom from responsibility" (Empey & Stafford, 1991, p. 28). A new concept of childhood slowly emerged from its roots in the views of 15th- to 17th-century reformers, who insisted that newer standards of morality for children be enforced. These were embodied in treatises and manuals written in the 17th and 18th centuries to guide parents. Standards by which parents were judged included proper supervision, disciplining rather than pampering, modesty in moral considerations, parental diligence, and obedience of children to authority (Empey & Stafford, 1991, p. 36). Signs of these principles were evident in the work of the gentleman reformers in the early 1800s.

Other standards pertaining to childhood were developed in the late 19th and early 20th centuries, including nurturance rights, educational rights, and distinctive legal rights (Empey & Stafford, 1991, pp. 56-58). Rights to life, food, clothing, and shelter were bestowed on children. Formal education replaced the apprenticeship system. Child labor laws soon were enacted. The distinctive legal rights of children emanated from English medieval doctrine giving the crown the right to intervene in family matters on behalf of children to protect property rights of the young. Due process rights did not apply to them in the same manner as to adults because adults needed protection from unreasonable and arbitrary actions. Rather, legal authorities would need broad discretionary powers "to inquire into the most private of family and personal matters, to protect children's dependent and unequal status. If children were to be properly raised, and their nurturance rights ensured, the state required legal means— part criminal and part civil—to make this possible" (Empey & Stafford, 1991, p. 57). For this humanitarian perspective, the progressive reformers came to be labeled negatively as "child savers" (Platt, 1969).

Some states already had begun holding separate court hearings for children, as early as 1870 in Suffolk County, Massachusetts, and 1877 in New York (Bremner, 1970, vol. 2, pp. 485-501). Indiana and Rhode Island quickly followed suit (Sussman & Baum, 1969). The juvenile court thus evolved on parallel tracks in the Northeast and Midwest. In the meantime, the probation function was created—later to be incorporated into the emerging juvenile and criminal justice systems. John Augustus, the father of probation, was its ingenious originator by virtue of having bailed a Boston drunkard out of jail in 1841, with the court's permission to provide for him while engaging in reformation efforts. Augustus also took in juveniles. He bailed them out of jail and worked with them, with the agreement of the court that their cases would be continued "as a season of probation." Five or 6 months later, Augustus would bring the boys into court at one time. "The judge expressed much pleasure as well as surprise, at their appearance, and remarked, that the object of law had been accomplished and expressed his cordial approval of my plan to save and reform" (Augustus, quoted in Moreland, 1941, p. 5).

Childhood principles were crystallized by the progressive reformers in their creation of the juvenile court. They viewed it as serving broader purposes than the criminal court. The juvenile court was expected to raise the standards of child rearing and ensure that children were not exploited or maltreated. This responsibility included monitoring families and schools, the main institutions charged with rearing children. If they failed, the juvenile court would assume the parental role (Empey & Stafford, 1991, p. 64). Simultaneously, the court was expected to apply scientific knowledge in curing the emotional ills of children and contribute to the prevention of delinquency by

serving as a catchment for children of poor, uncaring parents (Schlossman, 1977, pp. 57-63). The juvenile court was expected to advance the emerging conception of childhood by enforcing new laws pertaining to child care and the behavior of children embodied in the new concept of childhood.

The Chicago Women's Club was instrumental in officially creating the first juvenile court. In the late 1800s it worked to improve the criminal justice system and the conditions in jails. Finding its efforts in these areas inadequate, and as a result of the influence of Addams and other reformers, the Women's Club turned its reformist zeal to improving the conditions in which children were confined. Its members came up with the idea of establishing a special court and separate correctional procedures for children (Krisberg & Austin, 1993, p. 29). The Women's Club believed that a separate juvenile court could be an effective instrument for the advancement of youth welfare, that it could succeed where institutions had failed. Thus, its members saw the juvenile court as "the cornerstone of a comprehensive child care system" (Finestone, 1976, p. 45).

Supported by other philanthropic groups, such as the Chicago Bar Association, the Chicago Women's Club drafted a bill creating a juvenile court. The Illinois Juvenile Court Act was passed by the Illinois legislature in 1899 (Ill. Laws, 1899, 131-137). As envisaged in the new statute, the juvenile court was to represent a radical departure in the treatment of the delinquent. It was to treat wayward youth first as children, and second as offenders. It was to approximate the manner in which benevolent parents would deal with their offspring, in a caring but firm manner. The criminal court experience focused on the offense was transformed in the Illinois Act into a judicial setting focused instead on the offender functioning through the medium of personal relationships. Adjudication proceedings involved a hearing in which the judge explored the child's problem with the child, his family and friends, and the probation officer.

The juvenile court established a tradition of paying much less attention to the criminal act itself, instead looking at general circumstances lying behind the offender's misconduct. The goal was to identify the cause of the behavior and then administer the appropriate rehabilitative measures. For disturbed children who were the victims of faulty socialization, the court developed a rehabilitative/treatment model of justice. In the more serious cases, the juvenile court relied on more punitive measures to pursue the overall goal of remediating delinquent behavior (Maloney, Romig, & Armstrong, 1988, p. 47).

"Acting in the best interests of the child" was the predominant theme of the juvenile court movement; therefore, "no reason existed to formulate legal regularities of defendant rights, due process, and constitutional safeguards that marked the adult judicial process" (Maloney et al., 1988, p. 48). Law violations by juveniles were not viewed in the same way as those by adults. Juvenile misbehaviors were not to be held against them in later life. The mission of the court was to guide juvenile delinquents toward responsible and productive adulthood, not punish them (National Center for Juvenile Justice, 1991, p. 8).

The Illinois statute did not authorize incarceration of juveniles in adult prisons. It provided that children over 10 years of age could be committed to the state reformatory (sec. 9) and that children under 12 years of age could not be committed to a jail or police station (sec. 11). The statute further provided that

> when any child shall be sentenced to confinement in any institution to which adult convicts are sentenced it shall be unlawful to confine such child in the same building with such adult convicts, or to confine such child in the same yard or enclosure with such adult convicts, or to bring such child into any yard or building in which such adult convicts may be present. (sec. 11)

Within 10 years of the 1899 Juvenile Court Act, the definition of delinquency was broadened in several Illinois legislative acts. "Peculiarly juvenile offenses" were added, including frequenting areas where gaming devices were operated, incorrigibility, and growing up in idleness or crime. Later, running away from home, loitering, and using profanity were added to the list (National Center for Juvenile Justice, 1991, p. 8). Although similar behaviors were offenses for adults (telling fortunes, gambling, begging, lewd and disorderly behavior, loitering), the important distinction is that comparable offenses on the part of juveniles drew a different legal response. Crime, punishment, deterrence, and retribution were in the lexicon of the criminal justice system, not in that of the juvenile justice system. The juvenile court was to protect youngsters from misbehaviors and rehabilitate them through the use of such mechanisms as probation, detention, treatment, and incarceration, if necessary. The last of those responses, which originated with the Houses of Refuge, was still viewed as a means of protecting children from the vagaries of urban life.

Between 1900 and 1910, thirty-two states enacted legislation establishing juvenile probation. By 1912, 22 states had juvenile courts, and by 1925 all but two states had established them (Krisberg & Austin, 1993, p. 30). By 1930, every state except Wyoming had legislatively authorized juvenile probation, and in most states the courts were assigned administrative responsibility. At that time, 15 states still had not legislatively authorized probation for adults (Hurst, 1990).

The probation innovation, coupled with the advent of the "medical model" of treatment, provided a community-oriented approach to juvenile justice (Finestone, 1976; Hagan & Leon, 1977; Schlossman, 1977). Delinquency came to be viewed as a social disease that could be cured through early intervention and treatment using psychiatric and casework tools. Probation officers were the treatment agents. Their task was to prevent delinquents from becoming criminals by helping them in the community, thereby avoiding the necessity of institutional confinement. As Boston Judge Harvey Baker (1910) explained, probation officers would care for children over long periods of time.

Fox (1970, p. 1207) argues that the logical basis for the creation of juvenile courts was the humanitarian concern, more specifically, the delinquency prevention rationale supporting the House of Refuge concept. In this respect, juvenile courts could be viewed as an extension of institutions. More generally, the juvenile court provided a social response to the threat that lower-class youth posed to the security of middle-class society (Finestone, 1976, pp. 49-50). Above all, the middle classes wanted control over the children of the poor. Granted, reformers possessed genuine idealism. "However, as this idealism waned, the court became institutionalized as a legally sanctioned comprehensive instrument of paternalistic and impersonal social control" (Finestone, 1976, p. 49).

Juvenile courts also served a very utilitarian purpose: providing relief from institutional overcrowding. As Miller and Ohlin (1985, pp. 14-15) contend,

> The juvenile court movement . . . helped enormously in relieving overcrowding by creating an alternative control option with the rapid growth of supervised probation in the community. Probation offered a more benign, individualized form of treatment and control.

The new juvenile court inherited the *parens patriae* philosophy bestowed on reform schools. The juvenile court had authority to place children on probation, institutionalize them, or place them in foster homes or orphanages. Unpaid probation officers assisted judges and supervised youngsters.

Most important, establishment of juvenile courts reversed a 100-year tradition in the United States of handling juvenile offenders in criminal courts. Before their creation, none of the states had statutory provisions requiring that juveniles be treated any differently from adults. As Hutzler (1982, p. 25) states,

> Only "infants," those below the age of reason [presumed to be age 7] and therefore incapable of criminal intent, were exempt from prosecution and punishment. Children over the age of seven stood trial in criminal court for their crimes and could be sentenced to prison, or even death, if convicted.

In establishing the juvenile court, reformers achieved the main objective that they had sought since the beginning of government in the United States: removing juveniles from the harsh criminal justice system. The underlying justification for a separate system was that children and adolescents, by virtue of their age and immaturity, "are not fully responsible for their antisocial behavior and can, if humanely treated in proper rehabilitation programs, become productive members of society" (Hutzler, 1982, p. 26).

One of the distinctive features of the new juvenile court was that it controlled its own intake, unlike the criminal justice system, which received clients at the discretion of the district attorney. Legal considerations, centered on the *offense*, governed intake in the criminal justice system. By contrast, *offender* considerations governed juvenile court intake, including social, psychological, and educational factors. The intake and adjudication process sought to determine the source of problem behavior, providing the basis for treatment efforts. The criminal justice system premise that "punishment should fit the crime" had no place in the juvenile court disposition for a misguided child.

> Whatever the conduct that brought the child to the court's attention, the juvenile court judge was to consider the broad range of social facts regarding the child and his family and to direct treatment "in the child's best interests" and in accordance with his needs. (Hutzler, 1982, p. 27)

Hence, juvenile courts rejected fixed terms of confinement in favor of the indeterminate sentence. Children were released once their rehabilitation was complete.

The juvenile court persisted in its focus on the individual and the family from 1900 to the 1930s, dominated in its treatment philosophy by biological, Freudian, and medical approaches (Empey, 1985). Then, from the 1930s through the 1960s, treatment emphasis gradually shifted to consideration of extrafamilial factors: poverty, discrimination, inequality, and the role of peer groups. Finally, in the 1970s, interest in the family as a source of delinquency was revived, along with recognition that other sources of failures in the socialization process included the school and other youth-serving institutions (Empey, 1985, pp. 26-27).

Little is known about the operations of the juvenile justice system during the period from the beginning of the 20th century to the 1960s. According to Finestone (1976, pp. 54-76) and Krisberg and Austin (1993, pp. 35-51), the period was characterized by application of the newly emerging science of delinquency control in both delinquency prevention experiments and juvenile courts. Psychiatry, psychology, and sociology provided the tools that the reformers hoped would cure, rather than punish, child misbehavior (Hutzler, 1982). During this period, juvenile reform schools sprang up all over the country, and increasing numbers of youths were committed to them. Experimentation with other forms of institutionalization of juveniles continued (McCorkle, 1952; Weeks, 1958). For example, shortly before the beginning of World War II, California centralized its correctional institutions under the California

Youth Authority (CYA; Krisberg & Austin, 1993, p. 46). Under the CYA model, criminal courts committed youths aged 16-21 to the CYA, which determined appropriate dispositions. During the 1940s and 1950s, Wisconsin and Minnesota developed variations of the CYA concept (Krisberg & Austin, 1993, p. 46). Other states continued experimentation with different treatment approaches, including guided-group interaction and group therapy. "Correctional Administrators and social scientists hoped for a significant breakthrough in treatment, but it never came" (Krisberg & Austin, 1993, p. 47).

Likewise, the juvenile court ran into problems:

> Despite the early success of its sweep across the nation . . . the juvenile justice movement faced serious ordnance and supply problems. The new weapons of diagnosis and treatment with which the campaign began never achieved their anticipated accuracy or effectiveness, and the monetary resources needed to pursue the new strategy effectively were never provided. The failure of the movement to achieve its ultimate objective— the solution to juvenile misbehavior— eventually began to erode public confidence in the juvenile court. (Hutzler, 1982, pp. 27-28)

The Third Reform Movement: Delinquency Prevention and Alternatives to the Juvenile Justice System

The Juvenile Justice and Delinquency Prevention (JJDP) Act of 1974 (P.L. 93-415) embodied the results of the third juvenile justice reform movement: prevention and development of alternatives to the juvenile justice system. Several developments during the 1960s and 1970s led to the JJDP Act of 1974. Most influential were the President's Commission on Law Enforcement and Administration of Justice, a survey conducted by the National Council on Crime and Delinquency, several Supreme Court decisions, the National Advisory Commission on Criminal Justice Standards and Goals, and Massachusetts juvenile corrections reforms.

The Crime Commission

In keeping with its mandate to focus on the justice apparatus, the President's Commission on Law Enforcement and Administration of Justice (called the Crime Commission, established in 1965) examined the workings of the existing system of juvenile justice and made suggestions for improving it. It made the first comprehensive assessment of the American juvenile justice system. More specifically, the Crime Commission focused on the juvenile court and found it to be ineffective. "It has been proven to be true for a variety of reasons that the promise of the juvenile courts to help the child, to rehabilitate him, to lead him into a healthy and constructive life has not been kept" (President's Commission on Law Enforcement and Administration of Justice, 1967a, p. 30).

Two factors in particular appear to have influenced the thinking of the commission. The first was the presumed failures of the juvenile court. Information gathered in the course of the commission's inquiry pointed to extensive detention of children in jails, the lack of due process, assembly line justice, excessively large probation caseloads, crowded reformatories, and mounting evidence that juvenile correctional programs did not appear to be effective (Empey, 1978, p. 531; Empey & Stafford, 1991, pp. 333-338). Except for procedural inadequacies, rising crime rates and social unrest were considered the main evidence that the juvenile court was ineffective. "Though it is obvious that the juvenile court alone could scarcely have been responsible for these events, many Americans began to believe that it was incapable of dealing with them" (Empey & Stafford, 1991, p. 339).

The second factor was the growing popularity of labeling theory in the late 1960s. Its proponents (Becker, 1963; Lemert, 1951, 1967; Tannenbaum, 1938) argued that most juveniles would mature out of delinquency if left alone. They charged that agents of control exacerbate delinquency by setting into motion a self-fulfilling prophecy in officially labeling youth as "bad" or "delinquent." As a result of over-dramatization of initial wayward (minor) acts, youths repeatedly labeled "delinquent" by police, judges, and probation officers come to see themselves as they are labeled by officials; hence, the likelihood of subsequent delinquent behavior is increased, through the dynamics of the self-fulfilling process. These theorists pointed to the presumed failure of juvenile courts as evidence that the system has a harm-ful effect, that identifying and labeling children as "bad" or "delinquent" only made the prob-lem worse. Ironically, the term "delinquent" was coined to avoid the stigma attached to the label "criminal."

Lemert in particular laid a foundation for the growth of labeling theory in the 1970s, when it would be translated into public policy, most ef-fectively by Schur (1973) in his "radical non-intervention" notion. Although his proposition targeted mainly "victimless" offenders such as prostitutes and drug addicts, Schur (1971, 1973) got the attention of juvenile justice law-makers as well, who applied the concept to mi-nor delinquents in distinguishing them as "status offenders." System nonintervention in their lives would become the favored policy (see Empey, 1978, pp. 341-368).

Lemert (1967, p. 96) urged the Crime Com-mission to adopt the view that "If there is a de-fensible philosophy for the juvenile court, it is one of judicious nonintervention . . . an agency of last resort for children, holding to a doctrine analogous to that of appeals courts which re-quire that all other remedies be exhausted be-fore a case will be heard." The commission's recommendations favored small correctional units, a variety of treatment alternatives, addi-tional due process projections, decriminaliza-tion of victimless crimes, and deinstitutionali-zation of large correctional facilities (see the chapter on juvenile delinquency, pp. 55-89 and table of recommendations, pp. 293-310, in President's Commission on Law Enforcement and Administration of Justice, 1967a; see also the task force report, 1967b). The commission rejected the contention that "the time has come to jettison the experiment" and concluded, "What is required is rather a revised philosophy of the juvenile court, based on recognition that in the past our reach exceeded our grasp" (Presi-dent's Commission on Law Enforcement and Administration of Justice, 1967a, p. 81). It rec-ommended several steps to improve the ad-ministration of juvenile justice:

The formal sanctioning system and pro-nouncement of delinquency should be used only as a last resort. . . . Alternatives already available, such as those related to court intake, should be more fully exploited. The range of conduct for which court intervention is authorized should be narrowed. "Serious consideration . . .

should be given to complete elimination of the court's power over children for noncriminal conduct." The cases that fall within the narrowed jurisdiction of the court and filter through the screen of prejudicial, informal disposition modes would largely involve offenders for whom more vigorous measures seem necessary. . . . While rehabilitative efforts should be vigorously pursued in defer-ence to the youthfulness of the offenders and in keeping with the general commit-ment to individualized treatment of all offenders, the incapacitative, deterrent, and condemnatory purposes of the judge-ment should not be disguised. Accord-ingly, the adjudicatory hearing should be consistent with basic principles of due process. (1967a, p. 81)

As a means of handling minor offenders in the community in lieu of juvenile court, the Crime Commission recommended that com-munities establish neighborhood youth-serving agencies, called Youth Services Bureaus, lo-cated in comprehensive neighborhood com-munity centers. These bureaus would receive juveniles (delinquent and nondelinquent) re-ferred by the police, the juvenile court, parents, schools, and others. These agencies would act as brokers of all community services for young people and would also fill service gaps, espe-cially for less seriously delinquent juveniles (President's Commission on Law Enforcement and Administration of Justice, 1967a, p. 83).

The commission also offered recommenda-tions aimed at improving detention and incar-ceration. It suggested that state legislation should be enacted restricting both the authority to detain and the circumstances under which detention is permitted. Low-security commu-nity residential centers and similar shelters were recommended for children for whom de-tention is made necessary in the absence of ade-quate parental supervision (1967a, p. 87). Cor-rectional authorities should develop more extensive community programs providing spe-cial, intensive treatment as an alternative to in-stitutionalization (1967a, p. 171).

The commission's recommendations clearly called for a juvenile court of more restricted scope. Diversion of youth from the juvenile jus-tice system was encouraged. Moreover, limita-tions on confinement of juveniles were urged. Equally important, the commission offered a delinquency prevention rationale and mechanism. It reasoned that juvenile delinquency could be prevented through early intervention and provision of services outside the juvenile justice system. The favored service delivery mechanism was neighborhood centers it called Youth Service Bureaus.

The NCCD Juvenile Corrections Survey

In 1966, at the request of the President's Commission on Law Enforcement and Administration of Justice, the National Council on Crime and Delinquency (NCCD) surveyed state and local correctional agencies and institutions throughout the United States. This was the first systematic survey of juvenile facilities. The survey revealed widespread use of detention facilities to hold in custody juveniles accused of noncriminal conduct—often without court petitions. Wide variations in detention rates and lengths of stay exacerbated the situation. The NCCD (1967, p. 129) concluded, "Confusion and misuse pervade detention. It has come to be used by police and probation officers as a disposition; judges use it for punishment, protection, and storage" of youngsters.

The survey results led the NCCD to recommend that "No child should be placed in any detention facility unless he is a delinquent or alleged delinquent and there is a substantial probability that he will commit an offense dangerous to himself or the community or will run away pending court disposition. He should not be detained for punishment or for someone's convenience" (p. 211). The NCCD's survey also documented similar misuse of juvenile reformatories. "In theory, training schools are specialized facilities for changing children relatively hardened in delinquency. In practice, . . . they house a nonselective population and are primarily used in ways which make the serving of their theoretical best purpose . . . beside the point" (p. 143).

As a result of the survey, the NCCD recommended standards restricting use of juvenile institutions. "No child committed under noncriminal proceedings should be housed in institutions with those convicted under criminal proceedings. . . . Dependent and neglected children should not be committed to or placed in training schools or other facilities for delinquents" (p. 211).

Supreme Court Decisions

In 1954, the Supreme Court of Pennsylvania sanctioned the juvenile court's due process restrictions *In re Holmes* (348 U.S. 973). The Court reasoned that because juvenile courts are not criminal courts, constitutional rights granted to persons accused of crime are not applicable to children. Satisfaction with this ruling did not last long. By the 1960s, reformers began to question the legitimacy of withholding due process protections from juveniles. The issue was framed in terms of the effectiveness of treatment versus due process: Do adolescents receive individual treatment the juvenile courts were created to provide? If not, why are they not afforded the same due process protection that adults enjoy (Ketcham, 1961)?

Four U.S. Supreme Court decisions between 1966 and 1971 brought about important changes in the administration of juvenile justice. In 1966, in *Kent v. United States* (383 U.S. 541), for the first time, the Court required due process rights for juveniles, in its ruling that a juvenile cannot be waived to criminal court without the granting of procedural due process. It found evidence, in Justice Abe Fortas's words, "that the child receives the worst of both worlds: that he gets neither the protection accorded to adults nor the solicitous care and regenerative treatment postulated for children" (p. 566). Thus, the Supreme Court required a formal waiver hearing before a juvenile could be transferred to criminal court.

The following year, the Supreme Court's landmark ruling, *In re Gault* (387 U.S. 1, 1967), granted other due process rights to juveniles facing loss of freedom (through incarceration) including notice of the charges, right to counsel, right to confrontation and cross-examination, and the privilege against self-incrimination. These and other "due process" rights already enjoyed by adults in the criminal justice system were extended to juveniles in the juvenile justice system for the first time (see Grisso, 1980; Holtz, 1987; Kobetz, 1971; National Center for Juvenile Justice, 1991). The *Gault* case, however, applied only to some preadjudication procedures and to the adjudication hearing, not the disposition stage of juvenile court proceedings. Tailoring treatment to the individual child was not affected.

Prior to 1970, the standard for determining guilt in delinquency proceedings was a "preponderance" of available evidence; that is, "more likely than not." In 1970, the Supreme Court held, *In re Winship* (397 U.S. 358), that due process required that the state prove "beyond a reasonable doubt" facts establishing a juvenile's delinquency. As in the *Gault* ruling, *Winship* did not apply to procedures beyond the adjudication stage.

Equally important, in the *Gault* ruling, the Supreme Court made it clear that the juvenile court was not to be equated with the criminal proceedings of adult courts. A number of decisions extracted some measure of informality the juvenile justice system had been granted in the handling of juveniles, yet the separateness of the system was not successfully challenged. Thus, juvenile courts survived the attack on *parens patriae* while losing some ground on denial of due process. In 1971, the Supreme Court ruled in *McKeiver v. Pennsylvania* (403 U.S. 528) that there is no requirement of a jury trial in juvenile court proceedings. This decision supported *parens patriae* by limiting due process rights. As late as 1984, the Supreme Court reaffirmed *parens patriae* in *Shall v. Martin* (467 U.S. 253), in which the Court ruled that juveniles charged with serious crimes are subject to preventive detention. The court thus recognized that, unlike adults, juveniles are continuously in some form of custody and if parents fail, the state can assume the parental role. The juvenile court had survived the attack of civil libertarians and their allies on the Supreme Court, but not without the price of loss of informality (Hutzler, 1982, p. 28).

The National Advisory Commission

The National Advisory Commission on Criminal Justice Standards and Goals (1973) was established in 1971 to formulate the first national criminal justice standards, goals, and priorities that would constitute a "national criminal justice strategy." Appointed by the administrator of the Law Enforcement Assistance Administration in the United States Department of Justice, it completed its work in 1973.

Its exhaustive study of the U.S. crime problem led the National Advisory Commission to conclude that the first priority should be given to preventing juvenile delinquency, to minimizing the involvement of young offenders in the juvenile and criminal justice system, and to reintegrating delinquents and young offenders into the community (National Advisory Commission on Criminal Justice Standards and Goals, 1973, p. 23). Controlling crime committed by juveniles while at the same time providing treatment was the crux of the problem as viewed by the National Advisory Commission:

> The United States has a long tradition of dealing differently with juveniles than with adults who are in difficulty with the law, in the hope that juveniles can be re-channelled into becoming law abiding citizens. However many of the methods of dealing with juveniles in this country have come to be viewed either as counterproductive or as violations of the rights of children. Thus there is a pressing need for national standards to improve the quality of juvenile contacts with the system. (National Advisory Commission on Criminal Justice Standards and Goals, 1973, *Report on Corrections*, p. 247)

The commission focused in particular on detention center problems. It found that "persons in need of supervision" (PINS), or "minors in need of supervision" (MINS)—who later came to be called "status offenders"—composed at least 50% of most detention populations (*Report on Corrections*, p. 257; United States Children's Bureau, 1964). It also estimated that possibly more than 100,000 juveniles were held in jails and police lockups each year (*Report on Corrections*, p. 258).

The National Advisory Commission's standard for Detention and Disposition of Juveniles recommended that

> the delinquency jurisdiction of the court should be limited to those juveniles who commit acts that if committed by an adult would be criminal, and that juveniles accused of delinquent conduct would not under any circumstances be detained in facilities for housing adults accused or convicted of crime. The decision to detain prior to adjudication of delinquency should be based on the following criteria. Detention should be considered as a last resort where no other reasonable alternative is available. Detention should be used only where the juvenile has no parent, guardian, custodian, or other person able to provide supervision and care for him and to assure his presence at subsequent judicial hearings. Detention decisions

should be made only by the court or in-take personnel, not police officers. Juveniles should not be detained in jails, lock-ups, or other facilities used for adults. (*Report on Corrections*, p. 259)

In this recommendation, the National Advisory Commission identified a particular category of offenders that would become the subject of much debate, "status offenders," and defined them as juveniles who committed offenses not considered crimes if committed by adults. It expressed the belief that juvenile court effectiveness would be enhanced if it were authorized to incarcerate only delinquents whose offenses would be crimes if committed by adults (*Report on Courts*, p. 293). Thus, the National Advisory Commission reinforced the Crime Commission's recommendation delimiting juvenile court jurisdiction over noncriminal misbehavior, but it went a step further in urging that these children not be incarcerated.

Revolutionary Reform in Massachusetts

Large juvenile reformatories had been under attack virtually since their creation. Although they were established to rehabilitate juvenile offenders, critics charged that they were "warehouses" and "schools of crime" that produced high recidivism rates; that they were custodial, not therapeutic; and that they denied their inmates due process (Krisberg & Austin, 1993).

These issues came to a head in Massachusetts. In 1969, the state's Director of Youth Services resigned following a series of crises in the state's reformatories. His successor, Dr. Jerome Miller, took office with a mandate to develop new programs. Over the next 2 years, Miller (1973) established "therapeutic communities" within the state's existing reformatories, but adherents of the old custodial philosophy resisted his reforms. By 1971, Miller concluded that therapeutic communities could not be run successfully within the traditional reformatories. He closed the reformatories and replaced them with a network of decentralized community-based services (and a few small secure-care units for violent juvenile offenders). Miller's reformed system resembled what was called for by the 1967 Crime Commission and by the National Advisory Commission (Bakal, 1973; Coates & Miller, 1973; Coates, Miller, & Ohlin, 1973, 1978; McEwen, 1978; Miller & Ohlin,

1985; Miller, Ohlin, & Coates, 1977a, 1977b; Ohlin, Coates, & Miller, 1978).

Twenty-five years later, the community-based system Miller initiated in Massachusetts is still in place (Arnaud & Mack, 1982; Austin, Elms, Krisberg, & Steele, 1991; Lerner, 1990; Loughran, 1986). During this period, the state's Department of Youth Services has developed a sophisticated network of small (15-bed) secure facilities for violent offenders (who constitute only 15% of all youths placed in the state's juvenile correctional system) and a wide range of community-based residential and nonresidential programs for the remainder of its 1,700 committed youth. The Massachusetts changes constituted the most sweeping reforms in youth corrections in the United States since the establishment of juvenile reformatories in the 19th century and juvenile courts in the 20th century. Miller demonstrated, to Congress and the nation, that juvenile corrections need not be centered on large reformatories. He struggled to make juvenile institutions work, concluded that effective treatment within them was an unworkable concept, and closed them in Massachusetts. Through these actions, he called attention to the failure of previous juvenile justice reforms. Juvenile court reliance on institutions was not working. He called for alternatives to juvenile prisons. By the success of his actions, Miller demonstrated that community-based juvenile corrections was a workable concept.

The Fourth Reform Movement: Just Deserts

The fourth, and still active, reform movement, which Empey and Stafford (1991, pp. 443-464) call "neoclassical," is the product of two philosophical approaches: utilitarian and just deserts philosophy. Utilitarian philosophy is represented mainly in the writings of Van den Haag (1975) and Wilson (1983a, 1983b). These scholars' thinking is predicated on two main principles: that punishment deters people from committing crimes, and that punishment is indispensable for maintaining the social order. Although a deterrent effect of punishment was not demonstrated before or since the extensive National Academy of Sciences study (Blumstein, Cohen, & Nagin, 1978; Zimring & Hawkins, 1973), Van den Haag and Wilson argue a general deterrent effect. In the words of an English judge, "Men are not hanged for stealing horses, but that horses may not be stolen" (Van den Haag, 1975, p. 61). Especially severe punishments are believed to have a deterrent effect. In the view of a former OJJDP administrator, Alfred Regnery (1986, pp. 43-44), "If that's the way they want to behave, the only way to deal with them is to let them feel the sting of the justice system."

In their second principle, Van den Haag and Wilson see punishment as retribution, fair payment to society in return for crimes committed. Retribution demonstrates society's willingness to pay its debts by punishing the offender and reinforces social sentiments against crime, helping to preserve the social order. Van den Haag and Wilson believe that the justice system should concentrate its efforts on punishing criminals, not rehabilitating them. Implications of utilitarian philosophy for juvenile justice include decriminalizing status offenses, lowering the age of accountability for crime, abolishing the juvenile court, determinant sentencing, and using preventive incapacitation (Empey & Stafford, 1991, pp. 446-447).

The foundation for the "just deserts" philosophy was provided by the American Friends Service Committee in its *Struggle for Justice: A Report on Crime and Punishment in America* (1971). The committee concluded that the individualized treatment model, the ideal toward which reformers had been working, was theoretically faulty, systematically discriminatory in administration, and inconsistent with some of our most basic concepts of justice. Receiving impetus from the "war on crime" during the late 1960s and early 1970s (Graham, 1970), just deserts advocates initially directed their reforms at the criminal justice system (Cederblom & Blizek, 1977; Fogel, 1979; Fox, 1970, 1974; Gaylin & Rothman, 1976; Von Hirsch, 1976). They quickly expanded their focus, however, to include the juvenile justice system (Feld, 1983; Fogel & Hudson, 1981; Rosenheim, 1976; Thompson & McAnany, 1984), because of its stronger emphasis on the rehabilitative ideal (Allen, 1981).

Like utilitarian philosophers, just deserts advocates assume the ineffectiveness of the juvenile justice system. Both groups would abolish the juvenile court and have the criminal justice system adjudicate juvenile offenders, incarcerating them in adult prisons, as appropriate, commensurate with the seriousness of offenses. They would, therefore, have the system concentrate on "doing justice" (Gaylin & Rothman, 1976) rather than attempting to rehabilitate delinquents. Unlike utilitarian philosophers, who argue the value of punishment for deterrent purposes, just deserts advocates see virtue in punishment itself, because the individual deserves it. Whereas utilitarian philosophy sees the individual as wicked, just deserts philosophy sees the state as the wicked party, particularly because of its asserted abuse of discretion. Thus, just deserts philosophy supports these principles: mechanized justice (to avoid doing harm by abuse of discretion), sentencing the offender rather than the offense, legal punishment as a "desert" (Von Hirsch, 1976, chap. 7), parsimonious interference in the lives of convicted offenders, and abandonment of delinquency prevention efforts. The implications of these principles for juvenile justice are to decriminalize status offenses, lower the age of accountability, abolish the juvenile court, use determinate sentences, punish rather than rehabilitate offenders, and grade punishments according to the seriousness of the crime and the offender's prior record (Empey & Stafford, 1991, pp. 456-457).

People from a variety of perspectives contributed to the just deserts philosophy (Empey & Stafford, 1991, p. 455), including scholars studying the weaknesses of prisons (Gaylin, Rothman, and Von Hirsch), a practicing correctional administrator (Fogel), and legal scholars (Feld and Fox). Considerable impetus was provided to their philosophy by program evaluation reviews that found few rehabilitation programs to be effective (Greenberg, 1977; Lipton, Martinson, & Wilks, 1975; Palmer, 1978; Sechrest, White, & Brown, 1979). The most influential among these was the comprehensive review conducted by Martinson and his colleagues, published initially by Martinson (1974). The general conclusion of these reviews was that "nothing works." Thus, strong support was provided for the just deserts philosophy.

Just deserts reformers concentrated their efforts in the Juvenile Justice Standards Project, initiated in 1971 by the Institute of Judicial Administration (IJA) at New York University, later cosponsored by the American Bar Association (ABA). These came to be known as the "IJA-ABA Standards" (1980). In addition to the Crime Commission and Supreme Court decisions, drafters of the IJA-ABA Standards were influenced by just deserts advocates such as Fox (1970, 1972), an influential investigative report

(James, 1967) that uncovered abuse of authority in juvenile courts, but also by labeling theorists including Becker (1963), Lemert (1951, 1967), and Schur (1973)—all of whom advocated a more restricted role for the juvenile justice system in America's crime control apparatus. The 23 volumes of IJA-ABA Standards (1980) covered every aspect of juvenile justice administration, such as rejection of the medical or rehabilitative model of the juvenile court, procedural safeguards (for intake, adjudication, and dispositions), plea bargaining, recognition of children's rights, proportionality in dispositions, determinate sentencing, use of least restrictive alternatives, and restrictions on use of parole and aftercare supervision (see Empey & Stafford, 1991, pp. 469-472 for a detailed discussion).

The positions of the IJA-ABA Joint Commission were countered, to little avail, by those of the Twentieth Century Fund Task Force on Sentencing Policy Toward Young Offenders (1978). It conducted an exhaustive review of available data and research on criminal and juvenile justice system policies governing the handling of serious and violent juvenile offenders. Concluding that "the theory behind the juvenile court is not merely obsolete; it is a fairy tale that never came true" (Zimring, 1978, p. 6), it fashioned a "discrete policy toward youth crime" guided by four principles: culpability (the older the adolescent, the greater the degree of responsibility), diminished responsibility (less punishment for crimes committed by younger adolescents because of their diminished capacity to control their conduct), providing room to reform (leaving young offenders' life chances intact), and proportionality (punishment proportional to the seriousness of the offense). The Twentieth Century Fund Task Force rejected calls for abolition of the juvenile court and recommended instead rethinking and reform of juvenile court principles and processes.

Just deserts philosophy and practice grew in the 1980s and 1990s because of rising crime, prison overcrowding, and disenchantment with the prospects of successful treatment programs. More generally, the social unrest of the 1960s and 1970s, expressed in the form of civil rights protests, urban riots, campus rebellions, and opposition to the Vietnam War, led to the popular conclusion that the dominant progressive philosophy of the past half century had contributed to anarchy, not order (Empey & Stafford, 1991, pp. 338-339). "As a result, Rich-ard Nixon promised in 1968, if elected president, to wage a war on crime, even if young people had to be numbered among the enemy. The pervasive feeling was that the nation was in danger of losing everything. The only solution, therefore was to return to a more retributive concept of justice, favoring legal punishment rather than rehabilitation" (p. 339). The War on Crime would soon be heated up.

Ironically, the neoclassical philosophers, in their zeal to bring about equity in juvenile jurisprudence, came to advocate an old approach to juvenile delinquency that previously had been rejected by progressives of the late 19th century: classical criminology (Beccaria, 1963; Bentham, 1948). That school of thought repudiated rehabilitation, in the belief that punishment would deter crime, provided that it was certain and swift, as well as coupled with punishments graded according to offense seriousness. As an alternative to beheading and other means of exacting a death penalty, prisons were built as a more humane option, for adults and juveniles. Neoclassical thinkers' choice to confine juveniles in adult prisons is exactly what the progressive reformers found abhorrent, leading them to create the juvenile justice system.

Utilitarian and just deserts philosophies sought to bring an end to the optimistic era the progressive reformers established. The progressive era was "a period in American history that was based on hope and dedicated to the proposition that delinquency and crime, like other social problems, could be addressed by compassion and mercy, by knowledge and imagination. Now, however, it appears that none of these are of use to anyone" (Empey & Stafford, 1991, p. 460).

Juvenile Justice Today

The modern juvenile justice field is dominated by two competing philosophical models, just deserts and family court. On one hand, just deserts philosophies have gained strength over the past decade. On the other hand, the juvenile court has become more institutionalized as a "juvenile and family court." The latter development requires explanation.

Impetus for reformulation of the traditional juvenile court into a juvenile and family court came from standards development in the 1970s. In addition to the IJA-ABA standards, three other major sets were developed for juvenile justice in the 1970s (totaling 30 volumes, Allen-Hagen & Howell, 1982). One set pertains to corrections (developed by the American Correctional Association). Two others address the general administration of juvenile justice. These are the National Advisory Committee (NAC, 1980) *Standards for the Administration of Juvenile Justice and Delinquency Prevention*, and the set developed by the National Advisory Commission on Criminal Justice Standards and Goals (NACC, 1973). The NACC standards reconceptualized the traditional juvenile court in recommending adoption of a family court structure that would "provide for an integrated family court that would minimize duplication of efforts and provide for comprehensive treatment of family problems. The family court structure better enables the court to view juvenile behavior as part of a much broader framework and focus on the family as a whole" (NACC, 1976, p. 16).

The NACC standards redefined the clientele of juvenile and family courts as "families with service needs" and urged the court to use its legal powers to "command the assistance and cooperation of institutions serving children and families" (p. 313). These principles were expanded and reaffirmed periodically in publications of the renamed National Council of Juvenile and Family Court Judges (NCJFCJ) in Edwards (1992), Hofford (1989), and Whitlatch (1987). The stronger emphasis on rehabilitation is evident in the *Desktop Guide to Good Juvenile Probation Practice* (National Center for Juvenile Justice, 1991). In 1994, the NCJFCJ issued a statement of its basic principles and vision for the family court:

> A unified family court, housed in a centrally located family court center, should be established in every jurisdiction. . . . The court would manage an array of family related cases, including juvenile delinquency, dependency, status offenses, paternity, custody, support, mental health, adoption, family violence, and marital dissolution. . . . The court facility must serve as the center for the coordination and provision of services and resources to children and families in the community. The family court center would provide intake, evaluation, and referral to an array of public and private services, many of which may be located on site. . . . The family court must retain the impor-

tant delinquency functions of the traditional juvenile court. Delinquent behavior needs to be addressed through a balanced approach which includes protection of the community, constructive punishment, accountability and development of competency that will enable the child to become a contributing member of society. (National Council of Juvenile and Family Court Judges, 1994, p. 2)

Thus, the original concept of the juvenile court has been reaffirmed. The current status of juvenile justice reforms, however, can be characterized as a "schizoid revolution" (Empey & Stafford, 1991, pp. 465-487) because of the dominance of these competing just deserts and family court philosophies. The fundamental issue is how the United States views adolescents. Are they immature children who, consistent with the early 19th century view of childhood, deserve the benefit of a developmental perspective and a second-chance opportunity to mature? Or should they be seen as part of the criminal element of our society, deserving of punishment in a system that views them as if they were adults? Assessment of the results of this competition must await the end of this volume.

Summary

The history of U.S. delinquency policy began with disregard for childhood. Neither it nor adolescence had yet been defined; thus, no distinction was made in application of penal measures to juveniles and adults. Public beatings and torture gave way to imprisonment. More enlightened reformers created juvenile reformatories as alternatives to prisons. Initially viewed as a first resort, reformatories also handled juveniles convicted in criminal court. These gradually came to be seen as a last resort in a continuum of social controls, although their use as such never materialized.

Progressive understanding of the sources of juvenile delinquency coupled with repudiation of incarceration provided the way for creation of the juvenile court and, with it, the juvenile justice system. The new apparatus, created nearly 100 years ago, was to serve as an alternative to handling juvenile delinquency in the criminal justice system. Interventions focused on the offender rather than the offense. Elimination of the life chances of juveniles came to be considered a serious matter. The promise of rehabilitation, through early intervention that remediated the sources of problem behavior in the community, family, school, peer group, and individual, provided the impetus for growth of the juvenile justice system. Incarceration, however, continued to be a favorite response.

The modern era opened with attacks on the juvenile court, blaming it for not eliminating adolescent misbehavior. Its informal procedures, intended to help it achieve a primary goal of acting in the best interests of the child, came into question. Libertarians and labeling theorists accused the juvenile court of defeating its own purposes in the application of controls to juvenile misbehavior. The unique American experiment was almost jettisoned. Instead, public policy called for alternatives to the juvenile justice system: prevention, diversion, and alternatives to incarceration. Confinement of adolescents who had not committed a crime was repudiated, along with jailing of juveniles. Humane alternatives to incarceration were encouraged.

Then came the current reform movement, returning to the pre-Industrial Revolution policies of placing juveniles in the criminal justice system and adult prisons. Just deserts and punishment have become the favored public policies, over prevention, treatment, and rehabilitation. Once again, punishing the offense rather than the offender is the object of current crime policy.

2

Landmark Federal Legislation

This chapter reviews the fourth juvenile justice reform movement, delinquency prevention and provision of alternatives to the juvenile justice system. It culminated in the Juvenile Justice and Delinquency Prevention (JJDP) Act of 1974 (P.L. 93-415). This federal legislation wrought the most significant and controversial advances in the evolution of the juvenile justice system.

Developments chronicled in Chapter 1—the President's Commission on Law Enforcement and Administration of Justice (1967a), the National Council on Crime and Delinquency (NCCD) Corrections Survey (1967), the National Advisory Commission on Criminal Justice Standards and Goals (1973), and several Supreme Court Decisions—led to a new federal presence in the juvenile delinquency field in the form of the landmark JJDP Act. This act, however, was preceded by federal legislation in the 1960s that was much narrower in scope. This earlier legislation had been stimulated by growing juvenile delinquency and disenchantment with the juvenile justice system.

Previous Federal Juvenile Delinquency Legislation

Federal involvement in juvenile delinquency was not significant before the 1960s (Committee on Education and Labor, 1974, p. 3). Although a Children's Bureau was established in 1912, it paid minimal attention to juvenile delinquency. It did little more than collect data on juvenile court handling of children, although its mandate included investigating the operations of juvenile courts. In 1948, President Harry Truman convened the Mid-Century Conference on Children and Youth. It addressed methods for improving juvenile courts and social services (Raley, 1995). As a result, an Interdepartmental Committee on Children and Youth was established to coordinate federal agencies' programs in these areas. Presidential requests in 1955, 1956, and 1957 for legislation to combat delinquency (which had evidenced growth in the postwar era) were rejected by the Congress (Committee on Education and Labor, 1974, p. 63).

The White House Conference on Children and Youth (Proceedings of the White House Conference on Children and Youth, 1960) spurred federal activity. It provided the impetus for the Crime Committee on Juvenile Delinquency and Youth Crime, established in 1961. This entity, consisting of representatives of federal departments, launched delinquency prevention experiments in several cities—patterned after the Mobilization for Youth model. These soon were absorbed, however, in the War on Poverty programs initiated by President Lyndon Johnson in the mid-1960s (Miller & Ohlin, 1985, pp. 20-21).

Mobilization for Youth (MYF), founded in New York City in 1962 (Bibb, 1967), was the first project funded under the federal Juvenile Delinquency and Youth Offenses Control Act of 1961. This massive program, covering 67 blocks, was funded jointly by the Crime Committee on Juvenile Delinquency and Youth Crime, the National Institute of Mental Health, the Ford Foundation, and the City of New York. Designed to test Cloward and Ohlin's (1960) "opportunity theory," it aimed to change the opportunity structure for delinquent youth. MYF operated four service divisions: the World of Work (creating and accessing work opportunities), the World of Education (improving education and increasing educational achievement), Individual and Family Services (helping youths and families access social services through Neighborhood Service Centers), and Specialized Services to Groups, including gangs. Unfortunately, Cloward and Ohlin's theory could not be tested because of poor program implementation (Miller, 1985) and because it was aborted as a result of a change in federal priorities following the assassination of President Kennedy (Miller, 1990). MYF nevertheless represented a pioneering approach to delinquency prevention that was broad in scope and instigated federal involvement in the field.

The Juvenile Delinquency and Youth Offenses Control Act of 1961 (under which the MYF program was funded), and the 1964 and 1965 amendments to it, aimed to demonstrate new methods of delinquency prevention and control. It helped support such innovative programs as the Neighborhood Youth Corps, the Legal Services Corporation, and Head Start. These served as models for later programs under President Lyndon Johnson's War on Poverty (Raley, 1995). Only $19.2 million was appropriated, however, and little was accomplished toward the main purpose of the law (Committee on the Judiciary, 1974, p. 27). It was followed by the Juvenile Delinquency Prevention and Control Act of 1968, designed to provide federal funds to states and localities to improve their juvenile delinquency services. Its effectiveness was questionable (Jordan & Dye, 1970; Polier, 1973) and was further diminished by a controversy regarding "block" (general) grants to the states (Committee on Education and Labor, 1974, p. 4). It was amended in 1971, renamed the Juvenile Delinquency Prevention Act, and extended through 1972.

The new act created an Interdepartmental Council to Coordinate Federal Juvenile Delinquency Programs. All of these legislative acts in the 1960s were administered by the Department of Health, Education, and Welfare (HEW). HEW concentrated mainly on development of Youth Services Bureaus, which were intended to provide coordinated youth services for diverted youth. HEW developed a national juvenile delinquency strategy but never requested funding for state juvenile services (Hurst, 1990). Congress concluded that the office HEW established to implement the Juvenile Delinquency Prevention Act, the Youth Development and Delinquency Prevention Administration (YDDPA), failed to implement the new act effectively, resulting in more extensive juvenile justice funding under the Law Enforcement Assistance Administration (LEAA) (Committee on Education and Labor, 1974, pp. 21-22, 30-33).

The LEAA was a new federal agency created by the Omnibus Crime Control and Safe Streets Act (Omnibus Crime Act) of 1968 (42 U.S.C. 3782) in the U.S. Department of Justice to spearhead the "War on Crime" declared by President Richard Nixon in 1968 (Caplan, 1976; Empey, 1974; Harris, 1972; Jacob, 1974; Milakovich & Weis, 1975; Murphy, 1972; Reiman, 1979; Tonry, 1994a, 1994b; Vorenberg, 1972). The War on Crime is a figure of speech that requires some explanation.

> It is supposed to indicate that the community is seriously imperiled by forces bent on its destruction and calls for the mounting of efforts that have claims on all available resources to defeat the peril. The rhetorical shift from "crime control" to "war on crime" signifies the transition from a routine concern to a state of emergency. (Bittner, 1970, p. 48)

The Omnibus Crime Act authorized funding to juvenile courts and correctional systems, and it encouraged screening status offenders out of the juvenile justice system. LEAA funded delinquency programs of a wide variety under its broad authority. Agreement was reached between the attorney general and the secretary of HEW that LEAA would limit its program activities to the juvenile justice system, and HEW would concentrate on programming outside the juvenile justice system (Committee on Education and Labor, 1974, p. 4). By the end of 1970, more than 40 of LEAA's State Planning Agencies created under the Omnibus Crime Control and Safe Streets Act were administering the state component of HEW's Juvenile Delinquency and Control Act Program (Committee on the Judiciary, 1974, p. 30). Congress expanded LEAA's authority in 1971 and 1973, requiring the agency to place an even greater emphasis on juvenile delinquency. LEAA funding for delinquency prevention and control programs increased during 1972-1974 (Committee on the Judiciary, 1974, p. 31).

Congressional Hearings on the Juvenile Justice and Delinquency Prevention Act

In 1974, the United States Congress enacted new legislation that crystallized the fourth reform movement: delinquency prevention and alternatives to the juvenile justice system. Three years of hearings preceded development of the Juvenile Justice and Delinquency Prevention Act of 1974 (JJDP Act). The results of these hearings (Hearings Before the Subcommittee to Investigate Juvenile Delinquency, 1972-1973, 1973; Hearings Before the Subcommittee on Equal Opportunity, 1974) were summarized in the U.S. Senate Judiciary Committee's Report on its version of the JJDP Act (S. 821; Committee on the Judiciary, 1974, pp. 20-24) and in the U.S. House of Representatives Committee on Education and Labor's report on the House version of the JJDP Act (H.R. 15276; Committee on Education and Labor, 1974).

Senator Birch Bayh, chairman of the Senate Judiciary Committee and chief architect of the JJDP Act, made the following assessment of the juvenile justice system in his Senate floor speech arguing for passage of the new legislation:

Sadly, we must conclude that our present juvenile justice system has proven itself incapable of turning these young people away from a life of crime. The recidivism rate for persons under 20 is the highest of any age group, close to 75% within 4 years. . . . Our overcrowded, understaffed juvenile courts, probation services and training schools rarely have the time, energy, or resources to offer the individualized treatment which the juvenile justice system should provide. . . .

The tragedy of the failure of the juvenile justice system is further compounded by the fact that nearly one-half of the juvenile court's caseload involves noncriminal offenses, such as dependency, neglect, and status offenses including incorrigibility, waywardness, and beyond control, which are crimes of which only children can be guilty. Due to the juvenile court's jurisdiction over these noncriminal offenses the treatment of such offenses as truancy and runaway along with such serious crimes as robbery and burglary has meant that children who are guilty of serious offenses [do not receive adequate rehabilitation services].

The result has been not the decriminalization of crimes committed by adolescents but the criminalization of such social and adjustment problems as running away and incorrigibility. Once a young person enters the juvenile justice system for whatever reason, he will probably be picked up again for delinquent acts and eventually he will, more often than not, graduate to a life of crime. . . .

It is often vital that the youth be reached before becoming involved with the formal juvenile justice system. In the first instance, preventive services should be available for identifiable, highly vulnerable groups to reduce their expected or probable rate of delinquency. If children commit acts which result in juvenile court referral, then an attempt should be made to divert them from the juvenile court. When youth commit serious crimes and must clearly be subjected to the jurisdiction of the juvenile justice system, then the preferred disposition should be community-based treatment.

Given the history of failure in preventing delinquency, there is a compelling need for a thoroughgoing national response to this problem. It is essential to prevent children from coming under the jurisdiction of the juvenile court or being involved with the traditional juvenile correctional system, if that is possible, for being labeled as delinquent or predelinquent. All alternatives to counterproductive involvement of young people in the juvenile justice system must be realized at every point of decisionmaking— from arrest through detention, court appearance, commitment, probation, and parole. If the child must go into the juvenile justice system for a serious offense, then alternatives for different needs and circumstances should be available to the juvenile court. This bill provides, at the State and local levels, where this battle must be won, long overdue alternatives for youth both outside and inside the juvenile justice system. (Bayh, 1974a, p. S13488)

It is evident from Senator Bayh's statement that the Congress incorporated labeling theory and notions of utilitarian philosophy in its assessment of the juvenile justice system. Other references in the legislative history further illustrate the extent to which Congress was influenced by these viewpoints, specifically Schur's (1973) "radical nonintervention" notion.

First, most children and youth mature and develop into positive and productive members of society. . . .
Second, it is well documented that youths whose behavior is noncriminal . . . have inordinately preoccupied the attention and resources of the juvenile justice system. Nearly 40 percent (one-half million per year) of the children brought to the attention of the juvenile justice system have committed no criminal act, in adult terms, and are involved simply because they are juveniles. . . . These [are] status offenders. . . .
Third, if the status offender were diverted into the social service delivery network, the remaining juveniles would be those who have committed acts which, under any circumstances, would be considered criminal. (Committee on the Judiciary, 1974, pp. 22-23)

Allen Breed, president of the National Association of State Juvenile Delinquency Program Administrators, made the case for labeling theory and nonintervention in his testimony before the Senate Subcommittee on Juvenile Justice (Committee on the Judiciary, 1974, pp. 23-24):

The structural and procedural system has two built-in patterns that tend to be self-defeating. First, the youth in need is identified and labeled. As he is labeled, certain sanctions are imposed and certain critical stances assumed. The sanctions and the stance tend to convince the individual that he is a deviant, that he is different, and to confirm any doubts he may have had about his capacity to function in the manner of the majority. Second, as the label is more securely affixed, society's agencies (police, schools, etc.) lower their

level of tolerance of any further deviance; the curfew violator who is an identified parolee or probationer may go into detention; the non-labeled offender will frequently go home; and the misbehaving probationer will be remanded to the vice-principal's office faster than his non-probation fellow. As these discriminations are made, the youth is further convinced of the difference and of society's discrimination. If the unacceptable behavior continues and the youngster penetrates further into the justice and correctional apparatus, he is subjected to an increasing degree of segregation from others of his kind—from special schools to detention to state correctional school—each step invites a greater identification with the subculture of the delinquent, and so, again, his anti-adult-antisocial-peer-oriented values are reinforced and confirmed and the socializing conformity-producing influences of the majority society are removed further from him. Thus, as the state's "treatment" is intensified, so too is the rejection, both covert, and overt, and as we try harder to socialize the deviant, we remove him further from the normal socializing processes. Our objective must be, therefore, to minimize the youngster's penetration into all negative labeling, institutional processes. To this end, we must exploit all of the available alternatives at each decision point, i.e., suspension, expulsion, arrest, detention, court wardship, commitments, parole revocation. At each critical step, we should exhaust the less rejecting, the less stigmatizing recourse before taking the next expulsive step.

Moreover, the U.S. Senate was influenced by those who believed that juvenile justice system reforms should go further in the direction of "deinstitutionalization" (removal of juveniles from secure incarceration settings). This argument was made poignantly by Dr. Jerome Miller, commissioner of Youth Services in Massachusetts, who had recently closed the state's juvenile reform schools and replaced them with community-based programs funded in large part with LEAA funds (Hearings, 1972-1973, p. 35). He testified:

I am of the opinion that the primary and most crucial need, if we are to deal effectively with serious delinquency in contemporary American society, is to reform and restructure, at the most basic levels, the juvenile correctional system. Although there can be little question that ultimately, delinquency prevention and diversion programs will be the backbone of a reconstituted juvenile justice system, such programs will not be effective until such time as we have provided alternatives for those youngsters who are most deeply involved in the juvenile justice system. (Hearings, 1972-1973, p. 61)

Miller recommended full deinstitutionalization of reformatories by virtue of having demonstrated in Massachusetts that reform schools could be replaced by community-based programs. His actions and testimony provided considerable impetus for provision of alternatives to confinement in the juvenile justice system. These looked more promising (Empey, 1974). Moreover, empirical evidence of training schools' ineffectiveness was available. Lipton, Martinson, and Wilks's (1975; see also Martinson, 1974) comprehensive review of correctional programs had just been completed, concluding that "nothing works." Lerman (1970b, 1971) and others (Lerman, 1970a) had arrived at similar conclusions. Training school and prison rehabilitation state-of-the-art was summarized best by Keller and Alper (1970):

The rate of failure from our fixed institutions for young and old offenders has remained more constant through the years than any other index upon which we rely—cost of living, Dow Jones, or the annual precipitation of rain. An average of the recidivism rates reported by the most reliable researcher runs consistently in a range of from one-half to two-thirds. No other facility created by our society for dealing with any other area of social pathology which showed such a consistently high rate of failure could so long endure. (p. xi)

Reasons for the failure of prisons and training schools were unclear. Empey (1967) suggested that the theory underlying custodial confinement was faulty. He said, "Until improvements are made in the theories which underlie treatment, changes in correctional structures, by themselves, will be unlikely to produce dramatic reductions in delinquency and criminality. Instead, we will have more refined failure" (p. 6).

Howard James's (1967) Pulitzer Prize-winning exposé of juvenile correctional institutions also got Congress's attention. In fact, the last words printed in the 1973 volume of Hearings Before the Subcommittee to Investigate Juvenile Delinquency on the JJDP Act, just prior to its introduction to Congress, was an excerpt from James's book:

What is needed most is a national effort— a binding together of all groups interested in the problems of children, all working for the same goal, all pressing for reform. Such a group, if it spoke with a single, concerned voice, could move mountains. (Hearings, 1972-1973, p. 928)

The Congress was not completely persuaded of the efficacy of alternatives to incarceration for serious offenders.

Juvenile justice officials are increasingly recognizing the need for alternative forms of treatment for serious youthful offenders which are community-based. Custodial incarceration in large statewide institutions has proven to be ineffective as a treatment method; however, evaluation of community-based alternatives has indicated some initial successes but as yet has not been conclusive. (Committee on the Judiciary, 1974, p. 25)

Congress thus opted for the "least restrictive alternative" for all juvenile offenders in the JJDP Act and required deinstitutionalization of status offenders (DSO) and nonoffenders (dependent and neglected). The Congress reasoned, however, that if the system were reserved for the most serious and dangerous delinquents, it could do a better job with its scarce resources. Nonoffenders, status offenders, and nonserious/nonviolent offenders should not occupy beds in detention centers and reform schools. Their needs should be met through alternative programs, including shelter care, foster homes, group homes, and community-based alternatives to incarceration.

The "statement of the problem" contained in the report of the Committee on the Judiciary

(1974) identified four major policy positions that undergirded the JJDP Act. First, public policy must give priority to juvenile delinquency prevention. The committee noted that "the problem of juvenile delinquency must be dealt with in an effective and meaningful manner if we are to reduce the ever increasing levels of crime and improve the quality of life in America." The committee quoted the National Advisory Commission on Criminal Justice Standards and Goals: "The highest attention must be given to preventing juvenile delinquency, to minimizing the involvement of young offenders in the juvenile and criminal justice system and to integrating delinquents and young offenders into the community" (1974, pp. 20-21).

Second, status offenders must be provided with services outside the juvenile justice system. "Nearly 40 percent (one-half million per year) of the children brought to the attention of the juvenile justice system have committed no criminal act, in adult terms, and are involved simply because they are juveniles. . . . These [are] status offenders. . . . These juvenile status offenders generally are inappropriate clients for the formal police, courts, and corrections process of the juvenile justice system. These children and youth should be channeled to those agencies and professions which are mandated and in fact purport to deal with the substantive human and social issues involved in these areas" (Committee on the Judiciary, 1974, p. 23).

Third, increased juvenile justice system resources and attention must be focused on the serious juvenile offender. Congress expected that the juvenile justice system would be more effective if its limited resources were concentrated on more serious offenders. "If the status offender were diverted into the social service delivery network, the remaining juveniles would be those who have committed acts which, under any circumstances, would be considered criminal. It is essential that greater attention be given to serious youth crime, which has increased significantly in recent years" (Committee on the Judiciary, 1974, p. 24). The disproportionate involvement of juveniles in all major crime categories was emphatically noted by the Committee on the Judiciary (1974):

> Juveniles under 18 are responsible for 51% of total arrests for property crimes, 23% of violent crimes, and 45% of all serious crime. From 1960 to the present, arrests of juveniles under 18 for violent

crimes, such as murder, rape, and robbery, increased 216%. During the same period, arrests of juveniles for property crimes, such as burglary and auto theft, increased 91%. Between 1960 and 1970, total juvenile arrests (under 18) increased almost three times faster than adult arrests. Recidivism rates for juvenile offenders are estimated to range from 60% to 75% and higher. . . . With regard to the increasing rate of juvenile crime, recent crime data indicate that serious juvenile crime is increasing at a lower rate; however, the problem remains largely intractable. (p. 21)

Fourth, community-based programs must be developed to provide program alternatives to incarceration. "The need is present to comprehensively assess the effectiveness of traditional institutional procedures for dealing with certain juvenile offenders. . . . [and] the search for alternatives to institutionalization of juvenile offenders must be continued. . . ." (Committee on the Judiciary, 1974, pp. 24-25). Community-based programs using the least restrictions possible, located near the juvenile's home, seemed to hold the most promise.

The Judiciary Committee's discovery that nearly 40% of incarcerated juveniles had committed no criminal act startled the Congress. Senator Hruska (1974) observed that "The figure is staggering in recognition of the detrimental effects that incarceration has been shown to produce with first offenders and juveniles." Thus, Congress was provided an empirical basis for challenging the informal operations of juvenile courts that made possible the widespread incarceration of status offenders and nonoffenders. Outraged, Congress seriously considered eliminating juvenile court jurisdiction over status offenders. Having been influenced by the work of the National Advisory Commission on Criminal Justice Standards and Goals, the Judiciary Committee recognized the need to grant constitutional rights to juveniles involved in the formal system. Thus, the JJDP Act amended the Federal Juvenile Delinquency Act (which had remained virtually unchanged for 35 years) to "provide basic procedural rights for juveniles who come under Federal jurisdiction and to bring Federal procedures up to the standards set by various model acts, many state codes and court decisions" (Committee on the Judiciary, 1974, p. 19).

The Need for System Improvements

Congress concluded that things had gotten out of hand in the juvenile justice system. It was not meeting its (individualized justice) promise. The question was, What kinds of changes would revive the promise? In the view of the Congress, the solution lay in three arenas: delinquency prevention, system improvements, and development of alternatives to juvenile justice system processing.

Effective delinquency prevention programs were necessary to reduce the flow of juveniles into the system. In the congressional view, today's dependent and neglected kids become tomorrow's status offenders, who subsequently become delinquents. It was imperative that the cycle be broken, through a combination of community services and avoidance of labeling of these kids as "bad," thereby setting into motion a self-fulfilling prophecy that might enhance the likelihood of subsequent delinquency and criminality. Community control of delinquency therefore was preferred. In making this choice, Congress adopted the approach recommended by the Crime Commission (1967a), giving top priority to delinquency prevention by addressing community conditions, school failure, family problems, and unemployment. In many respects, the Congress adopted the view of Chicago's progressive reformers, that juvenile delinquency emanates from undesirable community and family conditions, and that community-generated solutions hold the most promise (Platt, 1970). Youth Service Bureaus, advocated by the Crime Commission, and other "major innovations in coping with this predelinquent or potentially delinquent behavior" were identified as ways of "delivering needed services or attention in such a way and at a time that may be crucial in preventing the development of a criminal career" (Committee on the Judiciary, 1974, p. 23).

Juvenile justice system improvements also were seen as a top priority. The Judiciary Committee found four major problems surrounding juvenile justice system operations.

> First, juvenile justice systems tend to be fragmented, bifurcated, and localized in their institutional responses to delinquency. . . . Second, the need is present to comprehensively assess the effectiveness of traditional institutional procedures for dealing with certain juvenile offend-

ers. . . . Third, the search for alternatives to institutionalization of juvenile offenders must be continued. . . . Fourth, in large measure, the agencies and institutions of the juvenile justice system have not been held accountable, and have not been well monitored. (Committee on the Judiciary, 1974, pp. 24-25)

The committee concluded that it was

> necessary, therefore, to provide a comprehensive and coordinated focus to the issues surrounding juvenile delinquency prevention, control, and offender rehabilitation with a balance reflected by: assistance to those agencies and professions charged with the responsibility for developing the positive potential of young people, thereby reducing the likelihood of youthful criminal justice system involvement; assistance in the development of State and local mechanisms designed to channel juveniles, for whom the criminal justice system is inappropriate, away from and out of the system into human problem-solving agencies and professions; and assistance to police, courts, and correctional agencies together with community resources, in their efforts to control and reduce crimes committed by juveniles, to improve the quality of justice for juveniles, and to deal effectively and humanely with offenders. (p. 22)

The U.S. House of Representatives held hearings in 1974 on the JJDP Act (Hearings Before the Subcommittee on Equal Opportunity, 1974). Congressman Claude Pepper summed up the predominant theme of the testimony heard by the Committee on Education and Labor (1974, p. 5) when he described federal support and coordination of juvenile justice programs as a "national disgrace." The committee had found that

> almost half of all serious crimes committed in this nation are committed by juveniles. Yet only about 15% of the resources of the LEAA and $10 million of the Department of HEW's Office of Human Development's resources are allocated for the prevention and treatment of youth crime. Further, these relatively meager federal efforts are fragmented and poorly coordi-

nated. As a consequence, efforts by the states and localities to address this important problem reflect the tentative, ill-defined approach of the federal government. (Committee on Education and Labor, 1974, p. 1)

Whereas the Senate Judiciary Committee viewed delinquency prevention in terms of providing services for dependent and neglected youths and others who otherwise might enter the juvenile justice system, the House Education and Labor Committee saw the need for more fundamental delinquency prevention efforts. Consequently, provisions were included in the House version of the JJDP Act for drug abuse education and prevention, alternative education programs, youth-initiated programs, youth rights and responsibilities programs, and advocacy programs. The Education and Labor Committee hypothesized that juvenile delinquency could be prevented by working "to keep youngsters in elementary and secondary schools, preventing unwarranted and arbitrary suspensions and expulsions and school 'push-outs' " (Committee on Education and Labor, 1974, p. 9).

The Committee on Education and Labor also saw a link between adolescent running away from home and delinquency. The problem, however, was conceptualized in a unique manner:

Testimony . . . revealed that, contrary to the overly romanticized and popular view, children run away from home because of problems in relation to their families. It is an expression of a search for a constructive resolution to these difficulties. Indications are that, far from becoming perpetrators of criminal acts, the youth are more often the victims of crime. (Committee on Education and Labor, 1974, p. 9)

In general, Congress saw preventing youth from coming into contact with the juvenile justice system as essential to delinquency prevention. In his final argument for congressional passage of the JJDP Act, Senator Bayh (1974b) said,

the juvenile justice system has proven itself incapable of turning these people away from lives of crime. Our goal is to make the prevention of delinquency a No. 1 national priority of the federal govern-

ment, and in so doing save tens of thousands of young people from the ravages of a life of crime, while helping them, their families and society.

Congress thus agreed with the National Advisory Commission on Criminal Justice Standards and Goals (1973) that the highest priority must be given to preventing juvenile delinquency, to minimizing the involvement of children and adolescents in the juvenile and criminal justice systems, and to reintegrating delinquents into the community.

Philosophy of the JJDP Act

In its preamble to the JJDP Act, Congress stated the following "findings":

(1) juveniles account for almost half the arrests for serious crimes in the United States today;

(2) understaffed, overcrowded juvenile courts, probation services, and correctional facilities are not able to provide individualized justice or effective help;

(3) present juvenile courts, foster and protective care programs, and shelter facilities are inadequate to meet the needs of the countless, abandoned, and dependent children, who, because of this failure to provide effective services, may become delinquents;

(4) existing programs have not adequately responded to the particular problems of the increasing numbers of young people who are addicted to or who abuse drugs, particularly nonopiate or polydrug abusers;

(5) juvenile delinquency can be prevented through programs designed to keep students in elementary and secondary schools through the prevention of unwarranted and arbitrary suspensions and expulsions;

(6) states and local communities which experience directly the devastating failures of the juvenile justice system do not presently have sufficient technical expertise or adequate resources to deal comprehensively with the problems of juvenile delinquency; and

(7) existing Federal programs have not provided the direction, coordination,

resources and leadership required to meet the crisis of delinquency. (P.L. 93-415, Sec. 101(a))

Professional Associations and Public Interest Groups

The JJDP Act was endorsed by many of the major organizations working in the field of youth development and delinquency prevention, such as the National Council on Crime and Delinquency, the National Council of Juvenile Court Judges, the National Youth Alternatives Project, the American Institute of Family Relations, the American Parents Committee, B'nai B'rith Women, the National Council of Jewish Women, the National Association of State Juvenile Delinquency Program Administrators, the National Governors Conference, the National League of Cities, and the U.S. Conference of Mayors.

It also was supported by the Interagency Collaboration on Juvenile Justice, consisting of the Boys' Clubs of America, Boy Scouts of America, Camp Fire Girls, Future Homemakers of America, Girls' Clubs of America, Girl Scouts of the U.S.A., the National Board of YMCAs, the National Board of the YWCAs, the National Federation of Settlements and Neighborhood Centers, the National Jewish Welfare Board, and the Red Cross.

Federal Agency Location of the Program

Utilitarian and labeling concerns sparked a congressional debate regarding whether the new program should be located in the Department of Justice, in its Law Enforcement Assistance Administration (LEAA), or in HEW. In the utilitarian and labeling views, placement of the JJDP Act office in LEAA could well mean a continuing overreach of the juvenile justice system into the lives of nonoffenders and minor offenders, harmfully labeling them as delinquent. Congress expressed misgivings regarding the Justice Department's ability to address delinquency prevention because of its main focus on the juvenile justice system. At the same time, congressional dissatisfaction with HEW's efforts in this area was manifest (Committee on the Judiciary, 1974, pp. 28-29).

That LEAA had well established its role in the juvenile delinquency field, primarily through the awarding of block grants to the states under the Omnibus Crime Control and Safe Streets Act of 1968, was a persuasive factor. The agency reported that it had spent nearly $140 million on a wide range of juvenile delinquency programs in 1972 (Committee on the Judiciary, 1974, p. 34). Congress also expressed concern that

the creation of the program in HEW would only further fragment and divide the Federal juvenile delinquency effort and delay the development of needed programs. What is needed now is more coordination and less confusion.

LEAA, through its programs, is the only agency able to provide the leadership and funding for the continuum of responses which must be made to deal with juvenile crime. . . . These goals can only be achieved by tying in juvenile and criminal justice efforts with the larger social service and human resource networks of the States and units of local government. LEAA is actively pursuing these goals. (Committee on the Judiciary, 1974, p. 33)

In addition, Congress felt that the need to focus the juvenile justice apparatus on the serious juvenile offender argued for placing the program in LEAA. "The social control of the juvenile and criminal justice system must be applied in dealing with this offender, and LEAA is the only Federal agency providing substantial assistance to the police, the courts, and the corrections agencies in their efforts to deal with juvenile crime" (Committee on the Judiciary, 1974, p. 34).

An important factor in the debate was the respective agencies' responses to a congressional query regarding what each already was doing in the area of research, training, and information dissemination; what they would do if the provisions became law; how long it would take to establish the program; and how much money they would put into it. LEAA responded the next day; HEW finally responded more than a month later, after considerable prodding (Quie, 1974, p. H8794). Congress took this event to indicate the greater level of interest in the program in the Justice Department.

Senator Bayh forged a partnership with Senator Hruska, the "father of LEAA," agreeing to locate the new agency within the Department of Justice (Raley, 1995). That is where the new

Office of Juvenile Justice and Delinquency Prevention (OJJDP), created by the JJDP Act, was established. President Gerald Ford signed the Juvenile Justice and Delinquency Prevention Act of 1974 (P.L. 93-415) into law on September 7, 1974.

Four Major JJDP
Act Requirements

The most controversial feature of the JJDP Act is the four mandates that it required states to meet to be eligible to receive funds under the act. In an unprecedented step in federal involvement in crime and delinquency policy, Congress determined that the conditions these mandates targeted were not in the best interests of the nation and were beyond the capability of the states to correct. Congress therefore intervened to require deinstitutionalization of status offenders, separation of juveniles from adults in confinement, jail and lockup removal, and reduction in the disproportionate confinement of minorities.

Deinstitutionalization
of Status Offenders

Hearings that Congress held pursuant to drafting the JJDP Act brought to the surface the surprising extent of child and adolescent detention. The NCCD's (1967) survey showed that nearly 320,000 children and adolescents were held in juvenile detention centers in 1965. Almost 90,000 were held in adult jails. The census of children's institutions reported by Pappenfort and Kilpatrick (1970) found that during 1967, nearly 900 children of elementary school age were in detention, as were 254 children under the age of 6, of whom 81 were infants. Other studies reported that conditions of confinement were deplorable, including overcrowding, inadequate diet, questionable disciplinary measures, and overly long confinement—no different from detention conditions reported 40 years earlier (Rosenheim, 1973). For example, an investigative panel looking into confinement conditions in New York City's Spofford Juvenile Center found "inadequate light and heat . . . faulty plumbing, poor lighting . . . leaky roofs, cracked hot-water pipes, and inadequate insulation" (NCCD, 1967, p. 8).

The NCCD's (1967) survey also confirmed the previously acknowledged variations in detention practices. "Juvenile court jurisdiction in most States is so broad that almost any child can be picked up by the police and placed in detention. . . . Because of confusion between court and child welfare functions, many legal definitions of delinquency make no distinction between crime and child neglect" (NCCD, 1967, p. 126). Rubin (1961, p. 49) illustrated the varied acts or conditions included under the "delinquency" heading in American juvenile court laws that might result in detention or jailing of juveniles. These included

Violates any law or ordinance

Immoral or indecent conduct

Immoral conduct around schools

Engages in illegal occupation

Associates with vicious or immoral persons

Growing up in idleness or crime

Enters, visits house of ill repute

Patronizes, visits policy shop or gaming place

Patronizes place where intoxicating liquor is sold

Patronizes public poolroom or bucket shops

Wanders in the streets at night, not on lawful business

Wanders about railroad yards or tracks

Jumps train or enters car or engine without authority

Habitually truant from school

Incorrigible

Uses vile, obscene, or vulgar language (in public place)

Absents self from home without consent

Loiters, sleeps in alleys

Refuses to obey parent, guardian

Uses intoxicating liquors

Deports self so as to injure self or others

Smokes cigarettes (around a public place)

In occupation or situation dangerous to self or others

Begging or receiving alms (or in street for purpose of)

Research illustrated the use of informal juvenile court procedures that resulted in excessive detention and incarceration of status offenders in training schools and other residential facilities (Ferster, Snethen, & Courtless, 1969; Pappenfort & Kilpatrick, 1970). These and other studies were reviewed by Rosenheim (1973) in her chapter that influenced congressional thinking. She made the case that in many states where there are no detention facilities and temporary shelter facilities, juveniles are held in adult jails or incarcerated in juvenile training schools. Pappenfort and Kilpatrick (1970) reported that in 1965, there were only 54 temporary shelters in the United States, holding 1,832 children, compared to 11,000 in detention.

Rosenheim (1973) made a persuasive argument for development of shelter care facilities and other programs that would serve as alternatives to detention, jailing, and incarceration of status offenders. She documented consistent misuse of detention, in three ways: It was resorted to when another form of care would be more appropriate, it was used out of convenience or to satisfy the cautious instincts of officials when they believed a child should be separated from the family while awaiting a court appearance, and it was used as punishment.

The 1974 JJDP Act required that states receiving funds under it must "provide within two years . . . that juveniles who are charged with or who have committed offenses that would not be criminal if committed by an adult shall not be placed in juvenile detention or correctional facilities, but must be placed in shelter facilities" (Sec. 223(a)(12)). The shelter facility placement requirement was relaxed in the 1977 amendments, and "nonoffenders" (dependent and neglected children) were added to the mandate. At the urging of the National Council of Juvenile and Family Court Judges, in 1980 Congress amended the JJDP Act's deinstitutionalization of status offenders (DSO) requirement to make an exception for status offenders and nonoffenders found to have violated a "valid court order (VCO)." Juvenile court judges believed that this exception was needed, particularly in the case of chronic runaways, who habitually violate court orders. The VCO provision can be applied to status offenders once procedural requirements are met, including court hearings, confrontation rights, the right to notification of charges against them, and the submission of a written report by another agency other than law enforcement or another court. It permits courts to confine status

offenders in detention centers for limited periods of time, but VCO violators may not be adjudicated delinquent and removed from the deinstitutionalization requirement under the VCO provision (Holden & Kapler, 1995, p. 8).

Separation of Juveniles From Adults in Confinement

Congress was appalled by the extent of juvenile confinement in adult jails and the conditions it found under which juveniles were being incarcerated with adults, particularly in jails and police lockups (Hearings Before the Subcommittee to Investigate Juvenile Delinquency, 1973). Three studies had documented the deplorable circumstance. The NCCD's (1967) jail survey conducted for the 1967 Crime Commission documented the scope of the problems surrounding the jailing of juveniles. Conducted in 1965, it revealed that

> the estimated number of children of juvenile court age held in (admitted to) county jails and police lockups in 1965 was over 100,000. . . . Ninety-three percent of the country's juvenile court jurisdictions covering about 2,800 counties and cities . . . have no place of detention other than a county jail or police lockup. Less than 20 percent of the jails in which children are held have been rated as suitable for adult Federal offenders. Nine states forbid placing children in jail, but this prohibition is not always enforced. In 19 states the law permits juveniles to be jailed if they are segregated from adults, but this provision also is not always adhered to. Children under 7 years of age have been held in substandard county jails for lack of shelter care in foster homes. Some of the youngsters had committed delinquent acts; some were merely dependent or neglected. Juvenile detention is frequently used as an immediate punishment for delinquent acts. (NCCD, 1967, pp. 121-122)

An Illinois jail study (Mattick & Sweet, 1969) found that juveniles represented about 6% of the inmates, although other studies reported juvenile jail populations as low as less than 1% (California) and as high as 45% (Virginia) (Mattick, 1974, p. 796). Nearly 70% of the Illinois county jails were 50 years old or older.

Most contained double bunks. Nearly a third had no medical facilities, and 64% had "first aid" only. Elementary commodities such as soap, towels, toothbrushes, and clean bedding, if available, were in short supply. The older jails posed a public health problem. They were havens for rodents, body lice, and other vermin. Mattick concluded that "If cleanliness is next to godliness, most jails lie securely in the province of hell" (1974, p. 802).

Rosemary Sarri, then codirector of the National Assessment of Juvenile Corrections project, presented testimony based on preliminary results from the project's 1972 analysis of juvenile codes in the United States (Sarri, 1974; see also Sarri, 1973, 1981; Sarri & Hasenfeld, 1976; Vinter, 1976; Vinter, Downs, & Hall, 1975), which showed that only 5 states absolutely prohibited jailing of juveniles and that 13 required that juveniles be held in separate sections of jails (Hearings Before the Subcommittee to Investigate Juvenile Delinquency, 1973, p. 31). Other widely recognized studies showed extensive incarceration of juveniles in adult jails, including Abbott (1916), Fishman (1923), Sumner (1971), and several NCCD studies (1967).

Downey (1970) summarized 23 studies that the U.S. Children's Bureau sponsored during the 1960s that examined 18,000 cases (in 18 states) of children in jail. He found that most state laws that were intended to protect children "from the evils of jail" did not keep children out of jail. Downey concluded that most children held in jail do not need to be locked up anywhere. They are unnecessarily confined for many reasons, including the use of jail for punishment or "treatment," poor court policies, and lack of open shelter care facilities. His review showed an apparent intent to keep children out of jail, for all the state laws contained a phrase like "no child shall be held in any jail, police lockup," but this phrase was usually followed by another qualifying one such as "unless ordered by the court" or "unless they are held in quarters separate and apart from any adult." About 40% of the children were jailed for acts that would not have been violations of law if committed by an adult.

The National Advisory Commission on Criminal Justice Standards and Goals (1976, p. 667) and the American Bar Association (1980) both urged standards prohibiting comingling of juveniles and adults. The National Sheriff's Association (1974, p. 31) urged full segregation from adults when jail detention

could not possibly be avoided, and the American Correctional Association had promulgated a standard calling for separate living quarters for juveniles housed with adults (1977, p. 177).

The Senate version of the JJDP Act (S. 821), introduced by Senator Bayh in 1973, called for removal of juveniles from adult jails (Sec. 403(a)(13)). When introducing the bill, Senator Bayh stated:

> The bill contains an absolute prohibition against the detention or confinement of any juvenile alleged or found to be delinquent in any institution in which adults— whether convicted or merely awaiting trial—are confined. Juveniles who are incarcerated with sophisticated criminals are much less likely to be rehabilitated. The older offenders become the teachers of graduate seminars in crime. . . . There is no reason to imprison adults and juveniles together. Only harm can come from such a policy, and this bill would forbid it completely. (Hearings Before the Subcommittee to Investigate Juvenile Delinquency, 1973, p. 262)

The final version of the JJDP Act, in Section 223(a)(12), required only separation of juveniles from adults in confinement. Complete separation was required, so that there was no sight or sound contact with adult offenders in the facility, including sallyports; entry/booking areas; hallways; and sleeping, dining, recreational, educational, vocational, and health care areas (OJJDP, 1995c, p. 26).

Jail and Lockup Removal

In 1980, the JJDP Act was amended (42 U.S.C. Sec. 5633(a)(14)) to require removal of juveniles from adult jails and police lockups. This provision drew its impetus from two main sources: OJJDP staff and public interest groups.

After 5 years of experience in implementing the JJDP Act separation requirement, OJJDP staff came to the conclusion that the act should be amended to require removal of children from adult jails and institutions. A detailed OJJDP staff position paper (Wood, 1980) helped obtain U.S. Department of Justice and congressional support for the amendment.

The OJJDP staff position paper cited several studies that documented the extent of juvenile jailing. A survey of nine states by the Children's Defense Fund (1976) found that only 18% of juveniles held in jails had been charged with a criminal offense, 4% had committed no offense at all, and 88% were there because of property offenses.

The LEAA's 1970 jail census (LEAA, 1971), the first of its kind, showed that 7,800 juveniles were confined in U.S. jails on a given day in March 1970. By 1972, this census (LEAA, 1974) found that the number had increased to 12,744. These figures did not include police lockups. Higher figures came from other sources. The National Assessment of Juvenile Corrections Project (Sarri, 1974) estimated the number to range from 120,000 to 500,000.

The OJJDP's staff position paper (Wood, 1980) offered several rationales in support of its recommendation. Costs associated with jail removal would be less than those required to separate juveniles from adults in jails and institutions. An OJJDP study (Dykatra, 1980) supported this position. Another OJJDP study (Flaherty, 1980) found the suicide rate among jailed juveniles to be seven times as high as the rate among juveniles held in detention centers. Experience had shown that juveniles did not receive basic services (counseling, medical, recreational) in facilities constructed and operated for adults. The position paper cited (pp. 271-272) several recent Supreme Court and state court decisions that brought constitutional considerations to bear on various issues associated with confinement of juveniles, including *Robinson v. California* (cruel and unusual punishment), *Sheldon v. Tucker* (failure to use the least restrictive alternative), *Baker v. Hamilton* (denial of due process), *Cox v. Turley* (cruel and unusual punishment), *Swansey v. Elrod* (cruel and unusual punishment), *Baker v. Hamilton* (cruel and unusual punishment), and *Lollis v. New York State Department of Corrections* (cruel and inhumane treatment).

A groundswell of opposition to jailing juveniles began much earlier, in the 1960s. In 1961, the National Council on Crime and Delinquency (NCCD, 1961) opposed placing juveniles in adult jails and lockups, as did the President's Commission on Law Enforcement and Administration of Justice (1967a, p. 87). In the late 1970s, a National Coalition for Jail Reform (1980) was formed, funded by the Edna McConnell Clark Foundation. Its impressive membership of 28 organizations included the American Civil Liberties Union (National Prison Project),

American Correctional Association, National Sheriff's Association, American Public Health Association, John Howard Association, National Association of Counties, National Center for State Courts, National Council on Crime and Delinquency, National League of Cities, and the National Moratorium on Prison Construction. On April 25, 1979, it adopted, by consensus, the position that no person under age 18 should be held in an adult jail, following its basic premise that "the first step in reforming the jails is to remove people who don't belong there" (Subcommittee on Human Resources, 1980, p. 308).

The jail removal amendment also was supported by the U.S. Justice Department (in the Carter Administration), through the testimony of then Deputy Attorney General Charles B. Renfrew. He stated, in part:

> It has long been recognized . . . that children require special protections when they come into contact with the criminal justice system. An initial reason for the development of juvenile courts was to provide such protections and separate children from the adult criminal justice system. One area where we have failed to provide the necessary protection, however, is the placement of juveniles in adult jails and lock-ups. . . . The jailing of children remains a national catastrophe.
>
> Separation has been particularly difficult to accomplish in county jails and municipal lock-ups because adequate separation, as intended by the Act, is virtually impossible within most of the facilities. As a result, juveniles are often isolated in what are the most undesirable areas of the facilities, such as solitary cells and drunk tanks. . . . The requirement of the Act that juveniles and adults be separated in all institutions is laudatory, but with respect to jails and lock-ups we must go further than separation. (Subcommittee on Human Resources, 1980, pp. 38-39)

Section 223(a)(14) of the JJDP Act was amended in 1980 to prohibit holding juveniles in jails and law enforcement lockups in which adults may be detained or confined. The jail removal amendment to the JJDP Act was supported by the Subcommittee on Human Resources of the Committee on Education and Labor, U.S. House of Representatives, in the course of the 1980 reauthorization of the JJDP Act. The Committee on Education and Labor Report (Subcommittee on Human Resources, 1980, p. 24) stated that "the committee believes, based on evidence presented during hearings on H. R. 6704 (the House bill reauthorizing the JJDP Act), that the time has come to go further [than separation]." Four factors were identified in the Committee Report that "prompted" the amendment: statistics on inappropriate placements, evidence of harm to juveniles, the growing body of constitutional law, and the expressed belief that properly planned and implemented removal of juveniles from adult jails and lockups is economically feasible (pp. 24-25).

Disproportionate Minority Confinement

Enactment of the fourth JJDP Act requirement, reducing disproportionate minority confinement (DMC), is attributable mainly to the support of the Coalition for Juvenile Justice. This organization (formerly called the National Coalition of State Juvenile Justice Advisory Groups) performs JJDP Act functions, including provision of technical support to its member organizations (the State Advisory Groups required in the JJDP Act) and advising the president, Congress, and the OJJDP administrator regarding OJJDP operations and legislation. The Coalition for Juvenile Justice has exercised enormous influence in these areas (Coalition for Juvenile Justice, 1993).

Perhaps the greatest accomplishment of the Coalition for Juvenile Justice is its successful effort in securing enactment into law of the DMC requirement. At the insistence of the coalition, Congress directed, in the 1988 Amendments to the JJDP Act, that specific attention be given throughout the act to disproportionate representation of minority youth in the juvenile justice system, particularly in detention facilities, secure correctional institutions, and adult jails and lockups (Sec. 223(a)(23)). The coalition documented the DMC problem in its 1989 report (Coalition for Juvenile Justice, 1989). It called attention to the disproportionate confinement of minority youth, that 55% of youths confined in public detention and correctional facilities were minorities, and that the percentage had been increasing since 1979. Of equal concern, the coalition (pp. 13-15) worried that lack of legitimate economic opportunities for minority youngsters might increase their involvement in the illegal drug trade and exacerbate the DMC problem. Its concern turned out to be prophetic (see Coalition for Juvenile Justice, 1994; Johns, 1992; Mann, 1993; Meddis, 1993a; Tonry, 1994a, 1994b).

An OJJDP study of disproportionate minority confinement (Pope & Feyerherm, 1993) supported the need for the DMC efforts. This study documented disproportionate confinement of minorities across the country. Pope and Feyerherm (1993, p. 3) concluded that there was "substantial support . . . that both direct and indirect race effects operate within certain juvenile justice systems." Other studies carried out in California (Austin, Dimas, & Steinhart, 1992), Florida (Bishop & Frazier, 1988, 1990), Georgia (Lockhart, Kurtz, & Sutphen, 1991), Missouri (Kempf, Decker, & Bing, 1990), and Pennsylvania (Kempf, 1992), as well as a literature review (Pope & Feyerherm, 1990), produced strong evidence that minority youth were overrepresented in the juvenile justice system. Advocates used these studies to illustrate the need for strengthening the DMC requirement (see Coalition for Juvenile Justice, 1993; OJJDP, 1994; Rhoden, 1994; and Roscoe & Morton, 1994, for a history and overview of the overrepresentation problem and OJJDP responses).

In 1992, Congress made DMC the fourth JJDP Act mandate, requiring that states receiving JJDP Act formula grants provide assurances that they will develop and implement plans to reduce the overrepresentation of minorities in the juvenile justice system (42 U.S.C. Sec. 5633(a)(23)) when the proportion of minority youth in confinement exceeds the proportion those groups represent in the general population. To meet the DMC mandate, states must complete three phases required in the OJJDP Formula Grants Regulation (28 CFR 31)—problem identification, problem assessment, and program intervention—within established time frames.

Since enactment of the JJDP Act in 1974, states have maintained eligibility to receive "formula" grant funding (based on their proportion of the total U.S. population under age 18) by making sufficient progress toward achieving the act's goals. In the 1992 JJDP Act amendments, Congress added a financial incentive to accelerate states' progress toward full compliance with the four mandates by requiring that 25% of a state's formula grant allocation be withheld annually for each mandate with which the state is not complying. In addition, the new amendment required that a noncomplying state direct the remainder of its formula grant funds to achieving full compliance (42 U.S.C. Sec. 5633(c)(3)(A) and (B)).

State Compliance

A state's participation in the JJDP Act Formula Grants Program is voluntary. To be eligible for the program, a state must submit a comprehensive 3-year plan setting forth the state's proposal for meeting the mandates and goals outlined in the JJDP Act. Each state determines its strategy and program priorities based on the characteristics of its particular juvenile justice system. The state's plan is amended annually to reflect new programming and initiatives to be undertaken by the state and local units of government.

Of the 57 eligible states and territories, 55 currently are participating in the JJDP Act Formula Grants Program. Each state submits an annual compliance monitoring report, which details its progress toward implementing its plan and achieving or maintaining compliance with the mandates of the JJDP Act. The level of compliance determines the state's eligibility for continuing participation in the program. Data for the annual monitoring report are collected by the state from secure juvenile and adult facilities. Verification of the data is required.

Data from the 1993 monitoring reports show an overwhelming majority of states and territories in full compliance with the first three major mandates (OJJDP, 1995d). Fifty-four states and territories are in full compliance with the DSO mandate, with zero or de minimus (minimal) exceptions; 55 states and territories are in full compliance with the separation mandate, with zero or de minimus exceptions; 53 states and territories are in full compliance with the jail removal mandate, with zero or de minimus exceptions; and 11 states have completed the first DMC phase, 7 have completed two phases, and 28 have entered the third phase. The time frame for state compliance with the DMC mandate varies by state according to the specific phases. Figure 2.1 shows the reduction in state violations of the DSO, separation, and jail removal mandates between the baseline years and 1993. The baseline years are 1975 for DSO and separation, and 1980 for jail removal. Percentage re-

ductions in violations for each mandate are 98% for DSO, 99% for separation, and 96% for jail removal.

Figure 2.2 shows the dramatic decrease in detention of status offenders since the OJJDP was established in 1975. In that year, 40% of juvenile court cases were detained. In 1992, only 7% of status offenders were detained. Throughout this period, about 20% of delinquency cases were detained. The decline in detention of status offenders represents the most significant change in the administration of juvenile justice brought about by the JJDP Act.

These accomplishments are unprecedented in the history of federal social legislation. Never before have such significant changes been brought about in the states in the administration of governmental structures and legal processes in social systems. Excepting the creation of reform schools and juvenile courts, these are the most significant changes in the history of juvenile justice in the United States. How and why did these changes occur? What factors account for such sweeping changes?

Obstacles to JJDP Act Success

Formidable obstacles to the JJDP Act reforms had to be overcome. Funding for these reforms was very limited. The OJJDP's budget has never exceeded $165 million (the amount of its 1995 allocation), most of which goes to the states in the form of block grants under the Formula Grants Program. During the early years of the JJDP Act, OJJDP's appropriation ranged from $25 million to $100 million, most of which is allocated to the states. The states, nevertheless, have not received funds sufficient to serve as a significant financial incentive to accomplish the JJDP Act mandates.

The OJJDP's presidentially appointed leadership has changed frequently since its establishment, disrupting national leadership supporting the JJDP Act reforms. Since the office was established in 1975, it has had 19 permanent or acting administrators. Many of them, especially during the Reagan and Bush Administrations, were not committed to the goals and mandates of the JJDP Act (for example, see the writings of former administrator Regnery, 1985, 1986; see also Brodt & Smith, 1988, for a rejoinder).

State and local governments have had few resources with which to fund programs to help

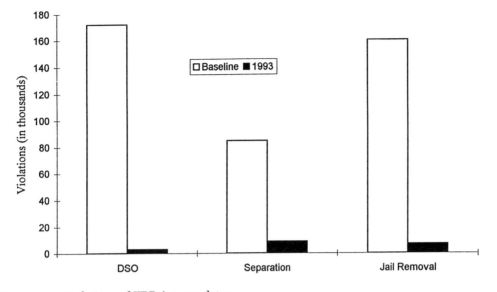

Figure 2.1. Violations of JJDP Act mandates

SOURCE: "Meeting the Mandates," Office of Juvenile Justice and Delinquency Prevention (1995), *Juvenile Justice, 2*, 25-28.

implement the JJDP Act reforms (Guarino-Ghezzi & Loughran, 1996, p. 91; Krisberg & Austin, 1993). State corrections budgets increasingly have been raided for the purposes of prison and jail construction beginning in the 1970s, rather than for the purpose of supporting juvenile justice reforms. Prison and jail construction costs consume 85% of the $25 billion annually spent on corrections in the United States (NCCD, 1993). Juvenile courts and detention receive the smallest proportional amount of juvenile justice system budgets. Youth workers are the most underpaid in the entire field.

Moreover, utilitarian and just deserts philosophies appear to have dominated juvenile justice policy during the period in which DSO, separation, and jail removal have been accomplished. How is it possible that achieving compliance with these mandates could occur while philosophies emphasizing punishment and deterrence are dominant? What factors account for this possibility as well as overcoming this and other obstacles to these juvenile justice reforms?

Reasons for JJDP Act Success

First, professionals in the juvenile justice system and their respective associations have made enormous contributions to achieving compliance with the DSO, separation, and jail removal mandates. The following organizations, and others, representing almost all the professionals in the juvenile justice and youth services system, as well as youth workers, have long been firmly committed to the JJDP Act mandates and have provided extensive training for their membership in how to accomplish them: the American Correctional Association, the American Jail Association, the American Youth Work Center, the Council for Correctional Administrators, the International Association of Chiefs of Police, the Juvenile Justice Trainers Association, the National Association of Juvenile Correctional Administrators, the National Collaboration for Youth, the National Council of Governments, the National Council of Juvenile and Family Court Judges (NCJFCJ), and the National Juvenile Detention Association.

The second key to accomplishing the JJDP Act mandates is the infrastructure it created to implement the act. State advisory groups required by the JJDP Act, appointed by the governors and consisting of representatives of the juvenile justice system, local units of government, private organizations, and youth members, play an active role in the development and approval of state plans, project funding, and other related activities. These bodies also re-

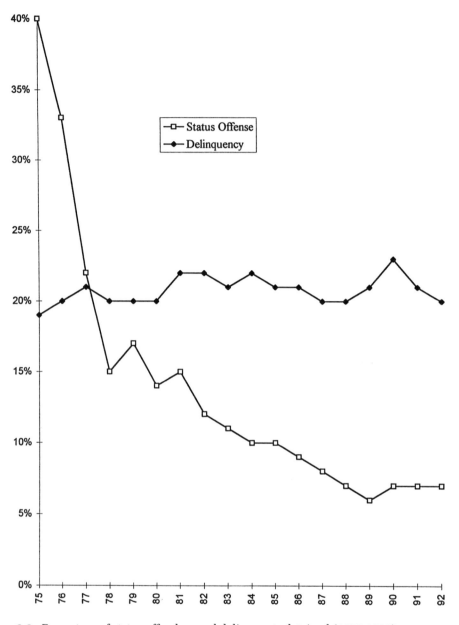

Figure 2.2. Percentage of status offenders and delinquents detained (1975-1992)

SOURCE: *Juvenile Offenders and Victims: A National Report* (p. 147), Snyder and Sickmund, ©copyright 1995 by National Center for Juvenile Justice. Reprinted with permission.

DATA SOURCE: *National Juvenile Court Data Archive: Juvenile Court Case Records 1975-1992* (machine-readable data files), National Center for Juvenile Justice (1994).

view the compliance monitoring reports submitted to OJJDP along with their Formula Grant Program applications. As noted earlier, the Coalition for Juvenile Justice that represents, trains, and serves the state advisory groups has played a key role in accomplishing the JJDP Act mandates as well as advocating retaining them in the JJDP Act. This infrastructure has led and supported much analysis of the delinquency problem and comprehensive planning at the state and local levels based on the JJDP Act mandates. In addition, the JJDP Act has led to increased public awareness of juvenile justice and delinquency prevention issues, the creation of forums for juvenile justice issue discussions, initiation of a cooperative planning process, development of flexible networks of community services to address the changing needs of youth, and adoption of state legislation and policies (Brown, 1995).

The third main factor is the specific program focus on juvenile justice the JJDP Act fostered at the state and local levels. It required that not less than 75% of state JJDP Act funds be allocated to "advanced techniques in developing, maintaining, and expanding programs and services designed to prevent juvenile delinquency, to divert juveniles from the juvenile justice system, and to provide community-based alternatives to juvenile detention and correctional facilities" (Sec. 223(a)(10)). The act linked these "advanced techniques" to its DSO, separation, and (later) jail removal mandates. Achievement of the three mandates thus was supported by JJDP Act funds. A recent review showed that during 1991, 51% of Formula Grant Program funds were used to reach compliance with JJDP Act mandates, 16% for prevention, 7% for serious and violent youth crime, 4% for drug programs, and 22% for a wide range of other purposes (Brown, 1995, p. 24).

Consistent legal support in the Department of Justice for adherence to JJDP Act legal requirements is the fourth factor. The DOJ's Office of Justice Program legal counsel has steadfastly supported state compliance with the major JJDP Act mandates. The states, by and large, have responded positively to the sense of justice and fairness embodied in the JJDP Act mandates and to evenhandness in OJJDP implementation of the act.

Fifth, the JJDP Act inspired effective programs. In outlining advanced program techniques such as involvement of youth and parents in the design and evaluation of programs, use of the least restrictive alternatives, locating programs near juvenile offenders' homes and communities, and urging evaluation of programs, the JJDP Act promoted progressive programming. Although a wide variety of effective and promising programs has been developed over the past 20 years, this progress did not begin with the JJDP Act. The juvenile justice field already had been improving treatment and rehabilitation programs for juvenile offenders.

Sixth, dedicated juvenile justice specialists (state employees with responsibility for planning and program development under the JJDP Act block grant program) have played a key role in some states. Throughout the country, dedicated youth workers tirelessly implement a wide variety of youth service programs, for very low pay and few, if any, benefits. For this, they receive little recognition, yet the programs in which they work are the very programs that come to be recognized as promising and effective.

OJJDP Contributions to the Juvenile Justice Field

Because it is not the purpose of this book to tout OJJDP programs, only a brief review of major program initiatives is made here. This review is also limited in its coverage, to the principal thrusts of the JJDP Act: delinquency prevention, alternatives to incarceration, and improving the juvenile justice system. The number and scope of projects is so large that an exhaustive and systematic evaluation of their lasting effects would require a major research project of its own. Only a few selected programs, therefore, are reviewed here as illustrative cases of JJDP Act contributions to the juvenile justice field in these three areas.

Delinquency Prevention

OJJDP has undertaken five major delinquency prevention experiments, all of which were funded in the late 1970s and early 1990s. One of these aimed to increase the delinquency prevention capacity of youth service organizations. The OJJDP provided funding to national organizations, which in turn sought to strengthen their local affiliates' delinquency prevention services. Although this program was not evaluated, it did not appear to increase delinquency prevention services significantly, but capacity building, youth advocacy, and youth involvement in programs operated by the national organizations appeared to increase (Research and Action, 1981).

Two large-scale OJJDP delinquency prevention programs focused on the school context. The first of these, the School Crime Reduction Initiative, sponsored jointly with the U.S. Department of Education, funded more than 200 teacher-student teams to assess delinquency problems and develop prevention approaches. Evaluation of the program (Grant & Capell, 1983), using reports from more than 35,000 students and 7,000 teachers, showed that school teams were most effective in preventing personal victimization in school, classroom disruption, and fear of crime. They were not, however, successful in reducing theft and drug use.

In the second OJJDP school program, Delinquency Prevention Through Alternative Education, 18 delinquency prevention models were funded in 15 cities, targeting schools serving grades 6 through 12 in relatively high-crime communities with high delinquency rates. Program models varied from secondary prevention programs that provided services to high-risk youths outside the school to interventions within the school that targeted high-risk youths for special services. Services ranged from purely educational interventions to counseling and work-related instruction. Evaluation of the program (Gottfredson, 1987) showed the program to be somewhat successful. It helped schools become safer and less disruptive. The number of schools in which nonattendance declined exceeded the number in which it increased, and the number of schools in which expectations for continuing schooling increased exceeded the number in which they declined.

OJJDP's fourth delinquency prevention program attempted to prevent delinquency in the community. This massive program involved 168 private youth agencies in 68 cities. About 20,000 youth were served by these programs in 2 years. A national evaluation of the program (Krisberg, 1981) found it to be a dismal failure. Although grantees were encouraged to choose from several prevention strategies, they chose instead to reinforce and expand traditional services they previously provided, mainly recreation, counseling, employment, and education. At-risk youth were not targeted. The programs lacked formal intake procedures; therefore, little delinquent behavior was prevented.

OJJDP's fifth delinquency prevention program was a product of its Assessment Center on Delinquent Behavior and Its Prevention, funded in 1976. After 3 years of reviewing studies of delinquency and program evaluations, the Assessment Center developed a theoretical model of delinquency prevention, the Social Development Model (Weis & Hawkins, 1979), and designed and implemented the Seattle So-

cial Development Project, which has produced a breakthrough in delinquency prevention (see Chapter 9). Unfortunately, the OJJDP was not allowed to enjoy the fruits of the developmental work it supported. Funding for the Seattle Social Development Project was terminated in 1981 by OJJDP Administrator Alfred Regnery, under whose administration OJJDP turned away from delinquency prevention toward punitive approaches to delinquency (see Regnery, 1986). Largely because of the fifth juvenile justice reform movement's emphasis on punishment and deterrence (see Chapter 1), which Regnery ushered into the OJJDP, the office did not support major delinquency prevention programs designed specifically for this purpose until Congress mandated that it do so in the 1992 amendments to the JJDP Act. These amendments created the Title V Delinquency Prevention Program (see OJJDP, 1995f, 1996), which is now being implemented in every state (see Chapter 9).

Alternatives to the Juvenile Justice System

The OJJDP's initial efforts to divert juveniles from the juvenile justice system were effective in accomplishing this administrative aim but were not particularly successful in achieving the longer-term objective of reducing delinquency. The office's first program, Deinstitutionalization of Status Offenders, supported 13 DSO projects that served more than 16,000 youths in their first 2 years of operation. The two main objectives of this massive program were providing alternatives to confinement of status offenders in detention centers and reformatories, and recidivism reduction. Its national evaluation (Kobrin & Klein, 1983) showed that a reduction in secure placement of status offenders was accomplished in most sites, but DSO clients showed a slightly higher recidivism rate than preprogram control groups. Alternative services for status offenders were not necessarily productive.

Two other findings were equally important. The evaluation strongly suggested that the "pure" status offender is relatively uncommon; most juveniles in both the experimental and preprogram group evidenced a mixed pattern of status and delinquent offenses. About 10% of the status offenders were found to be chronic offenders. Finally, considerable "net widening" appeared to occur. Funded programs appeared to serve many youths who otherwise would not have been detained or incarcerated. The experiment proved that accomplishing DSO was more difficult than many observers believed. Perhaps the most difficult part was providing effective alternative services.

A subsequent review (Schneider, 1985b; see also Schneider, 1986) of more than 70 empirical DSO studies generally substantiated the national DSO evaluation results. Although this review confirmed substantial reductions in confinement of status offenders in public correctional facilities, unintended side effects were apparent. Commitments to private correctional institutions increased substantially. Moreover, "relabeling" status offenders as delinquents appeared to be a common occurrence. Schneider called for concerted efforts to improve the quality of services for status offenders.

The OJJDP's first experience with diversion proved to be very similar to the DSO experiment, as foretold by Klein (1979). Eleven programs were funded, of which four were intensively evaluated. At these four sites, arrested youths, more than 1,300 in all, were assigned randomly to either outright release, referral to a diversion program, or normal processing by the juvenile justice system. The national evaluation of the program (Dunford, Osgood, & Weichselbaum, 1982) found evidence that three of the four programs had reduced the penetration of youths into the justice system. It appeared that the diversion programs were less coercive and more oriented to meeting clients' needs than were comparable justice agencies. Diversion programs were no more successful, however, in avoiding stigma than normal justice processing or outright release. Nor did diversion services appear to improve social adjustment or reduce recidivism. Diversion with or without services was about equally likely to reduce recidivism. Considerable evidence of "net widening" was found. Osgood's (1983) reanalysis of the data, separating minor offenders from those with more serious offense histories, showed no difference in diversion program effectiveness. Diversion would remain an elusive prospect for delinquency reduction.

In addition to Dunford et al.'s evaluation of the OJJDP's national diversion program, several other studies of DSO and diversion have refuted labeling theory (see Rausch, 1983; Thomas, 1976). In sum, juvenile justice system processing appears to be no more stigmatizing than alternative programs. Recidivism is equally as likely whether juveniles are processed normally in the juvenile justice system or diverted to alternative programs (Dunford et al., 1982).

The OJJDP's National Restitution Program consisted of 41 projects at 86 sites. Restitution consisted of monetary repayment, community service, or a combination of both. Nearly 20,000 juvenile offenders were referred to the 41 programs over a 2-year period. About half of the referred youngsters had been adjudicated delinquent for serious or very serious offenses. Nine of the programs were evaluated (Schneider, Griffith, & Schneider, 1980; Schneider & Schneider, 1980; Schneider, Schneider, Griffith, & Wilson, 1982). Individual projects were very successful in seeing that offenders completed court-ordered restitution (85% of the cases were closed in full compliance with restitution requirements). On the average, juvenile offenders repaid 75% of the ordered dollar amount, with 90% of the monies repaid coming from themselves. There were virtually no differences between serious and minor offenders in successful completion of restitution orders. Nor did prior offense seriousness appear to strongly affect the reoffending rate. The reoffense rate, measured in terms of new court contacts while under program supervision, was 9% the first year and 14% the second. In three out of four sites, restitution program youth had statistically lower recidivism rates than did control group youth during a 3-year follow-up period, illustrating a clear suppression effect.

In another study of four sites in which youths were randomly assigned into restitution and into traditional dispositions, Schneider (1986) found that on the whole, restitution may have a small but important effect on recidivism. She concluded that not all programs will be able to achieve this effect, because of program management and strategy, community circumstances, or other factors.

Because of the success of the restitution program, the OJJDP served as a catalyst in the development and expansion of the restitution movement. At the time the program was launched, there were only 15 formal juvenile restitution programs in existence (Schneider & Schneider, 1977). By 1985, 65% of large juvenile court jurisdictions and 33% of small ones had formal restitution programs (see Schneider,

1985a; Schneider & Schneider, 1980; Schneider & Warner, 1989). A National Restitution Association was soon formed (recently renamed the National Restorative Justice Association). It remains very active in promoting restitution programs (Bazemore & Umbreit, 1994).

Improving the Juvenile Justice System

In addition to its success in implementing the major mandates of the JJDP Act reviewed earlier in this chapter (DSO, separation, and jail removal), and in addition to its current work toward reducing the disproportionate confinement of minority youth, the OJJDP has made other major contributions to improving the juvenile justice system. The OJJDP has supported training for every component of the juvenile justice system: police, prosecution, court, detention, and corrections. The most substantial of these efforts, supported since the OJJDP was established in 1975, is the professional training and technical assistance provided by the National Council of Juvenile and Family Court Judges, not only for judges but also for other juvenile court personnel. Illustrative training materials include the *Desktop Guide to Good Juvenile Probation Practice* (NCJJ, 1991) developed by the NCJFCJ's National Center for Juvenile Justice (NCJJ), which is used extensively in training judges, intake officers, and probation officers. The NCJFCJ also provides extensive training for court, social service, and other child care workers under its Permanency Planning Project, to reduce use of foster care except as a last resort. The OJJDP recently began providing training for line detention center and correctional staff. The *Desktop Guide to Good Detention Practice*, prepared by the National Juvenile Detention Association, is used to train detention care givers and managers (Roush, 1996a).

Providing information, training, and technical assistance on alternatives to incarceration and detention has been a central thrust of the OJJDP's program development from the beginning. This work began with a national assessment of detention and alternatives to its use (Young & Pappenfort, 1977). This assessment found overuse of secure detention in many parts of the country, concluding that a large proportion of detained youth could be released to their parents or other adults to await court action. Secure holding arrangements are essential for a small proportion of alleged delinquents who constitute a danger to others. Residential and nonresidential programs appear about equal in their ability to keep youths trouble-free and available to court. Home detention was found to be successful with delinquents and some status offenders. The latter group sometimes require substitute care because of family conflicts. Young and Pappenfort urged that intake decisions be guided by clear, written criteria, together with close monitoring to guard against overuse.

For 15 years, the OJJDP has supported the adoption of nationally recognized standards for the administration of all aspects of juvenile justice (Allen-Hagen & Howell, 1982). New work on standards development is focused on improving conditions of confinement, which OJJDP's national assessment (Parent, Leiter, Livens, Wentworth, & Stephen, 1994) showed to be urgently needed. This program involves the development of performance-based standards for detention centers and reformatories in the areas of safety, security, order, treatment programs, health, and justice. State juvenile code revisions to improve the administration of juvenile justice also have been encouraged throughout the OJJDP's history, resulting in improvements in virtually every state. Technical assistance is now being provided to state legislatures by the National Conference of State Legislatures.

Juvenile and family court handling of abuse and neglect cases has been greatly improved by virtue of the Court Appointed Special Advocates Program (Slott, 1991). This national program provides trained volunteers who assist courts in investigating dependency and neglect cases. The National Incidence Study of Missing, Abducted, Runaway, and Thrownaway Children (Finkelhor, Hotaling, & Sedlak, 1990) revealed that only about 3% of all missing children are abducted by a stranger. Most are living in conflict-ridden families, often accompanied by abuse and neglect. Results of this research have been incorporated in training programs for child protection agencies in investigating parental abduction cases, which stem mainly from custody disputes associated with separation and divorce.

An interstate placement study (Hall et al., 1982; see also Hall, Hamparian, Pettibone, & White, 1981, pp. 3-165) documented excessive and inconsistent policies and practices in out-of-state placement of children and adolescents. A few states were found to have nearly a thousand children placed in other states. Several states drastically curtailed their interstate placements following the study, which helped reverse the 100-year-old practice.

Juvenile justice system handling of learning disabled (LD) children also has been improved as a result of a research and development program that initially discovered that LD children are no more likely than non-LD children to commit delinquent acts, but they are twice as likely to be adjudicated delinquent (Broder, 1980; Murray, 1977; Zimmerman & Broder, 1980). This discovery pointed to the need to improve LD screening mechanisms and training for juvenile justice professionals. The OJJDP sponsored the needed training in workshops around the country. This led to the establishment of a Learning Disabilities Institute in Phoenix.

One of the OJJDP's most significant contributions to improving the juvenile justice system is in the area of aftercare, perhaps the most poorly developed program area in the entire system. The first contribution in this area was made in the OJJDP Violent Juvenile Offender (VJO) program, developed to provide highly intensive treatment for violent and serious offenders in a correctional setting. Its design included a structured reintegration component (Fagan, Rudman, & Hartstone, 1984). The second aftercare model resulted from a national assessment of intensive supervision programs (Krisberg, Neuenfeldt, Wiebush, & Rodriguez, 1994). This model (illustrated in Chapter 9) incorporates phased stepdown following secure confinement of dangerous juvenile offenders. The third aftercare model that the OJJDP developed was the result of a national assessment of aftercare programs (Altschuler & Armstrong, 1994a, 1994b, 1994c, 1995). It is being tested in several sites.

Not all studies of JJDP Act implementation have been positive (see Altschuler & Luneburg, 1992; Howell, 1995c for discussions of related issues). The next section discusses problems in programming for status offenders. Other obstacles have impeded success in improving the administration of juvenile justice. These include racial bias (Bishop & Frazier, 1992; Pope & Feyerherm, 1993), a lack of programming for minority youth and disproportionate attention to the problems of white youth at the expense of mi-norities (Kempf et al., 1990; Woodson, 1977, 1981), gender bias in processing and a lack of effective programs for females (Bishop & Frazier, 1992), unacceptable conditions of confinement in detention centers and reformatories (Parent et al., 1994) and in adult jails (Soler, 1988), lack of due process protections in the juvenile justice system (Forst, 1995), lack of job and skills training for adolescents (American Youth Work Center, 1993; Howard, 1995), and the absence of a national youth gang policy (Miller, 1990). This listing is by no means exhaustive. The juvenile justice system and alternative programs also suffer from a severe lack of monetary and staff resources (National Conference of State Legislatures, 1996). Juvenile justice is on the bottom rung of state and county budgets.

The Other Side of Status Offenders

The National Academy of Sciences' review of DSO (Handler & Zatz, 1982) resulted in the following conclusions.

1. The vast majority of adjudicated status offenders have been removed from reformatories.

2. There has been a decline in the use of preadjudicatory detention for youths who have been charged with status offenses.

3. Fewer youths who are labeled status offenders are entering the juvenile justice system.

4. For those status offenders who are diverted to some other service system, the predominant forms of out-of-home care are group home and foster care arrangements. It is unclear, however, what is happening to status offenders who do not enter the juvenile court system or diversion programs. Many of the state and local respondents Handler and Zatz interviewed expressed the opinion that these youths are being ignored altogether.

The National Criminal Justice Association (NCJA) (Holden & Kapler, 1995) recently assessed the past 20 years of implementing the DSO mandate. It concluded that "over the past two decades, the JJDP Act has fundamentally changed the way our Nation deals with troubled youth. . . . The key to this transformation can be found in the JJDP Act's central mandate:

DSO" (p. 3). The NCJA concluded that although the majority of states have achieved compliance with the DSO mandate and remain committed to its purposes, maintaining state compliance "likely will depend in large part on how firmly installed it has become in laws, policies and practices," while states are facing "escalating pressures for more punitive approaches to resolving the violence problem" (Holden & Kapler, 1995, p. 9).

Development of effective services for status offenders represents another formidable challenge. The presumed difference between status offenders and delinquents is a myth. A majority of juvenile offenders commit both types of offenses (Datesman & Aickin, 1985; Kobrin & Klein, 1983; Thomas, 1976; Weis, 1979). Similarly, the most serious and violent juveniles also commit status offenses with considerable regularity (Thornberry, Huizinga, & Loeber, 1995). For these and other reasons, Empey and Stafford (1991, pp. 502-504) argue that effective intervention requires the availability of juvenile and family court resources to deal with runaways and other chronic status offenders. Juvenile court intervention will be needed less often, provided that integrated services are made available early in the development of problem behaviors (see Chapter 9).

3

Who's to Blame for Violent Crime?

This chapter reviews a wide variety of data sources and studies to assess what is known about the relative proportion of serious and violent crime in the United States for which juveniles and adults are responsible. Hidden adult crime is examined in the third section, followed by a reconsideration of the relationship between age and crime. Finally, a research agenda is suggested that might produce more accurate information on who is to blame for serious and violent crime in the United States.

The Perception

In a 1993 *USA Today*/CNN/Gallup poll (Meddis, 1993b), an astonishing 73% of adults said juveniles who commit violent crimes should be treated the same as adults. Why have we come to blame juveniles for violent crime in the United States?

Misleading statements frequently are fed to the public that distort the juvenile contribution to crime in the United States. Here is a sampling. Teenagers are said to commit murders in a much greater proportion than their numbers in the general population (Cullen, 1995). Fox (see Butterfield, 1995) described the United States as being in the calm period before a crime wave that will result in a "blood bath" of adolescent violence shortly after the turn of the

century. "Over the next 10 years more juvenile 'superpredators' will be flooding the nation's streets" (DiIulio, 1996, p. 25). A *Time* magazine story (January 15, 1996) reflected criminologists' warnings of "teenage time bombs" (see also Guest & Pope, 1996). Blumstein (1995a) warned that the 18-year-olds, currently today's adolescents, who are responsible for the higher homicide rates may continue reckless offending as they get older. It is said that legislators are merely responding to public pressure to enact strong measures against youth crime (Fox, in Potok & Sanchez, 1995).

The empirical basis for these assertions is questionable, yet such statements are all too often taken as facts and incorporated into public policy statements. For example, former Senator Robert J. Dole made reference in a campaign speech to today's newborns becoming tomorrow's superpredators (quoted in Harden, 1996). Dole called for more prosecution of juveniles as adults, an end to parole for violent crimes, and for states to build as many prisons as it takes to protect the public (quoted in Harden, 1996). An April 1996 *Los Angeles Times* poll, however, indicated that voters did not appear to see crime as a top priority for presidential candidates. Only 9% of those surveyed believed Dole and Clinton should focus on crime, whereas 18% mentioned the economy and 16% health care (Harden, 1996).

AUTHOR'S NOTE: The author is indebted to the National Center for Juvenile Justice for providing access to the spreadsheet files for figures and tables in two NCJJ reports: *Juvenile Offenders and Victims: A National Report* (Snyder & Sickmund, 1995), and *Juvenile Offenders and Victims: 1996 Update on Violence* (Snyder, Sickmund, & Poe-Yamagata, 1996). This chapter draws significantly on both of these reports.

Three criminologists are promoting dire forecasts of a juvenile crime wave in about 2005-2010 (Blumstein, 1995a, 1995b, 1996; DiIulio, 1996; Fox, 1996), based on a demographic explanation that consists of two hypotheses (Block, 1986, p. 12). The first one is that increases and decreases in the number of crimes are directly attributable to increases and decreases in the number of crimes committed by young people, especially by young black males. Second, the reason for the pattern of crime increases and decreases by young people is the corresponding patterns of increases and decreases in their numbers. The main problem with their demographic explanation is that it has been proven wrong before. A number of criminologists predicted a decrease in homicides by young people in the 1980s because their numbers would be decreasing (see Block, 1987, p. 12). Their prediction was wrong. Homicides among young people increased. Other criminologists and demographers correctly questioned the demographic prediction (see Block, 1987, p. 13). For example, Shin (1981) concluded that the age, sex, and race structure of the population accounted for at most 10% of the homicide rate change from 1930 to 1975.

"It might seem, at first glance, that if a certain group in the population commits crimes at a higher rate than other groups, and if the size of this population group changes, then the number of crimes would change correspondingly. However, the real situation is more complex" (Block, 1987, p. 12). Many other social and cultural factors account for crime, violence, and homicide, as we shall see. Before examining these, let us take a look at the reality of juvenile violence.

The Reality of Juvenile Violence

In 1994, less than one-half of 1% of all juveniles (ages 10-17) in the United States were arrested for a violent offense (Figure 3.1). Only 6% of all juveniles were arrested for any offense. Among all juvenile arrests in 1994, only about 7% were for an FBI Violent Crime Index offense (Snyder et al., 1996, p. 14). Even these small numbers likely exaggerate the actual number of guilty juveniles represented in arrest statistics, because juveniles often are arrested in groups. This point is supported by examination of crime "clearances" by arrest of juveniles.

Offenses Cleared by the Arrest of a Juvenile

The Federal Bureau of Investigation (FBI) tracks the number of reported crimes that result in an arrest, or crimes "cleared." In other words, a crime is *cleared* once someone is charged with that crime (see Snyder & Sickmund, 1995, p. 99). Based on 1994 clearance data, juveniles were responsible for 14% of all FBI Violent Index Crimes and 25% of all Property Index Crimes (FBI, 1995; Snyder et al., 1996). Surprisingly, juveniles were responsible for only 10% of all murders in 1994 (Table 3.1). Among the four Violent Index Crimes (murder, rape, robbery, and aggravated assaults), the juvenile share was largest for robberies (20%), which includes a significant proportion of minor offenses such as extortion involving small monetary amounts. Among the four Property Index Crimes (the remaining four offenses in Table 3.1), juveniles were disproportionately represented in arson offenses, which also includes a significant proportion of minor offenses such as setting small isolated fires. These percentages are much lower than those that do not take into account the percentage of all arrests cleared by the arrest of a juvenil.

The percentage of Violent Index Crimes cleared by the arrest of a juvenile (14%) is slightly above the proportional representation of juveniles of the most crime-prone age in the U.S. population. In 1994, persons age 10 to 17 represented 11.3% of the total population. Surprisingly, juveniles are underrepresented in the percentage of murders cleared by the arrest of a 10-17-year-old (10%) in 1994. Young adults, on the other hand, are disproportionately represented among murder victims. In 1994, persons age 18 to 34 made up 26% of the U.S. population, yet they represented 54% of all persons murdered (according to the FBI Supplemental Homicide Reports; see Perkins & Klaus, 1996, p. 3).

Snyder and Sickmund (1995, p. 99) illustrate the proper interpretations of "clearance" versus "arrest" data.

Let us try to answer the question: "What proportion of all burglaries are committed by juveniles?" The UCR reports that 20% of all burglaries cleared in 1992 were cleared by the arrest of persons under age 18 and that 34% of persons arrested for burglary in 1992 were under age 18. How

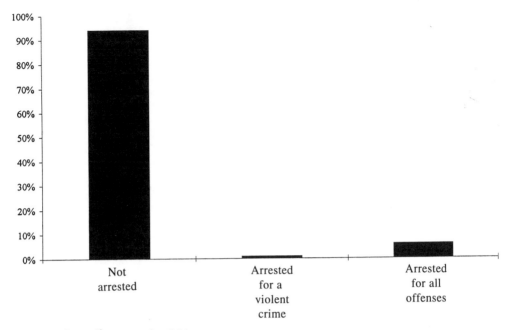

Figure 3.1. Juvenile arrests in 1994

SOURCE: *Juvenile Offenders and Victims: 1996 Update on Violence* (p. 14), Snyder, Sickmund, and Poe-Yamagata, ©copyright 1996 by the National Center for Juvenile Justice. Reprinted with permission.
DATA SOURCE: *Crime in the United States 1994*, Federal Bureau of Investigation (1995).

do we reconcile these very different percentages?

First, can we be certain that the 13% of all burglaries that were cleared in 1992 are like all the burglaries committed? It could be argued that juveniles are less skilled at avoiding arrest. If so, cleared burglaries are likely to contain a greater percentage of juvenile burglaries than would those that are not cleared.

But even if we assumed that the offender characteristics in the 13% of cleared burglaries are similar to those of the 87% not cleared, how do we reconcile that large difference between the juvenile clearance and arrest percentage (20% vs. 34%)?

The key to this difference can be found in the fact that, more so than adults, juveniles tend to commit crimes in groups (Reiss, 1988; Zimring, 1981a). Assume a police department cleared five burglaries, one committed by a pair of juveniles and the other four committed individually by four different adults. The juvenile proportion of burglaries cleared would be 20% (1 in 5), while 33% of per-

sons arrested for burglary would be a juvenile (2 in 6).

Clearance and arrest statistics answer different questions. If you want to know how much crime was committed by juveniles, the clearance data give a better indication because they count crimes, not arrestees. However, if you want to know how many persons entered the justice system, use the arrest data.

Most public representations of growing juvenile crime inappropriately use arrest data, resulting in an exaggeration of the proportion of serious and violent crime that should be attributed to juveniles. At the same time, those interested in showing the growth in juvenile crime often neglect to point out that in 1994 adults accounted for 86% of the clearances for violent crimes, and for 9 out of 10 clearances for murder. Violence and murder are overwhelmingly adult crimes.

The Tyranny of Small Numbers

In their analysis of increases in arrests for violent crimes between 1985 and 1994, Snyder

TABLE 3.1 Percentage of Crimes Cleared by the Arrest of a Juvenile, United States, 1994

Offense	Percentage
Murder	10
Aggravated assault	13
Forcible rape	14
Robbery	20
Burglary	21
Larceny-theft	25
Motor vehicle theft	25
Arson	48

SOURCE: *Juvenile Offenders and Victims: 1996 Update on Violence* (p. 13), Snyder, Sickmund, and Poe-Yamagata, ©copyright 1996 by the National Center for Juvenile Justice. Reprinted with permission.

DATA SOURCE: *Crime in the United States, 1994*, Federal Bureau of Investigation (1995).

and his colleagues (Snyder et al., 1996) illustrate the "tyranny of small numbers" principle that he and Sickmund developed earlier (Snyder & Sickmund, 1995, p. 110):

The number of violent crimes reported to law enforcement agencies increased 40% between 1985 and 1994. Knowing that over this same period, juvenile arrests for violent crime grew 75%, while adult arrests increased 48%, some may conclude that juveniles were responsible for most of the increase in violent crime. However, even though the percentage increase in juvenile arrests was more than the adult increase, the majority of the growth cannot be attributed to juveniles.

An example shows how this apparent contradiction can occur. Of the 100 violent crimes committed in 1985 in a small town, assume that juveniles were responsible for 10, and adults for 90. If the number of juvenile crimes increased 70% in 1994, juveniles would be committing 17 (or 7 more) violent crimes. A 50% increase in adult violent crimes would mean that adults were committing 135 (or 45 more) violent crimes. If each crime resulted in an arrest, the percentage increase in juvenile arrests would be more than the adult increase (70% versus 50%). However, 87% of the increase in violent crime (45 of the additional violent crimes) would have been committed by

adults. Juvenile arrests represent a relatively small fraction of the total; consequently, a large percentage increase in juvenile arrests does not necessarily translate into a large contribution to overall crime growth.

Using FBI reported crime and clearance statistics, Snyder et al. (1996, p. 20) estimated that juveniles committed 137,000 more Violent Crime Index offenses in 1994 than in 1985, while adults committed an additional 398,000. Juveniles, therefore, were responsible for about one-fourth (26%) of the growth in violent crime between 1985 and 1994 whereas adults were responsible for nearly three-fourths (74%) of the increase in violent crime clearances during this period.

Snyder and his colleagues illustrate the "tyranny of small numbers" in another comparison of juvenile and adult contributions to violent crimes during the 1985-1994 period (Snyder et al., 1996, p. 20). Their analysis showed that if juveniles had committed no more violent crimes in 1994 than in 1985, violent crime in the United States would have increased 30% instead of 40%. If juveniles had committed no more murders in 1994 than in 1985, murders in the United States would have increased 15% instead of 23%. Therefore, juveniles were responsible for about one-third of the increase in murders during the period 1985-1994 (Figure 3.2).

Another example serves to illustrate how the "tyranny of small numbers" creates a distorted view of juvenile offending. Greenfeld and Zawitz (1995) note the increase of more than 100% in the number of juvenile arrests for weapons offenses between 1985 and 1993 (from 30,000 to 61,000). The 33% growth they report in adult weapons arrests, however, actually meant that adults accounted for most of the additional weapons violations. Compared to the 31,000 additional juvenile arrests, adults were responsible for nearly twice as many (about 57,000) additional weapons violations arrests in 1993 than in 1985 even though their percentage growth was only about a third of the juvenile percentage increase.

The "tyranny of small numbers" has led the media and others to exaggerate the contribution of juveniles both to the total volume of violent crime in the United States and to the increase over the past decade. Juveniles thus have become the scapegoat for extremely high levels of violence in this country. To put juvenile vio-

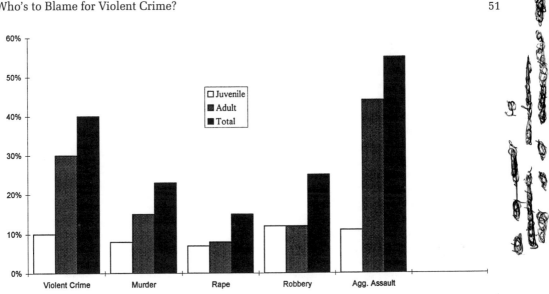

Figure 3.2 Percentage changes in adult and juvenile violent arrests, 1985-1994

SOURCE: *Juvenile Offenders and Victims: 1996 Update on Violence* (p. 20), Snyder, Sickmund, and Poe-Yamagata, ©copyright 1996 by the National Center for Juvenile Justice. Reprinted with permission.

DATA SOURCE: *Crime in the United States 1985*, Federal Bureau of Investigation (1986), and *Crime in the United States 1994*, Federal Bureau of Investigation (1995).

lence in a broader perspective, let us look at overall violence in the United States.

The Extent of Violence in the United States

For reasons that are not well understood, the United States has an extremely high level of violence. "Several countries have levels of violence that approach our own, but no other country has our level of lethal violence" (Block & Block, 1991, p. 49). According to the American Medical Association (Hutson et al., 1995, p. 1031), "the United States has the highest homicide rate in the industrialized world. During the last 25 years, the United Sates has experienced a dramatic increase in homicides, making homicide a major health problem." In fact, the homicide rate in the United States is many times higher than that of the Western industrialized country with the next highest rate (American Psychological Association, 1993, p. 13). As a result of the increase in homicide in our country, it is now the 10th leading cause of death in the United States (National Center for Health Statistics, 1994) and the second leading cause of death among males aged 15-34 (Centers for Disease Control and Prevention, 1994).

Homicide is expected to overtake motor vehicle fatalities as the leading cause of injury death in the United States by the year 2003 (Fingerhut, Jones, & Makuc, 1994).

In 1995, the American Medical Association (AMA) issued its first "Report Card: Violence in America," in which it graded the United States in four areas: family violence, sexual assault, public violence, and "virtual violence" (violence in entertainment; AMA, 1995). Four criteria were used in the AMA grading system: whether the problem was getting better or worse according to published statistical indicators, status of public awareness and attitudes toward the violence as measured by published survey and research information, effectiveness and availability of treatment and intervention programs as measured by published statistical and research information, and cost to society in dollars, pain, and human suffering as measured by published survey and research information. The overall grade the AMA gave the United States on violence was a "D."

The nation received its highest AMA grade on family violence among the four categories (a "C"), primarily because of increases in public awareness and reporting of offenses, as well as the availability of intervention and assistance programs. It concluded that the incidence of family violence continues to escalate. Sexual assault was awarded a "D" grade, principally because social myths about rape such as "no means yes" are still prevalent, impeding reporting and making apprehension and conviction of offenders difficult. Public violence received the lowest grade, an "F," mainly because of the pervasiveness of gang, drug, gun, and civil violence. The AMA graded the nation a "D" on virtual violence because of the lasting psychosocial effects of television, music, film, video, and computer violence on the individual, on which little progress toward reduction has been made.

How can the acceptability of violence in our society be explained? Supported by research showing that an increase in the acceptability of violence can be attributed to a lack of effective law enforcement (Campbell, 1921; McDowall & Loftin, 1983), the Blocks (1991) argue that citizens may become convinced that society is unable to protect them. They may feel compelled to provide their own protection. Ironically, the end result of these actions "may be rapid increases of levels of violence in the community as a whole" (p. 48), as Loftin (McDowall & Loftin, 1983) found to be the case during the early 1960s to the mid-1970s in Detroit. The Blocks suggest that the same process may explain sharp recent increases in violence in some neighborhoods of Washington, D.C., and Chicago (p. 48).

Another reason for general acceptance of violence in our society may be widespread violence among adults. We next examine hidden adult crime.

Hidden Adult Crime

Adult Victimization of Children

Doleschal's (1970) call to examine adult "hidden crime" has largely been ignored over the past 25 years, except from the viewpoint of victims, measured by the National Crime Victims Survey (NCVS). The NCVS, however, inadequately measures such "hidden crimes" as spouse abuse and child abuse. These are violent offenses against children and spouses that are largely hidden from the public and the criminal justice system.

Children suffer more serious family violence victimizations than do adults (Finkelhor & Dziuba-Leatherman, 1994b). Adults reported that they inflicted almost twice as much severe

TABLE 3.2 Family Violence Victimization Rate per 1,000 Children Versus Adults, 1985

Perpetrator-Victim Relationship	Any Violence	Severe Violence[a]
Spouse to spouse	158	58
Parent to child	620	107

SOURCE: *Physical Violence in American Families: Risk Factors and Adaptations to Violence in 8,145 Families*, Straus and Gelles, ©copyright 1990 by Transaction.

DATA SOURCE: National Family Violence Resurvey, 1985.

a. Includes kicking, biting, hitting with fist or object, beating, and using or threatening to use knife or gun.

violence against a child in their household than they did against their adult partner (Table 3.2; Straus & Gelles, 1990; Straus, Gelles, & Steinmetz, 1980). The second National Study of the Incidence and Prevalence of Child Abuse and Neglect (NIS-2) estimated that official reports were made on 1.4 million children believed to be harmed or at risk of harm by maltreatment in 1988 (Sedlak, 1990). Of these, more than 900,000 suffered "demonstrable harm" as a result of maltreatment.

The National Center for Child Abuse and Neglect's (1996a) national reporting system shows that in 1994, state Child Protective Service (CPS) agencies received 2 million reports of alleged child maltreatment, involving 2.9 million children. Among these reports, CPS investigations determined that slightly more than 1 million were "substantiated" or "indicated" maltreatments. Reports of child maltreatment increased by 14% from 1990 through 1994, while the number of substantiated cases grew by 27%. Reports of alleged child maltreatment have increased steadily at about this rate since 1980. Between then and 1993, child abuse and neglect reports increased 155% (NCCAN, 1995). What is worse is that the number of maltreated children who were seriously injured increased at a faster rate. Between 1986 and 1993, this number nearly quadrupled from approximately 143,000 to more than 572,000 (NCCAN, 1996b).

Most (53%) of the children maltreated in 1994 suffered neglect, 26% experienced physical abuse, 14% were sexually abused, 5% suffered emotional abuse, and 22% were subjected to other forms of maltreatment. Parents are about as likely to abuse an older child as a younger one. Nearly one-third of substantiated cases are age 10-17, compared to just over a third who are under age 6. One-half are white. Within the 43 states reporting to the NCCAN (1996a), 1,111 children died as a result of abuse in 1994. This number increased 8% from 1993, when 1,028 children were reported to have died as a result of abuse or neglect (NCCAN, 1995).

Linebaugh (1984, p. 19) estimates that there are as many as 2.5 million child sexual molestations in the United States each year. This may well be the most underreported of all crimes committed in this country. Less than 1% of all perpetrators are brought into the criminal justice system (Linebaugh, 1984, p. 19). Most perpetrators are known to the child (most often a very young girl), typically the child's father, stepfather, sibling, or family acquaintance. Child molesters and pedophiles are notorious chronic offenders (Lanning, 1984). Some victimize hundreds of children before they are stopped, generally only temporarily. There is no known cure. There is a leniency gap in the punishment of adults for sexually abusing an infant or child versus another adult. The largest discrepancy is in court dispositions (J. Roberts, 1987). Probation is imposed more than twice as often in cases involving children as in cases involving adults. Incarceration is imposed in 89% of adult sexual victimizations versus 69% of child victimizations. The majority of sentences in child victim cases are for less than a year; 77% of adult victimizations are for more than a year.

Greenfeld's (1996) analysis also shows that offenders who victimized adults received longer sentences than offenders who victimized juveniles. Child murderers were only about half as likely (10%) to be sentenced to death as inmates who murdered another adult (19%). What is worse is that nearly a third (29%) of the child predators were multiple violent child offenders. Nearly 38% of them had multiple murder victims. Overall, child predators got longer sentences than adult victimizers for murder, kidnapping, and manslaughter, but shorter sentences for rape and sexual assault, which were more common.

As many as 3.3 million children are estimated to witness spouse abuse each year, including fatal assaults with guns and/or knives as well as hitting and slapping (Osofsky & Fenichel, 1994). Family violence constitutes a major risk factor for delinquency and violence. Thornberry (1994) found that more exposure to family violence increases the risk of violent

offending by children in the home. Three different indicators of family violence were examined: partner violence, family climate of hostility, and child maltreatment. Children exposed to all three types of family violence reported more than twice the rate of youth violence as those from nonviolent families. In a study using official records, Widom (1992) found that abuse and neglect during childhood increases the likelihood of arrest as a juvenile by 53%, arrest as an adult by 38%, and the likelihood of committing a violent crime by 38%.

Snyder (1994; see Snyder & Sickmund, 1995, pp. 28-29) estimates the number of child victimizations that the National Crime Victims Survey may miss because it does not survey any victims under the age of 12. Using South Carolina data reported between 1991 and 1993 under the FBI National Incident-Based Reporting System (NIBRS), he estimates that about 600,000 violent victimizations of children below age 12 occurred in 1992. If the South Carolina NIBRS data are representative of the actual ratio of younger-to-older child victimizations, then Snyder (1994) estimates that the NCVS is missing 51% of violent sex offenses against juveniles under the age of 18, 9% of robberies, 26% of aggravated assaults, and 22% of simple assaults (Table 3.3). The number is much larger if one takes into account emotional abuse. Miller, Cohen, and Wiersema (1996) estimate that 794,000 children were sexually, physically, or emotionally abused in 1990.

Snyder's (1994; see Snyder & Sickmund, 1995, pp. 28-29) analysis shows that 6 in 10 of the offenders in violent crimes against juveniles (under age 18) in South Carolina are acquaintances and over 2 in 10 are family members (Table 3.4). The percentage of family member offenders increases to 50% for children age 5 and younger. The probability that the offender is a family member declines substantially for older juveniles, as the proportion of victimizations by acquaintances and strangers increases.

How serious are these violent victimizations of juveniles? Snyder's (1994) analysis shows that 44% of child victims (under age 12) of violent crimes reported to law enforcement agencies in South Carolina received an injury that required medical attention. If victimized, juveniles were less likely to be injured than were adults, and children were less likely to be injured than were older juveniles. Adults were injured in 51% of their violent victimizations,

TABLE 3.3 Criminal Victimizations Reported to Police in South Carolina, 1991 to mid-1993, by Age (percentages)

Victim's Age	All Violent Offenses	Murder	Sex Offense	Robbery	Aggravated Assault	Simple Assault
5 and younger	1	3	12	<1	1	1
6-11	3	<1	16	1	3	3
12-17	12	5	27	7	12	12
18-24	26	24	18	23	26	28
25-54	53	56	26	59	55	54
55 and older	3	11	1	11	3	3
11 and younger	5	4	28	1	4	4
17 and younger	17	9	55	8	16	16
18 and older	83	91	45	93	84	84

SOURCE: *Juvenile Offenders and Victims: A National Report*, Snyder and Sickmund, ©copyright 1995 by the National Center for Juvenile Justice. Reprinted with permission.
DATA SOURCE: *The Criminal Victimization of Young Children*, Snyder (1994).
NOTE: Detail may not add to 100% because of rounding.

older juveniles in 45%, and children younger than age 12 in 39% of their violent victimizations referred to police. Among children, injury occurred in a greater proportion of crimes committed by family members than by strangers and other offenders. Among older juveniles, injury was about equally as likely if the offender was a family member (43%), an acquaintance (46%), or a stranger (43%) (Snyder & Sickmund, 1995, p. 29).

When did these victimizations occur? Snyder (1994) developed a 24-hour profile of the risk of violent victimization for different age groups. Juveniles ages 6-17 were at greatest risk of violent victimization by nonfamily members at 3-4 p.m. (Figure 3.3). Violent victimization by family members were most common about 8-9 p.m., with another peak at noon-1 p.m. for youngsters under the age of 6 (Snyder & Sickmund, 1995, p. 30). An analysis of National Crime Survey data (Whitaker & Bastian, 1991) shows that about half of all violent teenage victimizations take place on the street, in a school building, or on school property, such as a playground, parking lot, or school bus. About one-quarter occur on the streets, and 11% occurred near the victim's home. Respondents said that only 4% occurred at home. More than a third (37%) of all violent victimizations occurred at school. Almost all these school victimizations are perpetrated by other adolescents, and many appear to be connected to events at school such as bullying (Garofalo, Siegel, & Laub, 1987; Olweus, 1992).

A national self-report survey of 2,000 children and juveniles (aged 10-16) (Finkelhor & Dziuba-Leatherman, 1994a), from a random sample of households, suggests that the incidence of violent victimization of children and juveniles may be even greater than the South Carolina data indicate, because of underreporting of victimizations to the police. One-quarter of the children and juveniles reported a completed violent victimization in the previous year, more than a third reported an attempted or completed victimization in the past year, and more than half reported an attempted or completed victimization at some time in their lives. These victimizations included assaults, sexual abuse, violence to genitals, and kidnapping.

Although two-thirds of all victimizations were disclosed to someone (Finkelhor & Dziuba-Leatherman, 1994a), only 25% were reported to an authority, and only 6% were reported to the police. Surprisingly, almost one-quarter (23%) of the sample experienced more than one type of victimization. Less than a third of all victimizations resulted in physical injuries, and only 1% of victims got medical attention. The majority of injuries (70%) resulted from nonfamily assaults.

Characteristics and Offending Histories of Adult Offenders

Little is known about adults who violently victimize children. "Behind closed doors" (Fontana, 1983, pp. 39-53) best describes the physi-

TABLE 3.4 Age and Offender Relationship in South Carolina Victimizations, 1991-1993 (percentages)

Offender Type		Victim's Age					
	All Ages	5 and Younger	6-11	12-17	11 and younger	17 and younger	18 and older
Family member	27	50	26	17	33	22	29
Acquaintance	53	41	59	64	54	61	51
Stranger	20	9	15	18	13	17	20
Total	100	100	100	100	100	100	100

SOURCE: *Juvenile Offenders and Victims: A National Report*, Snyder and Sickmund, ©copyright 1995 by the National Center for Juvenile Justice. Reprinted with permission.

DATA SOURCE: *The Criminal Victimization of Young Children*, Snyder (1994).

cal setting of child molestation and physical abuse. "The vast majority of child maltreatment cases are of the insidious variety in the sense that they are unseen or unrecognized at the time" (p. 39). Moreover, child abusers are often very cunning, careful not to break bones or leave other marks on the child. "Then there are the even more silent and less visible types of abuse, the in-family sex crimes, the torture-by-deprivation cases, the various subtle kinds of neglect and indifference; and the strange, often lethal accidents of very young infants and toddlers" (p. 39). FBI Special Agent Kenneth Lanning offers another reason that so little attention is given to child victimizers.

If you had an offender who was to cripple or physically handicap 100 children, if you had a guy who was breaking the legs of 100 little children, making them cripples for the rest of their lives, we would demand that that person be incarcerated for the rest of his life, or even executed. But yet, when the offender emotionally cripples and makes an emotional handicap of a child, we simply say, well, he didn't really hurt anybody. He's kind of a poor, unfortunate soul. He's sick. There's something wrong with him. We need to help him. Poor guy, he didn't hurt anybody. (Lanning, 1984, p. 28)

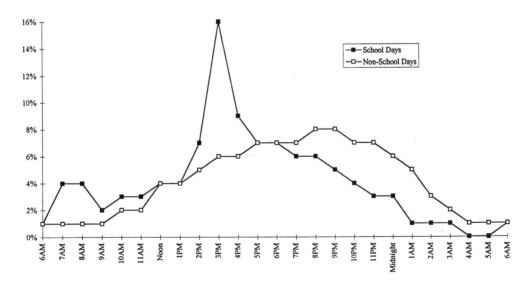

Figure 3.3. Percentage of violent victimizations at time of day (South Carolina)

SOURCE: *Juvenile Offenders and Victims: 1996 Update on Violence* (p. 27), Snyder, Sickmund, and Poe-Yamagata, ©copyright 1996 by the National Center for Juvenile Justice. Reprinted with permission.

DATA SOURCE: *National Incident-Based Reporting System 1991 and 1992* (machine-readable data files), Federal Bureau of Investigation (1993).

Some information is available on the offense histories and characteristics of adults convicted of violent offenses against children. Self-report responses from a nationally representative sample of male and female state prisoners (Greenfeld, 1996) shows that just under half (46%) of all prisoners had been convicted of one or more violent crimes, and that nearly 19% committed the single most serious of their violent crimes against a child. Among the latter group, nearly two-thirds (66%) raped or sexually assaulted their child victims. *Every one* of the prisoners serving time for crimes against juveniles self-reported having committed lewd acts with juveniles or abusing them. Nearly all (95%) also reported having committed statutory rape, and almost 86% said they had forcibly sodomized juveniles. Violent victimization of children, it is clear, is a fairly common occurrence among violent adult criminals.

More than half (55%) of these offenders' victims were age 12 or younger, substantiating the South Carolina data reported by Snyder (1994). The victims typically were children whom inmates knew, not random strangers. Nearly 86% of the offenders knew their victims. Over two-thirds of the victims were either their own child, a stepchild, or an acquaintance.

What about the characteristics of the offenders? Nearly two-thirds had been married, and almost 97% were males. Nearly 70% were white, and about 25% were black. Only 2% were under the age of 18 at the time they victimized juveniles. At the time of their arrest, the median age of child predators was 33. Child victimizers have several criminal history and social background characteristics that distinguished them from other prisoners. They have a less extensive criminal record than other prisoners, are older than other inmates, are more likely to have grown up in homes with both parents present, and more often have been sexually abused in childhood (Greenfeld, 1996).

A surprisingly large proportion (12%) were extremely chronic offenders, with 10 or more prior arrests (Greenfeld, 1996). Moreover, this was not the first conviction for the majority of them. More than half (55%) had a prior conviction for either a violent offense or a nonviolent one. Nearly 25% had a prior violent offense conviction. In other words, many of these offenders had a violent history before the current offense, and one-fourth were repeat violent offenders.

Adult Murders of Juveniles

More children are being killed by parents. Murders of children (under the age of 12) by family members increased 9% between 1980 and 1994. Among children under the age of 6, parents and other family members accounted for 44% of the increase, while acquaintances accounted for 41% (Snyder et al., 1996, p. 2). Children (age 12 and under) represent 4% of all homicide victims known to police from 1980 to 1994 (FBI, 1995, p. 287). Infants (1 year of age and younger) constitute 45% of all homicide victims age 12 and under during the past 15 years. Most (54%) were killed by a family member, and 25% were murdered by a friend or acquaintance. Almost half (47%) of the murdered children were beaten to death using hands or fists, 20% were killed with a firearm, and 11% were murdered by strangulation, asphyxiation, or drowning.

Spouse Abuse

An estimated 3-4 million women are battered every year by their husbands or partners (American Medical Association, 1995; Straus, et al., 1980). Based on the 1992 National Alcohol and Family Violence Survey (Straus, 1995), minor assaults reported by women and men increased since 1985, while severe assaults by women remained unchanged and severe assaults by men decreased. Straus suggests that the latter finding may be explained by decreasing willingness of men to report having assaulted their partner, perhaps because of growing public awareness of spouse abuse.

Local spouse abuse studies have shown high cumulative prevalence rates. Abbott, Johnson, Koziol-McLain, and Lowenstein (1995) surveyed women admitted to five Denver hospital emergency departments and clinics in 1993. The cumulative domestic violence prevalence rate among the patients was 54%. Cumulative prevalence rates of 22%-58% have been reported elsewhere (see Abbott et al., 1995). The Denver study showed that domestic violence was not restricted to indigent, uneducated, or minority women, as is commonly assumed. Prevalence rates differed little across demographic groups.

As of March 1994, all but five states had laws that, to a varying extent, require authorities (health care providers) to report domestic violence cases (Hyman, Schillinger, & Lo, 1995). Some statutes require "any person" to report; however, a great deal of controversy impedes progress in reporting the "dark secret" of spouse abuse. Many battered women believe that police intervention is not in the best interest of their safety and welfare (Bowker, 1983). "Practitioners may be caught between their obligations to society and their duties to the patient" (Hyman et al., 1995, p. 1784).

Age and Crime Victimization

Now that we have seen that a large proportion of adult criminality is not well represented in crime statistics, let us look at the relative involvement of juveniles and adults as victims. Are juvenile victimization rates higher than adult rates? Which is increasing most?

Juvenile Versus Adult Victimization

First, let us examine victimization data from the National Crime Victimization Survey. Recall that the NCVS does not survey children under the age of 12, nor does it include homicides. The large volume of child victimization reviewed above, therefore, is not reflected in the NCVS data. Adult victimizations also may be underreported because of the residential mobility of the most criminogenic populations and other difficulties associated with contacting high-rate offenders.

Between 1987 and 1992, violent victimization (rape, robbery, and assault) rates increased

TABLE 3.5 Violent Crime Victimization Rates (per 1,000 in 1992), United States

Age Group Crime	12-17	18-24	25-34	35+	Total
Robbery	10.9	13.0	7.7	2.9	5.9
Completed	6.4	8.0	5.1	2.2	3.9
Attempted	4.5	5.1	2.7	0.7	2.0
Assault	61.8	58.8	29.4	10.7	25.5
Aggravated	20.1	22.0	9.3	4.1	9.0
Simple	41.8	36.8	20.1	6.5	16.5
Total[a]	74.2	74.0	37.6	13.9	32.1

SOURCE: *Juvenile Victimization: 1987-1992*, Moone, ©copyright 1994 by Office of Juvenile Justice and Delinquency Prevention.

a. Includes data on rape not displayed as a separate category.

among all age groups (Moone, 1994). The increase was highest and similar among 12-17-year-olds and 18-24-year-olds. Victimizations of these two groups increased more than among any other ages. Young adults aged 18-24 had about the same violent victimization rate as juveniles during 1992 (Table 3.5), as measured by the NCVS. Young adults have about the same robbery victimization rate, 13% versus 11% for juveniles, and about the same aggravated assault victimization rate (22%) as juveniles (20%). The high assault victimization rate for juveniles, for the most part, is accounted for by the large number of simple assaults, which represent nearly half of all violent juvenile victimizations in 1992 (Table 3.6). Though violent, very few of these offenses result in physical harm. NCVS data, however, appear to underestimate the total volume of juvenile victimization, as noted above, because of the exclusion of children under 12 years of age from the survey.

TABLE 3.6 Violent Victimizations in the United States, 1992

	Total Victimizations	Juvenile Victimizations		
		Total	Percentage of Total	Percentage of Juvenile
Robbery	1,226,000	229,000	18.7	14.7
Completed	806,000	134,000	16.6	8.6
Attempted	419,000	95,000	22.6	6.1
Assault	5,255,000	1,293,000	24.6	83.3
Aggravated	1,849,000	420,000	22.7	27.1
Simple	3,406,000	873,000	25.6	56.2
All Crimes	6,621,000	1,552,000	23.4	100.0
Completed	2,410,000	523,000	21.7	33.7
Attempted	4,212,000	1,030,000	24.5	66.3

SOURCE: *Juvenile Victimization: 1987-1992*, Moone (1994).

NOTE: Detail may not add up to totals because of rounding.

Victimizations Per 1,000 in Age Group, 1991

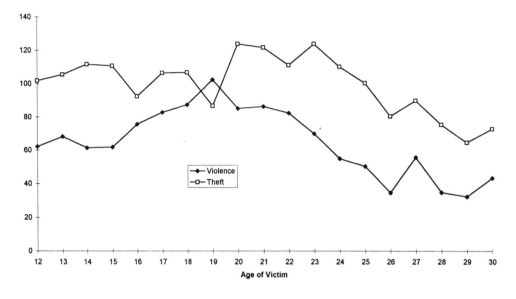

Figure 3.4. Risk of victimization by age

SOURCE: *Juvenile Offenders and Victims: A National Report* (p. 20), Snyder and Sickmund, ©copyright 1995 by the National Center for Juvenile Justice. Reprinted with permission.

DATA SOURCE: *National Crime Victimization Survey, 1991* (machine-readable data file), Bureau of Justice Statistics (1993).

Violent victimizations are most prevalent among older adolescents and young adults. Figure 3.4 (Snyder & Sickmund, 1995, p. 20) shows that violent victimizations peak at the age of 19, and that the risk of violent victimization is highest among persons from ages 15 to 24. Violent victimizations of young adults, however, are more serious than violent victimizations of adolescents.

The NCVS data show that victimizations of both groups are equally likely to result in injury (Snyder & Sickmund, 1995, p. 21). Once violently victimized, adult victims are twice as likely as juvenile victims to be injured seriously (14% versus 7%). Injuries requiring hospital stays of at least 2 days were three times more common for adults than for juveniles (3% versus 1%). Offenders in serious violent incidents against juveniles were less likely to be armed than in serious violent incidents against adults (67% compared with 72% for adults) and, when armed, less likely to use a handgun (19% compared with 24% for adults) (Snyder & Sickmund, 1995, p. 21).

Adult Offending Patterns

Now let us turn to information on adult offending patterns. We do not have any current longitudinal studies on self-reported adult offending in the United States; therefore, we must rely on the results of analyses of national data on arrests, prosecutions of adults, and surveys of incarcerated adults for information on adult offending patterns.

Snyder and Sickmund (1995, pp. 112-113) examined arrest rates among adults and juveniles for the 10-year period from 1983 to 1992. Figure 3.5 shows rate changes for all violent crimes and weapons arrests. Over the 10-year period, arrest rates for Violent Crime Index offenses increased substantially for young adults as well as for juveniles. The increase was largest among juveniles (60%), but the violent arrest rate increase even among persons ages 35 to 39 was 47%. Arrest rates for aggravated assault increased substantially in all age groups over the 10-year period (Figure 3.6). Although the increase was largest for juveniles (about 100%),

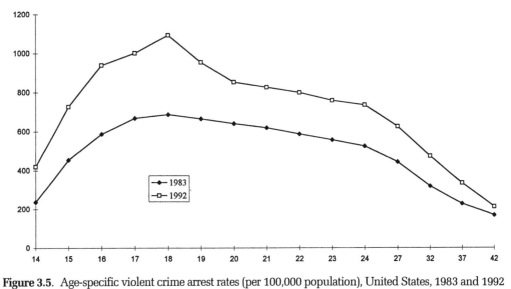

Figure 3.5. Age-specific violent crime arrest rates (per 100,000 population), United States, 1983 and 1992

SOURCE: *Juvenile Offenders and Victims: A National Report* (p. 112), Snyder and Sickmund, ©copyright 1995 by the National Center for Juvenile Justice. Reprinted with permission.

DATA SOURCE: *National Crime Victimization Survey, 1991* (machine-readable data file), Bureau of Justice Statistics (1993).

the increase for persons in their 20s was about 60%. (In 1992, arrests for aggravated assault represented two-thirds (68%) of all Violent Crime Index arrests.) It is interesting that arrest rates for murder decreased over the decade for persons over the age of 25 (Figure 3.7). Murder arrest rates increased most among juveniles and young adults, and the juvenile increase was

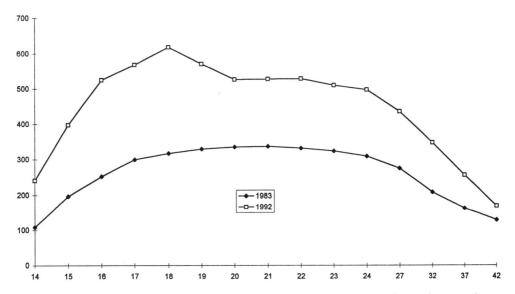

Figure 3.6. Age-specific arrest rates (per 100,000 population) for aggravated assault, United States, 1983 and 1992

SOURCE: *Juvenile Offenders and Victims: A National Report* (p. 112), Snyder and Sickmund, ©copyright 1995 by the National Center for Juvenile Justice. Reprinted with permission.

DATA SOURCE: *Age-Specific Arrest Rates and Race-Specific Arrest Rates for Selected Offenses 1965-1992*, Federal Bureau of Investigation (1994).

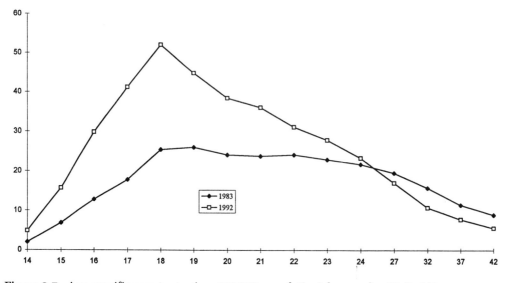

Figure 3.7. Age-specific arrest rates (per 100,000 population) for murder, United States, 1983 and 1992

SOURCE: *Juvenile Offenders and Victims: A National Report* (p. 113), Snyder and Sickmund, ©copyright 1995 by the National Center for Juvenile Justice. Reprinted with permission.
DATA SOURCE: *Age-Specific Arrest Rates and Race-Specific Arrest Rates for Selected Offenses 1965-1992*, Federal Bureau of Investigation (1994).

nearly double the average increase for young adults.

The fact that 18-24-year-olds have the highest homicide offending rate of all age groups is all but ignored. This fact remains so despite the recent increases in the juvenile homicide offending rate. In 1994, the rate among adolescents (ages 14-17) was 19 per 100,000 in the population. Among 18-24-year-olds, the rate was 25.3 per 100,000 (Fox, 1996, p. 4). Comparisons of these age groups rarely are made in media accounts of crime rates. Generally, the crimes rates of 10-17-year-olds are compared with rates for all adults above the age of 18. The result is that the 10-17-year-olds show a higher rate. This comparison makes juvenile rates look higher because the inclusion of all adults means that the elderly, who have very low offense rates, are included in the calculation. When rates for 0-17-year-olds are compared with those of people 18 and above, the adult group has a much higher rate.

Adults account for 81% of the increase in the total number of violent crimes reported to the police between 1983 and 1992 (Table 3.7). Juveniles account for only 23% of the increase. The increasing involvement of adults in violent crimes is indicated in arrest data on the age of offenders. According to the FBI Uniform Crime

Reports (1993b), on average, persons arrested for violent crimes in 1992 were about a year older than those arrested in 1972 (Table 3.8). The average age of arrestees in 1992 for each violent offense was 27 for murder, 29 for forcible rape, 24 for robbery, and 29 for aggravated assault. In 1992, the average age of property crime offenders was 25 years. Weapons offenders averaged 26 years of age, and persons arrested for drug abuse increased by 6 years in the 20-year period. The average age of weapons offenders declined from 29 to 26 over the 20-year span, and murder arrestees declined in age from nearly 30 to slightly over 27, reflecting increases in arrests of juveniles and other young persons for these offenses, despite the fact that the average age of the U.S. population increased by nearly 3 years during this period (Snyder & Sickmund, 1995, p. 109).

Adult Prosecutions

Little information is available on adult prosecutions. The Offender-Based Transaction Statistics (OBTS) program of the Bureau of Justice Statistics collects data from the states on criminal justice system processing of persons arrested for a felony. Perez (1991) analyzed data on felony arrest cases that terminated in 1988.

TABLE 3.7 Increase in Violent Crimes Attributed to Juveniles and Adults 1983-1992

			Change	
	1983	1992	83-92	% of Total
Total Reported Crimes	1,258,000	1,932,000	674, 000	100%
% Cleared by Juvenile Arrest	9.5%	12.8%		
Estimated Juvenile Crimes	119,000	247,000	128,000	19%
% Cleared by Adult Arrest	90.5%	87.2%		
Estimated Adult Crimes	1,139,000	1,685,000	546,000	81%

SOURCE: "Are Juveniles Driving the Violent Crime Trends?" H. N. Snyder. (1994). Fact Sheet #16. Washington, D.C.: Office of Juvenile Justice and Deliquency Prevention.

Perez's (1991) analysis (Table 3.9) shows similar percentages of felony offenders in all groups age 20-39, for violent offenses, property felonies, and weapons offenses (although the age span in each of the groups is not the same). Most surprising of all is the high percentage of felony offenders age 30-39. These adults represented about one-quarter of all offenders, violent offenders, property offenders, and weapons offenders. It is also surprising to see that persons age 40 and above represented 15% of all violent offenders and nearly 1 in 5 of all persons charged with assault. These data suggest that offending among older persons needs more attention.

Adult Drug Abuse

Drug abuse among adults is a growing problem. Since 1979, the average age of illicit drug users has increased from 24 years to 29 years (Substance Abuse and Mental Health Services Administration [SAMHSA], 1995). The extensive drug using cohorts of the 1970s, including those with severe problems, continue to get older. The proportion that are age 35 and older has risen steadily since 1979. In 1994, the rate of current illicit drug use was highest among persons age 18-21 and 16-17-years-old. Heavy drinking was most prevalent among persons age 18-25.

Drug-related emergency room visits, reported by the Drug Abuse Warning Network (DAWN), indicate that drug-related episodes

TABLE 3.8 Average Age of Persons Arrested, 1972 and 1992

Offense	1972	1992
Violent Crime Index	26.2	27.6
Murder	29.7	27.2
Forcible rape	24.8	28.6
Robbery	22.0	24.1
Aggravated assault	29.0	28.8
Property Crime Index	21.1	25.1
Burglary	19.9	23.5
Larceny-theft	21.8	26.2
Motor vehicle theft	20.1	21.8
Arson	20.5	22.8
Weapons	29.1	26.0
Drug abuse	22.3	28.5

SOURCE: Juvenile Offenders and Victims: A National Report, Snyder and Sickmund, ©copyright 1995 by the National Center for Juvenile Justice. Reprinted with permission.

TABLE 3.9 Age of Persons Arrested for Felony Offenses in 14 states, 1988

	Age and Percentage of All Arrests for Crime Type				
	Under 20	20-24	25-29	30-39	40 or Older
All offenses	14	25	22	25	13
Violent offenses	14	25	22	25	15
Homicide	16	25	20	22	15
Kidnapping	9	26	26	27	13
Sexual assault	10	20	20	28	21
Robbery	23	30	22	20	5
Assault	11	23	21	26	18
Property offenses	18	26	21	23	11
Drug offenses	12	27	25	27	9
Public order offenses	8	22	22	27	21
Weapons	18	27	21	22	12

SOURCE: Tracking Offenders, 1988, Perez (1991).

NOTE: The age of persons arrested for felonies was reported in 98% of the cases. Detail may not add to 100% because of rounding.

have been increasing about 6%-10% annually since 1991 (SAMHSA, 1994). Cocaine appears to be the primary cause for the increase in total drug-related emergency department episodes since the mid-1980s. Since 1988, cocaine-related episodes for persons aged 35-44 have more than doubled. Violence-related problems associated with drug abuse are most prevalent among 18-25-year-olds (11%), followed by 26-34-year-olds (7%), then 12-17 year-olds (5%). These problems include having arguments and fights with family members and friends (SAMHSA, 1995). Although the proportion of alcohol and other drug abusing adults who have children is unknown, children are not unaffected by these patterns.

All these data sources suggest the need to reconsider the relationship between age and crime. Although the age-crime curve "is the most basic fact of criminology" (Smith, 1995, p. 421), the reasons why onset of deviance is generally in the early teenage years and desistance occurs in the late teenage years or early 20s are not well understood. Neither is the difference between prevalence (the proportion of persons offending) and incidence (the number of offenses per person). The two measures often are used interchangeably (and erroneously) in thinking about age and crime. Farrington (1986a, p. 219) makes the important distinction: "the peak in the crime rate in the teenage years reflects a peak in prevalence [but] incidence does not vary consistently with age." Our review of adult offending supports his observation. We see a large volume (incidence) of offending well into the adult years, even violent offending. Much of the high incidence of adult offending may be a continuation of adolescent patterns of drinking and fighting (see Chapter 8). A lot of violent adult offending appears to take place in "youth" or "street" gangs, as we shall see in Chapter 6. Curiously, much adult crime occurs in adult groups that are not gangs. Still more occurs in the home in the form of violent attacks on children (their own) and spouses. Much research remains to be done toward developing a fundamental understanding of the incidence of adult offending.

New longitudinal data provide a basis for questioning the presumed age-crime curve among both females and males. These findings from the Program of Research on Causes and Correlates of Delinquency (Huizinga, Loeber, & Thornberry, 1995) show that serious violent (aggravated assault, robbery, gang fights, and rape) offending among girls peaks at ages 13-15, instead of at ages 15-17 as reported in the National Youth Survey (see Elliott, 1994a, p. 6). Data from all three sites show no decline in males' self-reported serious violent offending in late adolescence (Figure 3.8), in contrast with a peak in age-specific prevalence at age 17 in the NYS. The prevalence rates remain high (17%-20%) across the 17-19 age period. Further analysis of additional years of data will determine whether an anticipated downward age curve occurs as more of the sampled youngsters reach the late teenage years or whether the downward curve occurs in early adulthood. It is unclear whether we are seeing a change in age-specific prevalence or whether this observed pattern is a result of these new longitudinal studies, which are following the same subjects for a longer period of time (see Moffitt, 1993).

Summary

Although juveniles are slightly overrepresented in clearances for Violent Crime Index offenses overall, they are underrepresented in homicide clearances. In 1994, adults were responsible for 90% of FBI clearances for murder in the United States, and for 86% of violent crime clearances. Young adults (age 18-34) are overrepresented in murders. Although 18-34-year-olds represent a quarter of the U.S. population, they account for slightly over half of all murders. Juveniles are responsible for only about a quarter of the growth in overall violent crimes between 1985 and 1994, whereas adults account for nearly three-quarters of the increase in violent crimes. Juveniles account for only one-third of the increase in murders during the past 10 years, whereas adults account for two-thirds of the increase. Adults are overwhelmingly responsible for violent crime in the United States and for the increase over the past decade.

These conclusions suggest a research agenda. The arbitrary legal divide between juvenile and adult needs to be spanned to understand development of criminal careers that involve violence. Because adults account for an overwhelming proportion of all violence in the United States, research on adult violent crime should be a top priority. Their involvement should be addressed from two standpoints: first, the disproportionate involvement of

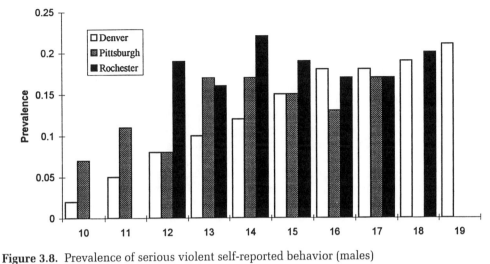

Figure 3.8. Prevalence of serious violent self-reported behavior (males)

SOURCE: *Recent Findings From the Program of Research on Causes and Correlates of Delinquency,* Huizinga, Loeber, and Thornberry (1995, p. 12).

young adults in homicides and other violent crimes, including the apparent prolongation of young adult criminal careers into later adulthood; and second, the high level of adult violent victimization of infants and children.

Criminological perspectives must be broadened to account for adult responsibility for juvenile delinquency and other adolescent problem behaviors. How can this be done? Incorporation of a developmental perspective of problem behavior would help increase our understanding of the intergenerational relationship of adult criminality to delinquent juvenile careers (see Chapter 8).

Adult violent offending appears to extend into older ages than previously thought, even into the 40s. It also appears that the rate of violent victimization of adults is increasing. Studies of adult chronic and violent offending are desperately needed. Ongoing longitudinal studies of juvenile chronic, serious, and violent offending in Chicago, Denver, Rochester, Pittsburgh, and Seattle should be extended into adulthood to address these issues.

Aggravated assaults account for most of the violent offenses among adults. What are the characteristics of these offenders? What background factors distinguish assaults and robberies from homicides? For two decades, Zimring (1977) has repeatedly asked the very important, yet unanswered, question: Under what conditions do assaults, robberies, and other offenses become homicides? Zimring (cited in Block & Block, 1991, p. 41) calls these various offenses "sibling" offenses to homicide. His discovery is that aside from gangland hits and contract murders, almost all homicides correspond to a "sibling" offense. In the nomenclature of Block and Block (1991), "expressive homicides, had they not had a fatal outcome, would have been assaults, and instrumental homicides would have been a robbery or a burglary" (p. 41).

Because most adult criminals have no juvenile justice system experience (Greenfeld, 1992; Langan & Greenfeld, 1983), these offenders need to be researched. Longitudinal cohort studies should examine the offender careers of those who begin late. How are they different (on causal variables) from juvenile offenders who continue their careers into adulthood? More research is also needed on adult offenders who begin their careers in the juvenile justice system. What characteristics distinguish graduates to the criminal justice system from juveniles who terminated their careers?

Finally, effective programs for preventing and reducing serious, violent, and chronic adult crime are needed. Have programs targeting them been found to be effective? A comprehensive strategy is needed for dealing with serious, violent, and chronic adults. Successfully targeting the most chronic, serious, and violent adult offenders, however, will not be easy. This has been attempted in the past without success. The Law Enforcement Assistance Administration undertook a Career Criminal Program in the late 1970s, based on the New York City Major Offense Bureau (Merola, 1975), that failed in its objective of targeting chronic adult offenders (Chelimsky & Dahman, 1981). Criminal defendants prosecuted under the Career Criminal Program were no more likely to be tried, to plead guilty, to be convicted, or to have the charges against them dismissed than would be expected under the routine processing by the local criminal justice systems of similar and noncareer criminal cases.

The program did not appear to influence the rate of incarceration among prosecuted defendants. The study authors (Chelimsky & Dahman, 1981) advised that the ability of a career criminal program to reduce crime is influenced by many factors. Most important, the group that is singled out by the program must contain those offenders responsible for most crimes and most likely to recidivate. They concluded that it is not yet clear how to identify the adult career criminal envisioned by the program.

This problem persists a decade later, after more than 100 jurisdictions have adopted some form of priority prosecution for career crimi-nals (Chaiken & Chaiken, 1991). In an assessment of priority prosecution in two jurisdictions, the Chaikens concluded that seven risk factors prosecutors used (pertaining to prior record, current charges, and current status in the criminal justice system) did not "validly and decisively distinguish high-rate offenders from others" (p. 5). Surprisingly, factors commonly believed to be predictive of dangerousness proved not to be, including use of a gun, number of adult convictions, previous incarceration, and prior arrest for drug distribution or possession. The authors recommended using additional criteria, in a two-step process, to distinguish the subset of dangerous offenders from others.

Studies of adult careers are sorely needed. "The conclusion that crime ceases in midlife may be premature; it is based on cross-sectional age comparisons of arrest and conviction rates. . . . Thus until longitudinal researchers collect self-reports of crime in the same individuals from adolescence to old age, the midlife disappearance of crime will remain an empirical question" (Moffitt, 1993, p. 679). Besides the evidence of chronic adult offending that we have reviewed, there is evidence that family violence offenses show a steady increase with age (Gottfredson & Hirschi, 1986). Arrest statistics reflect only the tip of the iceberg.

4

Juvenile Delinquency Trends
and Juvenile Justice System Responses

This chapter reviews juvenile delinquency (age 10-17, unless otherwise noted) trends over the past 15 years. This time frame is of particular interest because it is the period in which juvenile delinquency and violence is believed to have increased significantly. The aim of this chapter is to see how juvenile involvement in delinquency and violence has changed during this period. This chapter also examines juvenile justice system handling of offenders, to see how society has changed its responses to juvenile delinquency and violence.

Juvenile Violence Trends

Different conclusions can be drawn regarding juvenile violence trends depending on the source that is used to make this determination. Three main sources of juvenile violence trends are available: FBI Uniform Crime Report Supplemental Homicide Reports, the National Crime Victims Survey, and self-report studies. In this section, we review these sources of long-term information on juvenile involvement in violence and attempt to reconcile the different trends these sources suggest. Official (police, court, and correctional) data are reviewed in the next section, on juvenile justice system re-

sponses, because these sources represent societal responses to delinquency and crime. They should not be considered a measure of the incidence of delinquent behavior. We make an exception in the case of homicides. The FBI Supplemental Homicide Reports generally are used in criminological research as the best measure of criminal homicides.

Self-Report Measures

Surveys of the juvenile population in which respondents self-report their delinquent acts generally are recognized as the most valid measure of delinquent *behavior* and changes in adolescent involvement (see Elliott, 1995). The National Youth Survey (NYS) is a prospective study of a national probability sample of 1,725 youths age 11-17 in 1976. The panel was interviewed annually from 1976 to 1980, and every 3 years thereafter. At the time of the last interview, in 1993, the panel was age 27-33. Both self-report and official record data are available for all respondents.

Analyses of the NYS (Elliott, Ageton, Huizinga, Knowles, & Canter, 1983) over the 1976-1980 period (during which the median age of respondents increased from 14 to 18) indicate that the proportion of youth in the U.S. popu-

AUTHOR'S NOTE: The author is indebted to the National Center for Juvenile Justice for providing access to the spreadsheet files for figures and tables in two NCJJ reports: *Juvenile Offenders and Victims: A National Report* (Snyder & Sickmund, 1995), and *Juvenile Offenders and Victims: 1996 Update on Violence* (Snyder et al., 1996). This chapter draws significantly on both of these reports.

lation who reported involvement in some type of delinquent behavior annually (prevalence rate) remained relatively constant between 1976 and 1980, while the annual rate of offending (incidence rate) increased (Elliott et al., 1983, pp. 55-59). The overall incidence of delinquent acts increased by almost 50% during this period, while the incidence of serious delinquent offenses (FBI Index offenses) declined by 40%. Most of the increase in the overall rate of offending was in status offenses, public order offenses, carrying a concealed weapon, and drug trafficking. The delinquent offending rate within the youth population was very high throughout the 1976-1980 period.

NYS data cannot be used for recent trend analyses because the panel members are now adults; therefore, we must turn to the Monitoring the Future (MTF) Study, which measures illicit drug use and delinquency among a national sample of high school seniors (8th and 10th graders were added in 1991). Since 1982, students have been asked to report involvement during the past 12 months in 15 behavioral areas. Six questions covering violent acts are asked in the survey (arguing or fighting with parents, hitting an instructor or supervisor, getting into a serious fight at school or work, group fighting, hurting someone so seriously they needed medical attention, and using a weapon to take something). Osgood (1989) analyzed time trends for the period 1975 through 1985. Assault rates increased "noticeably" among these 17-year-olds during the 11-year period, although the trend was not consistent on a year-to-year basis. The most notable increases were in fighting at school or work and group fighting. There was no interpretable trend for robbery and most other offenses, except for theft, which declined. Using follow-up data the MTF survey collects after seniors leave school, Osgood (1989) found that rates of all types of behavior declined through age 23, except for assaults.

Johnston, O'Malley, and Bachman's (1995) subsequent examination of trends in the MTF survey over the 1982-1994 period found that seniors did not report more significant involvement in any of the 15 behaviors (except theft over $50.00) over the 13 years of the survey; in fact, they reported modest decreases in involvement in most behaviors (see Maguire & Pastore, 1995, pp. 258-259). Seniors' drug use declined significantly during the 1980s (except for a peak in cocaine use in 1984-1986) and began increasing again (except for alcohol use) in about 1992 (including 8th and 10th graders), but it has not reached previous high levels of the early 1980s. The increases since 1992 nevertheless are deemed to herald an upward trend because of the decline in adolescents' perceived risk, as shown in the National Household Survey on Drug Abuse (Substance Abuse and Mental Health Services Administration [SAMHSA], 1995).

Homicide Offenders

FBI Supplementary Homicide Report data provide the best trend data on juvenile homicide offenders. Analyses by Snyder and colleagues (1996, pp. 22-25) focus on the number of homicides in which there was enough information to identify the offender as a juvenile. Figure 4.1 shows the total number of juvenile homicide offenders between 1980 and 1994, by age. Altogether, there were more than 26,000 known juvenile homicide offenders during this period, peaking at just over 2,800 in 1994. This number represents about twice the number of juvenile homicide offenders 15 years earlier and about three times the number in 1984.

Most (88%) juvenile homicide offenders were 15-17 years of age, and the increase from 1984 to 1994 was almost entirely accounted for by this age group (Figure 4.1). Homicides by 12-14-year-olds increased slightly during the period, and murders by offenders under the age of 12 were fewer than 20 in most years and never higher than 35 in a given year (Snyder et al., 1996, p. 22).

Males account for almost all the increase in juvenile homicides from 1980 through 1994. Although the number of female homicide offenders increased 29% during this period (Snyder et al., 1996, p. 23), this is a negligible increase because of the small base in 1980.

What proportion of the increase in juvenile homicides is accounted for by black versus white youths? Figure 4.2 shows that throughout the 1980-1994 period, most juvenile homicide offenders were either black or white (with Hispanics represented in both groups). In 1980, about equal proportions of all juvenile homicide offenders were accounted for by black and white youths. By 1994, however, 61% of juvenile homicide offenders were black and 36% were white (Snyder et al., 1996, p. 22). This increase in black juvenile homicides appears to

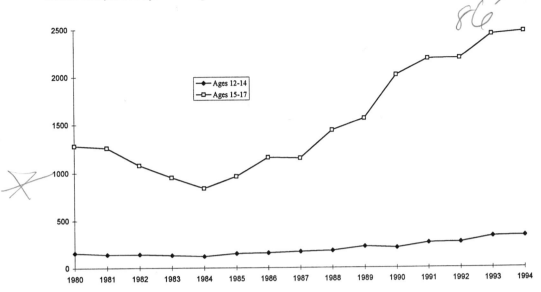

Figure 4.1. Age and number of juvenile homicide offenders, 1980-1994

SOURCE: *Juvenile Offenders and Victims: 1996 Update on Violence* (p. 22), Snyder, Sickmund, and Poe-Yamagata, ©copyright 1996 by the National Center for Justice, Office of Juvenile Justice. Reprinted with permission.

DATA SOURCE: *Supplementary Homicide Reports 1976-1994* (machine-readable data file), Fox (1996).

be related to the increase in gang-related killings during this period (see Chapter 6).

Who did juveniles kill? Most males killed acquaintances (47%) or strangers (32%) between 1980 and 1994 (Snyder et al., 1996, p. 23). Only 8% killed family members. The victim-offender relationship was unknown in the remaining 13% of cases. Juveniles tend to kill persons older than themselves. Three-fourths of the victims of 15-17-year-olds were age 18 and older in 1994, and more than a third (35%) were age 25-49 (Snyder et al., 1996, p. 24).

How did juveniles kill their victims? Figure 4.3 shows the increase from 1980 to 1994 in

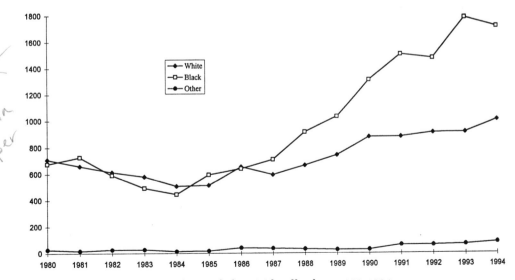

Figure 4.2. Race and number of juvenile homicide offenders, 1980-1994

SOURCE: *Juvenile Offenders and Victims: 1996 Update on Violence* (p. 22), Snyder, Sickmund, and Poe-Yamagata, ©copyright 1996 by the National Center for Juvenile Justice. Reprinted with permission.

DATA SOURCE: *Supplementary Homicide Reports 1976-1994* (machine-readable data file), Fox (1996).

Figure 4.3. Juveniles killed by firearms and other weapons, 1980-1994

SOURCE: *Juvenile Offenders and Victims: 1996 Update on Violence* (p. 24), Snyder, Sickmund, and Poe-Yamagata, ©copyright 1996 by the National Center for Juvenile Justice. Reprinted with permission.

DATA SOURCE: *Supplementary Homicide Reports 1976-1994* (machine-readable data file), Fox (1996).

juveniles' use of a gun to kill their victims, from 53% in 1980 to 82% in 1994 (Snyder et al., 1996, p. 24). Use of other murder weapons decreased slightly during the period. It appears that the availability of a firearm to settle disputes played a key role in the increase in juvenile homicides over the past 15 years. Although a suitable measure of firearm availability has not been developed, several studies indicate that firearms are readily available to juveniles (see Chapter 6).

Figures 4.4, and 4.6 show changes in juvenile murder arrest rates and aggravated assault

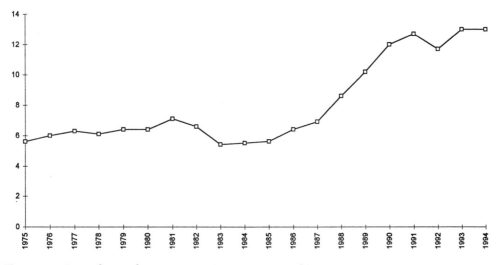

Figure 4.4. Juvenile murder arrest rates (per 100,000 aged 10-17), 1975-1994

SOURCE: *Juvenile Offenders and Victims: 1996 Update on Violence* (p. 18), Snyder, Sickmund, and Poe-Yamagata, ©copyright 1996 by the National Center for Juvenile Justice. Reprinted with permisssion.

NOTE: Arrest rates in 1993 and 1994 were estimated by the National Center for Juvenile Justice using data in the FBI's *Crime in the United States* reports and population data from the U.S. Bureau of the Census.

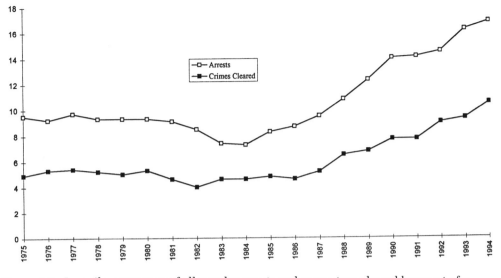

Figure 4.5. Juvenile percentage of all murder arrests and percentage cleared by arrest of a juvenile, 1975-1994

SOURCE: *Juvenile Offenders and Victims: 1996 Update on Violence* (p. 18), Snyder, Sickmund, and Poe-Yamagata, ©copyright 1996 by the National Center for Juvenile Justice. Reprinted with permission.

arrest rates over the past 20 years. Comparison of increases in arrest rates and clearances for murder (Figure 4.5) versus aggravated assault (Figure 4.7) indicates a sharper increase in murder arrests than in the "sibling aggravated assault offense (Zimring, cited in Block & Block,

1991, p. 41). In fact, the murder rate increase more closely resembles the increase since 1984 in the rate of juvenile weapons law violations (Figure 4.8), suggesting that the juvenile murder increase is accounted for by increased gun use.

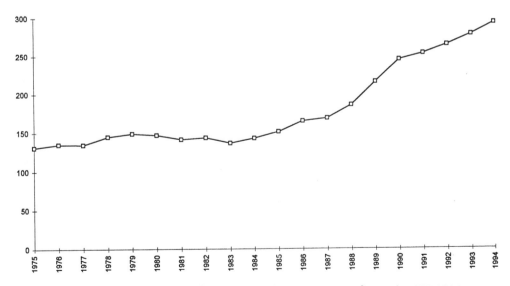

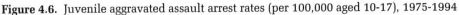

Figure 4.6. Juvenile aggravated assault arrest rates (per 100,000 aged 10-17), 1975-1994

SOURCE: *Juvenile Offenders and Victims: 1996 Update on Violence* (p. 19), Snyder, Sickmund, and Poe-Yamagata, ©copyright 1996 by the National Center for Juvenile Justice. Reprinted with permission

NOTE: Arrest rates in 1993 and 1994 were estimated by the National Center for Juvenile Justice using data in the FBI's *Crime in the United States* reports and population data from the U.S. Bureau of the Census.

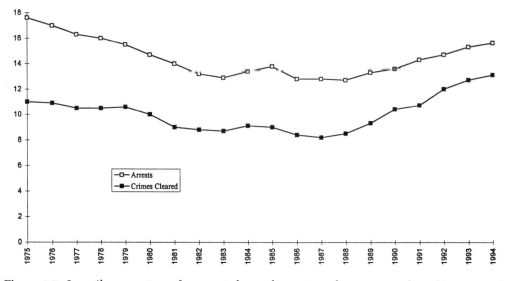

Figure 4.7. Juvenile percentage of aggravated assault arrests and percentage cleared by arrest of a juvenile, 1975-1994

SOURCE: *Juvenile Offenders and Victims: 1996 Update on Violence* (p. 19), Snyder, Sickmund, and Poe-Yamagata, ©copyright 1996 by the National Center for Juvenile Justice. Reprinted with permission.

This hunch was pursued by Zimring (in press) in his analysis of juvenile homicide trends during the period 1976-1992. He compared the total number of juvenile homicides to the number of juvenile gun and nongun homicides in each of the past 17 years. Almost all the increase in juvenile homicides was accounted for by the gun component of juvenile homicides. In fact, over the entire 17-year period, Zimring found a correlation of .9 between the percentage of all juvenile homicides committed with guns and the total juvenile homi-

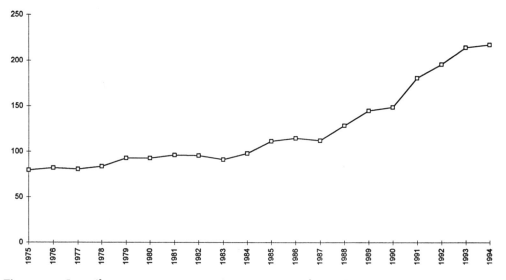

Figure 4.8. Juvenile weapons arrest rates (per 100,000 aged 10-17), 1975-1994

SOURCE: *Juvenile Offenders and Victims: 1996 Update on Violence* (p. 21), Snyder, Sickmund, and Poe-Yamagata, ©copyright 1996 by the National Center for Juvenile Justice. Reprinted with permission.

NOTE: Arrest rates in 1993 and 1994 were estimated by the National Center for Juvenile Justice using data in the FBI's *Crime in the United States* reports and population data from the U.S. Bureau of the Census.

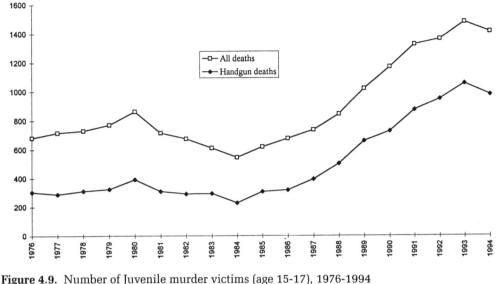

Figure 4.9. Number of Juvenile murder victims (age 15-17), 1976-1994

SOURCE: *Child Victimizers: Violent Offenders and Their Victims* (p. 19), Greenfeld (1996).

cide rate. Zimring (in press, p. 9) commented that "from a policy standpoint, [these data] make the identification of policy goals in youth violence what is called a 'no brainer.' It would be difficult to make up a set of weapon-specific homicide trends that would underscore the importance of guns more than [these]." Figure 4.9, showing the parallel between the increase in 15-17-year-old murders and handgun deaths, illustrates Zimring's point.

Analyses of juvenile homicide offending patterns from 1980 through 1994 show some interesting results (Snyder et al., 1996, pp. 24-25). Males were nearly twice as likely as females to kill with a gun. Older adolescents were more likely than younger juveniles to kill with a gun. Younger victims were less likely than older victims to be killed with a gun. More than three-quarters of juveniles who killed 15-17-year-olds and 18-24-year-olds used a gun. Guns thus appear to serve as an equalizer in assaults in which a younger person attacks an older one.

About half of juvenile murderers acted alone; however, juvenile group murders increased over the 15-year period more than lone killings. Over the entire period, lone murders rose 52% while multiple-offender homicides increased nearly 250%. The percentage of juvenile homicide offenders who had accomplices increased from 43% in 1980 to 55% in 1994. Group killings were more likely to involve use of a firearm (about 70%). The increase in group homicides reflects the growth in gang-related homicides from 1980 through 1994 (see Chapter 6). Most of the group killings (60%) during the 15-year period involved adult accomplices (Snyder et al., 1996, p. 25).

In most (80%) homicides involving juvenile offenders during 1980-1994, the offender and the victim were of the same race. Nearly all (90%) of the white offenders killed whites, and 76% of black offenders killed blacks. Group killings, however, were twice as likely as single-offender homicides to cross racial lines. In mixed-race killings involving groups, the most typical pattern (70% of all mixed-race group homicides) was blacks killing whites (Snyder et al., 1996, p. 25). These mixed-race group homicides are not likely to be gang-related because the latter typically involve killings within the same racial/ethnic group (see Chapter 6).

Victimization

Unfortunately, the BJS's analysis of National Crime Victimization Survey (NCVS) data do not separate juveniles from young adult victims; they lump juveniles with 18- and 19-year-olds. Thus, continuous analyses of NCVS data separating juveniles from young adults have not been performed. Two analyses of juveniles, however, have been made covering two separate 5-year periods.

Hindelang directed a project that analyzed NCVS data on 12-17-year-old victims (Danser & Laub, 1981; Hindelang & McDermott, 1981; Laub & Hindelang, 1981; McDermott & Hindelang, 1981; Sampson, Castellano, & Laub, 1981).In their first analysis of the NCVS data, McDermott and Hindelang (1981) showed that from 1973 to 1977, the total number and rate of personal crimes attributable to juvenile and youthful offenders remained relatively stable, although there was a slight increase in the number and rate of personal crimes attributable to adults. Guns rarely were used by juveniles in personal crimes, and there was no evidence that among juveniles weapon use generally, or gun use specifically, increased from 1973 to 1977.

Hindelang and McDermott (1981) noted that in recent years, juvenile criminal behavior had been portrayed by the media as both maliciously violent and increasingly common, particularly in urban areas. Their analysis of NCVS juvenile data did not support these perceptions. Juvenile crimes of rape, robbery, assault, and personal larceny were no more serious in 1977 than 5 years earlier. Moreover, the rate of offending for the personal crimes also did not show an increasing trend, despite a small increase in the juvenile arrest rate for violent crimes reported during the 1973-1977 period by the FBI.

In the second juvenile analysis, covering the period 1987-1992, Moone (1994) found that the juvenile violent victimizations increased 23% (Table 4.1), based on NCVS survey results, which exclude fatal assaults. Most (56%) of the victimizations juveniles reported in 1992, however, were simple assaults that do not involve a weapon and result in minor injury at most. In fact, the proportion of juvenile victimizations that resulted in serious injury declined from 11% to 7% from 1987 to 1991, and the percentage of serious violent incidents resulting in injury, hospital stays, and use of weapons remained essentially the same (Snyder & Sickmund, 1995, p. 23).

One gets a different picture of juvenile violence trends during the late 1980s and early 1990s, depending on whether NCVS victimization reports or UCR arrest data are used. Moone's analysis showed a 23% increase in re-

TABLE 4.1 Changes in Violent Crime Victimization Rates (per 1,000) of Juveniles Aged 12 to 17

Offense	Percentage Change	
	1987-1992	1991-1992
Robbery	35.3	6.1
Assault	21.2	4.4
Total	22.5	4.3

SOURCE: *Juvenile Victimization: 1987-1992*, Moone (1994).

ported violent victimizations from 1987 to 1992, only about half as large as the increase (47%) in juvenile arrests for violent crimes between 1988 and 1992 (FBI, 1993b, p. 223). Granted, comparing these data sources is much like comparing apples and oranges (and the time frames are not exactly the same), because one source is victims' accounts and the other is arrests of individuals. These trend data nevertheless should not show such a large discrepancy.

In his comparison of NCVS, UCR, and NYS self-report data for the period 1976-1980, Menard (1987) found that the UCR arrest data showed a very different trend compared to the NCVS victimization data and the NYS data. Among UCR Index offenses, arrest data indicated a predominantly upward trend over the 5-year period, whereas both victimization and self-report data showed decreases, if anything, other than random fluctuations over time. Menard (1987, p. 468) concluded that the self-report and victimization trends "that do appear are negative rather than positive, further emphasizing the difference between UCR and other sources of information on crime trends."

Because of the aging of the NYS sample, who are now young adults, the survey no longer provides national trend data specifically on juvenile offending. The mixed juvenile and young adult NYS data, however, demonstrate the low correlation between actual delinquent and criminal behavior and arrest data. Elliott's (1995) analysis of NYS data for 1976-1990, covering the age span of respondents from 11 to 30 years, revealed that the correlation between the frequency of FBI Index arrests and self-reported Index offenses was only .30, and the correlation between arrests and overall self-reported offending rates was only .38.

To determine whether the correlation was higher within the most chronic offending subgroup, Elliott (1995) examined the overlap between the worst self-reported offender group (those reporting 78 or more index offenses) and the worst 20% of persons arrested over the 25-year period (five or more arrests for index offenses). He found that fewer than a quarter of the worst arrest offenders were in the worst self-reported offender group. Elliott concluded that, "in essence, the individual arrest rates for index offenses do not appear to be representative of individual offending rates. And the worst self-reported offenders are not well identified by a high arrest rate" (p. 12). In general, comparing arrest and self-reported histories, he found that the arrest history seriously overestimates the proportions of burglaries and greatly understates the proportions of the serious violent offenses.

Elliott (1995, pp. 16-17) calculated the probability of arrest per self-reported violent offense as about .02. That is, there were only 2 arrests for every 100 self-reported aggravated assaults, robberies, and rapes. When self-reported violent offenses were restricted to more harmful offenses (involving either a weapon or an injury serious enough to require medical treatment), the probabilities of arrest increased to .09 for robbery and to .04 for aggravated assaults among males. The arrest probabilities, however, were much higher for black males than for white males. For robbery, the white male arrest probability was .04, compared to .29 for black males. For aggravated assault, the white male arrest probability was .02, compared to .11 for black males. "For both offenses, black males are approximately 6 times as likely to have an arrest for a self-reported violent offense as are white males over their adolescent and early adult years" (p. 18). These findings led Elliott (1995, pp. 19-20) to suggest that arrest and self-reported data

> provide substantially different pictures of onset, developmental course, offending patterns, specialization, and termination of criminal behavior. To rely almost exclusively on arrest studies when describing the dynamics of criminal behavior is indefensible. (p. 21)

Statisticians do not claim, though, that an arrest equals a crime (see Snyder & Sickmund, 1995, pp. 46, 98-99). Rather, they recognize that official statistics may underrepresent juvenile delinquency and suppress the actual picture of juvenile crime. "While official records may be inadequate measures of the level of juvenile offending, they do monitor justice system activity. An understanding of the size, characteristics, and variations in official statistics across time and jurisdictions provides a description of the caseloads of the justice system" (Snyder & Sickmund, 1995, p. 46).

Juvenile Justice System Responses

How has the juvenile justice system responded to juvenile delinquency over the past 15 years? Do its responses reflect the small increase in serious and violent juvenile delinquency that homicide, victimization, and self-reported data suggest? Our review of juvenile justice system responses covers arrests, juvenile court handling, detention and corrections, and conditions of confinement. First, though, let us examine the seriousness of delinquency that is represented in arrest data.

Arrests

Juveniles age 0-17 represented about 25% of the population in 1994. The 10-17 age group, who represented just over 11% of the U.S. population in 1994, accounted for 19% of all arrests, 19% of Violent Crime Index arrests, and 35% of Property Crime Index arrests (FBI, 1995). Most juvenile arrests (67%) are for Nonindex offenses (Table 4.2). Stealing (larceny-theft, which includes shoplifting) is the single offense for which juveniles were most likely to be arrested in 1994. Running away is the next most likely offense. Stealing, malicious mischief, misbehaving, running away, staying out late, drinking, drug use, and other miscellaneous offenses accounted for more than 60% of all juvenile arrests in 1994. Running away, minor assaults, disorderly conduct, drug-abuse violations, vandalism, curfew violations and loitering, and liquor law violations represent nearly half (44%) of all juvenile arrests in 1994.

The proportion of all Index Property Crimes accounted for by juveniles in 1994 (35%) is more than three times the representation (11%) of juveniles in the U.S. population (Snyder et al., 1996, p. 13). Among all Index Crimes for which juveniles were arrested in 1994, 83% were serious property crimes (Table 4.2). Larceny-theft alone accounted for over half (56%) of all juvenile Index Crime arrests in 1994, bur-

TABLE 4.2 Juvenile Arrests, 1994

Offense Charged	Estimated Number
Total	2,714,000
Crime Index Total	898,300
Violent Crime Index	150,200
Murder and manslaughter	3,700
Forcible rape	6,000
Robbery	55,200
Aggravated assault	85,300
Property Crime Index	748,100
Burglary	143,200
Larceny-theft	505,100
Motor vehicle theft	88,200
Arson	11,600
Nonindex offenses	1,815,700
Other assaults	211,700
Forgery and counterfeiting	8,700
Fraud	23,600
Embezzlement	1,000
Stolen property	44,200
Vandalism	152,100
Weapons	63,400
Prostitution and vice	1,200
Sex offenses	17,700
Drug abuse violations	158,600
Gambling	1,700
Offenses against the family and children	5,400
Driving under the influence	13,600
Liquor law violations	120,000
Drunkenness	18,400
Disorderly conduct	170,500
Vagrancy	4,300
All other offenses (except traffic)	422,300
Curfew and loitering	128,400
Runaways	248,800

SOURCE: *Juvenile Offenders and Victims: 1996 Update on Violence* (p. 10), Snyder, Sickmund, and Poe-Yamagata, ©copyright 1996 by the National Center for Juvenile Justice. Reprinted with permission.

DATA SOURCE: *Crime in the United States 1994*, Federal Bureau of Investigation (1995). Arrest estimates developed by the National Center for Juvenile Justice.

glary accounted for 16%, and motor vehicle theft for 10%. Larceny-theft offenses (theft of items of more than $50.00 in value), theft of automobile parts, and breaking and entering cars and buildings are the main serious property offenses for which juveniles are likely to be arrested. Among Index Crimes, juveniles are much more likely to be arrested for a property offense than for a violent crime.

Recall that, as discussed in Chapter 3, arrest data exaggerate the juvenile proportion of all arrests, because juveniles are more likely than adults to be arrested in groups and may be more easily apprehended. FBI clearance data therefore provide a better assessment of juvenile crime than do arrest data (Snyder & Sickmund, 1995, p. 117). Juveniles were responsible for 14% of all Violent Index Crimes cleared in 1994 and 25% of all Property Index Crimes cleared by arrest (Snyder et al., 1996, p. 13). Assessment of the juvenile contribution to the total volume of crime in the United States must take into account two other important considerations. First, juvenile crimes are demonstrably less serious than are crimes by adults in several major ways. They are less likely to involve use of a weapon, less likely to result in injury, and less likely to result in hospitalization (McDermott & Hindelang, 1981; Snyder & Sickmund, 1995, p. 21). A second consideration is that part of the increase in juvenile arrest is attributable to increased reporting of offenses by victims over the past 20 years (see Snyder & Sickmund, 1995, p. 98).

Crimes are more likely to be reported to the police if they involve injury or significant economic loss. Among victimizations reported to the NCVS in 1992, 92% of motor vehicle thefts, 70% of robberies with injury, 52% of simple assaults with injury, and 29% of attempted robberies without injury were reported to police (Snyder & Sickmund, 1995, p. 98).

In the case of juveniles, there is a significant time lag between the peak age at which juveniles are actively involved in serious and violent offending and peak arrest ages (Elliott, 1994a; Elliott, Huizinga, & Morse, 1986). The peak age for arrests for any offense is age 18, followed by age 19, then age 17. For violent crimes, the peak arrest age is 17, followed by age 18, then age 16 (FBI, 1995, p. 227). National self-report data (Elliott, 1994a) indicate a younger age peak in serious violent offending. Among males, the peak age is 17, followed by age 16, then age 18. Females peak earlier, at age 16. The later peak age of arrests may be explained partly by the increasing offending rates (incidence) between ages 18 and 25 (Elliott, 1994a, p. 7).

Arrests thus begin some time after offenders begin their criminal careers, as illustrated in findings from the Program of Research on Causes and Correlates of Delinquency (Huizinga et al., 1995). By the age of 14, 81% of chronic violent adolescents in Rochester, 97% in Denver, and 74% in Pittsburgh had begun committing violent offenses, but only slightly more

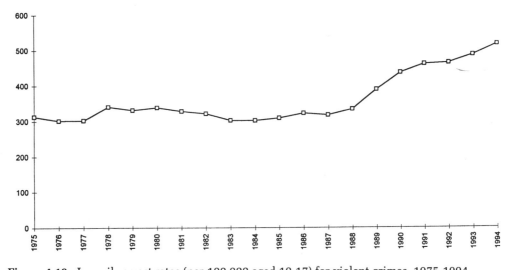

Figure 4.10. Juvenile arrest rates (per 100,000 aged 10-17) for violent crimes, 1975-1994

SOURCE: *Juvenile Offenders and Victims: 1996 Update on Violence* (p. 14), Snyder, Sickmund, and Poe-Yamagata, ©copyright 1996 by the National Center for Juvenile Justice. Reprinted with permission.

NOTE: Arrest rates in 1993 and 1994 were estimated by the National Center for Juvenile Justice using data in the FBI's *Crime in the United States* reports and population data from the U.S. Bureau of the Census.

than one-third of them in Rochester and Denver, and about half of them in Pittsburgh, had been arrested. Most of the chronic violent offenders are arrested at some point, however: two-thirds in Rochester and about three-fourths in Denver and Pittsburgh.

It is unfortunate that the juvenile and social services systems do not effectively intervene earlier in the careers of chronic violent offenders (see Chapter 8). In all three Causes and Correlates cities, children with the youngest ages of onset were found to be most likely to become chronic violent offenders. Among those who self-reported committing their first violent offense at the age of 9 or younger, 39% in Rochester, 41% in Pittsburgh, and 62% in Denver eventually became chronic violent offenders (Huizinga et al., 1995).

Arrest Trends

Changes in the arrest *rate* depict increases in juvenile delinquency most dramatically (Blumstein, 1995a, 1995b, 1996; Fox, 1996) because of "the tyranny of small numbers" (Snyder & Sickmund, 1995). Figure 4.10 indicates little change in FBI Violent Crime Index arrest rates from 1975 to 1987, then an increase of more than 50% from 1988 to 1994 (Snyder et al., 1996, p. 14). The increase from 1985 to 1994 was 75% (Snyder et al., 1996, p. 12). This in-

crease has captured media and political attention. How can we account for it?

First, let us examine specific offenses that make up the FBI Violent Crime Index: murder, rape, robbery, and aggravated assault. Juvenile arrests for these four offenses represented 14% of all violent crimes cleared in 1994 (Snyder et al., 1996, p. 14). Juvenile arrests for aggravated assault and robbery represent 94% of all their Violent Crime Index offenses in 1994 (Snyder et al., 1996, p. 10). Juvenile arrests for these offenses increased 97% and 57%, respectively, during the 10-year period (Snyder et al., 1996, p. 12). The increase in juvenile arrests for homicide contributed little to the 75% increase in violent crime arrests from 1985 to 1994, even though murders increased 150%, because homicides represent such a small proportion of all violent juvenile arrests, less than 3% in 1994 (Snyder et al., 1996, pp. 10, 12).

The main story in the volume of juvenile arrest increases between 1985 and 1994 is the increase in homicides. Increasing juvenile gun possession and use is the main factor explaining the greater lethality of assaults and robberies. As we saw earlier, the increase in juvenile homicides parallels the increase in homicides using firearms.

Juvenile weapons law violations have been increasing since 1983, with the sharpest upturn occurring after 1987. Between 1983 and 1992, the rate of weapons violations arrests among black youth increased 167%, whereas the increase among other races was 129% and that among whites was 106%. Overall, juvenile arrests for weapons violations increased 117% between 1983 and 1992 (Snyder & Sickmund, 1995, p. 108).

Preliminary analyses of official data and interviews in an 11-city study of juvenile arrestees (Decker & Pennell, 1995) show that 22% reported carrying a gun all or most of the time. Juveniles who had been shot at or threatened were more likely to report owning a gun. Nearly one-third (32%) of the juvenile males admitted using a gun in a crime, 50% reported that they had been shot at, and 38% believed that it was acceptable to shoot someone who hurts you.

The reasons for the increases in aggravated assault and robbery arrests are ill-understood. As we saw earlier in this chapter (Table 4.1), the increase in violent juvenile victimizations between 1987 and 1992 was 23%. Among reported violent juvenile victimizations, robbery increased 35%, while aggravated assault increased 31% (Moone, 1994). Increases in robbery and aggravated assault are linked to growing juvenile gun possession. By definition, robbery involves use of force, and aggravated assault is usually accompanied by use of a weapon of some type (FBI, 1995, pp. 26, 31). What else explains the increase in aggravated assaults and robberies?

Age. Age accounts for some of the growth of violent arrests among adolescents. Although the violent crime arrest rate among juveniles under the age of 15 increased significantly between 1983 and 1992 (Snyder & Sickmund, 1995, p. 112), because of the small statistical base at these ages, the contribution of violent crimes to overall juvenile violence hardly changed. Between 1985 and 1994, the proportion of all violent juvenile arrests accounted for by those under the age of 15 increased from 29% to 31% (Snyder et al., 1996, p. 12). Since 1980, the vast majority have been age 15 and older (Snyder et al., 1996, p. 22). The annual number of homicide offenders under the age of 12 throughout the United States has never exceeded 35 and has been below 20 in most years (Snyder et al., 1996, p. 22).

Female violence. Growing female involvement in violence appears to be a factor contributing to the growth in violent juvenile arrests. From 1985 to 1994, the number of female arrests for violent crimes increased 128%, compared to a 69% increase among males. Most of these female increases were for robbery (115%) and aggravated assault (137%) arrests. This female increase, however, did not make a significant contribution to the violent juvenile rate increase because of the small statistical base from which females began in 1985. For example, despite the significantly greater percentage increase in female robbery arrests (115%) compared to males (53%), the increase in the number of male arrests was more than seven times as large as that for females (Snyder et al., 1996, p. 11). It appears, nevertheless, that female violence is increasing, particularly in gang-related offenses, which are discussed shortly.

Race. Overall, between 1983 and 1992 the arrest rate for white youth increased 82%, versus an increase of 43% among black youth and an increase of 42% among youth of other races (Snyder & Sickmund, 1995, p. 108). Juvenile arrest rates for aggravated assault increased substantially across all racial groups during this period: 94% for whites, 116% for blacks, and 66% for other races. Although the robbery arrest rate is much higher among black than among other youths, the arrest rate among whites increased much more (61%) than among blacks (5%) and other youths (21%) between 1983 and 1992 (author's calculation using spreadsheet data provided by Snyder & Sickmund, 1995, p. 107). Homicide arrest rates increased faster among black (166%) than white (94%) youth during this period (Snyder & Sickmund, 1995, p. 106).

The nationwide arrest probabilities associated with committing the same offenses are much higher for black males than for white males (Elliott, 1995; see also Bridges & Weis, 1989). Inner-city black youths are much more likely to be arrested for any offense, including violent offenses.

Elliott's (1994a) analysis of National Youth Survey data showed that during the adolescent years, white and black juveniles had only small differences in age-specific prevalence rates. By the time the NYS subjects reached their late 20s, however, black adults' prevalence rates exceeded whites by a factor of about five. Searching for an explanation, Elliott (1994a, p. 19) suggested that because young black people are denied full adult status in our society and thus have fewer economic opportunities, they become "more deeply embedded in and dependent upon the gangs and the illicit economy that flourish in their neighborhoods."

Gangs. Youth gang violence has increased over the past decade. The United States has seen rapid growth of youth gangs since 1980. During this period, the number of youth gang problem cities has increased from an estimated 286 with more than 2,000 gangs and nearly 100,000 members (Miller, 1982) to about 2,000 cities, towns, and counties with more than 25,000 gangs and more than 650,000 members (National Youth Gang Center, in press). The latter numbers come from the National Youth Gang Center's nationwide survey. Nearly half (48%) of the jurisdictions reporting a gang problem said it was getting worse. Although it is clear that the numbers of youth gang problem cities, youth gangs, and youth gang members have increased significantly over the past decade, national data trend data are not available on the number of gang-related offenses. Miller (1982) estimated that during the 1970s, gang members in the largest gang problem cities accounted for about 11% of all arrests of male youth and 42% of arrests for serious and violent crimes. Curry and associates (1995, p. 27) estimate that there were 580,331 gang-related serious property and violent offenses in 1993, which is equal to about 35% of all FBI Index Property and Violent crime arrests of persons under the age of 30 in the United States in 1993 (author's calculation).

Specific jurisdictions have reported increases in gang-related crimes over the past few years, which accounts for part of the violent juvenile arrest increases—at least in certain large cities. In Chicago, street-gang-related offenses known to the police increased more than 300% from 1987 to 1994; violent offenses increased 130%, and drug or liquor offenses increased more than 700% (Block, Christakos, Jacob, & Przbylski, 1996). From 1990 to 1993, "the number of street gang-related murders in Chicago escalated far more than ever before" (p. 9), accounting for 16% of all Chicago homicides in 1993, up from an average of 7% per year. The increase occurred mainly from 1989 to 1993. Up until then, street gang murders numbered about 66 per year. The number nearly doubled during the 4-year period, to 129 in 1993.

From 1979 to 1994, the number of gang-related homicides in Los Angeles nearly tripled (Hutson et al., 1995). Drive-by shootings in Los Angeles increased by 39% in just 3 years, 1989-1991. Klein (1995, p. 118) attributes most of this increase to street gangs. Violent gang incidents increased 65% in San Diego from 1981 to 1988 (Sanders, 1994, p. 88). Other major cities have witnessed a different pattern. For example, gang homicides have been reported to have declined significantly in New York City (Dunston, 1990) and in Philadelphia in recent years (Spergel, 1995). Perales (1989) reported that in Houston, during 1987, there were no gang-related homicides. Houston police, however, have reported an increase in gangs, from 17 in 1988 to more than 100 in 1991 (Klein, 1995, p. 244). Youth gangs are widely believed to account for increasing violence in the inner cities (Hunzeker, 1993).

Growing youth gang problems have added to the growth of both juvenile and young adult arrests. The median age of a gang-related homicide victim in Los Angeles from 1979 to 1994 was 21 years; the peak age was 18 years (Hutson et al., 1995). In an earlier period, 1978-1982, median Los Angeles homicide perpetrators were over the age of 19, and victims were over the age of 23 (Klein & Maxson, 1989, p. 223). In Chicago, from 1990 to 1994, the risk of being either a gang homicide victim or an offender was greatest among 15-19-year-olds but also quite high among black and Latino 20-29-year-olds (Block, et al. 1996, pp. 24-25). Block and Christakos (1995), however, observed that gang homicide offenders are getting younger.

Miller (1982) estimated that gang homicides made up about 24% of all juvenile homicide arrests in approximately 60 cities during 1974-1979. His estimate was much higher for certain gang problem cities. Between 1972 and 1979, youth gang killings in Los Angeles, Chicago, and New York represented about 58% of all juvenile homicide arrests. Miller (1982) reported that gang-related killings in major gang cities increased from 181 in 1967 to 633 in 1980 (p. 85). The FBI (1995) reports that 38% of all juvenile homicides in 1994 were gang related. This figure appears to be low, especially in gang-ridden cities. For example, between 1979 and 1994, the proportion of all (adult and juvenile) Los Angeles homicides that were gang related increased from 18% to 43% (Hutson et al., 1995). Although incomplete, these data suggest that growing youth gang problems account for a significant portion of increasing youth violence arrests.

Wars on Crime and Drugs. A portion of the growth in juvenile arrests may be unrelated to changes in actual delinquent and violent behavior. Although research cannot prove or disprove it, few researchers would question that the War on Crime, hastened by the Nixon administration (see Chapter 2), and the War on Drugs, launched by the Reagan and Bush administrations (Bloom, Chesney-Lind, & Owen, 1994; Duke & Gross, 1993; Gardiner & McKinney, 1991; General Accounting Office, 1991; Johns, 1992; Mauer, 1990; Tonry, 1994a, 1994b; Wisotsky, 1986; Zimring & Hawkins, 1992), and its "zero tolerance" of drug law violations have resulted in more arrests of juveniles. Empey (1974) contends that although the War on Crime targeted juveniles, the attack on them was forestalled by labeling theory and an abiding interest in prevention that prevailed in the late 1960s and early 1970s. They would be targeted later, in the late 1970s and early 1980s, because of impetus provided by the "discovery" of the chronic juvenile offender, primarily as a result of the Philadelphia Birth Cohort Study (Wolfgang, Figlio, & Sellin, 1972). The War on Drugs targeted them as well as adults (see Weitekamp, Kerner, Schindler, & Schubert, 1995). Rationale for targeting juveniles in both of these "wars" was also provided by the changing philosophy of crime policy, from treatment and rehabilitation to punishment, and by the increases in juvenile delinquency observed in the 1980s.

Studies of the effects of the War on Crime and the War on Drugs have focused only on adults (see Austin & McVey, 1989; Blumstein, 1993; General Accounting Office, 1991; Langan, 1985, 1991; Lusane & Desmond, 1991; Tonry, 1994a, 1994b). The consequences for minority—especially black—juveniles are apparent in the arrest data presented above and in the juvenile justice system processing data to follow. The effects of the War on Drugs on arrest rates are illustrated in a debate instigated in Montgomery County, Maryland, by State's Attorney Andrew L. Sonner, who decided to stop prosecuting nonviolent drug users and small-time dealers (Mooar & Perez-Rivas, 1996).

Sonner alleged that Montgomery Court police were arresting drug suspects at random, apparently for the purpose of generating a greater number of arrests. It seemed to him that this had been police policy in the County for approximately ten years. Sonner's assessment, which he said was shared by other observers, is that this arrest policy was a failure. For one thing, it resulted in more jail overcrowding. For another, the policy resulted in more overload in court dockets. Finally, he concluded that the community received no benefit from the policy. It seemed that drugs are as readily available now as they were when the increased arrest policy was instituted.

Sonner said that in 1995, police presented the prosecutor's office with 524 drug cases, but that 27% of these cases were not strong enough for his office to prosecute. Overall, Sonner estimated that 40% of his office's resources were spent on drug cases.

The effect of such policies on incarceration of African Americans is illustrated in prison admissions. Figure 4.11 shows the percentage of admissions to federal and state prisons, by race. The percentage of blacks among those sent to prison nationwide increased from about 32% in 1960 to 54% in 1992, while the percentage of whites declined commensurately—despite no increase in violent arrests among blacks (Tonry, 1994b). A similar trend is apparent in juvenile corrections. From 1983 to 1991, the number of minorities held in public long-term institutional facilities increased 37%, while the number of whites dropped 23% (Snyder & Sickmund, 1995, p. 167).

Empirical evidence shows that black adult and adolescent drug use rates are no higher than white rates (Substance Abuse and Mental Health Services Administration, 1995). Moreover, black and white youth have similar self-reported delinquency rates (Elliott, 1994a), even in inner-city areas (Huizinga, et al., 1994, pp. 15-16). In his analysis of National Youth Survey data, Elliott (1994a, p. 18) found "little or no substantive race differences in the propensity for violence," as measured by self-reports, in contrast to a black adolescent arrest rate that is five times as high as the arrest rate for white youths. That arrest records seriously overstate the offending of blacks relative to whites has been well documented (Elliott, 1995; Geerken, 1994). This is a main reason that studies documenting the chronic juvenile offender have found race to be a defining characteristic (Tracy, Wolfgang, & Figlio, 1990; Wolfgang et al., 1972; Wolfgang, Thornberry, & Figlio, 1987).

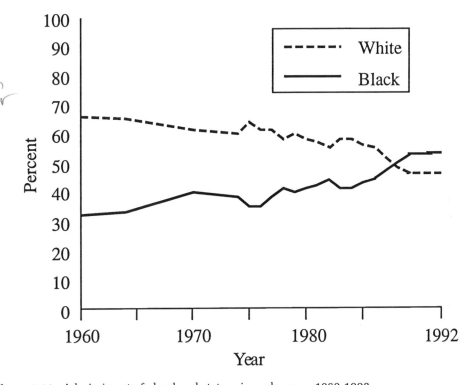

put in paper

Figure 4.11. Admissions to federal and state prisons by race, 1960-1992

SOURCE: "Racial Politics, Racial Disparities, and the War on Crime" (p. 483), Tonry, ©copyright 1994 by Sage Publications, Inc.
DATA SOURCES: Langan (1991), Gilliard (1992), Perkins (1992, 1993), and Perkins and Gilliard (1992).
NOTE: Hispanics are included in the black and white populations.

Juveniles are easier to catch than adults (Block et al., 1996, p. 27). Tonry (1994b) argues that arresting inner-city minority youth is particularly easier than arresting white suburban and urban working class youths because of three factors. First, drug sales in poor minority areas are likely to take place outdoors or in indoor public places such as bars. Second, dealers in inner-city areas have little choice but to sell to strangers and new acquaintances. Third, arrested drug dealers in inner-city minority communities are soon replaced because of the "nearly inexhaustible potential supply of young minority Americans to be arrested" (p. 487).

Juvenile Court Response

A dramatic increase in juvenile court handling of delinquency cases occurred in the period between 1985 and 1994. Table 4.3 shows that the total number of cases handled by juvenile courts increased by 41% in this 10-year period (Butts, 1996). Reflecting the small proportion of all juvenile offenses that are violent and

the few violent offenses that are brought to the attention of the juvenile justice system, only 22% of all juvenile delinquency cases handled by juvenile courts in 1994 were for person offenses. Among these, more than half were simple assault cases. The single most common type of offense brought into juvenile court in 1994 was larceny-theft, representing nearly 23% of all cases. Cases involving a Violent Crime Index offense represented only 8% of all delinquency cases in 1994.

The most significant increases in delinquency cases handled by juvenile courts between 1985 and 1994 were for weapons offenses (156%), homicide (144%), and aggravated assault (134%). During the second half of the decade (1990-1994), growth in delinquency cases handled by juvenile courts occurred mainly in drug law violations (a 69% increase) and in person offense cases (an increase of 38%). The increase in drug law violations represents a major shift, because from 1988 to 1992, the number of these cases handled by juvenile courts decreased 12% (Snyder & Sickmund, 1995, p. 126).

TABLE 4.3 Juvenile Delinquency Cases Handled in U.S. Juvenile Courts, 1994

Most Serious Offense	Number of Cases	Percentage Change 1985-1994
Total delinquency	1,555,200	41
Person offenses	336,100	93
Criminal homicide	3,000	144
Forcible rape	5,400	25
Robbery	37,000	53
Aggravated assault	85,300	134
Simple assault	177,700	91
Other violent sex offenses	10,000	65
Other person offenses	17,800	91
Property offenses	803,400	22
Burglary	141,600	5
Larceny-theft	356,200	17
Motor vehicle theft	59,300	69
Arson	9,500	37
Vandalism	118,600	46
Trespassing	61,200	21
Stolen property	28,600	1
Other property offenses	28,300	57
Drug law violations	120,200	62
Public order offenses	295,600	50
Obstruction of justice	108,400	59
Disorderly conduct	80,700	77
Weapons offenses	48,800	156
Liquor law violations	12,700	−34
Nonviolent sex offenses	9,600	−24
Other public order	35,500	10
Violent Crime Index[a]	130,600	98
Property Crime Index[b]	566,700	17

SOURCE: *Offenders in Juvenile Court, 1994*, Butts et al. ©copyright 1996 by the National Center for Juvenile Justice. Reprinted with permission.

a. Violent Crime Index: criminal homicide, forcible rape, robbery, and aggravated assault.

b. Property Crime Index: burglary, larceny-theft, motor vehicle theft, and arson.

Analysis of changes in the demographic characteristics of cases handled by juvenile courts shows a significant change in the gender and race of delinquency cases (Butts, 1996). Between 1985 and 1994, case rates for females increased 54% while male case rates increased 38%. The delinquency case rate for black youth was more than twice the rate for white youth in 1994. Over the 10-year period, the number of delinquency cases involving white youth increased 26%, while the number of cases involv-

ing black youth and youth of other races increased 78% and 94%, respectively.

Juvenile court statistics suggest that juvenile offenders are getting slightly younger. Between 1988 and 1994, delinquency case rates in the youngest age groups increased, mainly among 13-15 year-olds (see Butts, 1996, p. 3; Butts et al., 1996; Snyder & Sickmund, 1995, p. 130). Fewer 17-year-olds than 16-year-olds were handled in the nation's juvenile courts in 1994, despite the fact that more 17-year-olds than 16-year-olds were arrested that year. Two factors account for this anomaly (Snyder & Sickmund, 1995, p. 130). First, 11 states exclude 17-year-olds from the original jurisdiction of the juvenile court. Second, state legislatures permit or require older juveniles to be processed directly in criminal courts, either by specific offense exclusions or by concurrent jurisdiction provisions (see Chapter 5).

Reflecting their overrepresentation in arrests (Elliott, 1995), black juveniles were disproportionately represented in delinquency cases handled in 1994. Whereas black adolescents represented 15% of the juvenile population, they constituted 25% of all delinquency cases (Butts, 1996). Overall, in 1994 the delinquency case rate for black juveniles per 1,000 (119) was more than double the rate for white juveniles (45). Moreover, the black delinquency case rate increased 65% between 1985 and 1994, compared to a 22% increase for whites and a 31% increase for other juveniles (Butts, 1996, p. 4). The overrepresentation of black youth was most prominent in person and drug offense cases. The person offense case rate for black youth was nearly four times as high as the corresponding rate for white youth. The drug offense case rate for black youth was more than three times the rate for whites. Snyder and Sickmund (1995, p. 128), however, conclude that juvenile courts have not increased the level of racial disparity between blacks and whites compared to their disproportionate representation in arrest statistics.

A significant change occurred between 1985 and 1994 in the number of petitioned status offenders handled by juvenile courts—a 66% increase (Butts, 1996, p. 8). These cases include four status offense categories: runaway, truancy, ungovernability, and liquor law violations. For the most part, this increase probably reflects growth in the at-risk population (age 10-17), which began in 1989.

TABLE 4.4 Recidivism of Juvenile Court Referrals: Percentage Who Returned to Juvenile Court After Each Referral

Age at Referral 1	Number of Court Referrals							
	2	3	4	5	6	7	At Any Referral
All								
ages 41	59	67	71	74	77	77	56
10 61	84	96	97	*	*	*	71
11 60	85	91	92	98	*	*	72
12 59	83	89	97	98	95	98	72
13 57	82	90	93	95	97	96	73
14 53	77	86	91	92	94	96	70
15 45	69	80	84	89	89	91	66
16 33	55	68	73	77	81	82	54
17 16	27	36	41	45	48	50	30

SOURCE: *Juvenile Offenders and Victims: A National Report* (p. 158), Snyder and Sickmund, ©copyright 1995 by the National Center for Juvenile Justice. Reprinted with permission.
DATA SOURCE: *Court Careers of Juvenile Offenders*, Snyder, ©copyright 1988 by the National Center for Juvenile Justice. Reprinted with permission.
NOTE: Data are from Arizona and Utah.
*Too few cases to obtain a reliable percentage.

It may be surprising to some juvenile court critics to learn how effective it appears to be in rehabilitating youngsters. A court careers study conducted in Arizona and Utah (Snyder, 1988) shows that only the worst offenders have high recidivism rates. Table 4.4 shows that only 41% returned to court after the first referral, compared 'o 59% of those with 2 court referrals, and so on. Males were more likely to recidivate than females: 46% of males referred to juvenile court for the first time were referred again for a new offense, compared with 29% of females.

In an analysis of chronic offenders in this data set, Snyder (1988) reviewed cases with a 75% (or higher) probability of returning to court. Examination of the court records of these cases indicated that most youths with five or more referrals in their court career fall into this category; so do all youth age 14 or younger with two referrals in their careers and all youth 15 or younger with three referrals in their court careers. If these cases could be identified early, perhaps the offending careers of many of them could be forestalled, given the juvenile court's success with initial referrals.

Public and Private Juvenile Correctional Facilities

The main correctional facilities used to confine juveniles are public detention and correctional facilities. According to the Census of Public and Private Juvenile Detention, Correctional and Shelter Facilities (see Krisberg, DeComo, Rudenstine, & Del Rosario, 1996), admissions of juveniles to public and private facilities increased 28% between 1991 and 1993. Admissions for violent offenses increased most (77%) during this period, followed by drug offenses (62%), while admissions for serious property offenses decreased by 24% (Krisberg et al., 1996, p. 36).

A more comprehensive source of information on juveniles admitted to training schools became available in 1992. The State Juvenile Corrections System Reporting Program provided, for the first time, individual information on juveniles admitted to long-term state custody (Austin, Krisberg, DeComo, Rudenstine, & Del Rosario, 1994; DeComo, Krisberg, Rudenstine, &, Del Rosario, 1995; DeComo, Tunis, Krisberg, & Herrera, 1994). This source indicates a 7% increase in the number of juveniles admitted to state training schools between 1992 and 1993 (Rudenstine, 1995; Rudenstine & Moone, 1995). Part of this change could be accounted for by an increase in the number of reporting states, from 47 in 1992 to 50 in 1993.

This new data source also provides information not previously available, on the type of admissions. Among admissions for which the reason was known, 55% in 1992 and 1993 were new commitments. Most important, for the first time, we have information on recidivists (re-

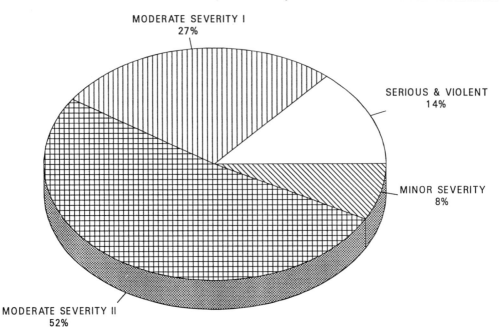

Figure 4.12. Estimated proportions of admissions to state juvenile corrections systems by severity of offense, 1992

SOURCE: "Trends in Juvenile Crime and Youth Violence" (p. 19), Howell, Krisberg, and Jones, in *Sourcebook on Serious, Violent, and Chronic Juvenile Offenders* Howell, Krisberg, Hawkins, and Wilson, ©copyright 1995 by Sage Publications, Inc.

DATA SOURCE: *Juveniles Taken Into Custody Research Program: FY 1992 Annual Report*, DeComo, Tunis, Krisberg, and Herrera, 1994. Reprinted with permission of the National Council on Crime and Delinquency.

NOTE: Estimates are based on 29 states for 1992. Serious and violent = murder, manslaughter, homicide, forcible rape, other violent sex offenses, sodomy, kidnapping, endangerment, robbery (with priors), and assault (with priors); Minor severity = shoplifting, technical (probation or parole), minor public order, status offenses, driving without license, minor traffic, dependency, and special court proceedings; Moderate severity = offenses not categorized in Serious and violent or in Minority severity, such as property, drug, public order, and traffic offenses (I = with prior state commitments, II = no prior state commitments).

commitments). During 1992, among all types of recommitments (parole violator, returned from nonstate supervision, and recommitment) on which information was available, 22% were previously incarcerated. The figure for 1993 is 19%.

The State Juvenile Corrections System Reporting Program shows two other important trends in the characteristics of juvenile offenders in reformatories. From 1992 to 1993, the percentage of training school admissions that were white decreased from 38% to 36%, while the proportion of training school admissions that were black increased from 43% to 46%. The percentage of all admitted youths that were Hispanic remained at 14% (Rudenstine, 1995; Rudenstine & Moone, 1995). We see a continuation of the trend of more use of reformatories to confine black youngsters.

This new data source also shows an increase in the proportion of person offenders admitted

to juvenile training schools from 1992 to 1993, an increase from 26% to 29%. Overall, however, the largest proportion of offenders are property offenders, 40% in 1993. Surprisingly, nearly 14% of 1993 admissions were public order offenders (Rudenstine, 1995; Rudenstine & Moone, 1995). Clearly, training schools are not being used to confine the most dangerous offenders.

A more detailed analysis of the offense histories of youths admitted to training schools using the State Juvenile Corrections System Reporting Program data, taking into account offense histories, substantiates this conclusion. DeComo and his colleagues (1994) compiled the offense histories of juveniles admitted to training schools in 29 states in 1992. Their analysis shows that only 14% of the 1992 admissions were for the most serious violent crimes (Figure 4.12). Only 27% (Moderate Severity I) had previously been committed to a

TABLE 4.5 Cumulative Estimated Prevalence of State Incarceration for All Juveniles Aged 10-17 (percentages), 1991

State	All	Male	Female	White	Black	Hispanic	Other
Ohio	1.55	2.75	0.28	0.83	6.53	1.20	0.26
Virginia	1.20	2.10	0.26	0.57	3.51	0.38	0.35
Missouri	1.08	1.86	0.27	0.74	3.32	NA	0.39
Tennessee	1.07	1.82	0.29	0.70	2.60	NA	0.24
Wisconsin	1.07	1.88	0.21	0.46	7.66	2.78	2.86
Louisiana	0.87	1.60	0.11	0.25	1.91	0.00	0.20
North Dakota	0.85	1.55	0.11	0.64	2.13	4.10	3.44
Texas	0.85	1.55	0.11	0.72	2.52	0.93	0.03
Utah	0.79	1.40	0.14	0.73	8.32	2.40	1.03
Iowa	0.73	1.33	0.09	0.62	4.54	1.85	1.17
California	0.69	1.27	0.06	0.69	2.66	0.88	0.18
New Jersey	0.69	1.18	0.18	0.35	2.20	1.18	0.11
New York	0.69	1.18	0.18	0.35	2.20	1.18	0.11
Illinois	0.67	1.23	0.07	0.37	2.04	0.81	0.06
New Hampshire	0.65	1.09	0.19	0.62	4.91	2.41	0.44
Massachusetts	0.56	1.05	0.04	0.28	2.73	1.68	1.95

SOURCE: "The Juveniles Taken Into Custody Research Program: Estimating the Prevalence of Juvenile Custody by Race and Gender" (p. 6), DeComo, ©copyright 1993 by the National Council on Crime and Delinquency. Reprinted with permission of the National Council on Crime and Delinquency.

training school and had a new commitment for property, drug, public order, or traffic offenses. The largest category (52%) of admissions (Moderate Severity II) was for these offenses and were first-time commitments.

Data gathered in the State Juvenile Corrections System Reporting Program also made possible another informative analysis. DeComo (1993) calculated prevalence estimates for incarceration in state training schools to examine interstate differences. His analysis reveals dramatically different prevalence rates by state (Table 4.5). Prevalence rates were unilaterally low across all the states for females. Rates for white youths were under 1% in all states, whereas the prevalence rates varied widely across the states for the other racial groups. Among black youths, prevalence rates ranged from a high of 8.3% in Utah to a low of 1.9% in Louisiana. Table 4.6 shows the estimated cumulative prevalence rates for the six race and sex subgroups. Black males have the highest prevalence rates of all subgroups in 15 of the 16 states. Again, wide variations for black males are observed, ranging from a low of 3.5 in Louisiana, to a high of 13.9 in Utah. Prevalence estimates are also substantially higher for Hispanic youths than for white youths in most states. Among females, prevalence estimates are highest for blacks in every state included in DeComo's analysis.

Juveniles in Detention

Because more than 10 times as many juveniles are admitted to detention centers as to training schools each year, let us look more closely at this method of confinement. Nearly 558,000 juveniles were admitted to detention centers in 1992 (Krisberg et al., 1996). Among these, 98% were held in public detention centers. About 20% of all delinquency cases in juvenile court during 1992 were detained, which is about the same rate as in 1988 (Butts et al., 1995). Overall, 25% of black juvenile court cases were detained in 1992, versus 22% of other races and 18% of whites. Cases involving black youth charged with drug offenses had the greatest likelihood of detention (47%), followed by black juveniles charged with person offenses (27%) and white youth charged with a drug offense (26%) (Snyder & Sickmund, 1995, p. 142).

Between 1982 and 1993, juvenile admissions to public detention centers increased 33%, and 1-day counts increased 58% (Krisberg et al., 1996). The increases were more than twice as high for males as for females. Admissions to private detention centers also increased. Between 1984 and 1992, juvenile admissions to private detention centers doubled (from nearly 6,000 to almost 12,000) (Krisberg et al., 1996).

TABLE 4.6 Cumulative Estimated Prevalence by State for All Juveniles Aged 10-17 (percentages) and for Combined Sex and Race Subgroups

State	All	White Male	White Female	Black Male	Black Female	Hispanic Male	Hispanic Female
Ohio	1.55	1.44	0.18	11.88	0.93	2.25	0.08
Virginia	1.20	0.96	0.16	6.34	0.60	0.46	0.30
Missouri	1.08	1.24	0.20	5.85	0.71	NA	NA
Tennessee	1.07	1.07	0.32	4.89	0.19	NA	NA
Wisconsin	1.07	0.77	0.13	13.86	1.15	5.21	0.29
Louisiana	0.87	0.45	0.04	3.54	0.24	0.00	0.00
North Dakota	0.85	1.16	0.09	4.76	0.00	7.34	0.00
Texas	0.85	1.30	0.10	4.68	0.28	1.72	0.10
Utah	0.79	1.28	0.15	13.92	1.28	4.37	0.31
Iowa	0.73	1.16	0.06	7.71	1.21	3.59	0.00
California	0.69	1.27	0.06	4.92	0.24	1.63	0.05
New Jersey	0.69	0.43	0.02	5.67	0.23	1.64	0.00
New York	0.69	0.58	0.10	3.88	0.53	2.09	0.22
Illinois	0.67	0.67	0.05	3.83	0.20	1.49	0.06
New Hampshire	0.65	1.05	0.18	7.64	1.72	3.71	1.08
Massachusetts	0.56	0.51	0.03	5.25	0.13	3.20	0.08

SOURCE: "The Juveniles Taken Into Custody Research Program: Estimating the Prevalence of Juvenile Custody by Race and Gender" (p. 6), DeComo, ©copyright 1993 by National Council on Crime and Delinquency. Reprinted with permission of the National Council on Crime and Delinquency.

One-day counts of juveniles in detention centers illustrate more clearly the disproportionate detention of minority youths. Minorities made up nearly two-thirds of the juveniles held in public detention centers on a given day in 1991 (Snyder & Sickmund, 1995, p. 144). In 1983, minorities represented 53% of the public detention population. By 1991, the proportion had increased to 65%. Blacks accounted for the majority of the overall increase in the minority detention population from 1983 to 1991 (Table 4.7).

Very little is known about detention. It is least studied in the juvenile justice system. Knowledge is lacking about such important issues as the types of facilities in which youths are detained, who initiates the detention decision, who reviews these decisions, and what criteria determine release. More important, we have virtually no knowledge of the effects of the juvenile detention experience on detained youth. What effect does the decision have on rehabilitation? On mental health? On long-term social adjustment? One thing is certain: Conditions of confinement in many juvenile detention centers present a threat to the health, safety, and well-being of many of the confined juveniles. We will return to this issue shortly.

It also is apparent that juveniles in detention centers possess a wide range of common problems. Figure 4.13 shows the percentage of juveniles in detention centers that facility administrators in 1991 estimated to have particular problems. More than 50% were assessed as having family, drug/alcohol abuse, peer, and depression problems. These problems as well as issues in conditions of confinement are being addressed in a new Juvenile Justice Personnel Improvement Project (Roush, 1996a).

Youths confined in training schools evidence personal problems similar to adolescents in detention centers. Training school administrators estimated similar proportions of their resident populations to have particular problems. More than 50% were assessed as having family, drug/alcohol abuse, peer, parental abuse, and disruptive behavior problems. In both the detention center and training school populations, facility administrators believed that about 40% of the youths were involved in a gang (see Synder & Sickmund, 1995, p. 146).

Juveniles in Jails

On June 30, 1995, an estimated 7,888 juveniles were held in adult jails, an increase of 17% in just one year (Gilliard & Beck, 1996). Juvenile admissions to jails decreased 38% from 1983 to 1988 (Bureau of Justice Statistics, 1988;

TABLE 4.7 Minorities Held in Public
Detention Centers, 1983 and 1991

Race/ ethnicity	Number of Juveniles Held		
	February 1, 1983	February 15, 1991	Percentage Change 1983-1991
Total juvenile residents	13,048	18,986	46
White (non-Hispanic)	6,157	6,629	8
Minorities	6,891	12,357	79
White Hispanic	1,943	3,574	84
Black	4,656	8,203	76
American Indian/ Alaska Native	154	227	47
Asian/Pacific Islander	138	353	156

SOURCE: *Juvenile Offenders and Victims: A National Report* (p. 144), Snyder and Sickmund, ©copyright 1995 by the National Center for Juvenile Justice. Reprinted with permission

DATA SOURCE: *Children in Custody Census 1982/83 and 1990/91* (machine-readable data files), Office of Juvenile Justice and Delinquency Prevention (1985, 1993).

Stephan, 1990) but then began increasing. In just 3 years, from 1992 to 1994, the number of juveniles in jail on a given day more than doubled (Maguire & Pastore, 1995, p. 533). The main reason more juveniles are being jailed is increased transfers to criminal court. More than three-quarters of juveniles held in jails in 1995 were tried or awaiting trial as adults (Gilliard & Beck, 1996, p. 10). These cases nearly doubled from 1993 to 1993 (from 3,300 to 6,018).

Juveniles in Prisons

In 1992, 5,212 youth under the age of 18 were admitted to state prisons (Perkins, 1994). Barely half (51%) of them were charged with a violent offense, mainly robbery (23% of the total), followed by assault (13%) and homicide (10%). Property offenses made up 31% of the total admissions, and 14% were committed for drug offenses. Burglary offenses made up 16% of the total. Only 3% were committed for weapons offenses. These data indicate a shift in offense seriousness for which juveniles are committed to state prisons. In 1989, only 36% of admissions were for violent offenses, 41% were

property offenders, and 15% were drug offenders (Perkins, 1992).

Conditions of Confinement

In the 1988 amendments to the JJDP Act, Congress required the OJJDP to conduct a study of conditions of confinement in secure juvenile detention and correctional facilities. The study (Parent et al., 1994) included surveys mailed in 1991 to all 984 public and private detention centers, reception and diagnostic facilities, training schools, and ranches. In addition, experienced juvenile correctional practitioners conducted 2-day site visits to a representative sample of nearly 100 facilities. Using nationally recognized correctional standards as a gauge, researchers assessed how juvenile offenders' basic needs were met, how institutional security and resident safety were maintained, what treatment programming was provided, and how juveniles' rights were protected (Allen-Hagen, 1993).

Based on standards conformance and related outcome measures, the study authors (Parent et al., 1994) concluded that serious and widespread problems existed in the areas of living space, health care, institutional safety and security, and control of suicidal behavior. Conditions of confinement appeared to be generally adequate in three areas: basic needs such as food, hygiene, and clothing; recreation; and living accommodations. Nineteen recommendations were offered to improve conditions in juvenile detention and correctional facilities.

More than 75% of the confined population were housed in facilities that violated one or more standards related to living space (facility design capacity, sleeping areas, and living unit size). Between 1987 and 1991, the proportion of confined juveniles living in facilities in which the daily population exceeded design capacity increased from 36% to 47%. Crowding was found to be related to higher rates of institutional violence, suicidal behavior, and greater reliance on the use of short-term isolation. Over the 12 months prior to the mail survey, Parent et al. (1994) estimated that juveniles injured 6,900 staff and 24,200 other juveniles; 11,000 juveniles committed 17,600 acts of suicidal behavior, with 10 suicides in 1990; more than 18,600 behavioral incidents required emergency medical care; more than 435,800 juve-

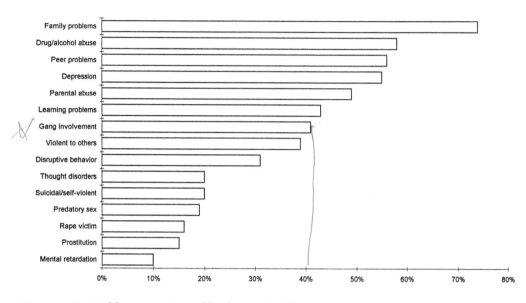

Figure 4.13. Problems experienced by detained adolescents

SOURCE: *Juvenile Offenders and Victims: A National Report* (p. 146), Snyder and Sickmund, ©copyright 1995 by the National Center for Juvenile Justice. Reprinted with permission.

DATA SOURCES: *Special Analysis of Data From the OJJDP Conditions of Confinement Study*, Leiter (1993).

NOTE: Administrators used the following response categories to indicate the proportion of juveniles having problems: 0-24%, 25-49%, 51-74%, 75-99%, and 100%. Midrange figures were weighted by the facility's juvenile population, and then the population proportions were calculated.

niles were held in short-term isolation (1 to 24 hours) and almost 84,000 were isolated for more than 24 hours; and 9,700 juveniles escaped from custody. The proportion of confined juveniles adjudicated of violent crimes was not related to injury rates (Allen-Hagen, 1993; Parent et al., 1994).

Most disturbing of all the study results, training schools holding nearly three-quarters of all adolescents in these facilities reported some use of mechanical restraints during 1990. The restraints used included anklets, security belts, straitjackets, and handcuffs. Most juveniles were in facilities that used handcuffs. More than a third of confined juveniles were in facilities that placed no time limits on use of mechanical restraints (Parent et al., 1994).

In announcing the study's release, Attorney General Janet Reno said, "This study puts an exclamation point on the obvious conclusion that America must not only take better care of its children before they get into trouble, but also not abandon them once they are in trouble"

(Allen-Hagen, 1993, p. 2). Conditions of confinement in adult prisons are worse (see Chapter 5).

Summary

In the first part of this chapter, we examined self-report and victimization data to determine whether or not violence by juveniles has increased. These sources suggest that it has. The question is how much. Self-report studies cannot provide a definitive answer because different surveys using methods that vary have been made over the past 20 years. A single survey has not measured delinquent behavior over the entire period. Based on the National Youth Survey and other self-report studies, Elliott (1994b, p. 1) estimates that over the past decade "there has been a relatively small increase (8%-10%) in the proportion of adolescents involved in some type of serious violent offending," but that the frequency of offending is about the same. In other words, Elliott suggests that the prevalence of delinquency has increased but that the incidence has not. More juveniles are committing serious deliquent acts, but not at a higher rate.

The only national victimization survey, the NCVS, indicates a 23% increase in violent juvenile victimization during 1987-1992. This increase is mainly in assaults, but most of these appeared to be simple assaults. We are left with a small increase, perhaps proportional to the 8%-10% increase in serious violent offending that Elliott estimates.

Neither self-report studies nor victimization surveys measure homicides; therefore, we must rely on the FBI Uniform Crime Reports and the FBI Supplemental Homicide Reports (1993a) for information on juvenile murderers. These have increased significantly over the past decade. This increase appears to be accounted for almost entirely by increased lethality of weapons; that is, more assaults and robberies turn out to be homicides because of the availability and use of firearms. This appears to be the case because the estimated increase in assaults and robberies does not come close to proportionality with the increase in homicides. Most of the increase may be owing to growing youth gang problems, although this cannot be determined because of the absence of a national gang reporting system.

Violent juvenile arrests have increased considerably, especially for robbery and aggravated assaults. The growth in homicides does not add a large increment because of the small numbers involved. Adults are responsible for 90% of all homicides in the United States and for three-quarters of the increase in the number of homicides in the past decade. Some of the increase in violent juvenile arrests is attributable to the War on Crime, the targeting of chronic juvenile offenders, and the trend over the past decade to punish rather than rehabilitate juveniles.

Our examination of juvenile court and correctional data indicates a growth in the number of juveniles processed over the past 15 years. This increase is accounted for by a mixed bag of factors. These include greater reliance placed on confinement instead of rehabilitation, growth of the at-risk population, a small increase in juvenile violence, and larger numbers of minorities coming into the juvenile justice system. The juvenile justice system appears to be keeping pace with the growth in serious and violent juvenile arrests. That is the good news. The bad news is that it appears to be accomplishing this at the expense of minorities. This is the most egregious and disturbing trend of all.

5

Removing Juveniles From the Juvenile Justice System

During the first half of the past 30 years, juvenile justice policy debates focused mainly on the front end of the juvenile justice system, on such issues as decriminalization of status offenses, due process for juveniles, deinstitutionalization, and diversion. Policy debates have shifted recently to the back end of the system, to the question of whether or not serious, violent, and chronic juvenile offenders should remain in the juvenile justice system or be transferred[1] to the criminal justice system. Several developments led to this change in focus on juvenile justice issues.

The 1960s saw the initiation of a major reform movement aimed at formalizing the juvenile justice system. It began with the President's Commission on Law Enforcement and Administration of Justice (1967a), which made the first comprehensive assessment of the United States' juvenile justice system. The President's Commission focused in particular on the juvenile court, declaring it to be ineffective. The Task Force on Juvenile Delinquency (of the commission) concluded "that the great hopes originally held for the juvenile court have not been fulfilled. It has not succeeded significantly in rehabilitating delinquent youth, in reducing or even stemming the tide of juvenile criminality, or in bringing justice and compassion to the child offender" (1967, p. 7). The commission saw little promise for rehabilitation through "treatment" because it believed that juvenile courts unnecessarily stigmatized youth by labeling them "delinquent," thus diminishing their chances of rehabilitation.

On the issue of waiver, the commission (Task Force on Juvenile Delinquency, 1967, p. 25) recommended that:

> To be waived, a youth should be over a certain age (perhaps 16); the alleged offense should be relatively grave (the equivalent of a felony, at least); his prior offense record should be of a certain seriousness; his treatment record discouraging. Waived youths would then be dealt with other than cursorily by the criminal court, and the juvenile court's action in transferring them would be based on an honest and open assessment of individual suitability.

Two United States Supreme Court decisions in the 1960s required changes in judicial waiver procedures. In *Kent v. United States* (383 U.S. 541, 1966), the Court required due process procedures in waiver proceedings, that a hearing be held on waiver cases, that the juvenile have the right to representation by counsel at the hearing, that the juvenile's attorney be provided access to all information used by the judge in deciding on waiver, and that the juvenile court's waiver decision be supported by a statement of reasons (p. 557). In its *Gault* decision (*In re Gault*, 387 U.S. 1, 1967), the Supreme Court mandated due process procedures in the adjudication of juveniles for delinquency when the juvenile faces possible confinement. Specifically, the Court required procedural safeguards for juveniles facing possible confinement, including notice of charges, the right to a fair and impartial hearing, the right to counsel, the opportunity to confront and cross-examine witnesses, and the privilege against self-incrimination (pp. 31-57). "In shifting the formal focus of juvenile courts from 'real needs' to legal guilt, *Gault* identified two crucial gaps between juvenile justice rhetoric and reality: differences between the theory and the practice of rehabilitation and between procedural safeguards afforded adults and those available to juveniles" (Feld, 1993, pp. 206-207).

Conservative juvenile justice reformers were spurred by implicit criticism of the juvenile court in the *Kent* and *Gault* decisions. "However, because *Kent* had failed to supply the solid legal foundation necessary for a judicial attack on discretionary waiver, reformers focused on legislative change instead" (Whitebread & Batey, 1981, p. 211). Model waiver statutes were developed. The 1968 *Uniform Juvenile Court Act* (United States Children's Bureau, 1968) and the *Legislative Guide for Drafting Family and Juvenile Court Acts* (United States Children's Bureau, 1969) were the most influential model statutes (Whitebread & Batey, 1981, p. 211). Both of these model acts incorporated certain restrictions on judicial waiver suggested by the Supreme Court in its *Kent* decision.

Just deserts reformers concentrated their efforts in the Juvenile Justice Standards Project, initiated in 1971 by the Institute of Judicial Administration (IJA) at New York University, later cosponsored by the American Bar Association (ABA). These came to be known as the "IJA-ABA Standards" (1980). In addition to the President's Commission and Supreme Court decisions, drafters of the IJA-ABA Standards were influenced in particular by the writings of Fox (1970, 1972), James (1967), Platt (1977), Rosenheim (1976), and Schur (1973), who advocated a more restricted role for the juvenile justice system in America's crime control apparatus. The IJA-ABA standards urged increased judicial waiver but recommended that, to be eligible for waiver, the juvenile must be charged with an offense punishable in criminal court by at least 20 years imprisonment, which the waiver decision maker finds is "serious" (IJA-ABA, 1980, Secs. 1.1B, 2.2A, and 2.2C).

The positions of the IJA-ABA Joint Commission were countered by those of the Twentieth Century Fund Task Force on Sentencing Policy Toward Young Offenders (1978). It conducted an exhaustive review of available data and research on criminal and juvenile justice system policies governing the handling of serious and violent juvenile offenders. The Task Force took the position that waiver should be confined to serious, violent crime cases, involving juveniles past their mid-teens, "where the minimum punishment necessary is substantially larger than that available to the juvenile court" (p. 10). All waiver decisions automatically would be reviewed by an appellate tribunal. A sentencing structure for juveniles in criminal court was recommended, guided by the principle "that the maximum sentencing options be significantly lower for violent young offenders than those for adults convicted of comparable crimes" (p. 16).

Positions taken by the Twentieth Century Fund Task Force soon were overshadowed by the "just deserts" philosophy (punishment commensurate with the crime) originally provided by the American Friends Service Committee in its report on crime and punishment in America (1971). It concluded that the individualized treatment model was theoretically faulty, systematically discriminatory in administration, and inconsistent with some of our most basic concepts of justice. Just deserts advocates initially directed their reforms at the criminal justice system (Cederblom & Blizek, 1977; Fogel, 1979; Von Hirsch, 1976), having been provided impetus by the "War on Crime" during the late 1960s and early 1970s (Graham, 1970). They quickly expanded their focus to include the juvenile justice system (Feld, 1983, 1984, 1987, 1988; Fogel & Hudson, 1981; Regnery, 1985, 1986; Thompson & McAnany, 1984; Tonry, 1994a, 1994b; Wizner, 1984; Wolfgang, 1982), because of its greater emphasis on the rehabilitative ideal (Allen, 1981).

Just deserts philosophy and practice grew in the 1980s and 1990s because of rising crime, prison overcrowding, and disenchantment with the prospects of successful treatment programs. Considerable impetus was provided by reviews of program evaluations that found few rehabilitation programs to be effective (Greenberg, 1977; Lipton et al., 1975; Palmer, 1978; Sechrest et al., 1979). The most influential among these was the comprehensive review conducted by Martinson and his colleagues, published initially by Martinson (1974). The general conclusion of these reviews was that "nothing works"; thus, strong support was provided for the just deserts philosophy.

The growth of juvenile violence in the 1980s and 1990s provided further justification for the transfer of juveniles to the criminal justice system. Between 1984 and 1993, arrests of juveniles for violent offenses rose by nearly 68%. Most of this increase occurred between 1989 and 1993, during which time juvenile arrests for murder increased 45%, arrests for robbery increased 37%, and arrests for aggravated assault increased 37% (FBI, 1994).

These developments over the past 30 years have led to significant changes in judicial and correctional handling of serious, violent, and chronic juvenile offenders. Growing numbers of juveniles recently have been transferred by means of judicial waivers and prosecutorial direct files, and state legislatures have specified more and more transferable offenses at younger and younger ages (Snyder & Sickmund, 1995, pp. 154-157). Although juvenile court judges have retained a focus on offender considerations in making the transfer determination, prosecutors and state legislatures have emphasized the serious and violent nature of the offense. The transfer decision thus has become a choice between courts with fundamentally different philosophical perspectives: either rehabilitation of the offender in the juvenile court or punishment for the offense in the criminal court.

What do we know about the outcomes of these competing philosophies? Assessing the results of studies of transfers of juveniles to the criminal justice system is the purpose of this chapter. Three main criteria guide this review. First, to what extent do each of the three transfer mechanisms (judicial waiver, prosecutorial direct file and legislative transfer) capture serious, violent, and chronic offenders? Second, to what extent do each of the respective transfer mechanisms protect the public by convicting serious, violent, and chronic offenders in criminal court and incarcerating them? Third, how effective is each mechanism in reducing recidivism?

Research Results

Judicial waiver studies are examined in this section, followed by comparative studies and research on legislative transfers.

Judicial Waiver Studies

Table 5.1 provides a summary of 36 studies of judicial transfer. Most are descriptive, focused on discretionary decision making by juvenile court judges and the ability of juvenile court judges to select for waiver the most serious and violent juvenile offenders. Many of them provide descriptive statistics. These and other results of these studies are summarized in the "major findings" column.

On average, about 42% of waived juveniles were serious property offenders and 47% were violent offenders in the study jurisdictions. More than three-fourths (77%) were convicted. Slightly more than half (52%) of waivers resulted in imprisonment, although small percentages were jailed in certain jurisdictions (by the author's calculations, based on percentages reported by Bortner, 1986; Eigen, 1981; Fagan, Forst, and Vivona, 1987; Federation for Community Planning, 1983; Gragg, 1986; Greenwood, Abrahamse, and Zimring, 1984; Greenwood, Lipton, Abrahamse, and Zimring, 1983; Greenwood, Petersilia, and Zimring, 1980; Hamparian et al., 1982; Heuser, 1985; Houghtalin and Mays, 1991; Kinder, Veneziano, Fichter, and Azuma, 1995; Lemmon, et al., 1991; Massachusetts Governor's Juvenile Justice Advisory Committee, 1981; McNulty, 1995; Nimick, Szymanski, and Snyder, 1986; Ohio Department of Youth Services, 1993; Podkopacz and Feld, 1995; Roy and Sagan, 1980; Rudman, Hartstone, Fagan, and Moore, 1986; Snyder and Hutzler, 1981; and Virginia Commission on Youth, 1994). Very few of these studies analyzed other aspects of the judicial waiver process or outcomes. These exceptions are discussed below.

Several studies were inspired by a popular issue that emerged during the 1970s: the presumed leniency of juvenile courts, called the "leniency gap" between juvenile and criminal courts. Greenwood and his colleagues (1980) argued that a determination of juvenile court leniency cannot be made without taking into account the seriousness of juvenile crimes compared to adult crimes, as well as the age of the offender (see also Greenwood, 1986).

To explore the effect of age and serious offending on criminal sanctions, Greenwood and his colleagues (1980) compared dispositions for three age groups (older juveniles, young adults, and older adults) in Los Angeles, Ohio, and New York City. In general, older juveniles (age 16-17) and young adults (age 18-20) charged with robberies were not convicted and sentenced more leniently than were older adults (age 21-25). Second, the degree of variation appeared to be crime-specific, affected mainly by the degree of violence in the charged offense. In a later study, Greenwood and colleagues (1984) found that juveniles with extensive records were incarcerated or sentenced to state facilities about as often as were the more serious young adults, and more often than older adults.

Influenced by the RAND research, Eigen (1981) examined risk factors for judicial waiver to criminal court in a unique Philadelphia study that focused not only on the likelihood of transfer but also on the resulting dispositions of samples of youths charged with murder and robbery. He compared two samples of youths (waived and not waived groups) and also compared waived youths with adults originally charged in criminal court. Using multivariate analysis techniques, Eigen found that no single factor mandated the decision to transfer either murderers or robbers. Surprisingly, neither the juvenile's age nor offense history significantly increased the transfer likelihood. Offense characteristics (the offender's role in the killing and crossing racial lines) increased the transfer risk most. In the case of robbery offenders, offender characteristics carried more weight, especially the youth's incarceration history, indicating a lack of amenability to treatment in the juvenile justice system.

As the number of prior adjudications increased, there was an attendant increase in sentence severity among both juvenile murderers and robbers. For both groups, the defendant's role in the crime was a significant factor. Among murderers, however, the most important factor in determining whether the defendant got probation or imprisonment was black youths' choice of a white victim. In comparison with adults, waived juveniles were sentenced to much longer terms of incarceration, for reasons that Eigen was not able to isolate.

Two national assessments of judicial transfers were conducted by the research arm of the National Council of Juvenile and Family Court Judges (NCJFCJ). Snyder and Hutzler (1981), at the NCJFCJ's National Center for Juvenile Justice (NCJJ), analyzed the handling of 360,000 juvenile cases in 10 states in 1979. Three interesting findings resulted. First, violent offenders were five times as likely as any other offense

category to be waived to criminal court and twice as likely to be incarcerated in the juvenile justice system. Second, substantially higher proportions of 16-17-year-olds were waived by judges in jurisdictions that permitted waiver of younger children. Third, in states without extended jurisdiction to age 21, judges waived cases about twice as often as in states with extended jurisdiction. Snyder and Hutzler suggested that "availability of [services], or [availability of juveniles] for treatment may be a crucial element in the concept of amenability to treatment" (p. 8).

Snyder and Hutzler also found that prior record was a better predictor of juvenile court dispositions than any other variable. Among violent cases with no prior referrals, about 15% were either waived or incarcerated in the juvenile corrections system. This proportion increased to about 22% with one or two prior referrals. If the violent offender had more than two prior referrals, the proportion waived or incarcerated increased to nearly 60%. In contrast, about 35% of serious property offenders with more than two prior referrals were either waived or incarcerated.

Another NCJJ study (Nimick et al., 1986) examined judicial waivers in 552 juvenile courts in nine states in 1982. Their analysis showed that cases referred for an index violent offense were most likely to be waived. Uniform Crime Report (UCR) Index violent offenses were more than four times as likely to be waived as Index property cases and were seven times as likely to be waived as nonindex offense cases. In general, they found that the probability of waiver increased with the seriousness of the alleged offense. Examination of the age of waived cases showed that 17-year-olds constituted two-thirds of all waived cases. Within each offense category, the probability of waiver increased with the age of the offender, regardless of offense.

To measure the impact of prior juvenile court history on the waiver decision, Nimick and colleagues analyzed the complete court careers of the 495 youth born between 1962 and 1965 who were waived by the juvenile court in Maricopa County (Phoenix). They found that waived juveniles tended to have a large number of prior referrals and an early age of onset. More than two-thirds had five or more court referrals. Nearly half began their court careers before the age of 14. Most of the waived youth had at least one prior delinquency or status offense adjudication,

(text continued on p. 95)

TABLE 5.1 Judicial Waiver Studies

Citation	Jurisdiction	Description	Major Findings
Barnes and Franz (1989)	A large metro county in northern California	Studied all waivers between 1978-1993	Waived violent offenders received more severe sentence in criminal court; property offenders received more lenient sentences
Bortner (1986)	A southwestern state	Studied all juveniles transferred between 1980-1981	61% property offenders; 47% violent offenders; 96% convicted; 31% imprisoned
Bortner (1992)	Arizona, two counties	Analysis of all transfers during 1990	Only 65% of motioned were transferred; few had extensive treatment in the juvenile system
Champion (1989)	Tennessee, Virginia, Mississippi, and Georgia	Examined all waivers during the 9-year period. Compare with Virginia Commission on Youth (1994)	Waivers increased 100% during the period; murder waivers decreased while property waivers increased
Eigen (1981)	Philadelphia	Compared waived with retained and adults—robbery and murder, 1970, 1973	88% of waived cases were violent offenders; 92-97% convicted; 91-100% imprisoned
Fagan, Hartstone, Rudman, and Hansen (1984)	Boston, Denver, Memphis, Newark, Phoenix, and Miami	Part of evaluation of OJJDP VJO Program, 1981-1984	All major felony offenders; 14% waived; those with prior adjudication twice as likely to be waived
Fagan et al. (1987) Fagan and Deschenes (1990)	Boston, Detroit, Newark, and Phoenix	Part of evaluation of OJJDP VJO Program, 1981-1984	Racial determinants not significant; 60% imprisoned
Federation for Community Planning (1983)	Ohio, statewide (see Ohio Department of Youth Services, 1993)	Examined characteristics and dispositions of all waived juveniles, 1981	40% were for property offenses; 39% were for violent offenses; 55% had 2-5 prior adjudications; one-half were black
Gillespie and Norman (1984)	Utah, statewide	Tracked dispositions of all waivers, 1969-1980	Nearly half for person offenses, three-fourths convicted; nearly half of these imprisoned
Gragg (1986)	12 jurisdictions	Part of evaluation of OJJDP Serious Habitual Offender Program	56% property offenses; 26% violent offenses; 59% had 2 or more prior adjudications; 60% had at least one prior felony adjudication

TABLE 5.1 *Continued*

Citation	Jurisdiction	Description	Major Findings
Greenwood et al. (1980)	Los Angeles, Franklin County, Ohio, and New York City (1971-1973)	Compared juvenile court dispositions of juveniles with young adults	72% convicted; 55% imprisoned
Greenwood et al. (1983)	Three large California jurisdictions (1971-1973)	Compared juvenile court dispositions of juveniles with young adults (robbery and burglary offenders only)	Criminal court sentences more severe except when juveniles had prior record; 30-75% convicted; 30-75% imprisoned
Greenwood et al. (1984)	Las Vegas, Seattle, and Los Angeles (1971-1973)	Compared juvenile court dispositions of juveniles with young adults (robbery and burglary offenders only)	Juveniles with extensive records sentenced more severely than adults; 45-75% convicted; 2-42% imprisoned
Hamparian et al. (1982)	Nationwide	Only nationwide transfer study, 1978	45% property offenders; 32% violent offenders; 90% convicted
Heuser (1985)	Oregon, statewide	Tracked 1980 cohort of juvenile and adult felony arrestees	75% of juveniles property offenders; averaged 10 prior referrals, 7% of which were violent offenses
Houghtalin and Mays (1991)	New Mexico	Studied all (49) waivers, 1981-1990	67% property or violent offense; only 35% previously incarcerated in juvenile corrections; 80% convicted; 64% imprisoned
Keiter (1973)	Cook County, Illinois	Examined all males transferred in 1970	92% were black, but whites not transferred had more serious offense histories
Kinder et al. (1995)	St. Louis, Missouri	Compared all waived cases with random sample of felony cases not waived, 1993	23% were property offenders; 50% were violent offenders; 23% were convicted; 6% were imprisoned
Lee (1994)	Maricopa County, Arizona	Studied factors related to waiver in a cohort of youth born in 1969	Prior waiver was the most important determinant of the current waiver decision
Lemmon, et al. (1991)	Pennsylvania, statewide	Studied dispositions of all 1986 transfers	Most were serious offenders with significant offense histories; 89% convicted; nearly all incarcerated in prison/jail

continued

TABLE 5.1 *Continued*

Citation	Jurisdiction	Description	Major Findings
Massachusetts Governor's Juvenile Justice Advisory Committee (1981)	Massachusetts, statewide	Tracked all serious and violent offenders committed to DYS in 1975, 1977, and 1979	90% of waivers serious or violent; varied by region and judge, 45% of waivers incarcerated
McNulty (1995)	Arizona, statewide	Studied all 552 juveniles waived to criminal court in 1994	39% were property offenders; 45% were violent offenders; 92% convicted; 43% imprisoned
Nimick, Szymanski, and Snyder (1986)	552 juvenile courts in nine states	Examined characteristics and dispositions in 1982	40% property offenders; 34% violent offenders
Ohio Department of Youth Services (1993)	Ohio, statewide (see Federation for Community Planning, 1983)	Examined characteristics and dispositions of all waived juveniles, 1992	18% were for property offenses; 62% were for violent offenses; 47% had no juvenile corrections experiences; two-thirds were black
Osbun and Rode (1984)	Minnesota, statewide	Compared transfers in 10 counties before and after new presumptory law	Law had little effect because it did not make transfer automatic
Pennsylvania Joint Council (1978)	Pennsylvania, statewide	Compared dispositions of waivers in 1974 and 1977	Slightly more waived juveniles were incarcerated in 1977 than in 1974
Phillips (1994)	Utah, statewide	Studied all (49) waivers during 1988-1993	More than half received prison sentences; average time served, 2 years
Podkopacz and Feld (1995)	Hennepin County, Minnesota	Studied all waiver decisions (330) 1986-1992	25% property; 42% violent; 94% convicted; 25% imprisoned
Poulos and Orchowsky (1994)	Virginia, statewide	Compared random sample of transferred youths with a stratified sample of nontransfers, 1988-1990	Number of prior property adjudications was best predictor of transfer; race was not an important factor
Roy and Sagan (1980)	Massachusetts, statewide	Examined dispositions of all 45 juveniles waived in 1979	Disposition took an average of 7 months; 45% imprisoned; blacks overrepresented
Rudman et al. (1986)	Boston, Memphis, Newark, and Phoenix	Part of evaluation of OJJDP VJO Program, 1981-1984	92% convicted; 76% imprisoned; adjudication and conviction rates about the same in juvenile and criminal court

TABLE 5.1 *Continued*

Citation	Jurisdiction	Description	Major Findings
Sagatun, McCollum, and Edwards (1985)	Santa Clara County, California	Compared waivers before and after 1976 presumptory legislation	Violent offenders as likely to be waived before law as after
Snyder and Hutzler (1981)	360,000 juvenile cases in 10 states	Analyzed dispositions compared with adults in 1979	35% property offenders; 60% violent offenders; all in both groups had 2 or more priors
Teilmann and Klein (1979)	California, statewide	Compared waivers before and after 1976 legislation adding presumptory offenses	Waivers increased 200% in just one year
Van Dusen (1981)	California, statewide	Compared waivers before and after 1976 legislation adding presumptory offenses	Waived juveniles received more severe penalties after the new law was enacted
Virginia Commission on Youth (1994)	Virginia, statewide	Analyzed all transfers during 1988-1990	35% were violent offenders; 31% were convicted; 63% were imprisoned

SOURCE: "Juvenile Transfers to the Criminal Justice System: State of the Art" (pp. 27-60), Vol. 18, Nos. 1 & 2, Howell, © copyright 1996 by Blackwell Publishers Ltd.

more than half had been placed on probation, and one-third had been placed in a juvenile facility.

Nimick and her colleagues also tested the relative importance of amenability to treatment in the waiver decision by examining the likelihood of waiver as affected by extended age of juvenile court jurisdiction. The rate of juvenile court referral was three times as high in courts with jurisdiction to only the 18th or 19th birthday than in the courts that had extended jurisdiction over youth until their 21st birthday, and more than four times the rate in those courts with the ability to retain jurisdiction past the 21st birthday.

In a nationwide study, Hamparian et al. (1982) examined the dispositions of judicial waiver, concurrent jurisdiction, and excluded offense cases waived to criminal court nationwide in 1978. With the exception of excluded offense states, they found that most juveniles transferred to criminal courts were charged with serious property offenses. Violent offense percentages were less than one-fourth of the judicial and prosecutorial referrals, and less than 5% in states with a maximum age of juvenile court jurisdiction below the age of 17.

Conviction rates were similar regardless of the transfer mechanism that was used. More than 90% of judicial waivers and concurrent jurisdiction cases resulted in convictions. Lengths of confinement appeared to be longer for judicial waiver cases than for concurrent jurisdiction cases. Juveniles convicted in criminal courts and sentenced to adult corrections facilities could expect longer periods of confinement than under juvenile court dispositions.

Hamparian and her colleagues (1982) also found that judicial waiver rates varied enormously from state to state, ranging from less than 1 per 10,000 juveniles in the general population to more than 13 per 10,000 in certain states. Higher waiver rates were observed in states that had original juvenile court jurisdiction over 16- and 17-year-olds. The most important factors in the referral decision were the seriousness of the offense, the extent of prior delinquency records, and the results of previous treatment efforts in the juvenile justice system.

In his Oregon study of a 1980 statewide cohort of adult and juvenile felony arrestees, Heuser (1985) used Oregon's Offender-Based

Transaction System data to track the flow of persons arrested in the state from arrest through juvenile and criminal justice system processing. The main subjects of the study were juveniles judicially transferred to the criminal justice system. Compared to nontransferred juveniles, waived cases were generally older (over 17 years of age), with an extensive juvenile court referral history involving largely predatory property crime.

Heuser examined the "juvenile justice system penetration" of the transferred juveniles to determine the extent to which treatment had been provided prior to the transfer decision. Waived juveniles' court records generally began at the age of 13 and were extensive (nearly 10 prior juvenile court referrals, on average). The most serious previous adjudicated offense was a property crime 85% of the time. Only half of the remanded juveniles had previous commitments to Oregon state training schools.

Heuser examined remand orders and other court documents to determine the criteria on which remand decisions were based (which could include more than one). These were low amenability to treatment (97%); number of prior referrals (59%); criminal "sophistication" of the juvenile (44%); seriousness of the instant offense (34%); evidence that the instant offense was committed in an aggressive, violent, premeditated, or willful manner (34%); and a history of running away (24%). Three or more of these criteria were cited in more than half of the transfers.

The Office of Juvenile Justice and Delinquency Prevention's (OJJDP) Habitual, Serious, and Violent Juvenile Offender Program provided the opportunity for Gragg (1986) to study the characteristics of juveniles waived, direct filed, or automatically transferred to criminal court in 12 jurisdictions during the first 6 months of 1985. All of these transfers were from a pool of juveniles targeted for increased sanctions under the program. Gragg compared the characteristics of juveniles transferred by judicial waiver, by prosecutorial direct file, and automatically by legislative criteria. Juveniles transferred by discretionary processes (judicial waiver and direct file) were on the average a year older than youths transferred automatically by legislative exclusion. About three-fourths of discretionary transfers were black, compared to 57% of automatic transfers. Waived youths had more than twice as many prior adjudications as direct files and statutory

exclusions. More than three-fourths of judicially waived youths had some prior correctional experience (which included nearly half of the chronic recidivists). Only 30% of the automatic transfers, however, previously had been sentenced to juvenile corrections. "Overall, cases that were transferred by waiver seem to most closely approximate the profile of the 'chronic offender' " (p. 31).

In conjunction with an analysis of all juveniles waived to criminal court in "a southwestern state" during 1980-1981, Bortner (1986) conducted an organizational analysis of the decision-making process. She found a low level of agreement regarding cases that should be transferred among key transfer decision makers, including the chief juvenile prosecutor, judges, and the chief juvenile court administrator. Although prosecutors' official criteria for deciding whether or not to request waiver included age, offense, and referral history, as means of identifying "dangerous and repetitive offenders," Bortner found the daily application of these guidelines to be "highly discretionary" (p. 61). She concluded (p. 62) that, "It cannot be demonstrated that those juveniles who are remanded are singularly dangerous or that they are intractable. Neither can it be demonstrated that the remand of these particular juveniles enhances public safety through incarceration or deterrence."

Several transfer studies were made in conjunction with evaluation of the OJJDP's Violent Juvenile Offender (VJO) Program (1981-1984), the main purpose of which was to test the effectiveness of a research and development program aimed at violent and chronic serious juvenile offenders. In the initial report, Fagan, Hartstone, and colleagues (1984) presented the results of analyses of juvenile court dispositions of referred juveniles who met the eligibility criteria for inclusion in the program (a major felony offense and one or more prior adjudications for a felony offense). The proportions transferred ranged from 1% in Newark to 44% in Miami. Fagan and his colleagues identified several factors that accounted for the variation in handling of serious and violent offenders in the different sites: inconsistent charging practices, collapsing several offenses into a single petition, variations in adjudication procedures, plea bargaining, and variations in handling parole revocations (pp. 129-133).

In the second VJO Program study report, Rudman and colleagues (1986) reported on the processing and outcomes of youths charged in the juvenile justice system with violent offenses and considered for transfer to the criminal justice system in four cities (Boston, Memphis, Newark, and Phoenix). It took 2.5 times as long for a violent youth to be transferred, convicted, and sentenced in the criminal court than to be adjudicated in juvenile court. The main cause of longer criminal justice system processing time was the lengthy appellate process. Most transferred youths remained in a juvenile detention center for the duration of the transfer proceedings. Youths convicted in criminal court received substantially longer sentences, on average about five times as long, than dispositions received by those retained in the juvenile justice system. The largest difference was found in murder cases.

In the third report on the VJO Program, Fagan and colleagues (1987) examined factors accounting for the judicial waiver decision. Race was not a determining factor in the four sites, except in homicide cases. Multivariate analyses revealed the most consistent contributors to the judicial waiver decision to be age at offense (older youth were transferred), age at onset of official delinquent careers (youths who started at younger ages were more often transferred), and a charge of murder (or armed robbery). Fagan and his colleagues concluded that judges "appear to focus on rational, concrete factors in the transfer decision" (p. 276).

Barnes and Franz (1989) analyzed the results of all waiver motions filed in a large metropolitan county in northern California. Factors accounting for the decision to waive juvenile court jurisdiction included seriousness of the offense, number and severity of prior offenses, and treatment history. In general, offense seriousness was the most important consideration in criminal court, whereas the number and nature of prior offenses and treatment history were more important factors in juvenile court.

A Virginia study (Poulos & Orchowsky, 1994) sought to identify the legal and extralegal factors that influence the juvenile court judge's waiver decision. The researchers compared a random sample of juvenile offenders transferred to criminal court in Virginia between 1988 and 1990 with a sample of transfer-eligible juveniles who were retained in the juvenile justice system. Poulos and Orchowsky used multivariate analysis to identify factors that accounted for the waiver decision. The single most important predictor of transfer was the

number of prior property adjudications. Other important factors included older age (17) at the time of the offense, previous commitment to a Virginia training school, previous adjudication for a felony-level offense, use of a firearm in the current offense, at least a ninth-grade education, residence in an urban area, and a violent or drug-related instant offense. Previous mental health treatment decreased the likelihood of transfer. Older offenders who used a firearm in their current offense increased significantly their likelihood of transfer. Race was not a significant predictor.

A later study in the state (Virginia Commission on Youth, 1994) of juveniles judicially transferred showed that the juvenile offender's age and a history of property offenses were the best predictors of transfer. Those sentenced to prison served an average of 17 months, compared to less than 8 months of time served by those handled in juvenile court and committed to juvenile institutions. Judges, prosecutors, and other officials throughout the state were surveyed to assess their views on a number of issues associated with the transfer decision. They said that (a) current offense and prior record are the most important factors in the transfer decision, (b) juvenile court judges should be able to impose longer determinate sentences for serious juvenile offenders, and (c) juvenile court postdispositional options are not adequate to deal effectively with serious juvenile offenders (p. 18).

An Arizona study by McNulty (1995) examined all juvenile cases referred to Arizona juvenile courts in 1994 and subsequently transferred to the criminal court for prosecution. McNulty's analysis focused on factors that predicted changes in the odds of a transferred juvenile receiving a sentence of incarceration or probation in the criminal court. Using multivariate analysis techniques, McNulty found that the following factors increased the odds of receiving a prison sentence: previous transfers to criminal court, an instant violent offense, minority status, and prior referrals to juvenile court. Surprisingly, age decreased the odds of being sentenced to incarceration: Younger juveniles were more likely to receive an incarcerative sentence. Juveniles charged with violent offenses were almost three times as likely to receive an incarcerative sentence as those who were not charged with a violent offense. Transferred black juveniles were approximately three times as likely to receive an incarcerative sentence, and Hispanic juveniles were almost twice as likely as white youths to be sentenced to incarceration.

McNulty also examined the extent to which juvenile court services had been exhausted for transferred juveniles. Nearly a third (30%) had more than 10 prior referrals. Less than half (43%) had previously been committed to the juvenile correctional facility, and 9% had previously been transferred to criminal court (the results of which were unknown). She found that prior services through the juvenile court (a diversion program, probation, intensive probation supervision, and commitment to the juvenile correctional facility) did not significantly change the odds of receiving either an incarcerative sentence or probation. Bortner's (1992) Arizona study of juveniles transferred in two counties during 1990 produced a similar finding.

Podkopacz and Feld (1995, 1996) conducted the most comprehensive and rigorous comparative study to date of the determinants and consequences of judicial waiver decisions. Their main objective was to examine judicial application of legislative criteria for transfer in the Hennepin County, Minnesota, Juvenile Court. Judicial discretion was guided by the state's juvenile code, which generally limited judicial waiver to the criteria set forth in the Supreme Court's *Kent* decision (generally, present offense, prior record, and past treatment efforts).

The data were collected during the period (1986-1992) in which Minnesota juvenile courts could order transfer only if there was probable cause to believe that the juvenile committed the alleged offense and the prosecutor demonstrated that the offender was not amenable to treatment. In addition, prosecutors could establish a "prima facie," or "rebuttable presumption"[2] case of eligibility for waiver when a youth committed any "serious" crime (which was not defined) and had an extensive prior record. Judicial discretion was not limited significantly by the "prima facie" provision, however, because evidence of a youth's amenability to treatment and lack of dangerousness could rebut the prosecution's case. Except for the "prima facie" provision, Minnesota's transfer strategy (judicial waiver on prosecutor's motions) is a fairly common strategy used in the United States.

Podkopacz and Feld included in their study all 330 judicial waiver decisions in the county

during the study period. In addition to analyzing the factors that influenced the waiver decision, they studied the background and characteristics of juveniles considered for transfer, the waiver process, dispositions, and recidivism. Transferred (215) and nontransferred (115) youths were compared in all of these areas.

Analyses of the process by which juvenile court judges reached waiver decisions on the prosecutor motions produced several interesting findings. First, the proportion waived by individual judges varied considerably, from 75% to 54%. Second, the juvenile court decided most of the referral motions without holding a full hearing, having negotiated informally the outcomes of more than 90% of all transfer motions. Third, multivariate analyses showed six variables to be most important in explaining judicial waiver decisions: (a) the recommendation that court services personnel gave the judge, (b) the judge who decided the case, (c) the age of the offender (older juveniles, generally age 17), (d) four or more prior delinquency placements, (e) the number of present offense charges, and (f) if the juvenile used a weapon in a felony person offense. Prior record appeared to influence the waiver decision more than the seriousness of the present offense, unless a weapon was used. The race of the offender was not found to be an important factor.

In general, these judicial waiver studies indicate that the most important factors in the referral decision are sex (males more likely to be waived), age (older offenders more likely to be waived), number and seriousness of the instant offense(s) (including weapon use), the number of prior court referrals and adjudications, and treatment history in the juvenile justice system. The latter variable involves a complex determination reflecting a wide range of considerations, in addition to the above factors (remaining years of eligibility for juvenile court jurisdiction, juvenile court staff recommendations, and other considerations). Studies using bivariate analyses find race to be an important determinant, whereas multivariate analyses do not, with one general exception (McNulty, 1995), and in murder cases (Eigen, 1981; Fagan et al., 1987).

Legislative Exclusion Studies

Only three states' legislative exclusion statutes have been studied. Singer (1993, 1994,

1996; Singer & Ewing, 1986; Singer & McDowall, 1988) evaluated New York State's 1978 juvenile offender (JO) law that lowered the eligible age of criminal justice system handling of juveniles to 13 for murder and 14 for other violent offenses. The new law automatically transferred these youths to criminal court. New York had already excluded 16-17-year-olds from the juvenile court in a 1976 Juvenile Justice Reform Act and required minimum sentences to secure facilities for designated offenses.

The 1978 law, as amended, labeled 13-15-year-olds charged with designated offenses as "juvenile offenders (JO)" and 16-18-year-olds as "youthful offenders," and it established a range of sentences within which the criminal court had flexibility. The court could transfer youths back to juvenile court (reverse waiver) at its discretion, guided by such criteria as the seriousness of the offense and circumstances surrounding it (Singer, 1996, p. 58). In short, "the get-tough reform proposed by the governor shifted the sources of legal discretion over violent juveniles from juvenile justice officials to criminal justice officials" (Singer, 1996, p. 59). The JO law required that murder cases be transferred to the criminal court. In the case of more ordinary offenses that did not involve murder, rape, or robbery with a weapon, the law allowed prosecutors and criminal court judges to consider circumstances beyond the characteristics of the offense in making the determination to prosecute a case or transfer it back to the juvenile justice system.

The New York JO law epitomizes the search for legal remedies for the serious, violent, and chronic juvenile offender. The state wanted to provide a more visible and understandable avenue of control and punishment for offenders like Willie Bosket, a 15-year-old who repeatedly committed violent crimes, even murder, without remorse (Butterfield, 1995; Singer, 1995, pp. 5-7). The JO law intended to target violent offenses that persons like Willie committed, to make offense criteria rather than the offender the main consideration in sentencing decisions, and to ensure that violent offenses did not go unpunished.

Singer and McDowall (1988) compared monthly juvenile arrest rates for violent crime in New York with rates in Philadelphia during the period 1974-1984, before and after the new law. The analysis showed that the new law did not reduce juvenile arrests. Singer and McDowall concluded that the law had little measurable effect on juvenile crime and thus did not produce the deterrent effect that lawmakers expected.

In another analysis, Singer (1993) identified predictors of prosecutorial referrals to the grand jury among all (103) designated JO arrests in Buffalo, New York, during 1978-1985. Multivariate analysis showed that the only significant offense-related variable was the extent of injuries. Once homicide cases were removed from the analysis, however, this variable was no longer important. The number of parents in the JO household was the only significant predictor of prosecutorial referral for non-homicide cases.

Singer (1994, 1996) also analyzed criminal justice system processing of all (nearly 10,000) juveniles (average age: 15) arrested under the JO law in New York State during the period 1978-1985. More than two-thirds of the JO arrests were for robbery, and more than two-thirds were black youngsters. Only 11% of juveniles had been arrested more than once. About 26% were convicted in criminal court, and 31% were reverse waived to juvenile court; the remainder were dismissed, acquitted, received another disposition, or were cases the prosecutor declined to prosecute. Conviction rates were higher for more serious offenses and for repeat offenders—although 41% of juveniles who were repeat violent offenders had their charges dismissed in criminal court. Singer (1996, p. 118) notes that the proportion convicted "is substantially lower than the proportion of arrested adults convicted in criminal court for the same kinds of offenses (60%)."

In a multivariate analysis of the determinants of conviction, Singer (1996, pp. 124-126) found age, gender, offense severity, and prior arrests to be the main explanatory factors. Race did not emerge as a main factor, even though black youths were more likely to be arrested for a designated offense, because infrequently arrested white youths generally were arrested for more serious offenses than black youths. Only 10% of all arrested juveniles who qualified for transfer to the criminal justice system were incarcerated, but the majority (58%) of convicted juvenile offenders received a sentence of incarceration, including 87% of juveniles charged with the most serious crimes and 80% of those with a prior designated felony arrest. Race was found to be a key factor in the incarceration decision. Most convicted (51%) white juveniles were sentenced to probation (despite their more serious offenses), whereas most (60%) black and most (59%) Hispanic juveniles were incarcerated. Multivariate analysis showed that the likelihood of incarceration for non-whites was nearly twice as great as for whites. Other than race, the strongest predictors of incarceration were offense severity variables. Age, race, offense severity, and prior arrests were the best predictors of sentence length.

The JO law required that sentenced juveniles be incarcerated in several maximum security institutions for juveniles and that academic and vocational education be provided along with psychological counseling. These institutions held about 100 juveniles and cost up to $80,000 per year per incarcerated juvenile. Singer (1996, pp. 165-186) conducted an assessment of one of these, the Mastern Park Rehabilitation Center, in Buffalo, created to imprison JO youths in lieu of state prisons. Although follow-up data were not obtained on youths placed there to serve their criminal court sentences, he interviewed inmates and facility officials and deemed the institution to be ineffective in rehabilitating or controlling youngsters. In fact, the facility was closed in 1994, following a Justice Department investigation of allegations that the civil rights of residents were violated repeatedly because of beatings by Mastern staff and ineffective supervision of youths placed there. Several staff members were arrested and indicted. Other state institutions were investigated for similar abuses (p. 185).

Singer concluded that New York's JO law was a failure. It did not reduce juvenile crime or eliminate individualized justice. At both the prosecution and sentencing stages, officials took into account the arrested juvenile's prior offense, family background and parental support, general demeanor, and age-related characteristics. Only 10% of juveniles transferred to criminal court were imprisoned. These were disproportionately black. "Justice by geography" was evident in that the seriousness of the offenses for which youths were arrested, the probability of conviction in criminal court or removal to juvenile court, and the length of their sentences depended on the county in which they were processed.

Singer saw the legislative experiment as "recriminalization" of juveniles that brought New York State full circle to a form of juvenile corrections that existed before the juvenile justice system was created. Political and organizational concerns dominated policies and procedures leading to the new law and in its implementation, including interests in maintaining the legitimacy of loosely coupled systems of juvenile and criminal justice. Although Singer (1996) acknowledged that "legislative waiver has the advantage of being offense-based and of preventing juveniles from entering criminal court for nonviolent offenses" (p. 193), he concluded that states can more effectively "respond to juvenile crime by both doing good and doing justice. A more tightly coupled system of juvenile justice is needed in which recriminalization is more narrowly focused and confined to the most serious of violent offenses." Other studies have documented the ineffectiveness of the New York law (Hairston, 1981; Roysher & Edelman, 1981; Sobie, 1981).

A Cook County, Illinois, study (Clarke, 1994) examined juveniles automatically transferred to criminal court for drug and weapons violations under several Illinois excluded offense statutes during 1991-1992. Clarke found that most of the transferred juveniles were not viewed by the criminal court as serious offenders. More than half received probation, supervision, or conditional discharge. Twelve percent were sentenced to incarceration in Illinois prisons, most of whom judges ruled eligible for boot camps. Among the remainder, 18% were found not guilty. Almost all (98%) the automatic transfers were black.

One study compared states with and without an automatic transfer provision. Jensen and Metsger (1994) assessed the deterrent impact of Idaho's 1981 statute that required the automatic transfer of juveniles aged 14-18 charged with murder, robbery, rape, mayhem, and assault or battery. The authors used official data gathered for 4-year periods just before and after enactment of the new law. Montana and Wyoming served as comparison states. Juvenile violent crimes increased in Idaho and decreased in the two comparison states, suggesting that the new law had no deterrent effect.

These studies do not provide a sufficient basis for drawing firm conclusions regarding the impact of legislative exclusion. It can be said, however, that they call into question the effectiveness of this transfer method in accomplishing the goals of selecting serious, violent, and chronic juvenile offenders for transfer and of ensuring more severe sanctions than are available in the juvenile justice system.

Prosecutor Transfer Studies

Evaluation of prosecutorial transfer (direct files) legislation has been done only in Florida. A 1981 Florida law (Fla. Stat. Ann. Sec. 3904(2)(e)(4)) gave prosecutors expanded transfer power with respect to 16- and 17-year-olds charged with any felony. Prior to the new law, prosecutorial direct files accounted for 48% of all transfers. In the first year after enactment of the new statute, the proportion jumped to 68% (in 1982), and it increased to 88% in 1987 (Bishop & Frazier, 1991).

The Florida Youth Services Program Office (1980) conducted a study of juveniles transferred by prosecutors to the criminal justice system in the state during 1978-1979. More than 70% of the cases involved felony charges, 34% of which were offenses against persons; 92% had prior referrals or encounters with the juvenile justice system. Examination of the dispositions of a random sample of 300 juvenile cases processed in the criminal justice system during 1979 showed that 62% were detained in the county jail before disposition, for an average period of nearly 4 months. Most cases (63%) were disposed of through plea bargaining; only 8% went to trial, and 62% were incarcerated in adult correctional institutions or in county jails. Of those sentenced to a correctional institution, 18% were sentenced for 3 years; 16% for 1 year; 14% for 4 years; 13% for 2 years; 12% for 5 years; and 11% for 4-6 months.

Thomas and Bilchik (1985) examined criminal court dispositions of juvenile offenders in Dade County, Florida, in 1981. Among those offenders on whom prosecutors filed charges that culminated either in a trial or a guilty plea, 90% were found guilty of serious felony offenses: 55% for crimes against property, primarily burglary; 17% for robbery; and 10% for felonious crimes against persons. Two-thirds of those found guilty were sentenced to a term of imprisonment (median length: 4 years). Almost all the remaining defendants (32%) were placed on probation.

A subsequent study by the Florida Governor's Task Force on Juvenile and Adult Criminal Dispositions and Coordination (1984) examined 1983 statewide direct file cases. The task force found that 50% of the most serious juvenile cases received prison terms, most for 1 to 5 years. An earlier study (August, 1981) produced similar findings. Among juveniles transferred in 1979, more than half (57%) were charged with property crimes, and 40% were sentenced to the state correctional system.

Bishop, Frazier, and Henretta (1989; see also Bishop & Frazier, 1991) conducted a Florida study of prosecutorial transfer in two counties. All cases in these two counties (a large urban area and a mid-sized urban area) were examined in which direct file proceedings were initiated by juvenile division state attorneys between 1981 and 1984. Only 29% of the transferred juveniles were charged with a felony person offense; most (55%) were charged with property felonies.

To explore the amenability to treatment issue, Bishop and colleagues (1989; Bishop & Frazier, 1991) examined the juvenile justice system history and offender careers of the transferred youths. Only 35% had been committed to a residential facility. Most (58%) had received some other type of juvenile court sanction, but 23% were transferred for a first offense. Over the 4-year period of the study, the trend was toward transferring youths with more extensive juvenile justice system and offense histories, although not more violent offenses.

Nearly all (96%) of the juveniles transferred over the 4-year period were convicted in criminal court. In 1981, 81% of those convicted were sentenced to incarceration, compared to 51% in 1984. Overall, some postconviction incarceration occurred in 61% of the cases, but prison sentences were ordered in only 31% of the cases. Among those receiving prison terms, 54% were sentenced to 1-3 years, 31% received 4-6-year sentences, and 15% received 7 or more years (Bishop et al., 1989; Bishop & Frazier, 1991).

Bishop and colleagues (1989; Bishop & Frazier, 1991) interviewed prosecutors to seek explanations of why few eligible youths are transferred, while so many of those transferred seem inappropriate. Telephone interviews were conducted with juvenile prosecutors in each of the state's 20 judicial circuits. Although generally pleased with Florida's 1981 law giving prosecutors expanded direct file powers, half wished the change had been more far-reaching (permitting direct files of youths under 16 years of age). Bishop and her colleagues categorized respondents into three groups: those favoring a "pure" just deserts model, a "modified" just deserts model, or a traditional rehabilitative model of juvenile justice. Prosecutors aligned with the "pure" just deserts model constituted the smallest group. They viewed transfer as serving to balance the scales of justice, providing punishment to juveniles that was due. Nearly half of the prosecutors fell into the second group of just deserts advocates. They felt as strongly as the first group that punishment was essential; however, they held the view that punitive measures would protect the community and prevent future crimes. The slight majority of respondents endorsed the traditional principles of juvenile justice, that transfer should be a last resort.

Surprisingly, Bishop and Frazier (1991, pp. 291-292) found little correspondence between prosecutors' stated philosophies and their own practices. Virtually every prosecutor, regardless of philosophical orientation, reported having increased the number of youths transferred after the 1981 law. Prosecutors espousing just deserts generally were no more likely to transfer youths than others favoring the traditional rehabilitative ideal. Many of the traditional philosophy prosecutors transferred as high a proportion of cases as others who advocated a punitive stance. Several of the "last resort" types, however, said they would transfer fewer youths if treatment programs were available, particularly residential programs in secure facilities that would satisfy public safety concerns.

The increase in prosecutor direct files in Florida did not change substantially the offense profile of transferred cases. As noted above, the Florida Youth Services Program Office (1980) found that about one-third of transferred cases prior to the 1981 Florida law were person felonies. In 1993, 29% of cases transferred to Florida's criminal courts involved a violent felony as the most serious charge (Snyder & Sickmund, 1995, p. 156).

In another Florida study, Frazier (1991) attempted to determine whether the juveniles selected for prosecutorial transfer to criminal court are more serious offenders than those whose cases are disposed in deep end juvenile justice programs. Comparison of direct file and retained groups showed that they were similar in age, gender, and ethnicity (although the ethnic differential was lowest in the direct file group). Both groups also looked similar in a composite measure of instant offense seriousness, prior offenses, prior delinquency dispositions, and number of prior delinquency referrals. The main difference in the two groups was that more serious offenders were found in the

"deep end" of the juvenile justice system (secure confinement) rather than in the direct file group. Prosecutors tended to select cases for transfer equally from low-, medium-, and high-risk categories. Frazier concluded that "given current available data, direct file cannot easily be justified on the grounds that it selects the most serious offenders for adult court" (p. 84).

A new Florida study (Bishop, Frazier, Lanza-Kaduce, & Winner, 1996) compared the recidivism of 2,738 juveniles transferred to criminal court with matched youths retained in the juvenile justice system. Although the follow-up period during which the samples could commit new offenses was 1 year or less, 30% of the transferred group were rearrested, compared to 19% of the nontransferred matches. Examination of the severity of rearrests showed that, of the transfers who were rearrested, 93% committed a felony compared to 85% of the nontransferred group. In a third comparison, the researchers found that transferred youths were likely to reoffend more quickly (135 days) than were the nontransferred juveniles (227 days). Finally, the nontransferred group showed a significantly greater tendency than transfers toward rearrest for a lesser offense. Bishop and her colleagues concluded that "overall, the results suggest that transfer in Florida has had little deterrent value. Nor has it produced any incapacitative benefits that enhance public safety" (p. 183). Despite the more prevalent incarceration of transferred youths, and for longer periods, they more quickly reoffended and at a higher rate than the nontransferred group, thereby negating incapacitative benefits achieved in the short run. Bishop suggests that as a result of transfer, juveniles are more likely to associate with other more seasoned offenders, which may partly explain the quicker and higher recidivism ("Adult Treatment of Juvenile Offenders," 1996).

Studies conducted in only one state do not provide an adequate basis for drawing conclusions regarding the efficacy of prosecutorial direct files (or any other transfer method). Rather, these results suggest the need to study the results of prosecutorial direct files in other jurisdictions, for the purpose of comparison. New research should examine the extent to which prosecutors are able to select for transfer the most serious, violent, and chronic juvenile offenders. Current research in Florida is evaluating the effectiveness of the state's "blended sentencing" approach to treatment of transferred juveniles (Thomas & Bilchik, 1985, pp. 477-478).

Comparative Studies

The first comparative study of juvenile and criminal justice system handling of juvenile offenders examined dispositions during 1975 in Buffalo, New York, and Pittsburgh, Pennsylvania. The study, conducted by the National Center for Juvenile Justice (reported by Young, 1981, pp. 313-314), compared handling of 16-year-old offenders under the New York system, where they were automatically adults, with Pennsylvania, where the 16-year-olds were handled in juvenile court. Random samples of 100 youth from each jurisdiction were included in the study. In Buffalo, the criminal court dismissed 74% of the offenders, whereas the Pittsburgh juvenile court dismissed 48%. About equal percentages were committed to incarceration in the two cities: 15% in Pittsburgh and 16% in Buffalo. The study also found that the juvenile court in Pittsburgh was twice as likely as the Buffalo criminal court to incarcerate a violent juvenile offender.

Snyder and Hutzler (1981) compared the flow of 1,000 adult felony cases through the criminal system and 1,000 serious (UCR Part I) juvenile offenders over 15 years of age through the juvenile court system in Washington, D.C., in 1977. They found that the juvenile court was far more likely than the criminal court to take some form of action on its most serious cases. Whereas less than 40% of adult felons referred to the district attorney were convicted and sentenced in the criminal court, 55% of the felony juvenile cases resulted in incarceration or court supervision. Among convicted adults and adjudicated delinquents, however, the criminal court was more likely to impose incarceration (57% versus 25%).

Greenwood and colleagues (1983) compared juvenile and criminal court dispositions of older juveniles (age 16-17) and young adults (age 18-21) charged with armed robbery or residential burglary in three large California jurisdictions. Although the study found that criminal court sentences were generally more severe, juvenile court dispositions were more severe when the juveniles had a prior record. For example, in Los Angeles, robbery cases that involved two or more aggravating factors were nearly three times as likely as those without aggravating factors to result in incarceration in juvenile court. Aggravating factors affected sentence severity much less in the Los Angeles criminal court than in the two other jurisdictions.

White (1985) compared the outcomes of cases involving juveniles charged with "dangerous" offenses (murder, rape, aggravated assault, robbery, and burglary) in the juvenile justice system with similar cases against young defendants in the criminal justice system. Comparisons were made in nine selected sites during 1980-1981. White found that juvenile courts waived about 5% of the dangerous cases filed with them. Criminal courts were slightly more likely to find offenders guilty, and criminal courts were more than twice as likely to incarcerate the young adults as were juvenile courts to incarcerate similar juvenile offenders. Confined young adults served considerably more time in adult prisons than did juveniles in reformatories and recidivated about 1.5 times more often than did juveniles. White (1985) concluded that the best mechanism for discriminating between those juveniles who should be tried as adults and those who should be adjudicated as juveniles appears to be judicial waiver.

In another cross-state comparison, Fagan (1995) studied the handling of serious and violent juvenile offenders in New York and New Jersey. New York's excluded offense law requires that felony cases of 15-17-year-olds originate in criminal court. Such cases normally would be handled in the juvenile court in New Jersey. His study was a natural experiment comparing the handling of juveniles in matched counties in the two states. The samples consisted of randomly selected adolescent felony offenders, ages 15-16, arrested for robbery and burglary during 1981-1982. Fagan tracked these cases through the respective systems in the two states, allowing a 4-year follow-up period.

Accountability for adolescent offenders transferred to criminal court was no greater than for juveniles retained in the juvenile court. In robbery cases, the rate of dismissal was significantly lower in juvenile court than in criminal court. Convictions were no more likely in the criminal court than were adjudications in the juvenile court. Punishment was swifter in the juvenile court (100 days to sentencing in juvenile court compared to 145 days in the criminal court). The likelihood of incarceration was initially greater in the criminal court but declined as the composition of court cases changed. Sentence lengths were almost identical. Recidivism rates appeared to be higher among criminal court cases. Reoffending occurred more quickly among transferred juveniles, who also were more likely to be returned to confinement. In an analysis of factors that might account for the greater deterrent effects of juvenile court handling, Fagan (1995, p. 254) suggested that more severe criminal court sanctions "may actually enhance the likelihood of recidivism." He concluded that "the effect of juvenile court over adult court case processing is positive and quite substantial" (p. 251). Fagen suggested that his findings raise new questions concerning efforts over the past decade to narrow the jurisdiction of the juvenile court.

A 10-state comparison (Butts & Connors-Beatty, 1992) of juvenile and criminal court dispositions of comparable cases during 1985-1989 was limited to violent offenses (homicide, violent sex offenses, robbery, and aggravated assault). Butts and Connors-Beatty compared outcomes for 16-17-year-olds in the 10 states' juvenile courts with dispositions for adults in 14 states included in the Bureau of Justice Statistics OBTS[3] system. Violent juveniles were more likely to receive some type of sanction in juvenile court than were adult violent offenders in criminal court, although the criminal court was more likely to incarcerate the adults. Juvenile courts petitioned 78% of all cases involving violent offenses, while criminal courts prosecuted 79% of such cases. Criminal courts incarcerated 32%, versus 24% in juvenile court. Overall, 53% of the violent offense cases handled in juvenile court were placed on probation, put in out-of-home placement, or waived to criminal court. In comparison, criminal courts ordered probation or incarceration in 41% of their comparable violent adult cases.

In their Minnesota study, Podkopacz and Feld (1995; see also Podkopacz & Feld, 1996) compared the dispositions received by youth retained in the juvenile court with those waived to the criminal court. The differences were significant in several areas. More than two-thirds (74%) of the retained juveniles were placed in confinement (54% were committed to a long-term juvenile correctional facility and 20% were placed in a short-term treatment facility), 14% were dismissed, and 12% were placed on probation. Among the juveniles waived to criminal court, 25% were imprisoned, 57% received a stayed prison term and were placed in

jail, 8% received only a jail term, 7% received probation, and only 3% were dismissed. Juveniles convicted in criminal court for presumptive offenses served about 4 years, whereas youths adjudicated in juvenile court for these offenses served about 9 months.

Examination of recidivism among the two groups also showed significant differences. Overall, 55% of all juveniles on whom prosecutors filed transfer motions were adjudicated or convicted of a new offense within 7 years. After restricting the analysis to juveniles who had 2 or more years of "street time" to commit offenses, 52% were adjudicated or convicted of a new offense. Comparison of the transferred juveniles with those not transferred revealed that 58% of the group referred to criminal court was convicted of a new offense, compared to 42% of the youths retained in juvenile court. Podkopacz and Feld offered three possible explanations for the lower juvenile court recidivism rate: (a) by emphasizing prior records, juvenile courts may have succeeded in identifying the most chronic offenders for transfer; (b) the greater effectiveness of treatment in the juvenile justice system; or (c) the failure of the criminal justice system to deter juveniles from committing offenses by applying more severe punishment.

Only one study has compared the experiences of youths while confined in juvenile correctional facilities and in prisons. In a research component of Fagan's evaluation of OJJDP's Violent Juvenile Offender Program, Forst, Fagan, and Vivona (1989) interviewed nontransferred youths subsequently incarcerated in juvenile training schools and youths transferred to criminal court, who were later imprisoned. The juvenile sample was interviewed on release, after nearly 3 years of confinement. Juveniles confined in prison were interviewed while incarcerated, after an average stay of nearly 2 years. All youths in the study were adjudicated for violent offenses between 1981 and 1984 in Boston, Memphis, Detroit, or Newark.

The youths' assessment of treatment services favored the juvenile training schools. Services in juvenile training schools were rated higher in three of five areas: medical care, counseling, and family relations. Respondents rated juvenile and adult facilities about the same for educational and vocational programs. Although property crime victimization rates were about the same for the two groups (over half of the residents), 37% of the juveniles in training schools versus 47% of juvenile prison inmates suffered violent victimization, much of it at the hands of staff. "Juveniles in adult prisons appear to suffer rape, aggravated assault, and other violent assaults at a far greater rate than juveniles who remain in the comparatively benign environment of a training school" (p. 9). Sexual assault was five times as likely in prison, beatings by staff were nearly twice as likely, and attacks with weapons were almost 50% more common. To compound the sexual assault problem, a recent study (Brien & Beck, 1996) found that the overall rate of confirmed AIDS among the nation's prison population is more than seven times the rate in the general population.

These studies have yielded the most definitive findings regarding the outcomes of juvenile justice versus criminal justice system handling of serious, violent, and chronic juvenile offenders. They provide a sufficient basis for several generalizable conclusions. On one hand, juveniles are more likely to receive some sanction in the juvenile court than in the criminal court. On the other hand, among those who receive sanctions in either court, the criminal court is more likely to confine youngsters, and for longer periods of time. As Bishop et al. (1996) concluded in their Florida study, however, the short-term gains achieved by incapacitation are offset by higher recidivism rates and more frequent offending among transferred juveniles.

National Trends

The number of juvenile cases handled in criminal courts is unknown. Only one nationwide study has been conducted—18 years ago. Hamparian et al. (1982) estimated that in 1978, more than 9,000 juveniles were judicially waived to criminal courts, more than 2,000 prosecutor transfers under concurrent jurisdiction statutes occurred nationwide, and more than 1,300 youths were prosecuted as adults because of excluded offense statutes. A reliable estimate could not be made of the number of juveniles tried in criminal courts as the result of lower maximum ages of juvenile court jurisdiction, which is the main mechanism for moving juveniles into criminal courts.

In 1989, an estimated 8,300 juvenile cases were judicially waived to criminal court. Judicial waivers increased 41% between 1989 and 1993, to 11,800. Waivers of person offenses increased 115%. The proportion of juvenile referrals judicially waived to criminal courts that were violent offense cases increased from 28% in 1989 to 42% in 1993. Property offense cases decreased from 49% of the cases waived in 1989 to 38% in 1993 (Butts, Snyder, Aughenbaugh, & Poole 1996; see also Snyder et al., 1996, pp. 28-29).

The proportion of all formally processed delinquency cases judicially waived to criminal courts increased slightly between 1989 and 1993 (from 1.4% to 1.5%), while the proportion of person offense cases increased from 2.0% to 2.7% and the proportion of drug cases decreased, from 2.8% to 2.2%. Although most (88%) judicially waived cases involved youths age 16 or older in 1993, this percentage decreased from 89% in 1988. The percentage of all judicially waived youth who were black increased during this period, from 49% to 52%, while the white percentage decreased from 49% to 45% (Butts et al., 1995; see also Snyder et al., 1996, p. 28).

Snyder and colleagues (1996) observe that the 58% increase in the number of person offense cases processed by juvenile courts between 1989 and 1993 cannot completely explain the increase in the number of cases judicially waived. They suggest (p. 28) that the greater increase (115%) in waived cases involves such other factors as

- an increase between 1989 and 1993 in the level of violence found in person cases;
- a general decline in the amenability of youth for treatment within the juvenile justice system;
- an increase in the willingness of juvenile courts to transfer eligible cases;
- a decline in available treatment options within the juvenile justice system; and
- an expansion of the pool of juveniles eligible for judicial transfer (e.g., a reduction in the minimum age at which a youth may be transferred).

As Snyder and Sickmund (1995, p. 155) note, in most states juvenile courts have original jurisdiction over youth through age 17. In eight states, however, the upper age of original juvenile court jurisdiction has been set at 16, and it is set at 15 in three states. This means that in these 11 states, youth 15 or 16 years of age or older are subject to criminal prosecution for any offense. The National Center for Juvenile Justice estimates that in 1991, 176,000 juveniles below the age of 18 were handled in criminal courts because state legislatures set the age of adult responsibility for crime at 16 or 17 (Snyder & Sickmund, 1995, p. 155).

No estimate is available of the number of juveniles transferred to criminal court as a result of state laws providing for "concurrent jurisdiction," in which prosecutors decide in which court to file charges. The number of states with such statutory provisions is increasing (Fritsch & Hemmens, 1995). Recall that Hamparian and colleagues (1982) estimated that there were 2,000 prosecutor "direct files" in 1978. In 1993, Florida prosecutors alone filed criminal charges in 7,000 cases involving offenders under the age of 18 (Snyder & Sickmund, 1995, p. 156).

The Virginia Commission on Youth (1994) surveyed all states' corrections agencies to obtain information on juvenile transfers within each state during 1988-1990. Only six states were unable to report data on transfers during this period. The number of juveniles transferred, convicted, and sentenced in criminal courts increased 39% between 1988 and 1990, from 5,797 to 8,067 in 43 states and the District of Columbia (Virginia Commission on Youth, 1994, p. 17). Transfers per capita of juveniles were calculated. These ranged from 4.88 per 10,000 juveniles in Connecticut to 0.0 in North Dakota (p. 17).

The General Accounting Office (1995) conducted a nationwide study of juvenile transfers to criminal courts, required in the 1992 Amendments (P.L. 102-586) to the Juvenile Justice and Delinquency Prevention Act of 1974 (P.L. 93-415). As of 1994, the GAO identified 47 states with judicial waiver laws, 10 states and the District of Columbia with prosecutor direct file laws, and 37 states and the District of Columbia with one or more statutory exclusion laws. A total of 21 states have provisions allowing criminal court judges to transfer cases from criminal court to juvenile court under certain statutorily specified circumstances (reverse waiver). In addition, 19 states allow a juvenile prosecuted and convicted in criminal court to receive a disposition as a juvenile under specified circumstances (pp. 7-8).

The number of juveniles transferred to criminal courts by either prosecutor direct file, legislative exclusion, or lower age of juvenile court jurisdiction could not be determined. The GAO estimated that 11,748 juvenile delinquency cases were judicially waived to criminal courts in 1992, compared to 7,005 in 1988, an increase of 33% (p. 10).

The GAO's analysis of statutory changes indicated that since 1978, 44 states and the District of Columbia have passed laws affecting which juveniles may be sent to criminal court. In 24 states and the District of Columbia, the laws tend to increase the number of juveniles potentially subject to transfer to criminal court. In 3 states, the new laws decrease the number of potential transfers. In 17 states, the new laws change the methods by which certain juveniles are sent to criminal court but may not affect the number of potential transfers (p. 19).

Data from six states were analyzed to assess the relationship between the probability of judicial transfer and selected case characteristics. This analysis showed that (a) older juveniles were more likely to be transferred than younger juveniles, (b) juveniles with prior referrals were more likely to be transferred, and (c) blacks were more likely than whites to be transferred in four of the six states.

The GAO used OBTS data to analyze the conviction rates and the number of juveniles prosecuted in criminal court in seven states for selected offenses in 1989 and 1990. The selected states represented a variety of transfer methods (judicial, legislative, and prosecutorial). Conviction rates ranged from 32% in New York to 100% in Minnesota for serious violent offenses. A similar pattern was observed for serious property offenses, ranging from 26% in New York to 97% in Minnesota and Vermont (p. 21).

A comparison was made between the conviction rates for 16-17-year-olds beyond the maximum age of juvenile court jurisdiction in their state and the rates for 18-24-year-olds in the same states and in five other states. This analysis showed that generally, for some offenses, juveniles were as likely as young adults to be convicted in criminal court. Among both age groups, the largest percentage of convictions were for property offenses in five of the seven states (pp. 22-23).

The GAO analyzed sentencing patterns in the original seven states. More than half of the juveniles sentenced in criminal court for serious violent, serious property, or drug offenses were incarcerated in four of the seven states. No consistent pattern was observed. For serious violent offenses, the percentages incarcerated ranged from 29% in Vermont to 98% in Minnesota. Comparison of 16-17-year-olds' (above the maximum age of juvenile court jurisdiction) incarceration rates with those of 18-24-year-olds in the same states (Missouri and New York) showed that incarceration rates for juveniles were higher than the rates for young adults (pp. 23-24).

A nationally representative sample of prosecutors was surveyed by the GAO to gather their opinions on the processing of juveniles in criminal court. A total of 226 responses was received, for an 84% response rate. Surveyed prosecutors were asked, "When considering whether to send or recommend sending a juvenile to criminal court rather than to juvenile court, what are the three most important factors that you are likely to consider?" Table 5.2 shows the percentages of the 226 respondents indicating that a particular item is one of the three most important factors. These responses are ambiguous. Whereas prosecutors attach great weight (85% of respondents) to seriousness of the offense (put in terms of drug involvement, guns, and destruction of property), they give relatively little weight (only 17%) to whether the offense was against other persons (put in terms of injury to others). Although none of the respondents indicated family background of the offender is important, Singer (1994, 1996) found this to be the most important explanation of prosecutor transfer motions in New York. Surprisingly, only 19% said the need to protect the community was important, only 5% said the prosecutive merit of the complaint was important, and only 5% attached priority importance to the availability of more serious punishments in criminal court. Further research will be required to resolve these apparent discrepancies.

Incarcerated Juveniles

This section presents data on juveniles incarcerated in juvenile justice system facilities and adult prisons. The aim is to assess the extent to which serious, violent, and chronic juvenile offenders are populating these respective systems of confinement.

Juveniles in Juvenile Justice Corrections Facilities

In 1992, an estimated 33,961 youngsters were admitted to state juvenile correctional facilities in 29 states that contributed data to the

TABLE 5.2 General Accounting Office Prosecutor Survey Results

Characteristic	Percentage
Family background of the offender	0
The offender's age	21
The offender's age in relation to the *upper* age of juvenile court jurisdiction	17
The offender's age in relation to the *extended* age of juvenile court jurisdiction	3
Sophistication and maturity of the offender	7
Seriousness of the alleged offense (e.g., involved drugs, guns, destruction of property)	85
Whether the offense was against other persons (e.g., involved victim injury)	17
Whether adult offenders were involved in the offense	1
Whether the offender is a repeat offender	57
The availability of more serious punishments in criminal court	5
The availability of a youthful offender facility	1
The need to protect the community	19
Whether the offender has been determined to be unamenable to rehabilitation	44
Prosecutive merits of complaint	5
Other factors	3

SOURCE: *Juvenile Justice: Juveniles Processed in Criminal Court and Case Dispositions*, General Accounting Office, 1995.

State Juvenile Corrections Reporting Program (DeComo et al., 1995). Of these, about 21% were committed for serious and violent offenses (UCR Part I). More than half of the juveniles admitted to these facilities in 1992 were charged with property and drug crimes and were experiencing their first commitment to a state institution.

The serious and violent juveniles who entered state juvenile facilities were principally charged with robbery or aggravated assault (35% and 40%, respectively), and 27% had previous histories of juvenile incarceration. About 11% of serious and violent juvenile offenders were committed for various types of homicide or manslaughter. Another 12% were charged with sex crimes.

These incarcerated serious and violent juvenile offenders were overwhelmingly males

(95%). More than half were black youths (56%), and 21% were of Hispanic ethnicity. Their modal age at admission was 16 years. These youngsters were most likely to be admitted to a secure training school (85%) and were released from the same type of facility after an average incarceration period of slightly more than 8 months. The majority of these youngsters received no diagnostic study or evaluation by the state juvenile corrections authority. Two-thirds were released to parole or aftercare services; 14% were completely discharged. One percent of this group were certified as adults and moved to the prison system.

Of those serious and violent juvenile offenders who were released in 1992 and might have returned to the juvenile corrections system (that is, they were 16 or younger at release), 25% were reinstitutionalized within 12 months of their release, which is comparable to the adult prison reincarceration rate (Beck & Shipley, 1987, 1989). The average time until readmission was slightly more than 5 months. Those released youths who were 14 years of age or younger were more likely to be returned to state facilities than older youths. This finding may reflect a combination of policy factors (the decision to keep these youths in the juvenile justice system), the very high level of risk factors exhibited by youngsters who are incarcerated early in their adolescence, and the longer period of eligibility. The returning youngsters were likely to have previous periods of state incarceration.

We saw in Chapter 4 that barely half (51%) of juveniles admitted to state prisons in 1992 were charged with a violent offense (Perkins, 1994). These data on juveniles in the respective systems suggest that neither system has a preponderance of the most serious, violent, and chronic juvenile offenders. Reincarceration rates appear to be similar, comparing serious and violent juvenile offenders to the total population of adult prisoners. Both systems are overpopulated with black youngsters.

New transfer laws will have a particularly deleterious effect on minority juveniles, especially black youngsters. For example, although only 15% of all U.S. juveniles aged 10-17 are black, in 1991 they accounted for 26% of all juvenile arrests, 49% of all violent juvenile arrests, 32% of all juvenile court referrals for delinquency, 44% of all adjudications for person offenses, and 52% of all cases waived to the criminal justice system by juvenile courts (Snyder & Sickmund, 1995, p. 91). The disproportionate representation of black youngsters in all stages of the juvenile justice system inevitably means that as transfers are increased, their greater prevalence in the pool of eligibles will result in disproportionate selection for transfer.

Summary

Zimring (1981b, p. 193) characterizes transfer to the criminal justice system as "the capital punishment of juvenile justice." It is the most severe disposition that can be given to youngsters in the juvenile justice system. It is important, therefore, to know the consequences of choosing this policy option.

It is surprising how little information is available on criminal justice system handling of juvenile offenders. For the most part, available studies cover only judicial waivers, yet these cases represent less than 10% of juveniles that are moved into the criminal justice system. Few studies have been made on the remaining 90% of juveniles tried in criminal court under legislative provisions and direct files by prosecutors under concurrent jurisdiction statutes. Moreover, nothing is known about the most frequently used mechanism for transferring juveniles into the criminal justice system, lower age of juvenile court jurisdiction. Snyder and Sickmund (1995, p. 155) estimate that in 1991, 176,000 juveniles below the age of 18 were handled in criminal courts because state legislatures set the age of adult responsibility for crime at 16 or 17. We know nothing about their fate.

The studies and data available to date do not provide an adequate basis for drawing final conclusions regarding the relative merits of the judicial, legislative, and prosecutorial processes for transfer of juveniles to criminal court. Use of the studies to inform public policy is limited for several reasons. There is a lack of conceptual clarity in much of the research. The same terms (waiver and transfer) are used to refer to many different policies and practices. It is difficult to disentangle the roles that multiple actors (prosecutors, defense counsel, judges) play in the transfer determination. Moreover, few of the studies address the important antecedent practices, police charging decisions and plea bargaining, that are so crucial to subsequent transfer results. Transfer is a sociolegal policy based on very little information. As Krisberg (personal communication, December 15, 1995) put it, "We have a policy (of increased use of the transfer mechanism) in search of a foundation."

The studies we reviewed suggest some general observations. First, there are enormous disparities from state to state and within states in the transfer of juveniles to the criminal justice system, with respect to offense severity, offense history, age, conviction rates, and incarceration rates. Most of this variation appears to be associated with political and organizational vagaries rather than differences in offenders from one jurisdiction to another. There is little agreement among transfer decision makers, a lack of formal transfer hearings, and inconsistent application of transfer criteria. Second, there are gross inequities in the transfer and incarceration of minority versus nonminority juveniles. Although it is clear that black youths are disproportionately selected for transfer, conviction, and incarceration in adult prisons, the sources of this disparity are spread throughout the system (see Fagan et al., 1987, for a detailed discussion). Third, there is an enormous disparity in the length of confinement from one state to another for transferred juveniles. In some cases, juveniles are confined for longer periods than adults for comparable crimes. Fourth, there are significant delays in the entire justice system process, even in programs that target chronic and violent offenders, that impede the administration of justice and system effectiveness. Fifth, generally fewer than one-half of the transferred juveniles have juvenile correctional treatment made available to them. Neither treatment nor graduated sanctions have been given the opportunity to fail for them, partly because of a lack of postdispositional programs. Sixth, the current trend is to transfer more and more juveniles to the criminal justice system (Torbet et al., 1996). Early in the history of this movement, the claim was made, in the absence of empirical support, that the criminal justice system was more effective than the juvenile justice system, as one basis for justifying more transfers. Evidence is fast mounting that the criminal justice system is much less effective in achieving public safety goals. The lack of treatment in adult prisons is the obvious explanation. Sherman (1993), however, argues that punishment increases the likelihood of recidivism when offenders perceive that authorities are acting unjustly. This is most likely to occur when the offender feels alienated, either from the sanctioning agent or the community the agent represents. Sherman hypothesizes that angry pride is provoked by the sanctioning agent, which predisposes the offender to repeat the sanctioned conduct.

Research to date suggests several unintended consequences of transfer of juveniles to the criminal justice system. While awaiting trial in criminal court, juveniles may be transferred from detention centers to adult jails in 42 states (Coalition for Juvenile Justice, 1994, p. 17). Many juveniles are confined in adult jails even though they may never be tried in criminal court or may be acquitted. Because of the lengthier criminal court processing time, such punishment raises issues of fairness and "right to treatment." Some states incarcerate small percentages of juveniles in jails in lieu of prison. Jailing cannot be said to contribute to rehabilitation and, more important, the juvenile suicide rate in jails is five times as high as the rate in the general youth population and eight times the rate for juveniles in detention centers (Community Research Center, 1980). Second, juveniles are far more likely to be violently victimized in adult prisons than in juvenile correctional facilities (Forst et al., 1989). Third, transferred juveniles create new problems for the adult corrections system (Forst et al., 1989), including development of treatment and reintegrative services, and protection from predatory inmates. Fourth, transfer of more and more juveniles to the criminal justice system will leave a residual group of less serious offenders in the juvenile justice system, the only group on whom substantial rehabilitation will be attempted. What are the long-term consequences of not providing adequate treatment for adolescents transferred to the criminal justice system? What will 15-17-year-old imprisoned juveniles' offending proclivities be like when they are released, say 5-10 years later, at ages 20-27? Given higher recidivism rates, more immediate offending, and more frequent offending among imprisoned juveniles following their release (Bishop et al., 1996; Fagan, 1995; Podkopacz & Feld, 1995, 1996; White, 1985), how much will their criminal careers be accelerated or prolonged? How much will their offending add to the overall volume of crime? As Rudman et al. (1986) put it, "we must ask if we are safer from a youth who has spent one to three years in a system designed to 'treat' him, or from a youth who has spent 10-15 years in a system designed to 'punish' him" (p. 94).

Much has been made of the "leniency gap" between juvenile and criminal courts. It does not appear to be significant with respect to the likelihood of sanctions. In contrast, little has been made of the "treatment gap" between juvenile and adult correctional systems. Forst and his colleagues' (1989) study of juveniles' experiences in both types of facilities stands alone. In addition to finding higher victimization rates of juveniles in adult prisons than in juvenile facilities, their study (Forst et al., 1989) shows that juveniles in reform schools evaluate more positively the medical care, treatment programs, and the maintenance of family contact in facilities designed for them.

Three main conclusions regarding the efficacy of particular transfer mechanisms can be drawn from this review. First, judges appear to be more adept than prosecutors or state legislatures in selecting serious, violent, and chronic offenders for transfer. In fact, only 9 of 23 states that enacted legislative waiver legislation between 1979 and 1995 included prior adjudications/convictions in their criteria (Fritsch & Hemmens, 1995). Second, judges appear more likely to incorporate graduated sanctions in their dispositions. Studies to date indicate that juveniles they select for transfer are more likely to have been exposed to juvenile justice system treatment. The fact that this proportion is not particularly high, however, suggests that judges need more postdispositional resources (Virginia Commission on Youth, 1994). Third, legislative exclusion of adolescents from juvenile court and prosecutorial transfer (direct file) appear to have very few positive features. The main one is that these mechanisms ensure that offenders are transferred for a violent offense. This benefit comes at a high price. It appears to be offset by greater disparity in the transfer of minority versus nonminority youth, because of the exclusive use of official records in making the transfer determination. The major disadvantage of increasing the role of prosecutors in making the transfer decision is that this method is subject to more potential for abuse than judicial waiver (Thomas & Bilchik, 1985, p. 478). Most judicial powers are exercised in open court and subject to appeal. Prosecutorial powers commonly are exercised in private. "Thus, whether for better or worse, the fact is that the most peculiar fea-

ture of our juvenile and criminal justice process is that it involves a fairly elaborate set of checks and balances on the conduct and the decisions of all but one set of actors: prosecutors" (Thomas & Bilchik, 1985, p. 478).

In sum, the United States needs a jurisprudence of transfer (Zimring, 1981b). The key substantive question, as Zimring (p. 193) put it, is this:

> When is it appropriate to treat the subjects of the juvenile justice system charged with serious offenses as if they were adults and banish them to prison for long terms? To put the matter less charitably, "When are juveniles not juveniles?"

Developing a jurisprudence of transfer presents a formidable challenge. The major obstacle is that we are not capable of defining into formal law the nuances of situation, intent, and social harm that characterize the seriousness of particular criminal acts (Zimring, 1981b). Transfer policies based on police arrests alone may mean that in many instances the most dangerous juvenile offenders are not sent to the criminal justice system. An unfortunate result of the Philadelphia birth cohort study (Wolfgang et al., 1972) is that it encouraged the use of official records only in the analysis of offender careers. Data on the numbers and characteristics of serious and chronic juvenile offenders in the juvenile justice system do not appear to provide an accurate representation of offender careers (Elliott, 1995; see Chapter 4). Elliot's discovery of a low correlation between official arrests and self-reported Index offenses indicates that arrested juveniles are not representative of actual serious, violent, and chronic juvenile offenders. Given this weak relationship, even if one were to assume a deterrent effect from imprisonment, the end result would be a minimal impact on overall crime levels.

Until such time as research demonstrates greater effectiveness of criminal justice system handling of juveniles, beyond the satisfaction retribution brings, it appears that our society would be better served by more judicious use of imprisonment for juvenile offenders. We have yet to give the juvenile justice system the resources needed to work effectively. Although we lack specific knowledge regarding what programs work best in rehabilitating serious and violent juvenile offenders with particular characteristics and at specific points in their careers, recent meta-analyses and other program assessments by Andrews and colleagues (1990); Brewer, Hawkins, Catalano, and Neckerman (1995); Farrington (1995); Krisberg, Currie, Onek, and Wiebush (1995); Lipsey (1992a); and Montgomery et al. (1994), have identified hundreds of promising programs, about two dozen of which can be said to be effective in preventing and reducing serious, violent, and chronic delinquency. This program information can be combined with advanced techniques for identifying offenders who represent the greatest threat to the public safety and tools that implement policy decisions regarding offenders who require secure confinement (which can be provided in juvenile facilities), thereby achieving the priority goal of ensuring public safety. A comprehensive strategy that can accomplish this is outlined in Chapter 9.

Notes

1. "Transfer" is used in this chapter as a generic term referring to all three vehicles for moving juveniles from the juvenile justice system to the criminal justice system (judicial waiver, prosecutorial direct file, and legislative exclusion).

2. Transfer is presumed for the most serious/violent offenses committed by 16-17-year-olds unless the juvenile can prove that he or she should remain in juvenile court. Presumptive offenses carry with them an expected or normal sentence for each particular offense, usually with a small amount of deviation.

3. Offender Based Transaction System.

Part II

Part II contains solutions to juvenile violence. We begin with youth gang violence in Chapter 6. The chapter includes an analysis of youth gang homicides and recommended program approaches for reducing these and youth gang problems in general. Chapter 7 reviews risk factors for youth violence. Chapter 8 presents "developmental criminology," a way of examining serious, violent, and chronic juvenile delinquency that should lead to a better understanding of offending. Finally, in Chapter 9, a comprehensive strategy for serious, violent, and chronic juvenile delinquency is presented. This chapter also illustrates how this comprehensive strategy can be implemented.

6

Youth Gang Homicides, Drug Trafficking, and Program Interventions

The Research Question

When the crack cocaine epidemic hit Los Angeles (and other cities) in the early- to mid-1980s, gang-related violence was reported to have increased in California (Philibosian, 1989). The two developments appeared to be interrelated. The popular theory promulgated in the media (Klein, 1995, pp. 120-121; Spergel, 1995, p. 47), by local governmental agencies (California Council on Criminal Justice, 1989), by the United States Congress (Clark, 1991; General Accounting Office, 1989), and by the executive branch of the federal government (Drug Enforcement Administration, 1988; Hayeslip, 1989; McKinney, 1988) was that youth gangs were instrumental in the increase in crack cocaine sales, and that their involvement in drug trafficking resulted in increased use of guns in these transactions and a growth in homicides.

A subsequent national conference concluded that "it is well known that gang members are key players in the illegal drug trade," and that "there is clear evidence . . . that the demand for drugs, especially crack cocaine, has led to the migration of Los Angles gang members across the country" (Bryant, 1989, pp. 2-3). The threat that youth gangs represented to the nation seemed apparent. "The fierce circle of drugs, profits, and violence threatens the freedom and public safety of citizens from coast to coast. It holds in its grip large jurisdictions and small ones, urban areas and rural ones" (Donahue, cited in Bryant, 1989, p. 1).

These views about gang involvement in drug trafficking seemed very plausible to law enforcement, the media, and political officials because of several assumptions (see Klein, Maxson, & Cunningham, 1991, pp. 623-625). Youth gangs seemed ideally suited for rapid, organized, and controlled distribution of crack cocaine. They already were located in the inner-city communities where the new drug was in demand. Their presumed organizational and territorial characteristics established their amenability to drug trafficking. Gangs must have been attracted to the distribution opportunity that crack cocaine, in its condensed form, provided at the neighborhood-level. Surely mid-level distributors would find youth gangs ideal for employment in the drug trade because of their violence readiness. Thus, it seemed that youth gangs could be instrumental in enforcing necessary control of drug trafficking territories. An escalation in the number of homicides would be one result.

Blumstein (1995a, 1995b, 1996; also see National Institute of Justice, 1995) has recently reintroduced a hypothesized process by which increased adolescent possession of firearms occurs, first suggested by Strodtbeck and Short

AUTHOR'S NOTE: This chapter summarizes two reports prepared by the author that review youth gang literature "Youth Gang Homicides and Drug Trafficking" (Howell, 1997a), and "Youth Gang Violence Prevention: What Works" (Howell, 1987b).

(1964, p. 134) in their classic study (Short & Strodtbeck, 1965) of Chicago youth gang behavior. Like Strodtbeck and Short, Blumstein contends that juveniles who participate in the illicit drug industry are very likely to carry guns for self-protection. His statement of the diffusion notion is that

> Since a reasonable number of juveniles can be involved in the drug industry in communities where the drug market is active, and since juveniles are tightly "networked," at school or on the street, other juveniles are also likely to arm themselves. Again, the reason is a mixture of self-protection and status seeking. Thus begins an escalation: as more guns appear in the community, the incentive for any single individual to arm himself increases, and so a local "arms race" develops. (1995a, p. 6)

Blumstein (1995a, 1995b, 1996) expands this notion, suggesting a connection among juveniles (mainly nonwhites), drug trafficking, and homicide. To support his hypothesis, Blumstein presents FBI Uniform Crime Report data on age-specific arrest rates for drug offenses and murder during the period 1965-1992. He argues that his hypothesis provides an explanation of the sharp increase in juvenile gun-related homicides during this period, especially among nonwhite youths (1995a, pp. 7-8; see also Fox, 1996).

Are the popular assumptions valid? Does Blumstein's hypothesis apply to youth gangs? This chapter first reviews research and data on the involvement of youth gangs in drug trafficking and homicides. The history of youth gang programming then is reviewed. Finally, suggestions are made for reducing youth gang homicides and gang participation.

Gang Drug Trafficking

The extent of gang involvement in drug use and trafficking has become a matter of debate (Howell, 1995a, 1997a; Klein, 1995; Moore, 1990; Spergel, 1995). A United States Congress study (General Accounting Office, 1989) concluded that during the latter part of the 1980s, the Crips and Bloods gained control of 30% of the crack cocaine market in the United States. Another federal agency, the Drug Enforcement Administration (1988) claimed links between

these Los Angeles street gangs and drug sales in 46 states. Police and FBI officials claimed that by the late 1980s, the Los Angeles Bloods and Crips had migrated to 45 other cities and set up crack cocaine trafficking operations (Skolnick, 1989, p. 13). According to Skolnick (1989), most of the drug trafficking in the two cities most often said to be gang migration cities, Kansas City and Seattle, attributed to Crips and Bloods has been carried out by older, former members of these gangs, and "wanna bes," (youngsters aspiring gang membership), although they may be supplied by the Los Angeles gangs. He reports evidence of extensive drug trafficking gangs in Southern California, based mainly on interviews with prison inmates.

Shortly after these reports were made, the Los Angeles County district attorney prepared a comprehensive report on youth gangs (Reiner, 1992). It concluded that "gang members are heavy drug users and even heavier drug sellers [than nongang youth], yet drugs and gangs are not two halves of the same phenomenon. Though they threaten many of the same neighborhoods, and involve some of the same people, gangs and drugs must be treated as separate evils" (p. 5). Reiner concluded that "most gang members are not drug dealers in any meaningful sense of the word" because of their infrequent involvement. Only one in seven gang members sells as often as 12 times a year (pp. 4-5). Reiner also concluded that "most L. A. gangs are not being transformed into organized drug distribution rings. Many individual gang members (and former members) are involved with drugs, but drugs remain peripheral to the purposes and activities of the gang" (p. 5).

Some researchers contend that proliferation of the drug trade gave many gangs a new purpose and contributed to their becoming more organized and businesslike (Sanchez-Jankowski, 1991; Skolnick, 1989; Skolnick, Correl, Navarro, & Rabb, 1990; Taylor, 1990a, 1990b). Anderson and Rodriguez (1984), Dolan and Finney (1984), Erlanger (1979), and Waldorf (1993) documented the economic opportunities drug sales provided to gang members. Spergel (1984) reported that youth gangs controlled drug sales in several Chicago neighborhoods. Philibosian (1989) documented Hispanic gang use and sales of PCP and marijuana. Chin (1989) reported active involvement of Chinese gang leaders in the New York City heroin trade. The Chicago Puerto Rican gang that Padilla

(1992) studied was extensively involved in drug trafficking; however, drug sales were not well organized. Taylor (1990b) contends that in Detroit, the drug economy has turned gangs into businesses, noting two developments: (a) an intermixing of juveniles, adults, males, and females in drug selling; and (b) out-of-state operations. Taylor thus (1990b) reports that the Detroit "scavenger" gangs of the 1950s-1970s have been transformed into "corporate" gangs involved in illegal money-making ventures, including drug trafficking.

Other research in New York City (Goldstein, 1985) has tied violence to drug dealing, but not to gangs. Inciardi (cited in Moore, 1990) reported that a media connection was made in Miami between gang activity and crack dealing. Miami grand juries empaneled in 1985 and again in 1988 (after a substantial increase in the number of gangs), however, found that youth gangs were not involved in crack dealing (Dade County Grand Jury, 1985, 1988). Decker and Van Winkle (1994, 1996) found St. Louis gang members to be extensively involved in cocaine trafficking; however, more than half of the members could not specify roles played by particular members in drug sales, and few reported that they joined the gang for the opportunity to sell drugs. The crack distribution network Adler (1995) studied in Detroit had virtually no gang involvement. Chin and Fagan (1990) found no evidence of drug trafficking among New York City gangs. Vigil and Yun (1990) report that drug dealing is shunned among Vietnamese gangs. Chein, Gerard, Lee, and Rosenfeld (1964) reported very low drug usage among the New York city gangs they studied, as did Robin (1967) in his research on Philadelphia gangs. Some studies have identified gangs that do not use or sell drugs (Chin, 1990a, 1990b).

Gang Drug Trafficking and Migration

Several studies have specifically examined the involvement of youth gangs in the crack cocaine epidemic. In the first of a series of Los Angeles gang studies, Klein, Maxson, and Cunningham (1988) examined the participation of street gangs in the sale of crack cocaine between 1983 and 1985, analyzing arrest data in community areas in which both crack and gangs were prominent. Gang arrests were compared to all arrests for cocaine sales (87% of which involved crack). Klein and his colleagues found

that all cocaine trafficking arrest incidents rose 375% during the study period, but this explosion was not dominated by gang involvement. Although the proportion of gang-related cocaine sales arrest incidents accounted for by gang-involved youth increased (from 9% in 1983 to 25% in 1985), this increase represented an insignificant proportion of the total increase in cocaine trafficking arrests.

In a later report on this study, Klein and colleagues (1991) specifically examined crack dealing in Los Angeles, covering the period 1983-1985. They tested two propositions: first, that youth gangs were ideally suited for distribution of crack cocaine, because of their presumed organizational and territorial characteristics; and second, that mid-level distributors employed them to enforce drug trafficking rules and control territorial domains (p. 625). Neither hypothesis proved to be correct. "During this three-year period, the explosion in cocaine sales was engaging a number of street gang members, but it was in no way dominated by gang involvement" (p. 628). "The increase in gang involvement was primarily at the low-volume, street level of sales" (p. 647).

Maxson (1995) conducted a similar study in Pasadena and Pomona, California, to see if gang drug traffickers in smaller cities near Los Angeles were changing the character of drug sales. Gang members were involved in about 27% of gang arrests for cocaine trafficking and less frequently in noncocaine drug sales (about 12% of arrests). Maxson characterized gang involvement in drug distribution in these two smaller cities as "substantial, but not overwhelming" (p. 11). She concluded that "the clearest policy implication emerging from this study is the suggestion for narcotics enforcement to move away from gang specialization" (p. 12).

One study has examined the presumed migration of youth gangs across the country to test the assumption that gangs have spread nationwide, primarily to expand drug trafficking operations. Maxson, Woods, and Klein (1995) conducted a nationwide gang migration survey of law enforcement agencies in 1,105 U.S. cities in 1992 to assess the extent to which gangs are migrating from major urban areas such as Los Angeles and Chicago to smaller cities and towns. Among the surveyed jurisdictions, 710 reported some gang migration. The most common migration pattern was for social reasons, including family moves to improve their quality of life and to be near relatives and friends.

Among all gang migration cities, drug market expansion and pursuit of other criminal activities were said by law enforcement agencies to be the primary motivation in about one-third of the cities. Migrants usually arrived individually rather than with gang companions. Migration preceded emergence of local gangs in only 5% of the cities. Within-the-region was the most predominant migration pattern. Respondents in most (60%) gang migration cities said the primary source of migrants was typically within 100 miles. Nearly two-thirds (63%) of the respondents in gang migration cities said the migrants came from Los Angeles area cities, one-third indicated Chicago area cities, and smaller percentages indicated New York (12%) or Detroit (10%) as migration sources. Some migration for drug market expansion and other criminal activities involves traveling longer distances. This type of migration is less likely to follow a regional pattern.

Maxson and her colleagues concluded that

it is now clear that the reasons for gang migration are far more complex than has been portrayed by the media and some enforcement agencies. Drug franchising is not the principal driving force. Normal family residential changes are paramount along with a not uncommon desire to move into less gang-oriented communities. (Maxson et al., 1995, pp. 115-116)

In a separate report on the migration study, Klein (1995, p. 96) concluded that most all gang problems are "homegrown."

Youth Gang Homicides and Drug Trafficking

Several studies of youth gang homicides related to drug trafficking have been conducted in Chicago and Los Angeles. Other studies in Boston, St. Louis, and San Diego also have investigated the relationship. We review them to see if gang homicide increases are linked to gang involvement in drug trafficking.

Chicago Studies

In their original Chicago gang homicide study, covering the period 1987-1990, the Blocks (Block & Block, 1993, p. 9) found that only 3% of gang-motivated homicides were

drug-related. They concluded that "the connection between street gangs, drugs, and homicide was weak and could not explain the rapid increase in homicide in the late 1980s." Most gang violence was emotional defense of one's identity as a gang member, defense of the gang and gang members, defense and glorification of the reputation of the gang, gang member recruitment, and territorial expansion.

In a separate study (Block, 1993) of Latino gang-related homicides in the 1982-1989 period, in which drug-related homicides increased in the general Chicago population, Block found that this increase was independent of the increase in street-gang-related homicides. "Only about 2% of Chicago street gang-related homicides involved a drug-related motive, and fewer still involved an offender and a victim who were under the influence of drugs at the time of the incident. In 1989, when Latino street-gang homicides increased, the proportion that were drug-related was even smaller" (p. 317).

The Blocks' meticulous gang research in Chicago has made enormous contributions to our knowledge of gang violence, especially homicides (Block, 1985a, 1985b, 1993; Block & Block, 1991, 1992, 1993; Block & Christakos, 1995). The following are perhaps their most important findings. Gang homicide occurs in spurts, unlike other types of homicide, which follow rather smooth trends. Gang homicides show trend patterns that vary from other homicide types in the city. There is a pattern of spurts in youth gang homicides that is evident in both Latino and black demographic groups. The two racial/ethnic groups, however, show different homicide incidence patterns, peaking at different points in time (Figure 6.1), suggesting that gang-related homicides are affected by unique factors that may not be related to other homicide types.

The Blocks' research has also shown that most gang violence is "expressive," related to defense of one's identity as a gang member, defense of the gang and gang members, defense and glorification of the reputation of the gang, gang member recruitment, and territorial expansion (although some of these activities serve instrumental purposes as well). A much smaller proportion of gang violence is "instrumental," involving formation and maintenance of a lucrative drug business and other entrepreneurial activities. Gang-related homicide patterns are driven by periods of escalation, re-

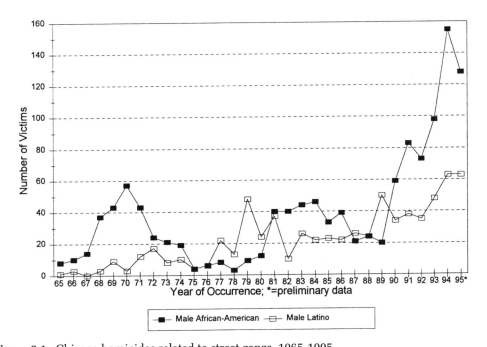

Figure 6.1. Chicago homicides related to street gangs, 1965-1995

DATA SOURCE: Chicago Homicide Dataset, a collaborative project of the Chicago Police Department, the Illinois Criminal Justice Information Authority, and Loyola University Chicago. Reprinted with permission.

taliation, and revenge, and are uniquely affected by such factors as weapon availability, the spatial arrangement of street gang territories, and characteristics of the drug market. Moreover, gang homicide patterns fluctuate significantly in relation to such factors and differ from one community area to another, despite the presence of similar gangs.

Los Angeles Studies

Two Los Angeles studies focused specifically on gang involvement in cocaine trafficking and related homicides. Klein and his colleagues (Klein et al., 1991) examined Los Angeles Police and Sheriff's Department data in community areas in which both crack and gangs were prominent during the major growth period for crack sales in Los Angeles (1983-1985). The proportion of firearms incidents connected to cocaine sales decreased from 34% in early 1984 to 21% in late 1985. Gang members were involved in crack distribution in about 25% of the arrest instances. Analysis of gang homicide investigative files revealed that 68% of all cases showed evidence of drug in-

volvement, compared to 56% of nongang homicides. Comparing gang and nongang homicides, they concluded that "the drug/homicide connection . . . is not basically a gang phenomenon" and that "the purported gang connection seems in most respects to have been considerably overstated" (pp. 646-647).

A subsequent study (Maxson, 1995) was conducted in Pasadena and Pomona, California (midsize suburban cities of Los Angeles), to test the popular perception of a close relationship between gangs, drug sales, and homicides. Both cities have a history of gang problems and more gang homicides than other midsize cities. Maxson's comparison of gang and nongang drug sales arrests revealed similar characteristics: Relatively small amounts of cocaine were involved, sales occurred on the street or in open settings, and firearms rarely were involved. Violence was present in only 5% of the sales incidents. Firearms were involved in only 10% of the incidents and showed a decreasing pattern of presence over time. Gang involvement did not increase significantly the violent character of drug sales.

Three youth-gang-related homicide studies have been conducted in Los Angeles by public health scientists. The first study (Meehan & O'Carroll, 1992) covered a period (1986-1988) during which the proportion of all Los Angeles homicides that were gang-related increased from 15% to 25%. The authors found that only 5% of gang-related homicides were narcotics related. Only 11% of narcotics-motivated homicides involved gangs. Empirical support could not be found in the data they examined for the popular theory that a substantial proportion of the increasing incidence of youth homicides in Los Angeles was attributable to the increasing involvement of gang members in illicit drug trafficking, drug use, or both. They concluded "that gang conflicts that result in a homicide are often independent of narcotics use and trafficking" and recommended that "gang activity and narcotics trafficking or use be addressed as separate, important risk factors for homicide rather than as interrelated cofactors" (p. 687). Meehan and O'Carroll also suggested that "it is quite possible that violence involving traditional youth street gangs that are loosely tied together by neighborhood allegiance is a phenomenon distinct from violence involving more highly organized institutional gangs or networks that exist for the purpose of marketing narcotics" (p. 687).

Hutson and his colleagues (Hutson et al., 1995) examined gang-related homicides in Los Angeles County during a 16-year period, 1979-1994. Over the entire period, gang-related murders represented 27% of all homicides. This figure increased from 18% in 1979 to 43% in 1994. In their epidemiological analysis, Hutson and colleagues attempted to isolate factors accounting for the increase in gang-related homicides. Several contributing factors were singled out, including an increase in the number of violent street gangs and gang members, increased gang violence, and an increase in the use of firearms in gang violence. Although some gang-related homicides occurred secondarily to drug trafficking, the study did not find drug transactions to be a major factor (p. 1034). Because the proportion of gang-related homicides involving firearms increased from 71% in 1979 to 95% in 1994, mainly because of the increased use of handguns, Hutson and his colleagues identified their use as a major factor contributing to the increase in gang-related homicides.

In a study of drive-by shootings in the city of Los Angeles in 1991, Hutson, Anglin, and Pratts (1994) found that an average of 49 drive-by shootings per month involving children occurred in the city in 1991. Among the total, 71% were gang members. A handgun was the most commonly used firearm (73%), and a semiautomatic weapon was used in 31% of the incidents (usually a 9 mm handgun). Analysis of arrest files led Hutson and his colleagues to conclude that, "contrary to the general assumption, drug trafficking is not a major causative factor [of drive-by shootings]" (p. 326).

Boston Study

Miller's (1994) analysis of Boston police arrest data covering 1984 to 1994 produced results similar to the Chicago and Los Angeles studies. Of 138 reported homicides categorized as "probably" or "definitely" gang related, only 10% involved drug use or dealing. Only 9% of 75 reported homicides categorized as "definitely" gang related involved drug use or dealing.

St. Louis Study

In their St. Louis study, Decker and Van Winkle (1996, pp. 185-186) found most gang violence, including homicides, to be "expressive," retaliatory, or situationally spontaneous. Although some violence was related to protection of drug turf and disciplining customers, most was related to gang members' proving their manhood, their toughness, or their hardness through initiations; to trespassing on rival territories; and to beating or shooting at the opposition. Violence erupts mainly over seemingly petty acts—disrespecting a color, stepping in front of another person, flashing hand signs, or driving through a rival neighborhood.

> Toughness, manliness, not backing down, are important values of their world and their psyches—to be upheld even at the cost of their own or others' lives. Whatever the "purpose" of violence, it often leads to retaliation and revenge creating a feedback loop where each killing requires a new killing. (p. 186).

San Diego Study

Sanders' (1994) San Diego study may be an exception to the research findings reported above. He reports that the rate of gang-related homicides in San Diego jumped from 3 per 100,000 population to 11 per 100,000 between 1985 and 1988, an increase he attributes largely to an increase in crack cocaine wars, mostly involving Crips and Bloods, sometimes against other gangs from Los Angeles. Sanders (1994) suggests that the increase in gang-related homicides is less related to traditional gang-motivated violence than to competition for money and turf in drug trafficking (i.e., crack cocaine wars), although he does not present substantiating data.

Discussion

Surprisingly, these studies do not support the popular image of youth gangs, that they were instrumental in the increase in crack cocaine sales and that their involvement in drug trafficking resulted in the growth of homicides. Studies conducted in Boston, Chicago, Los Angeles, and St. Louis suggest that these violent gang activities and narcotics trafficking should be viewed as separate, important risk factors for homicide rather than as interrelated co-factors. Three caveats must be offered. Some gang-related homicides are the result of drug trafficking, what Goldstein (1985) calls "systemic" crimes. Some gang homicides that might not be recorded as related to drug trafficking may be incidental to drug distribution; for example, when a gang member goes into another gang's territory to pick up drugs (Block et al., 1996). Although gangs may not be directly involved as an organization in drug trafficking, they may indirectly contribute by providing a protected environment for other groups to carry out drug trafficking operations (Short, personal communication, April 24, 1996).

There is little support for Blumstein's notion in the research we reviewed. At least for gang-related homicides, drug trafficking does not appear to be a major contributing factor. In fairness to Blumstein, he has not published a claim that his hypothesis applies specifically to youth gangs. Although his hypothesis may be valid for some gangs in certain cities, its generalizability seems very limited, perhaps to a few gangs that specialize in drug trafficking and to incidental situations. One reason that gang homicide studies provide little support for his hypothesis may be that the aggregate data Blumstein used to generate his hypothesis, the Uniform Crime Reports, are inadequate for examining local etiological processes such as the relationship among youth gangs, drug trafficking, and homicide.

The studies reviewed herein raise a more fundamental issue: the extent to which crack cocaine, as well as drug trafficking, is the province of youth gangs. There is no question that in some areas particular youth gangs are actively involved in drug trafficking. Moore (1990) concedes that some of the South Central Los Angeles gangs may well fit the popular stereotype, and, since 1985, more gangs may have become like this. It may be that some of the more loosely organized gangs will evolve to become organized criminal groups (Moore, 1988).

Some gangs that have a large, formal organizational structure are quite capable of managing drug trafficking operations. The Chicago Vice Lords specialize in drug trafficking (Block & Block, 1993). Moore (1990) contends that Detroit (Taylor, 1990a, 1990b) and New York (Sanchez-Jankowski, 1991) gang-trafficking organizations did not grow out of youth gangs; rather, they are criminal organizations that happen to call themselves gangs. Moore (1990) also makes a distinction between bona fide youth gangs and youthful criminal organizations (see Williams, 1989) that deal cocaine in New York. Fagan (1989) and others (Chin, 1990a, 1990b; Meehan & O'Carroll, 1992; Reiner, 1992; Spergel, 1995) suggest that drug trafficking is overwhelmingly controlled by adult criminal organizations. With respect to youth gang involvement in drug trafficking, Huff's (1993) conclusion appears to apply generally: that "the most common scenario appears to involve *individual* gang members in drug distribution networks that are neither gang controlled nor organized gang activities" (p. 10).

Moore's (1990) conclusions regarding Chicano involvement in drugs and violence seem applicable to youth gangs in general. She contends that the common stereotypes of the relationships among youth gangs, drugs, and violence are erroneous and sensationalized. Among Chicano gangs in East Los Angeles, violence is more a function of intergang conflict than of the drug trade. Her research on these gangs shows that most youth gangs are not involved in drug-related violent criminal activities. Where violence does occur, it stems from drug dealing by individual gang members or former gang members more than from activities of the youth gang as an organized entity. Her research suggests that the street groups extensively involved in criminal activities did not emerge from traditional youth gangs in Hispanic and black communities that existed before the crack cocaine epidemic. Rather, these groups grew out of criminal organizations formed solely for crack distribution and have few if any of the characteristics of traditional youth gangs.

Fagan's (1989) gang violence study of gang members in Los Angeles led to his conclusion that

> some [violent] incidents no doubt are precipitated by disputes over drug sales and selling territories, but the majority of violent incidents do not appear to involve drug sales. Rather, they continue to be part of the status, territorial, and other gang conflicts that historically have fueled gang violence. (pp. 660-661)

Fagan suggested that it may be that the most formally organized gangs are most extensively involved in drug use, drug trafficking, and violent crimes.

A surprising revelation in these studies is the limited extent to which assault weapons are used in gang-related homicides and drive-by shootings. The National Drug Intelligence Center informs us that "the semiautomatic pistol (especially the 9-millimeter) seems to be the weapon of choice for many street gang members, as opposed to military assault-style weapons" (NDIC, 1995, p. 2). None of the studies reviewed herein found extensive use of assault weapons by youth gangs. Hutson and colleagues (1995) found that assault weapons were used in only 3% of gang-related homicides in Los Angeles County during the period 1979-1994. In the study of Los Angeles drive-by shootings in 1991, only one of 677 shootings involved an assault weapon (Hutson, Anglin, & Pratts, 1994). The Blocks report increased used of automatic or semiautomatic handguns in Chicago gang-related homicides, especially from 1987 to 1993 (Block & Block, 1993; Block & Christakos, 1995).

Lack of gang use of assault weapons is not necessarily good news in the light of the rest of the weapon-related story. Gang homicides have increased significantly because of the proliferation of automatic and semiautomatic handguns. These are quite lethal. For example, in Chicago, from 1987 to 1990, virtually all the increase in gang-motivated homicides "seems attributable to an increase in the use of high-caliber, automatic, or semiautomatic weapons" (Block & Block, 1993, p. 7). In fact, Block and Block (1993) show that during a period in which there was no increase in street gang assaults, there was an increase in gang homicides, indicating that the lethality (deaths per incident) accounted for the greater number of homicides. Gangs have long been armed with some type of weapon (Newton & Zimring, 1969). As studies in the 1950s and 1960s show, homemade zip guns were very popular, but one never knew if they would fire, and if so, in what direction (Short, personal communication, April 24, 1996).

Gang Program Evaluations

Can the youth gang problem be solved? Miller (1974, p. 112) suggests that "it happens that great nations engage in national wars for almost identical reasons [that gangs do] . . . personal honor, prestige, and defense against perceived threats to one's homeland. . . . When a solution to this problem [of fighting nations has been found], we will at the same time have solved the problem of violent crimes in city gangs." Is there basis for more optimism than Miller expresses?

Miller (1990, p. 283) offers several factors that account for failure thus far to solve the youth gang problem in the United States. A comprehensive gang control strategy has not been developed, one that views the problem from a national perspective. Programs are implemented in the absence of proven theoretical rationales. Efforts to systematically evaluate program effectiveness have been virtually abandoned. Resources allocated to the gang problem are incommensurate with the severity of the problem.

Youth gang intervention is a formidable enterprise. Because we lack a clear understanding of why and how youth gangs form, preventing their formation is problematic. Gang interventions rarely are based on theoretical assumptions. This lack of knowledge impedes efforts to disrupt existing gangs and divert youth from them. Gangs dissolve and disappear for reasons that are poorly understood. In some cities, youths who join gangs leave them within about 1 year, yet we do not understand why. Future youth gang research must address the formation of gangs, disruptive forces, and factors that account for diversion of youths from gangs.

Evaluation of youth gang interventions is an equally complex undertaking. Not only must gang formation, dissolution, and diversion be shown, but also delinquency prevention or reduction. Because each youth gang is unique and each community is different in some respects, obtaining valid comparison groups or communities is difficult. Measurement problems abound. There is no commonly accepted definition of a youth gang; therefore, comparing study results is problematic. Most important, very few rigorous evaluations of youth gang programs have been undertaken.

With these caveats in mind, we recently reviewed the existing literature (Howell, 1997b). The general questions guiding this review were: What can we learn from what has been tried? What has failed? What looks promising? Space limitations here preclude discussion of the program literature. In sum, no single program has been demonstrated through rigorous evaluation to be effective in preventing or reducing gang violence. Like many other social problems, youth gang problems remain unsolved (Miller, 1990). The history of efforts to solve the youth gang problem in the United States is largely filled with frustration and failure. Three factors mainly account for this: the difficulties associated with gang intervention work, the complexity of program evaluation in this area, and the lack of evaluation studies.

Early in our nation's history, youth gang work emphasized prevention. These programs were followed by interventions designed to reintegrate particular gangs into conventional society, using detached workers. Detached workers were then put in automobiles, in crisis intervention programs. Then a major shift occurred as programs, led by the police, aimed to suppress youth gangs. These programs were followed by legislation that increased penalties for gang involvement and crime. Currently, a mixture of approaches is being tried across the nation, predominantly suppression activities. Despite the lack of demonstrated program success in gang work, our literature review suggested that youth gang problems can be reduced in prevalence and severity (Miller, 1990).

Recommended Gang Intervention Strategies

The research we reviewed (Howell, 1997b) suggests the need for three program strategies to deal with the youth gang problem. The first one targets gang problems directly in a community-wide approach to gang prevention, intervention, and suppression. The second one targets gang problems within a comprehensive strategy for dealing with serious, violent, and chronic juvenile delinquency. The third model targets gang-related (and -motivated) homicides. In implementing each strategy, program development should take into account the known risk factors for gang membership (Table 6.1) and risk factors for gang-related homicides (Table 6.2).

The Comprehensive Community-Wide Approach to Gang Prevention, Intervention, and Suppression Program

This program model was designed specifically to target youth gang problems, as the product of a nationwide assessment of youth gang prevention, intervention, and suppression programs in the late 1980s (Spergel, 1991, 1995; Spergel & Curry, 1993; Spergel, Curry, et al., 1994). Twelve program components developed by Spergel and his colleagues (Spergel, Chance, et al., 1994) are available for the design and mobilization of community efforts by police, prosecutors, judges, probation and parole officers, corrections officers, schools, employers, community-based agencies, and a range of grassroots organizations (Spergel, Chance, Ehrensaft, Regulus, Kane, & Alexander, 1992). Technical assistance manuals are available to support local program development (Spergel, Chance, Ehrensaft, Regulus, Kane, & Laseter, 1992). Variations of these models currently are being implemented and tested in Bloomington, Illinois; Mesa and Tucson, Arizona; Riverside, California; and San Antonio, Texas. An independent evaluation is being conducted by the University of Chicago.

The most promising gang violence prevention and intervention program is being conducted in the Little Village area of Chicago (Spergel & Grossman, 1994, 1995). Called the "Gang Violence Reduction Program," the program incorporates a complement of strategies based on the comprehensive model Spergel and his colleagues developed (Spergel, Chance, et

TABLE 6.1 Risk Factors for Gang Membership

Community	Social disorganization, including poverty and residential mobility (Curry & Spergel, 1988); organized lower-class communities (Miller, 1958; Moore, 1991); underclass communities (Bursik & Grasmick, 1993; Hagedorn, 1988; Moore, 1978, 1985, 1988, 1991; Moore et al., 1983; Sullivan, 1989); presence of gangs in the neighborhood (Curry & Spergel, 1992); availability of drugs in the neighborhood (Curry & Spergel, 1992; Hagedorn, 1988, 1994a, 1994b; Sanchez-Jankowski, 1991; Taylor, 1990; Moore, 1978; 1991); availability of firearms (Lizotte et al., 1994; Miller, 1982; Newton & Zimring, 1969); barriers to and lack of social and economic opportunities (Cloward & Ohlin, 1960; Cohen, 1960; Fagan, 1990; Hagedorn, 1988, 1994b; Klein, 1995; Moore, 1990; Short & Strodtbeck, 1965); lack of social capital (Short, 1996; Sullivan, 1989); cultural norms supporting gang behavior (Miller, 1958; Short & Strodtbeck, 1965); feeling unsafe in the neighborhood (Kosterman et al., 1996)
Family	Family disorganization, including broken homes, and parent drug/alcohol abuse (Bjerregaard & Smith, 1993; Esbensen et al., 1993; Vigil, 1988) troubled families, including incest, family violence, and drug addiction (Moore, 1978, 1991); family members in a gang (Curry & Spergel, 1992; Moore, 1991; Moore et al., 1983); lack of parental role models (Wang, 1995); low socioeconomic status (most all studies); poor families (Kosterman et al., 1996)
School	Academic failure (Bjerregaard & Smith, 1993; Curry & Spergel, 1992; Kosterman et al., 1996); low educational aspirations, especially among females (Bjerregaard & Smith, 1993); negative labeling by teachers (Esbensen & Huizinga, 1993; Esbensen et al., 1993); trouble at school (Kosterman et al., 1996); few teacher role models (Wang, 1995)
Peer Group	High commitment to delinquent peers (Bjerregaard & Smith, 1993; Esbensen & Huizinga, 1993; Vigil & Yun, 1990); low commitment to positive peers (Esbensen et al., 1993); gang members in class (Curry & Spergel, 1992); friends who use drugs (Curry & Spergel, 1992)
Individual	Early antisocial behavior (Kosterman et al., 1996); prior delinquency (Bjerregaard & Smith, 1993; Curry & Spergel, 1992; Esbensen & Huizinga, 1993); deviant attitudes (Esbensen et al., 1993; Fagan, 1990); street smartness (Miller, 1958); toughness (Miller, 1958); defiant and individualistic character (Miller, 1958; Sanchez-Jankowski, 1991); fatalistic view of the world (Miller, 1958); aggression (Campbell, 1984a, 1984b; Cohen, 1962; Horowitz, 1983; Miller et al., 1962; Sanchez-Jankowski, 1991); proclivity for excitement and trouble (Miller, 1958; Pennell et al., 1994); locura—acting in a daring, courageous, and especially crazy fashion in the face of adversity (Moore, 1991; Vigil, 1988); higher levels of normlessness in the family, peer group, and school contexts (Esbensen et al., 1993); social disabilities (Short & Strodtbeck, 1965); illegal gun ownership (Bjerregaard & Lizotte, 1995; Vigil & Long, 1990); early or precocious sexual activity (Kosterman et al., 1996), especially among females (Bjerregaard & Smith, 1993); alcohol and drug use (Bjerregaard & Smith, 1993; Curry & Spergel, 1992; Esbensen et al., 1993; Thornberry et al., 1993; Vigil & Long, 1990); drug trafficking (Thornberry et al., 1993); desire for group rewards such as status, identity, companionship, and protection (Fagan, 1990, Horowitz, 1983; Horowitz & Schwartz, 1974; Moore, 1978, 1991; Short & Strodtbeck, 1965)

al., 1994): suppression, social intervention, opportunities provision, and community mobilization, which are "employed interactively" (Spergel & Grossman, 1995, p. 3).The program targets mainly the older members (aged 17-24) of two of the city's most violent Latino gangs. These two gangs consist of about 1,000 peripheral and regular members and 200 hard-core violent youth, and they account for about 80% of the gang violence in the community.

The Gang Violence Reduction Program consists of two coordinated strategies: (a) targeted control of violent or potentially hard-core violent youth gang offenders, in the form of increased probation department and police supervision and suppression, and (b) provision of

TABLE 6.2 Epidemiology of Youth Gang Homicide

I. United States		Is one of the most violent countries in the world, 5th among 41 countries[a] Has highest homicide rate in the world[b]
	A. Prevalence	Gang members are 60 times as likely to die of homicide as are members of the general population (600 per 100,000 gang members)[c] In 1989-1993, 33% of L.A. gang-related homicides were drive-bys.[d] In 1985-1994, 7% of Chicago gang-motivated homicides were drive-bys[e]
	B. Incidence	The FBI reports 1,157 juvenile gang-related homicides in the United States in 1995[f] Chicago had 240 street-gang-motivated homicides in 1994[g] Los Angeles County had 803 gang-related homicides in 1992[h]
	C. Victim/ offender	75% of Chicago gang-related homicides are intergang; 14%, nongang victims, and 11%, intragang[i] Peak age of homicide offenders is 18[j] 64% of Chicago gang-related homicide victims are age 15-19[k] 82% of juvenile gang homicides in Los Angeles are intraracial[l] 63% of gang homicides in Los Angeles result from intergang interactions[m] 23% of Los Angeles drive-by shooting victims are innocent bystanders[n] 64% of gang homicide victims are gang members[o]
	D. Weapons	Firearms are used in 95% of gang-related homicides[p]; use of fully or semi-automatic weapons increased 13-fold in Chicago from 1987 to 1994[q]
II. Risk Factors		In addition to the risk factors for gang membership, fatalities mainly related to turf disputes in closely concentrated geographical areas within specific years and specific age groups[r]; expressive violence in relatively prospering neighborhoods with expanding populations, acts of instrumental violence (e.g., drug disputes) in disrupted/declining neighborhoods[s]; racial and class discrimination, immigrant adjustment, changing economic situation, drug market conditions[t]; setting and participant characteristics[u]; weapon availability/lethality, more gangs and gang violence[v]; and social disorganization (immigrant resettling).[w] Drug trafficking is not strongly correlated with youth gang homicides.[x]

a = Rosenberg and Mercy (1986); b = Hutson et al. (1995); c = Morales (1992); d = Hutson et al. (1995); e = Block et al. (1996); f = FBI (1996); g = Block et al. (1996); h = Klein (1995); i = Block et al. (1996); j = Block et al. (1996); k = Block et al. (1996); l = Hutson et al. (1995); m = Hutson et al. (1995); n = Hutson et al. (1996); o = Hutson et al. (1995); p = Hutson et al. (1995); q = Block et al. (1996); r = Block (1993); s = Block and Block (1993); t = Block and Block (1993); u = Maxson et al. (1985); v = Block and Block (1993); Hutson et al. (1995); Miller (1982); w = Curry and Spergel (1988); x = Block (1993); Block and Block (1993); Hutson et al. (1995); Klein et al. (1991); Hutson, Anglin, and Pratts (1994); Meehan and O'Carroll (1992); Miller (1994).

a wide range of social services and opportunities for targeted youth, to encourage their transition to conventional legitimate behaviors through education, jobs, job training, family support, and brief counseling. Managed by the Neighborhood Relations Unit of the Chicago Police Department, the project is staffed by tactical police officers, probation officers, community youth workers (from the University of Chicago), and workers in Neighbors Against Gang Violence, a new community organization established to support the project. This organization is composed of representatives from local churches, a job placement agency, youth service agencies, the alderman's office, local citizens, and other community groups.

Preliminary evaluation results (after 4 years of program operations) are positive (Spergel & Grossman, 1995). Project efforts have been associated with a decline, or at least a reduction in the rate of increase, in gang violence. In Little Village, gang-motivated violence increased by 32%, compared to an increase of 77% in the control area (p. 28). The reduction in drug selling was more than eight times as large for youth receiving combined services from police and gang workers, compared to program youth receiving noncoordinated or alternate forms of services (Spergel & Grossman, 1995, p. 21). Prior to initiation of the program, all gang members in both gangs reported an average of more than 26 violent crimes during the past 6 months, including homicides, drive-by shootings, aggravated gang batteries, and aggravated gang assaults (Spergel & Grossman, 1995, p. 11). Interviews with gang members served by the project for nearly 3 years show they committed an average of fewer than 12 violent crimes during the past 6 months. This model and other versions of the comprehensive model Spergel and his colleagues developed can be implemented and tested in other jurisdictions.

The OJJDP's Comprehensive Strategy for Serious, Violent, and Chronic Juvenile Offenders

Targeting gang problems within a community's comprehensive strategy for dealing with serious, violent, and chronic juvenile offenders is the second recommended approach. The OJJDP's "Comprehensive Strategy for Serious, Violent, and Chronic Juvenile Offenders" (Wilson & Howell, 1993) provides a framework for strategic community planning and program development. The OJJDP's *Guide for Implementing the Comprehensive Strategy for Serious, Violent, and Chronic Juvenile Offenders* (Howell, 1995b) is a resource for carrying out the OJJDP Comprehensive Strategy. It contains numerous promising and effective program models that will help prevent and reduce gang problems while targeting serious, violent, and chronic juvenile offenders.

The theoretical foundation of the Comprehensive Strategy is the "social development model" (Catalano & Hawkins, 1996; Hawkins & Weis, 1985), a risk-focused approach to delinquency that identifies risk factors contributing to delinquency, prioritizes them, and specifies ways to buffer and reduce those risks. The Comprehensive Strategy consists of prevention and graduated sanctions components, encompassing the entire juvenile justice and human service fields. The graduated sanctions component uses structured decision-making tools (risk and needs assessments) to achieve the best match between public safety risks that offenders pre-

sent and treatment needs in a continuum of sanctions and program options.

Youth gang members account for most offending by serious, violent, and chronic juvenile offenders in Rochester, New York (Bjerregaard & Smith, 1993; Thornberry, Krohn, Lizotte, & Chard-Wierschen, 1993), Seattle (Battin, Hill, Abbott, Catalano, & Hawkins, 1996), and Denver (Esbensen & Huizinga, 1993). Gang members and other serious, violent, and chronic juvenile offenders share common risk factors (Esbensen, Huizinga, & Weiher, 1993; Thornberry, et al., 1995). Because separate causal pathways to gang participation versus nongang serious and violent offending have not been identified, programs found to be effective or promising for preventing and reducing serious and violent delinquency in general may hold promise in combating gang delinquency and violence. Promising programs that might be included in a comprehensive youth gang program follow. These address known risk factors for gang participation.

Prevention component. The prevention component of the Comprehensive Strategy incorporates a risk- and protective-factor approach for systematically assessing community risk factors, identifying and prioritizing the most prevalent risk factors, and then selecting from promising and effective interventions those that best target the priority risk factors and strengthen protective factors. *Communities That Care* (Hawkins & Catalano, 1992) is a structured process for analysis of "risk" factors and the development of approaches that reduce them and buffer their negative effects by increasing protective factors. The major risk factors for gang involvement are found in the individual, family, school, peer group, and community domains (see Table 6.1). Promising programs that seek to reduce these risk factors and also increase protective factors are noted below.

A public education campaign is needed to educate national, state, and local leaders; parents; children; and adolescents about the risks associated with gang participation. This educational campaign should be based on the elevated risk of homicide among gang members—60 times the risk of homicide among the general population (Morales, 1992)—and focus particularly on inner-city and low-income areas of cities and towns.

Discouraging children and young adolescents from joining gangs is the most cost-effective approach to reducing serious gang crime (National Drug Intelligence Center, 1995). Two gang prevention curricula, Project BUILD (Thompson & Jason, 1988) and the Gang Resistance Education and Training (G.R.E.A.T.) curriculum (Esbensen & Osgood, 1997), have shown positive results.

A number of promising *family-based* early intervention programs have been identified (see Hawkins, Catalano, & Brewer, 1995, pp. 52-60; Horne, 1993), including pre- and perinatal medical care, intensive health education for the mother, child immunizations, parent training, child cognitive development activities, home visitation (Olds, Henderson, Tatelbaum, & Chamberlin, 1988), and home-based parent training and skills training for juveniles (Tremblay et al., 1992). These aim mainly to strengthen family management and can reduce the likelihood that offspring will join gangs (see Yoshikawa, 1995).

Promising *school* programs include the Perry preschool project (Schweinhart, Barnes, & Weikart, 1993); the Syracuse University Family Development Research Program (Lally, Mangione, & Honig, 1988); a variety of classroom organization, management, and instructional interventions, including school-based behavioral interventions (for a review and summary, see Brewer et al., 1995, pp. 70-77); graduation incentives for high-risk youths (Taggart, 1995; see also Greenwood, Model, Rydell, & Chiesa, 1996); and an anti-bullying program (Olweus, 1992).

Promising *peer group* and *individual-focused* programs include manhood development (Watts, 1991); employment training, education, and counseling (Corsica, 1993); conflict resolution and peer mediation in tandem (Hawkins, Farrington, & Catalano, in press); alternatives to gang participation (Klein, 1995); equipping peers to help one another (Gibbs, Potter, & Goldstein, in press; Leeman, Gibbs, & Fuller, in press); and techniques for separating youths from gangs (Hunsaker, 1981; Kohn & Shelly, 1991). The House of Umoja is a unique indigenous community program that provides a "sanctuary" from street life and gangs (Woodson, 1981, 1986). It helps target youths pursue alternatives to gang life through a comprehensive program that includes educational development, career development, employment assistance, and individual counseling. The program has evolved into the first "Urban Boystown," consisting of 23 homes on Frazier Street, Philadelphia. In addition to a job training center, a Security Institute is operated by House of Umoja, in which boys are trained in crime prevention and for employment as security officers in department stores and other businesses.

Community programs must increase social and economic alternatives to gang involvement. Promising programs include community reconstruction (Eisenhower Foundation, 1990), Empowerment Zones (revitalization of communities through economic and social services), and Enterprise Communities (promoting physical and human development). Empowerment Zones and Enterprise Communities are large-scale programs supported through the federal Department of Housing and Urban Development (see OJJDP, 1995b) that aim to reconstruct selected inner-city areas. Other programs are needed that help improve social and economic conditions in impoverished communities, providing "social capital" for young people (Short, 1996), enabling them to reach "turning points" such as gainful employment in pathways to success outside gangs (Sampson & Laub, 1993). Community norms supporting gang crime and violence also must be changed. Strengthening anticrime incentives and weakening procrime incentives may work (Miller, 1993).

Promising programs designed to prevent gang problems in particularly low-income areas and public housing projects include the Beethoven Project in Chicago's Robert Taylor Homes (Center for Successful Child Development, 1993); Neutral Zone (Thurman, Giacomazzi, Reisig, & Mueller, 1996); a Community Outreach Program (Kodluboy & Evenrud, 1993); and Boys and Girls Clubs: Targeted Outreach (Feyerherm, Pope, & Lovell, 1992).

Community policing is an essential component of a comprehensive gang prevention program. Several community policing programs appear to have realized some success in dealing with youth crime problems (see Cronin, 1994, for three promising models). One of these is the Norfolk Police Assisted Community Enforcement (PACE) program, focused in low-income housing areas. Although the PACE program has not been evaluated, crime has decreased by an estimated 29% in the targeted neighborhoods (Cronin, 1994). Police report fewer service calls and a significant drop in on-street drug trafficking and gunfire in the targeted areas. One key to the apparent success of the PACE program is the formation of partnerships between police and neighborhood organizations, empowering neighborhoods through community mobilization to develop—in concert with the police and other city agencies—solutions to gang and other crime problems. These solutions include social and human service needs.

Another community policing model that specifically targets youth gangs is the Reno, Nevada, program (Weston, 1993). Through the formation of a Community Action Team (CAT), the Reno Police Department involves minority neighborhoods, community service agencies, and political leaders in a community solution to the city's serious youth gang problem. The CAT program, developed in response to gang problems, had two strategies: (a) creation of a highly specialized team of officers to target the top 5% of violent gang members in a repeat offender program, and (b) a prevention and early intervention program that targeted the city's estimated 80% of local gang members who were not involved in criminal activity and not considered to be "hard core." Neighborhood advisory groups provide feedback from community residents, and an interagency group coordinates prevention and intervention resources. Although the program has not been independently evaluated, Weston (1993, p. 300) reports that "it would appear that limited violence and limited growth in gang membership is related to the many success stories resulting from intervention efforts." Neighborhood block watch also appears to be a useful community crime prevention technique (Lindsay & McGillis, 1986; Rosenbaum, Lewis, & Grant, 1986).

Successful prevention of gang problems cannot be accomplished without involving community leaders and neighborhood organizations, because of the integral relationship between gangs and community conditions and dynamics (Spergel, Chance, et al., 1994). Community mobilization, therefore, is a key component of a comprehensive gang prevention program. It is a process of consciousness raising, objective identification of gang problem dimensions, and developing a community commitment to take action. "The essence of the community mobilization process is to reinvigorate or reorganize community structures so that community energies and resources are developed to address the youth gang problem, and these resources are integrated and targeted on the gang problem" (Spergel, Chance, et al., 1994, p. 6).

It also is critical that gang prevention program developers solicit input from gang members. Gang leaders have identified program strategies they believe would be most valuable in their communities. These included gutting and burning abandoned structures, building counseling centers and recreation areas, beautifying of the neighborhood, renovating educational facilities, promoting tutoring programs and health care facilities, replacing welfare programs with state-sponsored employment, encouraging economic development programs, and increasing roles for residents in law enforcement activities (Bursik & Grasmick, 1993, p. 178).

Graduated sanctions component. The Graduated sanctions component should consist of structured sanctions, including priority arrest, adjudication, intensive probation, incarceration, and aftercare for juvenile offenders (see Howell, 1995a; OJJDP, 1995c). Vertical prosecution of adult chronic, serious, and violent gang offenders should be pursued in the criminal justice system (Genelin, 1993; Weston, 1993). A continuum of juvenile corrections treatment options can be provided in an Intensive Supervision Program (Krisberg et al., 1994). Improved assessment of gang involvement is necessary, especially among adolescents in juvenile detention and correctional facilities, in which gangs represent a formidable problem (see Howell, 1997c).

Interpersonal skills training appears to hold promise for improving social skills, reducing anger, and possibly reducing violence among street gang youth and with institutionalized populations, some of which have included gang members (Goldstein, 1993; Goldstein & Glick, 1994). In a recent experiment, Aggression Replacement Training (ART) was tested as a gang intervention program with 10 aggressive juvenile gangs in New York City. Goldstein and Glick (1994) report a reduction in arrest rates, as well as other evaluation results, supporting the effectiveness of a 2-year project using the ART intervention approach. In an 8-month follow-up, 13% of the ART group were rearrested, compared to 52% of the control group. On other measures, compared to the control group, the ART group showed significant improvements in community functioning and slightly better improvements in interpersonal skills and anger control. The ART model teaches gang members anger control and other skills, as well as attempting to turn their real-world reference group, the gang, from an antisocial group into a prosocial one (Gibbs et al., in press).

The Multisystemic Therapy (MST) Program appears to be a promising treatment and rehabilitation program for gang members even though it has not specifically targeted them. Because of the success of MST in treating multiple problems of serious and violent juvenile offenders in different settings (Borduin et al., 1995; Henggeler & Borduin, 1990; Henggeler, Cunningham, Pickrel, Schoenwald, & Brondino, 1996; Henggeler, Melton, & Smith, 1992; Henggeler, Melton, Smith, Schoenwald, & Hanley, 1993), MST appears to have applicability as a juvenile justice system rehabilitation approach for youth gang members. Treatment groups in various MST experiments have included gang members. This discovery provided the basis for fielding an experiment specifically targeting gang members. The MST model is currently being tested in Galveston, Texas, in the "Second Chance" program, which targets gang-involved youth (Thomas, 1996).

The "8% Early Intervention Program" in Orange County, California (Kurz & Moore, 1994), includes a gang component. It targets gang leadership and the most chronic recidivists through a coordinated program of gang interdiction, apprehension, and prosecution (Capizzi, Cook, & Schumacher, 1995). These three strategies are integrated and coordinated by TARGET (the Tri-Agency Resource Gang Enforcement Team), consisting of the Westminster Police Department, the Orange County district attorney, and the County Probation Department. The Gang Incident Tracking System (GITS) identifies and tracks gang members, providing the information base for the TARGET program, which supports gang interdiction, apprehension, and prosecution. TARGET uses intelligence gathering and information sharing to identify and select appropriate gang members and gangs for intervention. Civil abatement procedures are used to suppress the criminal activities of entire gangs.

Effective police and agency interventions can be enhanced by sound, current gang information. The Chicago Early Warning System (Block & Block, 1991, pp. 54-56) is a model for this purpose, and it can be replicated in other jurisdictions. This system, stimulated by earlier research in Chicago (see Curry & Spergel, 1988), is based on a statistical model that consolidates spatial information and uses auto-

mated "hot spot area" identification and other geographic statistics to predict potential crisis areas. The Early Warning System is used in the Chicago Police Department's "Police Area Four" project, in which the police identify problem areas, then target prevention efforts in those areas. Up-to-the minute information is necessary for targeting specific neighborhoods. Gang violence changes over time, following a pattern of escalation, retaliation, and revenge that often occurs across a spatial border that also changes over time (Block & Block, 1993). Information provided by the Early Warning System is used to inform police and community agency interventions to head off the cycle of retaliation and retribution, if possible, through the use of mediation and crisis intervention. The Chicago Early Warning System effectively supports the Little Village project (discussed above) by providing timely information on criminal gang activity (see Spergel & Grossman, 1995).

The main target crime in the Police Area Four project is gang-related homicides. Although conventional wisdom suggests that homicide cannot be prevented, the Blocks disagree (Block & Block, 1991, p. 57). They contend that homicides can be prevented by targeting efforts on (a) the "specific Homicide Syndromes [e.g., expressive] that are the most dangerous and have the highest chance of successful prevention, (b) specific neighborhoods in which the risk of being murdered is especially high, and (c) specific groups who are at the highest risk of victimization" (p. 57).

Reduction of gun access and use is an essential component of a comprehensive strategy. Recent studies have shown the proliferation and use of firearms among youth gangs (Block & Block, 1993; Maxson, Gordon, & Klein, 1985). Gang members are significantly more likely than nonmembers to own a gun illegally (Bjerregaard & Lizotte, 1995). Adolescents who own guns for protection are more likely to be involved in gangs and to commit serious crimes (Lizotte, et al., 1994); therefore, limiting gun access and use is an important means of reducing lethal gang violence.

Numerous proposals for firearms reduction have been made that merit testing (Cook, 1981a, 1981b, 1991; Cook & Nagin, 1979; Newton & Zimring, 1969; Office of Juvenile Justice and Delinquency Prevention, 1995e; Zimring, 1985, 1993, 1995; Zimring & Hawkins, 1987). Several approaches suggested recently have particular applicability to the youth gang firearm problem. Police seizures of illegally carried guns in "hot spot" areas have been found to reduce gun crimes, homicides, and drive-by shootings, though not significantly (Sherman, Shaw, & Rogan, 1995). "Coerced use reduction" may be effective (Kennedy, Piehl, & Braga, 1996). Undercover purchases of firearms from adolescents, control of the supply channels, creation of ammunition scarcity, bilateral buy-back agreements, and nonuse treaties with financial compliance incentives hold promise (Zimring, 1995). Interdicting supply channels may be more feasible than commonly assumed because of the newness of guns used in gang homicides and their purchase within the state (Kennedy et al., 1996; Zimring, 1976). Equally important, research is needed on the relationship between firearms and violent street gang activity, on the extent of youth gun ownership and use, and on patterns of acquisition of guns by minors in the gang gun inventory environment (Zimring, 1993, 1995).

Multiagency coordination of investigations, prosecutions, and sanctioning of criminal gang members is important for effective and efficient law enforcement. One model, the JUDGE (Jurisdictions United for Drug Gang Enforcement), targets drug-involved gang members in San Diego. The multiagency task force enforces conditions of probation and drug laws and provides vertical prosecution for probation violations and new offenses involving targeted offenders. Evaluation of JUDGE showed vertical prosecution to be a cornerstone for successful implementation and illustrated the advantages of a multiagency approach (Office of Justice Programs, 1996).

The gang program model that holds the most promise is likely to contain multiple components, incorporating prevention, social intervention, treatment, suppression, and community mobilization approaches. Involvement of all sectors of the community is essential (Bursik & Grasmick, 1993, pp. 148-180). To work, gang program components must be integrated in a collaborative approach, supported by a management information system.

A Strategy to Prevent and Reduce Youth Gang-Related (or -Motivated) Homicides

Because of recent increases in gang homicides, a third gang program strategy for targeting them is recommended. Reducing youth gang-related (or -motivated) homicides should

be a priority wherever they occur. Studies in Chicago and Los Angeles, however, indicate that these two cities disproportionately account for gang-related homicides in the United States. In Chicago, the number of street-gang-motivated[1] homicides increased almost five-fold between 1987 and 1994, from 51 to 240 (Block et al., 1996). *Gang-related* homicides in Los Angeles County more than doubled from 1987 to 1992, from 387 to 803 (Klein, 1995). Chicago and Los Angeles alone accounted for nearly 1,000 gang homicides in 1992. Hutson and colleagues (1995) concluded that "gang-related homicides in Los Angeles County have reached epidemic proportions and are a major health problem" (p. 1031).

The "Epidemiology of Youth Gang Homicides" (Table 6.2) summarizes demographic information and research on risk factors for gang homicides. The major risk factors are community conditions (weapon availability/lethality, social disorganization, racial and class discrimination, immigrant adjustment, changing economic situation, and drug market conditions), communities where gangs and gang violence are most prevalent, and where gangs are involved in turf disputes in closely concentrated geographical areas within specific years and specific age groups. Consideration of these risk factors, along with available knowledge of promising and effective programs, suggests a strategy that may work to prevent and reduce youth-gang-related homicides. They are preventable (Block & Block, 1993; Hutson, Anglin, & Mallon, 1992a, 1992b).

Chicago's "Gang Violence Reduction Program" appears to be a promising program model for targeting gang-motivated violence and homicides (Spergel & Grossman, 1994, 1995). It should be replicated and tested in other Chicago communities, in specific Los Angeles communities, and in other cities experiencing significant levels of gang homicides. One key to its success is the Early Warning System Geoarchive of the Illinois Criminal Justice Information Authority, which provides up-to-date information on "hot spots" of gang violence for targeted intervention efforts by the police and other agencies.

This literature review has identified other promising interventions that should be considered in designing a comprehensive gang homicide prevention and reduction program. These include a hospital emergency room intervention program for injured victims that could be established by adding a gang specialist to Suspected Child Abuse and Neglect Team—SCAN—now found in many hospitals (Morales, 1992), serving to initiate entry into programs to break the cycle of gang violence (Hutson et al., 1995), and counseling for victims of drive-by shootings to reduce the traumatic effects of victimization and discourage retaliation (Groves, Zuckerman, Marans, & Cohen, 1993; Hutson, Anglin, & Pratts, 1994; Pynoos & Nader, 1988).

Access to firearms by violent street gangs should be reduced by legislation, regulation, and community education, and by removing illegal guns from the possession of gang members. A number of promising strategies have been recommended (Block & Block, 1993; Cook, 1981a, 1981b, 1991; Cook & Nagin, 1979; Hutson et al., 1995; Kennedy et al., 1996; Sheley & Wright, 1993; Sherman et al., 1995; Wright, 1995; Zimring, 1976, 1993, 1995; Zimring & Hawkins, 1987). A firearm wounding and fatality reporting system should be established to determine sources of weapons and assist interdiction efforts (Teret, Wintemute, & Beilenson, 1992; see also American Academy of Pediatrics, 1992; Cristoffel, 1991; Kellerman, Lee, Mercy, & Banton, 1991).

Effective program strategies must be built on continuously updated information because of the frequently changing patterns (Block & Block, 1993). Short-term successes can be realized by targeting the causes of acute escalation in violence levels (Block & Block, 1993). As the Blocks have shown, programs must take into account the instrumental and expressive characteristics of gang violence. "For example, a program to reduce gang involvement in drugs in a community in which gang members are most concerned with defense of turf has little chance" (Block & Block, 1993, p. 9). Because juveniles tend to shoot others of their own ethnic group (Hutson et al., 1995), prevention programs must be culture-specific (Soriano, 1993) and age-appropriate (Block & Christakos, 1995; Centers for Disease Control and Prevention, 1990; Hutson et al., 1995; Hutson, Anglin, Mallon, & Pratts, 1994; Klein & Maxson, 1989).

Summary

Youth gang homicides represent a growing proportion of youth violence in certain cities. There is no question that in particular commu-

nities in certain cities, youth gangs are very actively involved in drug trafficking. A few youth gangs have established drug operations in distant cities and towns. Some studies show that youth gang members extensively use drugs, and many of them are involved in drug trafficking. Some homicides are a result of incidental contact with members of other gangs during a drug trafficking mission. As the Blocks have found in Chicago, most youth gang homicides result from impulsive and emotional defense of one's identity as a gang member, defense of the gang and gang members, defense and glorification of the reputation of the gang, gang member recruitment, and territorial disputes. Studies conducted in Boston, Chicago, Los Angeles, and St. Louis suggest that these violent gang activities and narcotics trafficking should be viewed as separate, important risk factors for homicide rather than as interrelated cofactors.

The "Comprehensive Community-Wide Approach to Gang Prevention, Intervention, and Suppression Program" developed by Spergel and his colleagues targets gang problems. It emphasizes community change as its main theoretical approach. The original model contains 12 program components for the design and mobilization of community efforts by police, prosecutors, judges, probation and parole officers, corrections officers, schools, employers, community-based agencies, and a range of grassroots organizations. Technical assistance manuals are available to support local program development. Variations of these models currently are being implemented and tested in five sites under OJJDP support. Another version of this comprehensive model, the "Gang Violence Reduction Program," has been implemented in Chicago and is showing very promising results.

The second approach, reducing gang delinquency by targeting serious, violent, and chronic delinquency, is accomplished by implementing the OJJDP "Comprehensive Strategy for Serious, Violent, and Chronic Juvenile Offenders." A number of program options are suggested, based on this literature review. This chapter organized these options under the prevention and graduated sanctions components of the Comprehensive Strategy.

Finally, a strategy to prevent and reduce youth gang-related (or -motivated) homicides is recommended. It incorporates program strategies that look promising for preventing and reducing gang homicides. The central program intervention is the Chicago "Gang Violence Reduction Program." To be effective, it must be supported by up-to-date information on "hot spots" of gang violence for targeted intervention efforts by the police and other agencies. Replication of the Early Warning System Geoarchive of the Illinois Criminal Justice Information Authority is recommended for this purpose. It is recommended that the proposed homicide reduction strategy be implemented in specific Chicago and Los Angeles communities, where gang homicides have reached epidemic proportions.

NOTE

1. Law enforcement agencies in Los Angeles and Chicago define gang homicides differently (see Maxson & Klein, 1990). In Los Angeles, the basic element is evidence of gang membership on the side of either the suspect or the victim. Maxson and Klein call this a "gang member" definition (p. 77). In Chicago, a homicide is considered gang-related only if the preponderance of evidence indicates that the incident grew out of a street gang function; that is, gang-motivated (Block et al., 1996, p. 2).

7

Risk Factors for Youth Violence

How can we account for the small increase (except for homicides) in juvenile violence over the past decade? This is the subject of this chapter. After examining the major risk factors for violence, we consider social and cultural changes that may help explain the increase.

Hawkins and Catalano (1992, 1993, 1996; see also Brewer et al., 1995; Hawkins, Catalano, & Miller, 1992; Loeber, Stouthamer-Loeber, Van Kammen, & Farrington, 1991) provide a comprehensive summary of risk factors for juvenile delinquency, violence, and other problem behaviors, based on their review of 30 years of research in these areas (Table 7.1). The major risk factor domains Hawkins and Catalano identify are the *community*, the *family*, the *school*, *individual characteristics*, and adolescent *peer groups*. The presence of a check mark beside a risk factor in the table means that experimental studies have documented the validity of the risk factor for the specified problem behavior. The absence of a check mark beside a risk factor may not mean that it is irrelevant, only that experimental research has not confirmed the relationship.

The literature on serious, violent, and chronic juvenile offending is being reviewed in the OJJDP Serious Violent and Chronic Offenders Study Group Project, under the direction of Rolf Loeber and David Farrington. That review, which also includes an assessment of effective interventions, will summarize available information on which interventions appear to work best at specific transition points in the developmental career of the serious, violent, and chronic juvenile offender. A detailed review of

that literature is not attempted here. Rather, the summary is intended to show that juvenile violence is grounded in cultural norms and social conditions in our society. For each risk factor, we first review indicators of general risk factors, then more specific ones.

Community Factors

Social and cultural context. "Violence is woven into the cultural fabric of American society" (American Psychological Association [APA], 1993, p. 22). We have an ambivalent relationship with violence (APA, 1993, pp. 22-23). On one hand, we abhor it in our communities, homes, schools, and public places. On the other hand, we condone violence in many ways. The U.S. frontier was blazed by rugged individualists. Media idols such as Arnold Schwarzenegger and Sylvester Stallone often glorify violence on individual and personal levels. Violence is graphically displayed and condoned in film, television productions, and music. These violent episodes are widely enjoyed. Our children covet and possess guns and war toys. They are given a plethora of opportunities from early ages to learn that violence is an acceptable means of resolving disputes.

Community poverty is a major contributor to youth violence. In 1992, 22% of all juveniles in the United States lived in poverty, consisting of 25% of all children under the age of 6 and 19% of youngsters ages 7-17 (Snyder & Sickmund, 1995, pp. 7-8). These figures represent nearly

TABLE 7.1   Risk Factors for Delinquency and Other Problem Behaviors

Risk Factors	Adolescent Problem Behaviors				
	Substance Abuse	Delinquency	Teen Pregnancy	School Dropout	Violence
Community					
Availability of drugs	✔				
Availability of firearms		✔			✔
Community laws and norms favorable toward drug use, firearms, and crime	✔	✔			✔
Media portrayals of violence					✔
Transitions and mobility	✔	✔		✔	
Low neighborhood attachment and community disorganization	✔	✔			✔
Extreme economic deprivation	✔	✔	✔	✔	✔
Family					
Family history of the problem behavior	✔	✔	✔	✔	
Family management problems	✔	✔	✔	✔	✔
Family conflict	✔	✔	✔	✔	✔
Favorable parental attitudes and involvement in the problem behavior	✔	✔			✔
School					
Early and persistent antisocial behavior	✔	✔	✔	✔	✔
Academic failure beginning in elementary school	✔	✔	✔	✔	✔
Lack of commitment to school	✔	✔	✔	✔	
Individual/peer					
Rebelliousness	✔	✔		✔	
Friends who engage in the problem behavior	✔	✔	✔	✔	✔
Favorable attitudes toward the problem behavior	✔	✔	✔	✔	
Early initiation of the problem behavior	✔	✔	✔	✔	✔
Constitutional factors	✔	✔			✔

SOURCE: *Communities That Care Planning Kit Leader's Guide*, Hawkins and Catalano, ©copyright 1996 by Developmental Research and Programs. Reprinted with permission.

18 million persons under the age of 18 (9 million whites, 5 million blacks, 3 million Hispanics, and nearly a million of other races). Moreover, poverty is worsening among minorities and whites alike. Between 1976 and 1992, the number of juveniles living in poverty increased 42%, accounted for by a 30% growth in the number of black children in poverty, compared to a 45% increase for white children (including predominantly white Hispanic children). The increase in this period was greatest among Hispanic children (116%). Minorities are disproportionately represented in poverty-stricken areas: 60% of both black and Hispanic juveniles living in inner-city areas are poverty-stricken.

Central cities contain 44% of all these children. Families with children were three times as likely to live in poverty in 1992 as those without children (Snyder & Sickmund, 1995, pp. 7-8). Adolescents who live in economically deprived areas characterized by extreme poverty, poor living conditions, and high unemployment are more likely to engage in crime and violence (Farrington, 1991; Yoshikawa, 1994).

The Annie E. Casey Foundation (1994) estimates that nearly 4 million American children are growing up in "severely distressed" neighborhoods. Characterized by poverty, female-headed households, high-school dropouts, and reliance on welfare, these neighborhoods put children at risk of drug abuse, delinquency, school failure, teenage pregnancy, child neglect and abuse, and family breakdown. Urban neighborhoods plagued by poverty and rapid population turnover, which disconnects people from their support systems, have higher rates of violence than other neighborhoods.

> To be poor in America is to be segregated, often in decaying inner cities, in which crime and the threat of crime confine the poor to fear and isolation at best and to injury and death at worst. Violence rates in central cities are 41.3 per thousand, but in suburbs and nonmetropolitan areas they are 25.2 per thousand. (APA, 1993, p. 23)

⌈Poverty, prejudice, and discrimination coexist in minority communities. These factors interact to produce negative psychological as well as economic consequences for members of minority families. Self-confidence and self-esteem are damaged, laying a foundation for anger, discontent, and violence.⌋Official records suggest a disproportionate propensity of minority group members to engage in serious and violent behavior (Wolfgang et al., 1987). Recent self-report studies, however, show no differences between minorities and nonminorities in poor areas of inner cities at young ages (Peeples & Loeber, 1994). By the time they are in their late 20s, significant differences in individual serious and violent offending rates appear among white and black persons, suggesting that "once involved in a lifestyle that includes serious forms of violence, theft, and substance use, persons from disadvantaged families and neighborhoods find it very difficult to escape" (Elliott, 1994, p. 19). Elliott concludes that "poverty is related less to the onset of violence than to the continuity of violence, once initiated" (p. 19). Aside from poverty, prejudice, and discrimination, how can the higher juvenile crime rates in the inner city areas be explained?

⌈The transition from a manufacturing to a technological and service-based economy in the United States drastically changed economic conditions, reducing the demand for low-skilled workers in an increasingly service-oriented, high-tech society, restricting their access to the labor market and blocking their upward mobility (Wilson, 1987), creating what Glasgow (1980) first called the "underclass." A major result of the changing economy was the migration of more affluent families out of the central cities to the suburbs and small towns. Many services moved with them, leaving a void in services for the remaining underclass population. Moore (1978, pp. 27-29) describes the underclass plight as being permanently excluded from participating in mainstream labor market occupations. As a result, members of the underclass must rely on other economic alternatives: low-paying temporary jobs, part-time jobs in the secondary labor market, some form of welfare or living off friends and relatives, or becoming involved in hustling or street crime (Moore, 1988). Others (Auletta, 1982; Bursik & Grasmick, 1993; Hagedorn, 1988; Jackson, 1991; Moore, 1978; 1985; Sullivan, 1989; Wilson, 1987) have argued that crime, delinquency, youth gangs, and youth violence have increased as a result of these postindustrial society conditions (see Bursik & Grasmick, 1993, pp. 142-146). Does empirical evidence support the link between community conditions and crime?

Specific risk factors. The influence of community factors on delinquent and violent behavior stems from the common assumption "that offences arise from the interaction between an individual, with a certain antisocial tendency or crime potential, and the environment, which provides criminal opportunities" (Farrington, 1993, p. 8). The few studies examining the link between community variables and individual offending, however, have had difficulty sorting out the influence of family variables. In fact, knowledge about individual, family, and neighborhood influences on delinquency "is rather fragmentary" (Farrington, 1993, p. 19).

Farrington (1993, p. 29) summarizes the evidence on community factors: Researchers have not "succeeded unambiguously in proving neighborhood influences on offending." Yet "it is hard to resist the conclusion that, because of inadequate definitions of neighborhoods and poor measurement of crucial neighborhood variables, the importance of the neighbourhood effects has been under-estimated up to the present time" (p. 28). It turns out that Farrington's observation was prophetic.

Recent research demonstrates neighborhood differences in offense levels. People in disorganized neighborhoods—characterized by high rates of crime and violence, high population density, physical deterioration, lack of natural surveillance of public places, and low levels of attachment to the neighborhood—are at higher risk for criminal and violent behavior (Sampson & Laub, 1994; Yoshikawa, 1994). In a preliminary analysis of Pittsburgh Youth Study data on boys' progression in individual pathways to crime in different types of neighborhoods, Loeber and Wikstrom (1993) detected neighborhood differences in the prevalence of involvement in overt and covert behaviors, and in their progression in pathways to serious and violent offending. "Boys living in low socioeconomic neighborhoods tended to advance further into a pathway than boys living in high socioeconomic neighborhoods" (p. 200).

Moreover, the three projects in the Program of Research on the Causes and Correlates of Delinquency recently identified specific neighborhood risk factors for juvenile violence: availability of firearms and crime, transitions and mobility, low neighborhood attachment, community disorganization, and extreme economic and social deprivation (Huizinga et al., 1995, p. 35). These studies also show that juveniles who live in underclass areas, regardless of race or ethnicity, have higher rates of self-reported delinquency than do youngsters living elsewhere (Peeples & Loeber, 1994). The study authors conclude that "living in underclass areas itself seems to increase the chances of delinquency, even when holding other factors constant" (p. 16). Few theorists have specified the linkage between community characteristics and delinquent behavior. Most point to "community disorganization" (Shaw & McKay, 1942). Others dispute the disorganization of inner-city minority neighborhoods (Miller, 1958).

Shannon pointed the way to an understanding of differential risk levels in communities, building on the work of the Chicago tradition of research begun by Shaw and McKay (1931). Although Shaw and McKay did not conclusively demonstrate the influence of neighborhood factors independent of family and individual influences (Farrington, 1993, p. 15), they pointed to the importance of diminished community control in socially disorganized neighborhoods and cultural transmission of antisocial values. Shannon pursued the latter proposition in his Racine study. This line of inquiry sets Shannon apart from most studies of the community-crime connection, which emphasize differential opportunities (Gottfredson & Taylor, 1986) rather than differential socialization in communities. Shannon (1991) found that the levels of self-reported delinquency and arrests were highest in inner-city and transitional areas.

Shannon (1988, 1991) also saw a cyclical process in certain communities in Racine, Wisconsin. In communities that fell victim to economic deterioration, residents moved out, followed by increases in juvenile delinquency, which in turn were followed by further economic deterioration. Shannon also found modest support for the hypothesis that different neighborhood milieus (inner city, transitional, stable, and middle/upper class) produced variations in delinquent and criminal behavior and even more disproportional societal reactions (arrests, court referrals, and incarceration) to delinquency and crime.

Numerous studies of gang violence have shown community variations (Hagedorn, 1994; Horowitz, 1983; Moore, 1990; Vigil, 1988) and that youth gangs serve as the carriers of neighborhood traditions and culture (Miller, 1958; Moore, 1991; Short & Strodtbeck, 1965). Block and Block (1992) found variations in homicide patterns during the same time frame to vary in different community areas of Chicago, that youth gang homicides have episodic peaks and troughs in specific neighborhoods, and that the patterns of yearly changes from one community to another were unrelated (pp. 84-85). In a subsequent study, Block and Block (1993) showed that neighborhood characteristics such as chronic social and economic problems were associated with specific types of gang crime. Youth gangs specializing in instrumental violence were most prevalent in disorganized and declining neighborhoods, whereas youth gangs specializing in expressive violence were most prevalent in prospering neighborhoods with expanding populations.

This latter finding confirmed Spergel's (1984) earlier observation that youth gangs emerge both in newly settled areas and in relatively stable, well-organized areas. In a later study, Curry and Spergel (1988) also found distinctly different gang violence patterns in various Chicago communities, showing that youth gang homicides tended to be correlated significantly with social disorganization and that other forms of delinquency were more directly related to poverty-stricken communities. Other studies suggest that factors giving rise to, or that change the character of, youth gangs transcend neighborhood influences (see Bursik & Grasmick's discussion, 1993, pp. 132-134).

In sum, research on youth gangs provides the most substantiation of the long-held belief in the significance of neighborhood factors in generating delinquency and violence. Studies documenting neighborhood variations in gangs and their different types of violence are persuasive. Likewise, general delinquency research, particularly Shannon's landmark study, convincingly shows delinquency traditions in specific neighborhoods and disproportionate societal responses to delinquent behavior in different neighborhoods. Most important, the longitudinal prospective cohort studies on causes and correlates have found disproportionate self-reported delinquency in underclass areas and have identified neighborhood-specific risk factors for violence. Bursik and Grasmick's (1993, p. 29) conclusion that "the neighborhood does have a significant effect on the probability of criminal behavior that is independent of the effects that can be attributed to the personal attributes of residents of the community" seems warranted.

Availability of firearms in the community is a specific risk factor for violence. There are several empirical bases. First, there is evidence that homicides increase because of the greater lethality that results from gun use. Block and Block (1993, p. 8) found in their analysis of gang-related homicides in Chicago during 1987-1990 that, although street gang assaults did not increase during the period, homicides did. The increase in deaths was attributed to an increase in the lethality (deaths per incident) of assaults. Automatic or semiautomatic weapons of high caliber replaced lower caliber weapons. Even the .38 caliber handgun, widely used in Chicago homicides since 1970, became less frequently used than higher caliber (such as 9 millimeter) guns.

[Second, guns bought for family protection represent a greater threat to members of the household than to outsiders. Guns kept in the home for self-protection are more than five times as likely to kill a family member, friend, or acquaintance than to kill an intruder (Kellerman & Reay, 1986). In Kellerman and Reay's 6-year study in King County, Washington, less than 1% of residential deaths where a firearm was kept involved an intruder shot during attempted entry, and less than 2% were killings in self-defense. For every case of self-protection homicide in-volving a firearm kept in the home, there were 1.3 accidental deaths, 4.6 criminal homicides, and 37 suicides involving firearms. Handguns were used in 70.5% of all these deaths.

Third, it should not go unnoticed that Kellerman and Reay's (1986) study showed that guns kept in the home for self-protection are 37 times as likely to be used in a suicide as in the killing of an intruder. "Self-destructive use of guns claims more lives than either criminal assaults or accidents in the United States—about 1,000 more deaths in 1990 than the total attributable to accident and homicides" (Zimring, 1993, p. 113).

Fourth, guns are readily available to adolescents. Youths now have access to more lethal weapons. In their survey of incarcerated youth from particularly high-violence urban areas, Sheley and Wright (1993, 1995) found that most of them owned a revolver at the time of their incarceration, and 65% said they owned three or more guns. Aside from presumed legally owned guns (hunting rifles and regular shotguns), the most common calibers were .38 and .357. Revolvers were closely followed in popularity by automatic and semiautomatic handguns, typically 9 millimeter or .45 caliber. Seventy percent of the inmates said they could easily get a gun on release.

In another component of the study, Sheley and Wright (1993, 1995; Wright, 1995) surveyed students (grades 9-12) in cities near the correctional facilities from which they drew the sample of incarcerated youths. The student sample consisted of classroom groups in schools identified as experiencing firearms incidents. The percentage who owned a gun is higher than one might expect, even among such a high risk group. More than half (55%) of the inmates and 18% of the students said they owned an automatic or semiautomatic handgun.

Both groups were asked how they would go about getting a gun if they wished to, and where they obtained the guns they owned. Family members, friends, and street people were the main sources from whom the adolescents and young adults believed they could get a gun (Table 7.2). This study would have been more helpful in understanding the role family members play in young persons' access to guns if respondents had been asked questions that would have enabled the study authors to distinguish illegally owned guns from legally owned ones. In the Rochester Youth Development Study, Lizotte and colleagues (1994)

TABLE 7.2 Means of Obtaining Guns

	Percentage of Inmates	Percentage of Students
Likely source if desired[a]	(N = 728)	(N = 623)
Steal from a person or car	14	7
Steal from a house or apartment	17	8
Steal from a store or pawnshop	8	4
Borrow from family member or friend	45	53
Buy from family member or friend	36	35
Get off the street	54	37
Get from a drug dealer	36	22
Get from an addict	35	22
Buy from gun shop	12	28
Source of most recent handgun[b]	(N = 640)	(N = 211)
A friend	30	38
Family member	6	23
Gun shop/pawnshop	7	11
The street	22	14
Drug dealer	9	2
Drug addict	12	6
"Taken" from someone's house or car	12	2
Other	2	4

SOURCE: "Gun Acquisition and Possession in Selected Juvenile Samples," Sheeley and Wright (1993, p. 6).
a. Item: "How would you go about getting a gun if you decided you wanted one?" (Multiple responses permitted.)
b. Item: "Where did you get your most recent handgun?" Respondents who owned handguns only.

found that about 10% of 9th and 10th grade Rochester inner-city boys owned guns (4% for sport and 6% for protection). Only 4% of sport owners self-reported committing a crime, compared to 30% of illegal owners.

The Centers for Disease Control and Prevention's (1993) New York City survey found that 22% of high school students carried a weapon (such as a gun, knife, or club) in the past month (up 2% from 1991). Nearly 12% of them had brought a weapon to school on at least 1 day in the past month. Callahan and Rivara's (1992) Seattle high school study illustrated how readily available handguns are to youngsters not considered to be at high risk. Thirty-four percent of the students reported easy access to handguns, and 6% reported that they owned one. Only 3% of all students but 33% of handgun owners reported that they had shot someone. Lizotte and colleagues (1994) found that 8% percent of the Rochester boys reported carrying guns regularly. The National School Safety Center (Stephens, 1994) reported a 25% increase in school-associated deaths in the 1993-1994 school year over the previous year.

The high rate of homicide in the United States is not solely the result of weapon avail-

ability, because the average rate of homicides committed without a firearm in the United States exceeds the total homicide rate in every other country for which information is available (Block & Block, 1991, p. 49). The Blocks also note that "neither are high homicide rates a simple function of high rates in the black community; white homicide victimization rates in the United States are higher than total homicide rates in European countries" (p. 49). They point to a growing body of research that "suggests that the prevailing attitudes in the United States condone violence to a greater extent than in other countries" (p. 49). One indicator is the level of violence on the job, which the National Institute for Occupational Safety and Health recently called an "epidemic," because it documented 1,071 murders and 160,000 physical assaults on the job in 1994 (Elias, 1996).

Fifth, gangs are more likely to recruit adolescents who own a firearm (Bjerregaard & Lizotte, 1995). The Rochester study found that more than half of the juveniles who reported being in a gang also said they owned guns for protection (Lizotte et al., 1994). A comparison of boys who owned guns for protection versus for sport showed that the former are eight times as likely to commit a gun crime, six times as likely to carry guns, almost five times as likely to be in a gang, more than four times as likely to sell drugs, and more than three times as likely to commit a street crime (Lizotte et al., 1994, p. 64). In their 3-year field study of 99 active gang members in St. Louis, Decker and Van Winkle (1996) reported that 80 of them owned guns. The mean number owned by the gangsters was more than four. Two-thirds of them (66) had used their guns at least once.

Sixth, drug trafficking is associated with firearms possession. Van Kammen and Loeber (1994b; see also Van Kammen & Loeber, 1994a) found that juveniles' initiation into selling drugs was associated with a significant increase in carrying a weapon. Late onset drug sellers became more deeply involved in carrying a concealed weapon when they initiated drug trafficking. More than half of the drug sellers at age 19 were carrying a gun, and this proportion increased to almost 80% for drug traffickers selling hard drugs. From another viewpoint, of all the young men at age 19 who carried a weapon, 64% were also involved in selling drugs. This proportion among juveniles in Rochester was only half as large (32%; Lizotte et al., 1994).

Seventh, firearms are increasingly the weapon of choice in homicides, whereas use of other weapons is decreasing (Snyder et al., 1996, p. 24). In 1967, less than half (47%) of all homicides were by a firearm (Mulvihill & Tumin, 1969, p. 235). In 1992-1993, 82% of homicides were committed by handgun (Zawitz, 1996, p. 4). Firearm-related deaths increased 60% from 1968 through 1991 (Fontanarosa, 1995), equaling or surpassing motor vehicle-related deaths in seven states and the District of Columbia (Centers for Disease Control and Prevention, 1994). Since 1990, firearm-related violence has been the leading single cause of death associated with brain trauma in the United States (Sosin, Sniezek, & Waxweiler, 1995). Of the approximately 50,000 deaths associated with brain trauma in 1992, 44% were attributable to firearms and 34% to motor vehicle crashes (Fontanarosa, 1995).

The growing availability and use of firearms in the United States have reached epidemic proportions (Hutson et al., 1995), although the National Rifle Association disagrees (see Blackman, 1992). Guns are more readily available than in times past to juveniles in the home and on the streets. Most of the well-publicized instances of children killing children are precipitated by immediate access to guns rather than by the arrival of a new class of child "superpredators," as DiIulio (1996) suggests. Strategies for reducing the availability of firearms to juveniles are identified in Chapter 6.

Family

General family conditions. We saw earlier that poverty has a growing and devastating effect on families (National Research Council, 1993, pp. 13-40). Family income is the main determinant of the settings in which children and adolescents spend their lives. Key social opportunities linked to housing, health services, neighborhoods, and schools are controlled by family income. Equally important, income shapes the most important of all settings in which children grow up: families (National Research Council, 1993, pp. 16-18). Poverty limits families' ability to purchase goods and services essential for healthy development, including adequate housing and food. Families living in these conditions are unable to provide the necessary emotional support and stimulation critical to healthy child development. Children of poverty-stricken families are at high risk for physical, mental, and developmental disabilities.

Children growing up in structurally weak families also are at a disadvantage. Between 1960 and 1990, the number of divorces in the United States nearly tripled. Effects of the broken home have been a controversial issue (see Farrington, 1996, pp. 86-88) since Bowlby (1951) popularized the hypothesis. Although a number of studies have found correlations between broken homes and delinquency, Farrington (1996, p. 91) suggests that it is not so much the broken home that produces crimogenic families as the parental conflict that causes it. He also suggests that "a loving mother might in some sense be able to compensate for the loss of a father" (p. 91). Farrington bases these observations on McCord's (1982) study showing that the prevalence of offending was similar among boys reared in broken homes without affectionate mothers (62%) and among those reared in united homes characterized by conflict (52%), compared to boys reared in united homes without conflict (26%) and boys reared in broken homes with affectionate mothers (22%). He also notes (p. 92) that researchers have had difficulty separating the effects of single-parent families from the effects of low-income families, because most of the studies focused on single-parent families living in poverty.

Teenage pregnancy is another general risk factor for problem behaviors. About 1 million teenagers become pregnant each year, 80% of whom are unintended (Centers for Disease Control and Prevention, 1996). Early childbearing is associated with many other adverse developmental outcomes that compromise the future of these children (National Research Council, 1993, pp. 18-20). Early sexual activity (especially among females) is linked to poverty, social disadvantage, and family disorganization (Leffert & Peterson, 1995), and also to high rates of delinquency involvement and gang participation (Thornberry, 1993; Bjerregaard & Smith, 1993).

Specific risk factors. Parental and family influences are classified in four domains (Loeber & Stouthamer-Loeber, 1986): family demographics (e.g., socioeconomic status), parental characteristics (e.g., antisocial personality), parenting techniques (e.g., lack of monitoring, inconsistent discipline), and parent-child relationships (e.g., parental rejection). Loeber and Stouthamer-Loeber (1986) concluded that lack of parental supervision was one of the strongest predictors of the development of delinquency and violence in offspring. Parental rejection also has been shown to be a key predictor of later adolescent aggression and delinquency (Farrington, 1991; Loeber & Stouthamer-Loeber, 1986; Olweus, 1980).

Other reviews examining the relationship of family factors to general delinquency identify poor parental management techniques, harsh or erratic parental discipline, parental disharmony, low parental involvement in the child's activities, large families, early and persistent childhood problem behavior in the home, low intelligence and educational achievement, and separation from parents (Loeber & Dishion, 1983; Loeber & Stouthamer-Loeber, 1987; Snyder & Patterson, 1987; Uting, Bright, & Henrickson, 1993). The three projects in the Program of Research on the Causes and Correlates of Delinquency identify specific family risk factors for juvenile violence: a family history of high risk behavior, family management problems, child maltreatment, and family conflict (Huizinga et al., 1995).

Prenatal and perinatal factors are also important predictors of delinquency and other problem behaviors (Farrington, 1996, pp. 83-85). These include absent biological fathers, low income, and welfare support. Early childbearing (as a result of teenage pregnancy), drug use during pregnancy, and perinatal complications are correlated with poor parenting techniques, child hyperactivity, impulsivity, low intelligence, and low school achievement, which in turn predict childhood behavior problems and later delinquency (Farrington, 1989a, 1994). Kolvin, Miller, Scott, Gatzanis, and Fleeting (1990) found that teenage mothers were twice as likely as young adults to have sons who became offenders by the age of 32. Teenage daughters of young mothers also tend to have psychological problems (Lerman & Pottick, 1995).

Studies have shown that criminal, antisocial, and alcoholic parents tend to have delinquent sons (Farrington, 1996; McCord, 1979, 1982; Robins, 1979; Robins, West, & Herjanic, 1975; Wilson, 1987). More important, West and Farrington (1973, 1977) discovered that parental offending is concentrated in a small proportion of families. Less than 5% of the 400 families in the Cambridge, England, study were responsible for about half of the criminal convictions of all family members, including fathers, mothers, sons, and daughters. Farrington (1979) also found that the existence of convicted parents and delinquent siblings was related to self-reported as well as to official offending.

In a recent study, Smith and Thornberry (1995) found that a history of childhood maltreatment significantly increases the likelihood of later self-reported juvenile involvement in moderately serious, serious, and violent delinquency (but not minor delinquency). Maltreatment also increased significantly the chances of being arrested and the frequency of arrests. Both of these findings stood up when race/ethnicity, social class, family structure, and mobility were held constant. Although the most egregiously maltreated youngsters (measured by frequency, severity, duration, and variety of maltreatment) exhibited the highest delinquency rates, the differences in delinquency involvement between the worst maltreated children and others were not large. This finding led Smith and Thornberry to conclude that "having a history of childhood maltreatment serious enough to warrant official intervention by child protective services is a significant risk factor for later involvement in serious delinquency" (p. 469).

It is important to note that Smith and Thornberry operationalized "maltreatment" very broadly, to include physical abuse, sexual abuse, emotional maltreatment, moral/legal maltreatment, educational maltreatment, physical neglect, and lack of supervision. In an earlier analysis, Thornberry (1994) found that children who experienced multiple forms of family violence in the home (child abuse, spouse abuse, and family conflict) were twice as likely to commit violent acts themselves. Among youths in nonviolent families, 38% reported involvement in violent delinquency. This rate increased to 60% for youths who experienced one form of violence, to 73% for those exposed to two forms of violence, and to 78% for adolescents exposed to all three types of family violence. Previous studies, which measured only official delinquency (see Smith and Thornberry, 1995, pp. 452-455 for a discussion of these), have not shown the strong connection to violence that the self-report measures in the Rochester study made possible.

The prevalence of serious delinquency is three times as high (36% vs. 11%) among children experiencing five or more family-related risk factors compared to children who experienced none of the risks (Smith, Lizotte, Thornberry, & Krohn, 1995). The risk factors Smith and her colleagues measured were low parental education, parental unemployment, family receipt of welfare, the respondent's mother having her first child before the age of 18, the respondent's family moving five or more times before he or she was 12 years old, family members experiencing trouble with drugs, family members experiencing trouble with the law, an official record of child abuse or maltreatment, and the respondent being placed in care outside the family. Despite the presence of five or more of these risk factors, nearly two-thirds of the high-risk youth were resilient to serious delinquency, which provides encouragement that the negative effects of risk factors can be reduced.

Hawkins and colleagues' (1995, pp. 48-50) review of risk factors for crime, violence, and substance abuse from conception to the age of 6 identifies several factors associated with later problems—including perinatal difficulties, minor physical abnormalities and brain damage, and other family-related factors such as parental drug and alcohol abuse, poor family management practices, and family conflict—that predispose infants and children to later violent, aggressive, and substance abuse behavior (see also Yoshikawa, 1994).

School Failure

The social context. Adolescents from low-income families and neighborhoods are at much higher risk of school failure than are suburban youths. Children who drop out or fail in school tend to be from poor families, living in single-parent households, and living in urban areas (National Research Council, 1993, p. 113). School failure is a risk factor not only for delinquency but also for violence and substance abuse (Hawkins, Catalano, & Miller, 1992; Hawkins et al., 1995, p. 49; Yoshikawa, 1994).

Although high school dropout rates have declined since 1972, they have increased recently among Hispanic youngsters (Snyder & Sickmund, 1995, pp. 14-16). In 1992, 11% of all 16-24-year-olds had dropped out of school before receiving a high school diploma. This rate was much higher for Hispanics (29%) than for blacks (14%) or whites (8%). Hispanics in middle- and low-income groups dropped out at a higher rate than whites or blacks. Youths who drop out of school have dismal employment prospects. Unemployed high school dropouts are at high risk for delinquency and criminal involvement.

The safety of the school environment is an important factor affecting school failure. Lab and Clark (1996) found in their survey of 44 public and private Ohio schools that more normative control measures, contrasted with coercive techniques, were associated with lower school victimization levels. Lab and Clark concluded that, even in the most crime-ridden communities, "islands of safety" can be created in schools using normative measures. Rutter, Maughan, Mortimore, Ouston, and Smith (1979) established that delinquency levels varied with school organization and practice, student achievement, and student behavior. An important implication of their research and other studies on the limited effectiveness of alternative education, specifically the practice of pulling students out of mainstream classrooms, is that school performance can be increased while reducing delinquency by mainstreaming students in improved schools (see Hawkins, Doueck, & Lishner, 1988, pp. 32-34).

School failure is not simply a unilateral decision on the part of the failing youngster. The strongest predictors of school failure are family income and educational background. Other factors explaining higher dropout rates among minority and low-income youths than among those not disadvantaged include inhospitable learning environments, poor and irrelevant instruction, and fewer resources than schools in more affluent neighborhoods (National Research Council, 1993, pp. 102-113).

Specific risk factors. Several reviews have been made of studies regarding school risk factors for delinquency (Gottfredson, 1981; Hawkins et al., 1988; Hawkins & Lishner, 1987; Maguin & Loeber, 1996). Maguin and Loeber's (1996) meta-analysis is the most comprehensive to date. They summarize the major risk factors identified in longitudinal and experimental studies. Poor academic performance is related not only to the prevalence and onset of delinquency but also to escalation in the frequency and seriousness of offending. Conversely, better academic performance is related to desistance from offending. More specifically, there is an incremental effect. The poorer the academic performance, the higher the delinquency. Maguin and Loeber (1996, pp. 246-247) estimate that the odds of delinquency involvement are about twice as high among students with low academic performance compared to those with high academic performance. Moreover, studies reviewed by Maguin and Loeber suggest that lower levels of academic performance are linked to a higher frequency of offenses, more serious offenses, and more violent offenses. These researchers also found some evidence that low academic performance is related to early onset of offending. All these findings were consistently stronger for males than for females, and for white youths than for black youngsters.

The link between early onset and low school performance has been confirmed for general delinquency in the Pittsburgh Youth Study (Huizinga, Loeber, & Thornberry, 1994, p. 15). The relationship between reading performance and general delinquency appears for first graders. More generally, school performance, whether measured by reading achievement or by teacher-rated reading performance, and retention in grade is related to delinquency. The Pittsburgh Youth Study also found that youngsters who are not highly committed to school subsequently have higher rates of street crimes, which in turn results in reduced levels of commitment to school (Huizinga, Loeber, & Thornberry, 1994, p. 15). The three projects in the Program of Research on the Causes and Correlates of Delinquency recently have identified school risk factors specifically for juvenile violence: early and persistent antisocial behavior at school, academic failure, and a lack of commitment to school (Huizinga et al., 1995). Other studies have found that how much students like school, spend time on homework, and perceive their coursework to be relevant, hold high educational aspirations, and feel bonded to school are related to delinquency (Elliott, Huizinga & Ageton, 1985; Elliott & Voss, 1974; Hirschi, 1969; Kelly & Balch, 1971). "The evidence on school failure, attitudes toward school, school misbehavior, and delinquency suggests that low-achieving students have an increased risk for school misbehavior and, ultimately, for involvement in delinquent behavior" (Hawkins et al., 1988, p. 33).

Individual Characteristics

An overview. Age and gender are the main individual characteristics accounting for differential rates of violence. Violence peaks in the adolescent years, and rates are higher among males than females (Elliott, 1994a). Aside from age and gender, most other individual characteristics fall into the mental health arena. About 12%, or 7.5 million, of our nation's 65 million children and adolescents are estimated to suffer from mental disorders (Institute of Medicine, 1994, p. 4). The Office of Technology Assessment (1991) estimates that the prevalence of diagnosable mental disorders among individuals under the age of 20 may be closer to 20%. These disorders include autism, attention deficit hyperactivity disorder, severe conduct disorder, depression, and alcohol and other drug abuse and dependence.

Poor mental health is not a condition that children and adolescents choose. The American Academy of Child and Adolescent Psychiatry (1990) warns that growing numbers of children and adolescents are at "exceptionally high risk" for developing a mental disorder because of abuse and neglect (2.9 million children), living in foster care arrangements (300,000 youths), and living with an alcoholic parent (7 million youngsters). In addition, Michaels and Levine (1992) estimated that by 1995, 37,000 children would be left motherless by the HIV/AIDS epidemic.

Family factors that constitute significant risk for increased childhood psychopathology include severe marital discord, social disadvantage, overcrowding or large family size, parental criminality, maternal mental disorder, and admission to child welfare services. Mental impairment rates are significantly higher for children from low-income welfare families, living in subsidized housing, and living in an area that has a high rate of community disorganization (Institute of Medicine, 1994, pp. 182-183; Lerman & Pottick, 1995). A prematurely born, low-birthweight baby (who may as a result have low intelligence) may be more vulnerable than a healthy sibling in a suboptimal family. Such a child may be disadvantaged in parent-child interactions. "Individual risk factors during childhood can lead to a state of vulnerability in which other risk factors may have more effect" (Institute of Medicine, 1994, p. 182).

The process by which individual characteristics play out, resulting in delinquency and violence, appears to derive from interaction between personal traits and the environment. Mothers of children with a difficult temperament may become increasingly permissive with them; this, in turn, results in a worse later childhood temperament (Olweus, 1980). Young children with a difficult temperamental style are difficult to socialize because they do not respond readily to parenting techniques such as reinforcement and reward. These children may be thrill seekers and drawn to peer group situations that provide excitement and adventure. Given the presence of other risk factors—such as poor parental monitoring, poverty, and the availability of a delinquent peer group—a fearless, uninhibited, or difficult temperament may predispose a child to a developmental trajectory of aggression and violence (Pepler & Slaby, 1994, p. 37).

Because of the diversity of adolescents' health and mental health needs, the fragmented U.S. health care system is unable to provide needed services. Adolescents are unlikely to know where to go for necessary services or how to access them. The adolescent health and mental health care system lacks a consistent entry point into the system, service coordination, adequate consultation and referral services by adolescent specialists, and comprehensiveness. "As a result, the health care system is poorly set up to help adolescents overcome problems resulting from poverty, dangerous neighborhoods, and an inadequate social environment including school and home" (National Research Council, 1993, p. 6).

Specific risk factors. Individual characteristics that are related to violence fall into four categories: constitutional factors, poor mental health, drug abuse, and antisocial behavior such as bullying.

Individual violence proclivity appears to be related to a set of constitutional factors that include a fearless and uninhibited temperament, a difficult temperament, impulsiveness, cognitive impairments, and low intelligence quotient (IQ). These factors "can interact with other factors to produce violence (Eron & Slaby, 1994, p. 7). Genetic variation in possible violence-related temperament factors may also contribute to violent behaviors (Eron & Slaby, 1994, p. 7). Based on knowledge accumulated to date, the most likely linkage between children's individual traits and aggression may be a function of acquired biological deficits—such as prenatal and perinatal complications (Brennan, Mednick, & Kandel, 1991), neonatal injuries (Kolvin et al., 1990), injury to the brain and neurological dysfunction (Rivara & Farrington, in press), and exposure to neurotoxins—or deficits in their social environments (Loeber, 1990).

Mental health as a risk factor for violence has not been well researched. The main problem is that it is hard to disentangle normal adolescent developmental problems from serious mental illness (Rutter, 1986). Clinical and delinquent populations show much higher prevalence rates than the general adolescent population. Achenbach and Edelbrock (1983) classified 35% of an East Coast sample of adolescent mental health referrals as delinquent, 46% as hyperactive, 33% as hostile-withdrawn, and 26% as aggressive.

Lerman and Pottick (1995) found higher delinquency prevalence levels and similar levels of other problems among boys referred to a Newark Family Crisis Intervention Unit: 60% were diagnosed as delinquent, 47% as hyperactive, 31% as obsessive-compulsive, 25% as hostile-withdrawn, and 22% as aggressive (verbal, interpersonal, and starting fights by physical assault). Girls evidenced a high prevalence of being delinquent (62%), cruel (47%), immature-hyperactive (45%), depressed (35%), and aggressive (31%). A study (McManus, 1984) of incarcerated juvenile samples found that 54% fit the adult diagnostic category of antisocial personality disorder. Several studies report no significant differences in psychopathology between delinquent and psychiatric treatment populations (Cohen et al., 1990; Lewis, 1980; Shanok, 1983), generally showing that racial bias mainly accounts for the choice of placements, a finding disputed by Kaplan and Busner (1992).

Lerman and Pottick (1995) suggest that prediction of delinquency among urban youth can be improved by including mental health measures. They found that the highest rates of cruel and assaultive behaviors occur when youths score high on both delinquency and aggression (verbal, interpersonal, and starting fights by physical assault). "Highly aggressive youth do not require the association of bad peers to be violent, but their level of cruelty and assaults are likely to increase in a high delinquent context that includes the support of bad peers" (p. 215).

Drug abuse is a pervasive individual risk factor among adolescents. Although the percentage of persons who reported using an illicit drug in the past month in 1994 was highest among those age 18-21 (15.2%), the group with the second highest rate was teenagers age 16-17 (14.5%) (Substance Abuse and Mental Health Services Administration [SAMHSA], 1995). Between 1994 and 1995, use of cigarettes and most illicit drugs increased among students in the 8th, 10th, and 12th grades (U.S. Department of Health and Human Services, 1995). From 1993 to 1994, the number of drug-related episodes among 12-17-year-olds resulting in visits to the emergency room increased 17% (SAMHSA, 1994). The percentage of youths 12-17 years old who perceive great risk in using illegal drugs has decreased since 1992 (SAMHSA, 1995). It is not surprising, then, that drug use among high school seniors began increasing in 1992.

Most studies identifying individual risk factors for delinquency have focused more generally on "antisocial behavior" as a personality deficit. A number of investigations indicate that antisocial behaviors are related to deficits in social skills, social cognition and inappropriate attributions of the meanings of social contexts and interactions, failure to empathize or take the role of others in interactions, and deficits in social problem-solving thinking (see Bullis & Walker, 1996). Other factors linked to antisocial behavior include learning disabilities (Zimmerman, Rich, Keilitz, & Broder, 1981), schizophrenia and bipolar disorders (Duchnowski & Kutash, 1996), severe emotional disturbance (Wagner, D'Amico, Marder, Newman, & Blackorby, 1992), abuse and neglect (Smith & Thornberry, 1995; Thornberry, 1994; Widom, 1989a, 1989b), and ADHD (At-

tention-Deficit Hyperactivity Disorder). Although the exact relationship of ADHD to delinquency onset and escalation is not clear, a number of studies have established a relationship (Loeber, Farrington, Stouthamer-Loeber, & Van Kammen, 1994; Loeber, Green, Keenan, & Lahey, 1995; Loeber, Keenan, Zhang, & Sieck, in press; Loeber et al., 1993). In addition to child maltreatment, the three projects in the Program of Research on the Causes and Correlates of Delinquency identify, as specific individual risk factors for juvenile violence, alienation and rebelliousness, early initiation of problem behavior, and favorable attitudes toward problem behavior (Huizinga et al., 1995).

Bullying is a form of aggression that predicts adult offending. Farrington (1993, p. 381) defines bullying as "repeated oppression, psychological or physical, of a less powerful person by a more powerful one." Work on bullying was pioneered by Olweus (1978, 1979, 1992, 1994), resulting in a nationwide Norwegian school program. Olweus established the relationship between adolescent bullying and adult offending, finding that more than half of bullies were convicted of criminal offenses by the age of 24 and that their offending rates were four times as high as rates among nonbullies. Farrington (1993, 1995) summarizes other evidence on bullying. It is surprisingly common. More than half of surveyed students have been bullied, and more than half have bullied at one time or another. Bullies tend to display aggression in different settings over many years. They tend to be impulsive and have low school attainment, low self-esteem, and poor social skills. Adolescent boys tend to physically bully others, whereas girls tend to psychologically bully. Both tend to come from families of low socioeconomic status, with poor child rearing techniques. Adolescent bullies tend to become adult bullies and later to have children who are bullies. In the Cambridge Study in Delinquent Development (Farrington, 1993), males who reported that they were bullies at the age of 14 also were likely to report that they were bullies at the age of 32.

A key issue that needs to be explored is the relationship between bullying and other forms of victimization. Garofalo and colleagues (1987) discovered that a large proportion of school-related victimizations stem from peer interactions occurring in the course of routine daily activities that escalate into victimizations. These include bullying, insults, and misguided mischief. Much of the peak in juvenile victimizations that occurs at the end of the school day is probably related to these kinds of events.

Peer Group

Overview. "One of the most stable and well-established findings in delinquency research is that the delinquent behavior of an individual is positively related to the actual or perceived delinquent behavior of that individual's friends" (Elliott & Menard, 1996, p. 29). The strong relationship between delinquent peer group members and delinquent behavior was well documented 65 years ago (Shaw & McKay, 1931) and is largely uncontested to this day. There is disagreement among researchers and delinquency theorists, however, with respect to the causal importance of peers (Warr, 1996, pp. 11-12). A main point of contention is that peers are involved in other legal things kids do; therefore, association with delinquent peers may not have causal significance (Warr, 1996, p. 12). Others argue that engaging in delinquent behavior and having delinquent friends are actually different measures of the same thing—that exposure to delinquent friends leads to delinquent behavior, or that delinquent behavior leads to acquisition of delinquent friends (see Elliott & Menard, 1996, p. 29; Keenan, Loeber, Zhang, Stouthamer-Loeber, & Van Kammen, 1995, pp. 715-716). Others contend that the process by which boys become associated with delinquent friends is analogous to "niche picking," seeking out peers who accept their behavior (Patterson, 1982). Farrington (1996, p. 98) suggests that "the major problem of interpretation is whether young people are more likely to commit offenses while they are in groups than while they are alone, or whether the high prevalence of co-offending merely reflects the fact that, whenever young people go out, they tend to go out in groups."[1] Longitudinal studies are necessary to disentangle the peer group deliquency relationship.

Peer groups appear to play an increasingly important role in adolescent socialization in our society. The reasons are linked to social and structural changes over the past two decades. The high divorce rate, growing numbers of single parents, increasing teenage births, and the increasing number of dual working parents (National Research Council, 1993) all serve to diminish parental socialization and control of adolescents. Sampson and Groves (1989; see also Sampson, 1992, 1993) suggest that weak family structures reduce informal controls in the neighborhood, by virtue of diminished family networks that serve to supervise and provide social control over youngsters. Sampson and Groves thus link high family disruption rates to the prevalence of disorderly teenage groups.

Specific risk factors. In their analyses of longitudinal, self-reported National Youth Survey data, Elliott and Menard (1996) convincingly demonstrate that "the onset of exposure to delinquent friends typically precedes the onset of one's own illegal behavior" (p. 28). Elliott and Menard (1996, pp. 25-26) describe the sequence as follows: "The typical progression for those who are non-delinquent and in non-delinquent peer groups is (1) movement into a slightly more delinquent peer group, (2) onset of minor delinquency, (3) movement into a more delinquent peer group, (4) onset of Index delinquency, and (5) movement into a predominantly delinquent peer group." When juveniles enter young adulthood, they tend to become less involved in both delinquent peer groups and delinquent behavior (Elliott & Menard, 1996). With respect to general delinquency, Elliott and Menard (1996, p. 43) found that less than 18% of the total sample began general or minor offending before their initial exposure to delinquent friends.

The sequential process Elliott and Menard describe appears to apply to serious and violent offending as well as to general delinquency. They found that in the vast majority of cases, exposure to delinquent friends precedes Index offending (Elliott & Menard, 1996, p. 43). In fact, only 1% of the total sample self-reported an Index offense before their exposure to delinquent friends (p. 43). The Program of Research on the Causes and Correlates of Delinquency identifies two specific peer group risk factors for juvenile violence: friends who engage in problem behavior and gang participation (Huizinga et al., 1995).

Gang studies in Denver (Huizinga, 1996), Rochester (Thornberry, in press), and Seattle (Battin et al., 1996) show that the influence of the gang on levels of violent offending is greater than the influence of other highly delinquent peers. Second, while in the gang, members commit serious and violent acts at a much higher level of frequency compared to before and after gang membership (Esbensen & Huizinga, 1993; Hill et al., 1996; Thornberry et al., 1993). Third, the influence of the gang is long-lasting. In all three sites, gang members' offending continued to be elevated after leaving the gang, although the level of offending dropped (Esbensen & Huizinga, 1993; Hill et al., 1996; Thornberry et al., 1993). Most notably, in Seattle drug use and trafficking rates remained nearly as high after leaving the gang as while active in it (Hill et al., 1996). In fact, gang member involvement in drug trafficking through the 10th grade predicted drug trafficking in the 12th grade (Howell, Hill, Battin, & Hawkins, 1996). Gang involvement thus influences delinquency involvement above and beyond the influence of delinquent peer groups. The contribution of youth gangs to recent increases in juvenile violence will be discussed shortly.

The delinquent peer group clearly plays a key role in the onset and escalation of delinquency and violence. The empirical evidence supports a causal relationship between bad peers and the onset of delinquency among good kids. Studies in Denver, Rochester, and Seattle suggest that gang peers contribute mainly to violence escalation rather than to onset because gangs tend to recruit adolescents who already are delinquent (Esbensen & Huizinga, 1993; Hill et al., 1996; Thornberry et al., 1993).

The dynamics of group interactions in gangs that contribute to violence escalation requires more study (Klein, 1995; Short & Strodtbeck, 1965; Thornberry et al., 1993). Goldstein and Soriano (1994, p. 322) suggest that certain adolescents have characteristics that may render them more susceptible to gang influences. These include status seeking behavior, marginality, independence striving, search for identity, heightened need for self-esteem enhancement, and challenge of authority. Keenan and colleagues (1995) found a strong correlation between boys' exposure to peers engaged in overt problem behavior and boys' subsequent initiation into overt behavior, which may help explain the rapid escalation in violence among boys who join gangs. Miller (1980) argues that gang members are uniquely susceptible to peer group pressure. Their susceptibility may be explained by the cohesiveness of gangs, which is related to selective recruitment, shared neighborhood residence, and within-group conformity pressures (Cartwright, Howard, & Reuterman, 1970). Another factor may be high levels

of egotism among gang leaders, the "dark side of high self-esteem" (Baumeister, Smart, & Boden, 1996). These factors may help explain why the youth gang context is clearly the most violent of all adolescent settings.

Other Social and Cultural Factors

In addition to the increasing risk factors for violence reviewed above, a number of social and cultural factors account for the small growth in juvenile violence over the past decade. These include demographic changes, diminished family and youth services, a new ethos of self-expression, the contagious nature of violence, the Wars on Drugs and Crime, and youth gangs. Each of these factors is examined in turn.

Demographic Changes

The number of juveniles age 15-17 began declining in 1986 and began to rise in 1991, when the children of "baby boomers" began reaching crime-prone years (Snyder et al., 1996, p. 15). This explains, in part, the higher number of arrests from 1986 to 1994, but not necessarily the higher violence growth rate among 15-17-year-olds. The increasing violence rate may be related to the fact that more youths of the same age are available. This "cohort effect" (Kleplinger & Weis, 1981; Smith, 1986) may account for much of the increase since 1991.

Easterlin (1978) argues that large cohorts may behave differently from smaller cohorts because of the increased competition for employment and lower relative economic and social well-being. Davis (1979) extends this line of reasoning, contending that larger cohorts experience less socialization and less supervision per child. The growth of this age group has put a strain on social institutions, including families, schools, churches, and youth serving organizations (see Sampson & Groves, 1989; Sampson, 1992, 1993). Increased demand for social services such as education has a negative impact on social adjustment. Larger cohorts also experience a relatively greater peer influence than adult influence, simply as a function of the greater availability of peers. In sum, members of larger cohorts are less prepared for conventional life than members of smaller cohorts (Kleplinger & Weis, 1981, p. 2).

Diminished Family
and Youth Services

In the Reagan and Bush Administrations, the War on Drugs diverted attention from severe social problems (Johns, 1992). Funding for a wide range of health and social services was decreased (Schorr, 1988), resulting in a "virtual abandonment" of the lower class (Johns, 1992) and fewer services for youth and their families at other social class levels as well. The prevailing attitude toward the poor throughout the 1980s was that poverty was their fault and that the government had no abiding responsibility to assist them (Murray, 1984). Consequently, the availability and quality of services for children and adolescents diminished, and this problem was exacerbated by the growing infant and child population during the 1980s. School systems were most visibly affected by the arrival of baby boomers' children. Classrooms became larger as schools bulged with the added student population. The quality of education suffered, as did academic achievement, particularly in inner-city areas (National Research Council, 1993). Supervision of youth likewise decreased. As a result of its comprehensive assessment of youth services, the Panel on High Risk Youth (National Research Council, 1993, p. 96) concluded that "institutions and systems initially designed to help high-risk youth . . . have instead become sources of risk," and that "as the fault lines widen, more and more young people are falling into the cracks."

A New Ethos

A new ethos, or ethic, of self-expression appears to have developed among adolescents. Each of the factors reviewed in this section has given impetus to an egocentric ethos. As in the 1920s, when immediate gratification replaced values of the Victorian era (Wilson, 1983a), the new ethos appears stronger than ever. More children and adolescents—competing for scarce services and opportunities, coming from more troubled families and devastated neighborhoods, and receiving less socialization and supervision, by default or design—over the past decade have become incivil. More adolescents have a tendency to resolve disputes by conflicts, as they had learned to do from their parents and others. More adolescents now join gangs, which flourish in the weakened social system, to increase their odds of social success

and meet their unsocialized needs. Most unfortunately of all, firearms are more readily available than ever before, for use as instruments of the new ethos.

In large measure, adolescents are taking their cues from adults. A 1996 national survey found that 89% of Americans think incivility is a serious problem, and three-fourths believe the problem has gotten worse in the past decade (Lawrence, 1996). The new ethos is expressed in many ways: political meanness, a baseball player spitting at an umpire, and insults hurled by talk-show hosts. Instances of hostility on the highways also have become more common (Twig, 1996).

The Contagious Nature
of Violence

The new ethos favoring violence is contagious. Chief among the findings of more than a half century of psychological research on aggression is that violence is largely learned behavior (Eron & Slaby, 1994, p. 5). It is contagious (Loftin, 1986). "It is clustered in space; it escalates over time; it spreads from one person to another. The empirical evidence for this is consistent, persuasive, and vast. . . . [It] may spread from . . . husband to wife, parent to child, family to friend. People who have been treated violently are more likely to treat others (including the person who victimized them) violently" (Block & Block, 1991, p. 37; see also Baird & Neuenfeldt, 1988; Feld & Straus, 1989; Singer, 1986; Thornberry, 1994; Widom, 1989a, 1989b). "Children who learn that violent behavior 'works' in families, on television, in violent pornographic literature, among peers, and in the community, it is argued, may have a greater potential to behave violently as adults" (National Research Council, 1993, p. 101).

Although violence begins among adolescents as aggressive behavior (Kazdin, 1987), a wide range of offenses typically follows, sometimes including violence (Loeber et al., 1993). One type of behavior in childhood, such as aggression, does not predict one specific type of behavior in adulthood, such as violence (Laub & Lauritsen, 1993, p. 245). In fact, "violent offenders and nonviolent offenders are virtually identical in childhood, adolescent, and adult features" (Farrington, 1991, p. 24). What distinguishes those who become violent as opposed to nonviolent remains problematic. Violence, particularly lethal violence, is not normally planned.

> Expressive violent acts begin as a fight, brawl, or argument that occurs relatively spontaneously, with little rational planning. Even those expressive confrontations that become lethal begin impulsively. Though the assailant may intend to kill at the moment of the event and may even have thought about it previously, the actual murder was not planned in advance. Therefore, the time, the place, the choice of weapon (if any), and even the participants tend to be those that happen to be available.
>
> Many expressive violent confrontations begin as an argument in which both parties, and often bystanders as well, participate. Often, similar incidents have occurred between the same participants numerous times in the past, and the history of these events is a silent partner in the current incident. In fact, at the outset of the confrontation, it may be difficult to distinguish between the person who later will become the victim, and the person who will become the offender. The loser of the confrontation is the person who dies; the "winner" becomes the offender. (Block, 1993, p. 289)

The Wars on Drugs and Crime

Chapter 4 argued that the War on Drugs and the War on Crime have resulted in increased arrests of juveniles, especially minorities. Do disproportionate arrests, adjudication, prosecution, and confinement lead to increased offending? Limited yet persuasive evidence suggests that this is so. Sherman (1993) argues that offending increases in reaction to unjust punishment. The increase, owing to the Wars on Crime and Drugs, is probably most pronounced among minority youth in inner-city areas. In his Wisconsin birth cohort study, Shannon (1991) found no evidence of deterrence based on severity of sanctions, but there was some evidence that future offense seriousness was reduced by frequent interventions. Institutionalization seemed to further accelerate delinquency (p. 91). Studies of shock incarceration have shown that it increases juvenile offending (Lipsey, 1992a). Taking a long-term perspective,

Moore, Garcia, Cerda, and Valencia (1978) documented the process of increased adult involvement in youth gangs following their imprisonment. Active involvement of ex-convicts increased the life of gangs and added an increment to the level of violence, partly because of their increased proclivity to violence following imprisonment and because their continuing involvement gave more visibility and history to gangs. The latter development stimulated the emergence of more violent young cliques, who wanted to outdo their predecessors (pp. 45-46).

We know very little about what arrest, detention, and confinement do to adolescents—how these experiences affect their prosocial development. The few studies that best address this issue have examined long-term confinement (Forst et al., 1989; Gold & Osgood, 1992; McEwen, 1978; Moos, 1975; Osgood, Gruber, Archer, & Newcomb, 1985; Street, Vinter, & Perrow, 1966). They emphasize a common theme, that effective treatment cannot be coerced. As Gold and Osgood (1992, p. 198) put it, "groups become more prosocial when staff permits them greater autonomy within the limits of standards for good behavior and institutional security."

Drug Use and Trafficking

Growing drug use may account for part of the increase in serious and violent juvenile arrests during the past few years. Blumstein (1995a, 1995b, 1996) suggests that the "crack cocaine epidemic" (Reinarman & Levine, 1989) that began in the early 1980s contributed significantly to the growth in juvenile violence and homicides. Chapter 6 reviewed studies of the growth of gang-related homicides to assess the extent to which an increase in these murders is related to drug trafficking. The concern here is with the possibility of a connection between juvenile drug use, drug trafficking, and the increase in juvenile violence.

The association between delinquency and drug use is well established (Elliott, Huizinga, & Menard, 1989), but the temporal order is not; nor is the relationship between drug use and violence. There is little evidence that drug use leads to delinquency, but serious drug use may prolong involvement in serious delinquency (Huizinga, Menard, & Elliott, 1989). Recent research on the relationships among drug selling, illegal drug use, serious theft, and violence in the Pittsburgh Youth Study suggests that drug

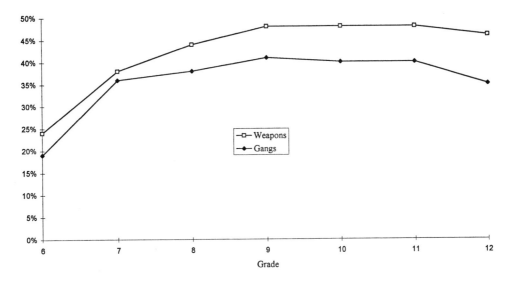

Figure 7.1. Student reports of gangs and weapons by grade, 1993

SOURCE: *Juvenile Offenders and Victims: 1996 Update on Violence* (p. 7), Snyder, Sickmund, and Poe-Yamagata, ©copyright 1996 by the National Center for Juvenile Justice. Reprinted with permission.
DATA SOURCE: *School Safety and Discipline Component: National Household Education Survey of 1993* (machine-readable data file), National Center for Education Statistics (1994).

use, serious theft, and violence precede drug selling (Van Kammen, Maguin, & Loeber, 1994). Van Kammen and her colleagues also found that selling illicit drugs started significantly later in adolescence than the other three behaviors. Initiation of drug selling was strongly related to previous involvement in multiple types of delinquency, rather than a single type. Being African American, living in a neighborhood with a high rate of drug-related offenses, and having friends who used and sold drugs increased the likelihood of drug selling by a factor of almost 10. These influences on drug selling were more powerful than previous involvement in either illegal drug use or violence.

Altschuler and Brounstein (1991) also found that drug-selling boys in the District of Columbia tended to commit more offenses, but mainly more personal crimes. In a study of adolescent crack cocaine dealing in two Florida housing projects (Dembo, Hughes, & Jackson, 1993), 67% of dealers reported having killed or hurt someone, and 82% indicated that adults used children to sell cocaine to avoid the harsh criminal penalties for adult offenders. Chapter 3 showed that initiation into selling drugs is associated with a significant increase in carrying a weapon (Van Kammen & Loeber, 1994a). This Pittsburgh study makes a strong case that drug

use leads to drug trafficking and that drug selling is strongly associated with other serious and violent crimes, but not necessarily that juvenile drug trafficking results in more frequent violent offending.

A recent analysis of longitudinal data in Seattle found that gang involvement in drug trafficking does not lead to increased violence (Howell et al., 1996). Surprisingly (given this finding), among nongang adolescents, involvement in drug trafficking did predict violence, but this single factor explained only 5% of the variance. It may well be that drug trafficking, serious property offending, and violent offending are expressions of the same antisocial tendencies (Van Kammen et al., 1994) that are part of a developmental rather than a causal pattern (Huizinga et al., 1989).

Youth Gangs

Chapter 4 reported the growing number of gang problem cities, youth gangs, and gang members. Gang problems are more prevalent in schools than in the past. In a 1989 school crime victimization survey (Bastian & Taylor, 1991) 15% of the students reported that there were street gangs in their school. In contrast, a 1993 school survey (National Center for Edu-

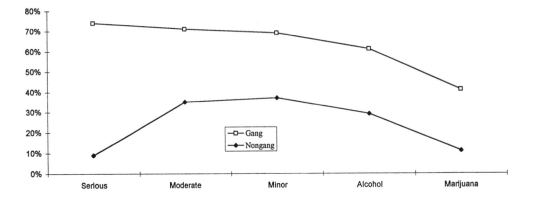

Figure 7.2. Percentage of Rochester gang and nongang youth self-reporting delinquency

SOURCE: "Gender Differences in Gang Participation, Delinquency, and Substance Use" (p. 342), Bjerregaard and Smith, 1993.

cation Statistics, 1995) found that 35% of students reported fighting gangs in their school (see Snyder et al., 1996). This education survey also suggested an association between the presence of gangs and weapons in schools (Figure 7.1). Students who reported gangs and weapons in school were about twice as likely to report having been victims of a violent crime (physical attack, robbery, or bullying). Lab and Clark's (1996) Ohio study suggests that the most significant detrimental result of gang presence in schools is their impact on school climate, resulting in more absenteeism as a result of fear, and a more control-oriented approach to discipline, which was correlated with higher levels of student victimization (especially theft).

Several studies show that gang delinquency is more violent, serious, and chronic than non-gang delinquency (Bjerregaard & Lizotte, 1995; Bjerregaard & Smith, 1993; Decker & Van Winkle, 1996; Dolan & Finney, 1984; Esbensen & Huizinga, 1993; Esbensen et al., 1993; Fagan, 1989, 1990; Robin, 1967; Spergel, 1984; Thornberry et al., 1993; Tracy, 1979). Longitudinal studies in Denver, Rochester, and Seattle show that from a cumulative perspective, gang members account for a significant proportion of all serious and violent delinquencies in gang problem cities. Denver gang members, representing 7% of adolescents from high-crime areas, self-report committing 55% of all street offenses (violent offenses, serious theft, and drug sales), 36% of all other serious offenses, and 43% of drug sales

(Esbensen & Huizinga, 1993). The percentage of delinquent acts committed by gang members in Rochester is much higher than reported in Denver (Thornberry, in press). Rochester gang members (20% of the urban adolescent sample) self-report committing 80% of all violent offenses, 90% of all serious delinquencies, and 73% of drug sales. The proportion of all offenses committed by gang members in a Seattle sample of adolescents is comparable (Battin et al., 1996). Gang members (15% of the sample) self-report committing 85% of robberies and 62% of illegal service offenses (drug trafficking and prostitution) committed by the entire sample. "Gangs are no longer just at the rowdy end of the continuum of local adolescent groups— they are now really outside the continuum" (Moore, 1991, p. 132).

Juvenile gang members commit serious and violent offenses at a rate several times higher than nongang adolescents. In Denver, gang members commit about three times as many serious and violent offenses as nongang youth (Esbensen & Huizinga, 1993). Even greater differences were observed in Rochester (Bjerregaard & Smith, 1993), where gang members committed about seven times as many serious and violent delinquent acts as nongang adolescents. In Seattle, gang youth self-report more than five times as many violent offenses as nongang youth (Battin et al., 1996). In Rochester, two-thirds (66%) of the chronic violent offenders were gang members for a time (Thornberry et al., 1995). Nearly three fourths of Rochester

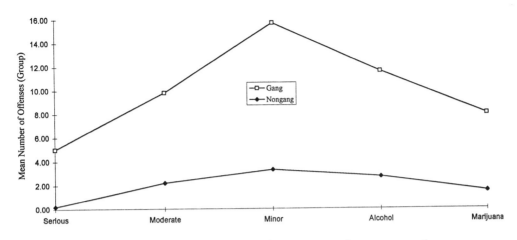

Figure 7.3. Incidence of delinquency among Rochester gang and nongang youth

SOURCE: "Gender Differences in Gang Participation, Delinquency, and Substance Use" (p. 342), Bjerregaard and Smith, 1993.

gang members reported involvement in serious delinquency, compared to only 9% of nongang youth (Bjerregaard & Smith, 1993). Figure 7.2 shows the percentages of gang and nongang youth who self-reported committing various offenses. Figure 7.3 shows the mean number of offenses (the group mean) committed by gang and nongang youth.

Still, violent offenses are rare in most gangs. Only one study has observed and counted gang members' behavioral acts to determine the proportion that is violent. Miller (1966) and a large cadre of field researchers documented the daily behavior of members of the most violent Boston gangs over a 2-year period. Of approximately 54,000 behaviors that were recorded, only 3% related to assaultive behavior (p. 100). Klein (1971) observed that gangs' involvement in delinquent episodes "is so infrequent that one must wait many months before sufficient offenses have taken place to provide the grist for the statistician's mill. This is perhaps the most important fact about gang behavior—most of it is nondelinquent" (p. 123).

Recent gang studies suggest increasing female involvement. The Denver Youth Survey (Esbensen & Huizinga, 1993, p. 571) has produced the highest statistic to date on female gang participation. During 1988-1992, from 20% to 46% of self-reported gang members were females. At young ages, the Rochester Youth Development Study (Bjerregaard & Smith, 1993) found that the prevalence rate for females (22%) was even higher than for males

(18%). These female participation rates are much higher than earlier estimates. In his national survey, Miller (1982) estimated that male gang members outnumbered females about 10 to 1 in the 1970s.

Self-report studies of female gang member involvement in delinquency show elevated levels when compared with nongang females. In Denver, Esbensen and Huizinga (1993) found that the likelihood of delinquency involvement was significantly higher among female gang members than among nongang females. Incidence levels, however, were not significantly higher. As in Denver, Bjerregaard and Smith (1993) found that Rochester female gang members were significantly more likely to engage in serious delinquency than were nongang females. In contrast to the Denver results, in every offense category, Rochester female gang members had significantly higher incidence rates than nongang females. Fagan (1990) also found high levels of involvement in serious delinquency among female gang members in Chicago, Los Angeles, and San Diego. Surprisingly, female gang members had higher prevalence rates than nongang males in all behavior categories, including violent offenses. Although different levels of female involvement in serious and violent gang delinquency have been reported, the higher levels of membership reported recently suggest that female gang participation and crime involvement bears closer scrutiny. Two noted female gang researchers express skepticism. Moore (1991, p. 41) suggests that "The general notion that gang girls have moved away from . . . 'traditional [auxiliary] roles' must be taken with a grain of salt." Based on her review of gang research, Chesney-Lind (1993) contends that there is little evidence to support the notion of a new breed of violent female gangsters "breaking into" this historically male-dominated phenomenon.

Many cities do not appear to have serious gang problems; therefore, other law-violating youth groups are responsible for a significant proportion of violent juvenile arrests (see Morash, 1983; Reiss, 1988). Unfortunately, little is known about these groups. The group context of juvenile offending has been well recognized since Shaw and McKay's (1931) finding that 82% of juvenile offenders in court committed their offenses with two or more companions. Miller (1982, p. 20) viewed the delinquent gang as one subtype of "law-violating youth groups." He identified 20 types of such groups, which include such nongang groups as predatory cliques/limited networks, burglary rings, robbery bands, larceny cliques and networks, extortion cliques, drug-dealing cliques and networks, and casual assaultive cliques.

Little is known about these other kinds of law-violating youth groups. Miller (1982) estimated that gangs made up about 2% of the total number of law-violating youth groups in the 1970s, and that 71% of all serious crimes committed by juveniles could be attributed to law-violating youth groups other than gangs. He also estimated that there were seven times as many law-violating youth groups as gangs in the typical locality. These groups were particularly active in such offenses as larceny, burglary, robbery, drug and alcohol violations, assault, disruption, disorderly conduct, vandalism, and arson. Gang members were arrested in significantly higher proportions for more violent crimes, including robbery, rape, assault, and weapons violations. Warr's (1996) recent study makes an important contribution to knowledge of adolescent group offending. In an analysis of National Survey of Youth (Gold & Reimer, 1975) data, he found that most adolescent offenses are committed with two or three others (except for group fighting, in which about four others were involved). The probability of committing different offenses within the same group, however, was small. Warr (1996, p. 33) found most delinquent groups to be "demonstrably transitory." National victimization data also show substantial adolescent group offending (Snyder & Sickmund, 1995, p. 47). More than one-half of serious violent juvenile offenses involved a group of offenders (compared to one-third of adult offenses).

Because of the proliferation of youth gangs in U.S. cities and towns, Miller's estimate of the proportion of serious and violent delinquency attributable to law-violating youth groups other than gangs (71%) may need to be revised downward. When he made that estimate, only 286 cities were known to have gang problems (Miller, 1982). By 1995, the number of known gang problem cities increased to 2,007 (National Youth Gang Center, in press), a nearly tenfold increase (part of which is accounted for by surveying more jurisdictions). In this recent survey, 58% of responding law enforcement agencies reported youth gang problems, including virtually all large cities and half of cities and towns with populations under 25,000 (National Youth Gang Center, in press). Unfortunately, data are not available on the proportion of all serious and violent youth crime accounted for by gang members across these localities. In the Seattle adolescent sample, Battin and her colleagues (1996) found that 24% of the total sample were members of delinquent groups, compared to 15% who were in a gang. With the exception of robbery (in which gang members accounted for 85% of all offenses), compared to law-violating groups, gangs accounted for about twice the proportion of all offenses as other delinquent groups.

Given the findings in the Denver, Rochester, and Seattle studies, it is reasonable to expect that the proportion of all serious and violent youth crime accounted for by gang members in the growing number of gang problem cities and towns is significant. Whether or not the relative proportion of all violent juvenile crimes committed by gangs is increasing in comparison with other group patterns is unknown. Moore (1991) observes that "the gang can be expected to be more deviant as the adolescent subculture in general becomes more deviant. This is one significant source of change: The adolescent gang 'leads' in ordinary adolescent trends" (p. 41).

The most important factor explaining the elevated level of violence in gangs is normative acceptance and encouragement of violence. "Violence that is internal to the gang, especially during group functions such as an initiation, serves to intensify the bonds among members" (Decker & Van Winkle, 1996, p. 270). Most youth gangs are governed by norms supporting the expressive use of violence to settle disputes (Short & Strodtbeck, 1965) and achieve group goals associated with member recruitment, impulsive and emotional defense of one's identity as a gang member, turf protection and expansion, defending the honor of the gang, retaliation, and revenge (Block & Block, 1993). Gang sanctioning of violence is also dictated by the gang "code of honor," a normative code that stresses the inviolability of one's manhood and defines breaches of etiquette (Horowitz, 1983; Sanchez-Jankowski, 1991). Violence is also a means of demonstrating one's toughness and fighting ability, and of establishing one's status in the gang (Short & Strodtbeck, 1965).

Summary

We have reviewed the major risk factors for delinquency and violence in this chapter. It is apparent from our review that adults are responsible for most of the risk factors for delinquent and violent juvenile behavior. Juveniles do not participate in the political process that controls social and economic conditions in communities. Adults are responsible for social disorganization, poverty, discrimination, and prejudice. Adults control the quality of family life, which is affected by community social conditions. Adults manage schools and are responsible for the control of violence in them, which can be minimized, even in the worst communities. Most individual characteristics that predispose children to delinquency and violence are either inherited, environmentally influenced, or responses learned from adults, beginning in the home. Poor mental health also appears largely to be inherited or a result of deprivation early in life. Adolescents choose delinquent peer groups, but the availability of delinquent peer groups and adolescents' wrong choices such as joining a gang appear to be affected by personal, family, social, and economic conditions. Moreover, adults indirectly contribute to a significant proportion of juvenile violence through their violent victimization of infants and children, perpetuating a cycle of violence.

Growing youth violence appears to be a developmental pattern linked to increases in risk factors. A key factor in the increase in juvenile violence is the growing influence of deviant peer groups, which seem to flourish when negative social and cultural risk factors are elevated. These peer groups include a wide variety of law-violating groups and gangs. Both gang and nongang violence has been fueled by the ready availability of firearms. The growth of gangs and other law-violating peer groups probably accounts for most of the increase in weapon-related violence.

Note

1. Reprinted with the permission of Cambridge University press.

8

The Case for Developmental Criminology

This chapter reviews briefly the history of developmental criminology and then highlights recent contributions of this approach to criminological research. The purpose is to show the value of developmental criminology in understanding the career of the serious, violent, and chronic juvenile offender. This is important for both research and program development purposes.

Chronic Juvenile and Adult Offending

The Cambridge Study in Delinquent Development (Farrington, 1995; Farrington & West, 1990), a prospective longitudinal survey of more than 400 London males from ages 8 to 32, provides valuable information on the link between juvenile and adult chronic offending. Based on the results of this landmark study, Farrington succinctly described the life cycle of delinquency, adult criminality, and regeneration:

> The Cambridge study found that the typical offender—a male property offender—tends to be born in a low-income, large-sized family and to have criminal parents. When he is young, his parents supervise him rather poorly, use harsh or erratic child-rearing techniques, and are likely to be in conflict and separate. At school, he tends to have low intelligence and attainment, is troublesome, hyperactive,

and impulsive, and often truant. He tends to associate with friends who are also delinquents.

After leaving school, the offender tends to have a low-status job record punctuated by periods of unemployment. His deviant behavior tends to be versatile rather than specialized. He not only commits property offenses such as theft and burglary but also engages in violence, vandalism, drug use, excessive drinking, reckless driving, and sexual promiscuity. His likelihood of offending reaches a peak during his teenage years and then declines in his 20s, when he is likely to get married or cohabit with a woman.

By the time he is in his 30s, the offender is likely to be separated or divorced from his wife and separated from his children. He tends to be unemployed or to have a low-paying job, to move frequently, and to live in rented rather than owner-occupied accommodations. His life is still characterized by more evenings out, more heavy drinking and drunk driving, more violence, and more drug taking than his contemporaries. Hence, the typical offender tends to provide the same kind of deprived and disruptive family background for his own children that he himself experienced, thus perpetuating from one generation to the next a range of social problems, of which offending is only one element. (Farrington, 1996, p. 69)

Farrington has provided a profile of the chronic adult offender, who has been the subject of little research in this country. Farrington and West (1993) examined the life histories of chronic offenders, those with six or more convictions. These 23 offenders, 6% of the entire cohort of 411 London males, accounted for 49% of all recorded convictions up to the age of 32. Their average offending history lasted more than 13 years, from the age of 13 to nearly 27. The average age for conviction of a violent offense was 22 years, higher than for any other offense, except drug violations. They were disproportionately likely to commit drug offenses (68%), robbery (59%), and fraudulent offenses (59%). The chronics were no more likely to be convicted of a violent offense than were non-chronics, indicating versatility in offending. The worst offenders at the age of 18 also tended to be the worst offenders at the age of 32 (Farrington, 1990).

Farrington and West (1993, p. 500) charted by age the frequency and seriousness of offenses for which the London chronic offenders were convicted. Offense convictions 5-7 occurred at an average age of nearly 18. Convictions for offenses 8-10 occurred at an average age of 20; offenses 11-15 at 23; and offenses 16-20 at about age 25. The average age at the last conviction was nearly 27. Offending got worse, rather than better, after the first conviction. "Convicted males became more aggressive and hostile towards the police, suggesting that one reason why a first conviction leads to increased offending might be because it results in increased hostility to the police" (p. 504).

The chronic offenders "were very different from non-chronic offenders, and from non-offenders in childhood, adolescence, teenage years, and adulthood. Ideally these results should form the basis of a theory of the development of chronic offenders, recognising that they are usually the most deviant cases on most variables" (Farrington & West, 1993, p. 521). In fact, Farrington and West found that most of the chronic offenders could have been predicted at the age of 10, on the basis of troublesome behavior and several background features. But what about false positives? Farrington contends that ameliorative intervention might have been justified for them as well, because most of the unconvicted vulnerable boys were leading relatively unsuccessful lives at the age of 32.

Other recent analyses of the Cambridge study data (Nagin, Farrington, & Moffitt, 1995; Nagin & Land, 1993) provide new information on chronic adult offenders. Results of these studies call for modifications in our previous understanding of the length of criminal careers. In their analysis of data on Farrington and West's Cambridge sample, Nagin and Land (1993) identified three groups of convicted juveniles and adults: high-level chronic, low-level chronic, and adolescent-limited offenders. According to official data (convictions), the high-level chronics and low-level chronics continued offending up to the latest data collection point (age 32), whereas the adolescent-limited offenders peaked at ages 16-17 and had their last conviction at the age of 21. The low-level chronics peaked at ages 22-23 but continued to have convictions as late as the age of 32. In contrast, the high-level chronics' convictions peaked at ages 18-19 but show a more gradual decline through the age of 31.

Career lengths were found to be longer using self-report measures. Nagin et al. (1995) found that the adolescent-limited group did not desist their offending at the age of 21, as indicated by convictions. At the age of 32, they self-reported extensive illicit drug use, heavy drinking, and getting into fights. Their offending behavior was indistinguishable from that of high-level chronics and low-level chronics. The adolescent-limited group, however, seemed to be careful to avoid committing crimes with a high risk of conviction that might jeopardize their work careers and familial attachments. This discrepancy between the official records of adults and their self-reports calls into question the accuracy of official records as a measure of adult offending (Elliott, 1995).

Moffitt (1993, p. 679) describes in summary fashion the "life-course-persistent" offender (based on three studies: Farrington & West, 1990; Robins, 1966; Sampson & Laub, 1990): "drug and alcohol addiction; unsatisfactory employment; unpaid debts; homelessness; drunk driving; violent assault; multiple and unstable relationships; spouse battery; abandoned, neglected, or abused children; and psychiatric illnesses have all been reported at very high rates for offenders who persist past age 40." She goes on to say (p. 679) that "the conclusion that crime ceases in midlife may be premature; it is based on cross-sectional age comparisons of arrest and conviction rates. . . . Thus, until longitudinal researchers collect self-reports of crime in the same individuals from adolescence to old age, the midlife disappearance of crime will remain an empirical question."

Most of the prospective longitudinal studies that have collected crime data on subjects into adulthood have been conducted in other countries (see Farrington, 1995). These include the Dunedin study in New Zealand (Moffitt, 1990a, 1990b, 1993; Moffitt, Mednick, & Gabrielli, 1989; Moffitt & Silva, 1988), the Newcastle Thousand-Family Study in England (Kolvin, Miller, Fleeting, & Kolvin, 1988; Kolvin et al., 1990), an English study (Rutter, 1981), a Canadian study (LeBlanc & Frechette, 1989), a Swedish study (Stattin & Magnusson, 1991; Stattin, Magnusson, & Reichel, 1989), a Stockholm study (Janson, 1977, 1982), and the Cambridge Study in Delinquent Development (Farrington, 1992, 1993, 1995; Farrington & West, 1993; Nagin & Farrington, 1992a, 1992b; Nagin & Land, 1993; Nagin & Paternoster, 1991).

Few longitudinal cohort studies have been conducted in the United States. The oldest studies are Cairns and Cairns in North Carolina (1991); Glueck and Glueck in Massachusetts (Glueck & Glueck, 1968); McCord in Boston (1979, 1980); Robins in St. Louis (1979); Sampson and Laub's reanalysis and followup of the Gluecks' sample (1993); Patterson in Oregon (Capaldi & Patterson, 1989; Patterson, Reid, & Dishon, 1990); Polk in the Pacific Northwest (1975; Polk & Halferty, 1966); Wolfgang, Thornberry, and Figlio in Philadelphia (1987); Shannon in Racine, Wisconsin (1988, 1991); Werner and Smith in Hawaii (1992); and the National Youth Survey (Elliott et al., 1985; Elliott et al., 1989). Although few of these studies are prospective, they nevertheless provide insights into criminal adult careers. Each of these data sets needs to be analyzed further to develop a more complete understanding of the developmental histories of criminal careers, the relationship between juvenile and adult offending (where feasible), and patterns as well as length of adult offending. The latter issue is particularly important because adults account for more than four-fifths of violent crime in the United States.

What do we know about the chronic adult offender in the United States? It is astonishing that little research has been conducted on this offender group in this country. Neither the Panel on the Understanding and Control of Violent Behavior (Reiss & Roth, 1993) nor the Panel on Research on Criminal Careers (Blumstein, Cohen, Roth, & Visher, 1986) profiled the chronic adult offender. Little is known about ages of criminal career termination and their lengths. Farrington's (1986a) review of the relationship between age and crime emphasizes the need to reconsider the age-crime curve and recognize the residual length of adult criminal careers. His unique analysis (pp. 196-197) of violent age-crime curves using FBI Uniform Crime Report data shows that in 1983, half of violent males have a peak of offending that occurs before the age of 15. For half of them, however, the average peak age is after the age of 32, the median age is 25, and the mean age is 28. Farrington (1986a, pp. 236-237) concludes that

> a court faced with an offender aged twenty-five, for example, cannot necessarily assume that person's criminal behavior will decline in the next few years as the aggregate curve does. The probability of termination may be lower at twenty-five than at eighteen, the expected residual career length may be higher, the incidence of offending may be just as great, and the seriousness of offenses may be higher.

Farrington (p. 189) suggests that "this has major implications for criminal justice policy since . . . the greatest potential incapacitative effect may be between ages thirty and forty, not at the peak age [18]."

A later and very exhaustive review of nearly 50 major studies on aspects of individual violent criminal careers (Weiner, 1989) resulted in the conclusion that "the bulk of serious violent crimes occur in late adolescence and, more so, early adulthood. Whether this clustering reflects greater participation at these ages, elevated individual violent crime rates, or both is uncertain" (p. 128). Weiner (p. 128) notes that studies have not yet linked analyses of high-rate offenders to offenders with long careers; "in short, little is currently known about the violent career criminal."

Developmental Criminology

Developmental models of crime and delinquency are most appropriate for studying juvenile delinquency and adult crime. First, these emphasize the social and psychological developmental processes in childhood and adolescence, which is a necessary theoretical framework for understanding the effects of social and cultural conditions. Second, developmental theories seek to explain the evolution of delinquency into adult criminality. Using longitudinal studies with repeated measurements, developmental theories capture a broad range of causes and correlates. These theories emphasize temporal ordering of changes in predictors with age, as well as the relationship between variations in offending and important transitions in the life cycle. This type of study increases the options for differentiating between risk factors or correlates and causes (LeBlanc & Loeber, 1993). Other contributors to a developmental perspective include Catalano and Hawkins (1996); Elliott (1994a); Elliott and Menard (1996); Farrington (1986a, 1996); Farrington and West (1993); Finkelhor and Leatherman (1994); Huizinga (1995); Huizinga, Esbensen, and Weiher (1991, 1994); LeBlanc and Frechette (1989); LeBlanc and Loeber (1993); LeBlanc, McDuff, and Tremblay (1994); Loeber and LeBlanc (1990); McCord (1979, 1980); Moffitt (1990b, 1993); Nagin and Farrington (1992); Robins (1966, 1979); Sampson and Laub (1990, 1993); Shannon (1988, 1991); Thornberry (1987, 1996); Thornberry et al. (1991, 1994); Tolan, Guerra, and Kendall, (1995); Tonry, Ohlin, and Farrington (1991); and Yoshikawa (1994, 1995).

Developmental approaches are not new to criminology. Early developmental models include labeling theory (Lemert, 1951), developmental stage models (Jennings, Kilkenny, & Kohlberg, 1983; Sullivan, Grant, & Grant, 1957), a social-psychological model (Jessor & Jessor, 1977), and psychodynamic theory (Feldman, 1969). Unfortunately, the search for causes of crime has been dominated by cross-sectional approaches and analysis of between-individual differences, which "has led to a near standstill in the identification of those correlates or risk factors of offending that are also most likely to be causes [and] hindered the development of new, empirically based theories and the development of another generation of much-needed innovative intervention and prevention strategies for reducing delinquency" (LeBlanc & Loeber, 1993, p. 233).

LeBlanc and Loeber (1993, pp. 233-235) challenge three main assumptions of theoretical approaches that lack a developmental perspective. First, these approaches assume that the same causes operate regardless of the age of the offender and for early onset as well as later onset. Second, these approaches assume that causal factors operate only in a close time frame with delinquent acts. Third, the approaches do not take into account the sleeper effects of causal variables. Loeber (1988) therefore called for use of a developmental framework in the study of crime and delinquency, which he and LeBlanc (1990) called "developmental criminology." It uses longitudinal studies with repeated measurements as a principal tool for differentiating between risk factors or correlates and causal factors. It examines within-individual changes in offending over time in relation to various dimensions of offending: activation, aggravation, and desistance. Finally, it emphasizes social processes over time, their temporal ordering, and changes in causal factors with age (LeBlanc & Loeber, 1993). Thus, developmental criminology is an orientation toward examining data from a developmental point of view. It views behavioral change as accounted for by a multitude of life events that must be examined in terms of the timing and duration of particular conditions at specific ages. These periods may be viewed as segments of "criminal careers" (Blumstein & Cohen, 1987; Blumstein et al., 1986).

A pioneering developmental model resulted from Jessor and Jessor's (1977) longitudinal study of adolescents. The resulting "theory of problem behavior" (Jessor, 1987) proposes that multiple problem behaviors are similar in the functions they serve for the adolescent, such as peer acceptance and achieving autonomy from parents. Stated otherwise, Jessor (1987) suggests that adolescents have a "behavior proneness" in which risky problem behaviors are associated; that is, they come in "packages" (Kazdin, 1996).

A recent developmental model, formulated by Sampson and Laub (1993) in their award-winning book, is an age-graded theory of informal social control that explains delinquency and crime over the life span. They show how age-based informal social controls operate in interpersonal bonds that link individuals to one another and to wider social institutions such as family, school, and work. These institutions play a mediating role between individual propensities for delinquency and crime and formal social controls. Key "turning points" are marriage and full-time employment, which Sampson and

Laub argue modify childhood pathways to crime or conformity in adulthood.

A new generation of U.S. prospective cohort studies is producing valuable information on the serious and violent offending, the subjects of which are now entering adulthood. Interestingly, every one of these studies incorporates a developmental perspective. They are The Denver Youth Survey (Esbensen & Huizinga, 1993; Esbensen et al., 1993; Huizinga, 1995; Huizinga et al., 1991; Huizinga, Esbensen, & Weiher, 1994), the Rochester Youth Development Study (Lizotte et al., 1994; Thornberry, 1996; Thornberry, Lizotte, Krohn, Farnworth, & Jang, 1991, 1994), the Pittsburgh Youth Study (Loeber, 1996; Loeber et al., 1991; Loeber et al., 1993), and the Seattle Social Development Project (Catalano et al., 1992; Hawkins, Arthur, & Catalano, 1995; Hawkins, Catalano, Morrison, et al., 1992; Hawkins et al., 1988; Hawkins, Von Cleve, & Catalano, 1991; O'Donnell, Hawkins, Catalano, Abbott, & Day, 1995). Provided that funding for these landmark studies is continued, they will no doubt provide valuable insights into both juvenile and adult criminal careers. Two other prospective studies are underway in Chicago, the Program on Human Development (see Sampson, 1993, pp. 163-164 for a description) and the Chicago Youth Development Study (Gorman-Smith, Tolan, Zelli, & Huesmann, 1996; Tolan, 1990). With the exception of the Seattle project, each of these appear to emphasize a developmental model in the course of analyzes the results, as the study authors were influenced by emerging developmental criminology.

There are significant advantages to prospective studies (Thornberry et al., 1995, p. 215). They produce valuable information on the causes of delinquency. They permit researchers to sort out which factors precede changes in offending and to predict these changes independently of other factors. Repeated measures permit identification of pathways to delinquency and changes in career patterns. The resulting information on offending careers and causal factors is very valuable in designing program interventions.

Let us review briefly some of the significant contributions of these projects to developmental criminology. It is infeasible to review but a few of their contributions. The aim is to suggest how the results of these important projects can be used to design comprehensive prevention and intervention strategies.

Stepping Stones to Adult Criminality

Farrington (1996) developed a "theory of offending and antisocial behavior" as a result of his research with West in the Cambridge Study. His theory emphasizes changing manifestation of problem behavior with age. The extent of delinquency and criminality depends on "energizing," "directing," and "inhibiting" processes. "The occurrence of offenses and other antisocial acts depends on the interaction between the individual (with a certain degree of antisocial tendency) and the social environment in a decision-making process" (Farrington, 1996, p. 109. For Farrington, the key to persistent offending is an "antisocial personality" that begins to develop in childhood and evolves into adulthood.

Farrington's (1986b) "stepping stones" model depicts events and conditions leading to criminality in a long-term prediction framework (LeBlanc & Loeber, 1993, p. 253). He used a range of factors, measured at different points in relation to chronological aging (childhood, adolescent, and young adulthood) to predict adult criminality. Two important findings resulted from application of Farrington's stepping stones model. First, he demonstrated a stepwise continuity in delinquent and criminal behavior. Troublesomeness and daring behavior at ages 8-10 predicted convictions at ages 10-13, which predicted self-reported delinquency at age 14, which, with convictions at age 14-16, predicted antisocial tendency at age 18. Convictions at ages 17-20 predicted convictions at ages 21-24. Second, Farrington identified a common set of predictors of offending at different ages: economic deprivation, family criminality, parental mishandling, and school failure. These indicators of a general antisocial tendency predicted adolescent aggression, offending frequency, and adult violence (Farrington, 1986b, 1989b; LeBlanc & Loeber, 1993, pp. 252-253).

Stacking of Problem Behaviors

In his initial contribution to developmental criminology, Loeber (1988, 1990, 1996) pioneered the notion that individuals experience "stacking" of problem behaviors (Figure 8.1).

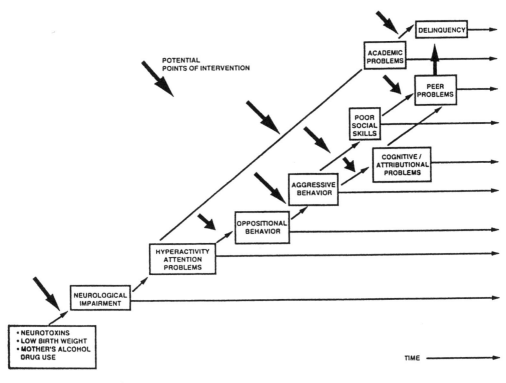

Figure 8.1. Developmental stacking of problem behaviors

SOURCE: "Development and Risk Factors of Juvenile Antisocial Behavior and Delinquency," R. Loeber, ©copyright 1990 by Clinical Psychology Review. Reprinted with permission of the author.

Loeber (1988) enumerated five characteristics of a developmental progression in problem behaviors. First, some behaviors have an earlier onset than others. Second, there is usually escalation in behavioral seriousness over time. Third, early behaviors usually are retained as new ones are added. Fourth, each behavior is best predicted by the developmentally adjacent behavior. Fifth, the ordering of behaviors in a pathway is invariant. His notion is supported by studies showing that a high variety of disruptive behaviors is a better predictor of problem persistence than is a low variety (Farrington, 1973; Kandel & Faust, 1975; Loeber, 1982, 1988; Robins, 1966). Loeber's "stacking" model illustrates the finding that early disruptive behaviors, like fighting at home and at school, predict the most delinquent youngsters (Loeber, 1996). Moreover, aggressive boys are more at risk than nonaggressive boys to diversify (and escalate) into concealing behaviors

and delinquent activities. Children with certain individual conditions like hyperactivity, who have attention problems, and who experience more difficulties with academic tasks than other children may be particularly at risk for other problems such as poor peer relations and delinquency. Loeber contends that hyperactive children may be particularly vulnerable to the stacking of other problem behaviors (p. 17).

Pathways to Delinquency and Serious Violent Offending

One of Loeber's most significant contributions to developmental criminology is his identification of "pathways" (Loeber et al., 1993). He conceived this way of examining a youngster's developmental history as an alternative to classification of offenders on the basis of a single offense, for example, as a violent offender, property offender, status offender, run-

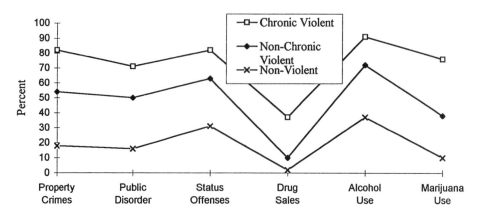

Figure 8.2. Involvement in delinquency by offender type (Rochester)

SOURCE: Thornberry, T. P., Huizinga, D., & Loeber, R. (1995). "The Prevention of Serious Delinquency and Violence: Implications from the Program of Research on the Causes and Correlates of Delinquency" (p. 225), Thornberry, Huizinga, and Loeber, in J. C. Howell, B. Krisberg, J. D. Hawkins, & J. J. Wilson (Eds.), *Sourcebook on Serious, Violent, and Chronic Juvenile Offenders*, ©copyright 1995 Sage Publications, Inc.
DATA SOURCE: Rochester data.

away, and so on. This later approach "does not necessarily reflect essential characteristics of the delinquent career" (Loeber, 1996, p. 14), which is often launched by a mix of problem behavior. A "pathway" is defined as a group of individuals that shares a behavioral development that is distinct from the behavioral development of another group of individuals (Loeber et al., in press). It is a dynamic (Huizinga, 1979) method of classification, an empirical model for examining the offender's career that allows one to make a distinction between youth who "experiment" and others who "persist" in a particular problem behavior (Loeber et al., in press). It recognizes that there is more than one pathway to delinquency (Loeber, 1988) and the well-established empirical fact of a wide diversity of offending among juveniles (Klein, 1984; Thomas, 1976), even among chronic violent offenders (Thornberry et al., 1995). Figure 8.2 illustrates the latter point with data from the Rochester Youth Development Study (Thornberry et al., 1995, p. 225).

A distinct pathway has been identified in the development of drug use. The first step involves the use of beer or wine, the second is marijuana use, and the third is use of hard drugs (Hamburg, Kraemer, & Jahnke, 1975; Kandel, 1980). Researchers, however, debate whether delinquency, like drug use, develops in an orderly manner (Loeber & Wikstrom, 1993; Loeber et al., 1993). Analyzing data on 10-16-year-olds

collected in the Pittsburgh Youth Study, Loeber and his colleagues (1993) designed an empirically based formulation of three basic but overlapping pathways in the development of disruptive child behavior (Figure 8.3): Authority Conflict Pathway, Covert Behavior Pathway, and Overt Behavior Pathway. Less serious disruptive behaviors (Authority Conflict) generally preceded the onset of moderately serious behaviors (Covert Behavior) which, in turn, preceded the onset of very serious acts (Overt Behavior) (Loeber & Hay, 1994; Loeber et al., 1993). A substantial group progressed in only one pathway. Self-reported and official delinquency rates were lowest among these youngsters. Youths moving simultaneously in two pathways (either Overt-Covert or Covert-Authority Conflict) had significantly higher rates of delinquency than those in only one pathway.

A subsequent analysis (Loeber et al., in press) found that, compared to experimenters, persisters tended to enter pathways at the first rather than later steps in the pathways. Almost all the boys who persisted in either the Overt or Covert Pathways had persisted in the Authority Conflict Pathway. The data suggested that among the most chronic offenders, authority conflict generally occurred first, followed soon by overt disruptive behavior, then by more serious covert behavior. About 75% of the most chronic offenders were persisters in stage two

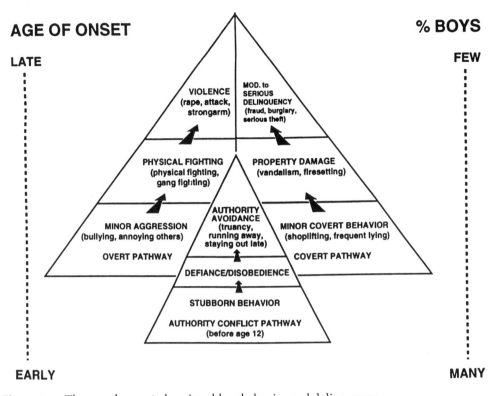

Figure 8.3. Three pathways to boys' problem behavior and delinquency

SOURCE: "Developmental Approaches to Aggression and Conduct Problems," Loeber and Hay, in M. Rutter and D. F. Hay (Eds.), *Development Through Life: A Handbook for Clinicians* (pp. 488-516), ©1994 by Blackwell Scientific. Reprinted with permission.

or three of any of the pathways. The authors caution that "a judgment about the long-term utility of the pathways necessarily has to await until all boys have passed through the peak period of high risk offending" (p. 26).

The findings to date indicate that boys in the initial step of a pathway are at less serious risk of persistence than are those in later steps. Later progressions are more predictable. All the boys who advanced to violence in the Overt Pathway had progressed through the intermediate stages of that pathway, compared to none of the experimenters (Loeber et al., in press). As Loeber and his colleagues (in press) suggest, more progress in this area would be of great value to authorities making a decision regarding with whom to intervene.

Loeber and his colleagues (1991) also used a dynamic model specifying stages of initiation, escalation, and desistance in juvenile offending to identify age-related shifts in offense correlates. They (p. 82) drew several tentative con-clusions from the study, which analyzed longitudinal data in the Pittsburgh youth study. Some correlates of offending, such as ADHD and a negative caretaker-child syndrome, show equal strength across late childhood and early adolescence. These may trigger initiation of offending at any point during that period. Other offending correlates such as school factors appear to increase in importance over time. The correlates of early initiation only partly overlap with those of late initiation. They also discovered that desistance correlates varied with the age of the offender. Loeber and colleagues (1991) point out that prevention programs need to take these findings into account to enhance their effectiveness.

Returning to the "stacking" model (Figure 8.1), Loeber (1996, p. 22) explains how it can be used to plan and design interventions. The bold arrows in Figure 8.1 indicate that preventive interventions can take place at different points. Treatment can be designed for intervention at several levels. Because of the likely variety of disruptive behaviors, the ideal would be to address most, if not all, the problem behaviors. For maximum effect, intervention probably would combine treatment and prevention. For example, an early intervention might target reduction of the likelihood of academic problems in hyperactive children (prevention). Another might be directed to children at risk of becoming chronically aggressive (intervention). In either case, "interventions can be optimized by a more precise knowledge of the course of antisocial development that is currently available" (p. 22).

Important Developmental Knowledge of Juvenile Violence

Developmental studies of juvenile delinquency have produced important knowledge in the past few years. The findings having the most important implications for future research and program development are the effects of multiple risk factors for multiple problem behaviors, interaction of risk factors, intermittency of violent offending, predictors of violent offending at different developmental stages, and identification of salient protective factors. We summarize these discoveries here because of their implications for program and policy development.

Multiple Risk Factors for Multiple Problem Behaviors

Professional associations in several fields have conducted comprehensive assessments of risk factors for juvenile delinquency and other problem behaviors that encourage a broad perspective of the origins of crime. Assessments of the plight of the poor in America and the victimization of children have been made by the American Bar Association (1993), the American Psychological Association (1993), the Carnegie Council on Adolescent Development (1989, 1992, 1995), the Children's Defense Fund (1991), and the National Coalition of State Juvenile Justice Advisory Groups (1993). Several other comprehensive assessments of youth problems have been made, including Cocozza (1992), Dryfoos (1990), Hamburg (1992), the In-

stitute of Medicine (1994), McCart (1994), the National Commission on Children (1991), Petersen and Chalk (1993), Romero and Brown (1995), and Schorr (1988). Each of these reviews describes the victimization of at-risk children as a result of exposure to multiple risk factors, mainly in families and communities.

The following generalizations regarding risks for delinquency and violence have important implications for risk-focused prevention (Brewer et al., 1995, pp. 64-65). First, as we saw in Chapter 7, risks are found in many domains, including the individual, family, school, peer group, and community. Second, exposure to a greater number of risk factors increases risk of crime and violence exponentially (Institute of Medicine, 1994; Rutter, 1980). These generalizations suggest that to be successful, prevention programming should use multiple strategies to reduce multiple risk factors and should address risks throughout development from conception through adolescence. Third, risk factors become salient at different points developmentally—some as early as the prenatal period, others in early adolescence. Agencies that traditionally administer categorical funds will need to find ways to collaborate in reducing a variety of risks at multiple levels across developmental stages if a risk-focused prevention approach is to reach its full potential. Finally, common risk factors predict diverse problems. Reviews of risk factors for other problem behaviors including substance abuse (Hawkins et al., 1992), teenage pregnancy (Dryfoos, 1990), and school dropout (Cairns, Cairns, & Neckerman, 1989) suggest that most of the risk factors for delinquency and youth violence also predict these problems. This means there may be an economy of preventive intervention in that programs that successfully address risk factors for delinquency and violence may also have benefits for preventing other problem behaviors. Thus, comprehensive risk-focused prevention initiatives should not be conceived from narrow categorical perspectives but should be designed and implemented to reduce overall levels of risk exposure at the individual, family, school, peer group, and community levels. Effects on a broad range of health and behavior problems including crime, violence, substance abuse, school dropout, and teen pregnancy should be evaluated.

Interaction of Risk Factors

Stress within the family exacerbates parents' antisocial tendencies, which in turn results in inconsiderate and sometimes violent reactions to those around them, as well as irritable discipline practices (Patterson & Dishon, 1988). Parents who use violence against each other and their children lead youngsters to think and solve interpersonal problems in antisocial ways (Dodge, Bates, & Pettit, 1990). Once established at home, aggressive behavior patterns are transferred to the school and peer contexts. Aggressive children seek out and associate regularly with other children who are like them and will accept them (Hymel, Wagner, & Butler, 1990; Patterson, 1982). Aggression results in rejection by nondelinquent peers (Coie, Dodge, & Kupersmidt, 1990), which in turn leads to further involvement in delinquency, more association with deviant peers (Pepler & Slaby, 1994) in coercive cliques (Cairns, Cairns, Neckerman, Ferguson, & Gariepy, 1989), and less association with popular and skilled members of the social group (Cairns & Cairns, 1991). Aggressive children disrupt classrooms and experience academic difficulties because of their off-task behavior (Pepler & Slaby, 1994). School failure leads to delinquency, violence, and gang participation (Bjerregaard & Smith, 1993). Adolescent involvement in group violence and vandalism is associated with criminality in adulthood (Farrington, 1991).

⌈Poor family life makes delinquency worse, which makes family life worse (Huizinga et al., 1994). This dynamic relationship is worsened if the parents or caretakers are exhibiting problem behaviors, as illustrated in an analysis from the Denver Youth Survey (Thornberry et al., 1995). Adolescents who have nondelinquent friends and parents with little or no problem behavior have, on the average, very low involvement in serious delinquent behavior. The addition of either delinquent friends or parents with problem behavior increases offending. Those who have both delinquent friends and problem parents have the highest levels of involvement in serious delinquency (p. 228).⌋

Just as low commitment to school, high commitment to delinquent peers, and low family attachment have been shown to lead to increases in delinquency, delinquency may lead to further deficits in each of these areas (Thornberry et al., 1995, p. 229). For example, Thornberry et al. (1991, 1994) have shown that youth who have low attachment to their parents have higher rates of subsequent delinquency. Higher delinquency involvement leads in turn to subsequent reductions in parental attachment.

Intermittency of Violence

Juvenile violence is rare, and chronic, serious, and violent juveniles are a very small subgroup of the total U.S. juvenile population. Thus, predicting juvenile violence is a difficult task. About 5% of all juveniles in each age group commit a serious violent offense each year (Elliott et al., 1987). Only 4% of adolescent males self-report three or more violent offenses per year for 5 years (Elliott et al., 1987). Less than one-half of 1% of all juveniles are arrested for a violent crime (Snyder et al., 1996, p. 14). The proportion involved and the frequency of violent behavior looks much larger among high-risk, inner-city youths if one takes a cumulative view. For example, in Rochester, about 15% of high-risk youth accounted for 75% of all violent offenses committed by the entire sample from the time they were age 13 to when they were 17 (Thornberry et al., 1995).

Despite the finding that a small subgroup of boys progresses in an orderly fashion over a long period of time from minor to serious forms of violence (Loeber et al., in press), involvement among the larger group of juveniles who engage in violence is characterized by intermittence or episodic involvement. Analyses of the Denver Youth Survey data (Huizinga, 1995; Huizinga et al., 1994; see also Thornberry et al., 1995, p. 224) reveal that among all who reported involvement for at least 3 years, the most frequent pattern was intermittency; that is, more than half of these offenders are not active every year. Among those committing the most serious violent acts, 47% offended only one time, 22% in two contiguous years, and 12% in three or more contiguous years. The chronic violent offenders, therefore, are a small subset of all serious violent offenders. A key finding of the analysis (Huizinga et al., 1994) was that there was a great deal of variation from year to year in involvement in different types of delinquency, even over multiple years. For example, being a serious offender in one year had little effect on being a serious offender in some other year later in the age period covered (7-17 years of age).

When patterns of delinquent behavior over periods of several years of age were used, however, a relationship between earlier and later offending was observed (Huizinga et al., 1994, pp. 215-216). These findings make difficult the determination of whether or not a particular juvenile charged with a violent offense is a chronic violent offender, or even might reoffend at all.

Violence Predictors at Different Developmental Stages

A new meta-analysis of longitudinal studies (Lipsey & Derzon, in press) identifies the best childhood predictors of violence. The main childhood predictors (measured at ages 6-12) of violence at ages 12-25 are early antisocial behavior and antisocial parents. Early antisocial behavior (the best predictor) includes delinquency and substance use, physical and verbal aggression (toward objects and others), and other problem behaviors (e.g., temper tantrums). Having antisocial parents (criminal, pathological, and violent) places lower-class boys at particularly high risk of violent behavior.

Interestingly, a somewhat different set of risk factors predicts violence in late adolescence and early adulthood when measured in early adolescence. Lipsey and Derzon's (in press) meta-analysis of longitudinal studies shows that these risk factors cover a wider range than is the case for childhood predictors. Five categories of risk factors, measured at ages 12-15, predict violence between ages 15 and 25. These are antisocial peers, prior antisocial behavior (delinquency, aggression, and physical violence), school attitudes/performance, psychological conditions, and parent-child relations. Both substance use and antisocial parents decrease noticeably in strength as predictors at the early adolescence point (Lipsey & Derzon, in press).

These findings are not surprising from a developmental perspective. During childhood, individual characteristics and family risk factors are most important. Later, during early adolescence, peer group and school risk factors become important, commensurate with greater exposure of the adolescent to these environments.

Protective Factors

Three classes of protective factors have been identified: factors inherent in the individual, factors related to the development of social bonding, and healthy beliefs and clear standards for behavior (Hawkins et al., 1992). Individual protective factors include female gender, high intelligence, a positive social orientation, and a resilient temperament (Rutter, 1985; Werner & Smith, 1982). Social bonding includes warm, supportive, affective relationships or attachments with family members or other adults (Garmezy, 1985). It also includes the development of commitment to the lines of action valued by a social institution such as family, school, or a religious organization. Healthy beliefs and clear standards include family and community norms opposed to crime and violence and supportive of educational success and healthy development. Whereas risk factors operate directly, "protective factors are hypothesized to operate indirectly through interaction with risk factors, mediating or moderating the effects of risk exposure" (Catalano & Hawkins, 1996, p. 153).

Because human aggression is largely learned, it can be reduced through learning (Eron, 1987; Slaby & Roedell, 1982). Bonding to individuals who exhibit prosocial behaviors increases the likelihood of learning nonviolent behaviors. Young people who are bonded to positive, prosocial family members, including adults outside the family (including teachers, coaches, youth leaders), and to prosocial friends are less likely to do things that threaten that bond such as using drugs, becoming violent, or committing crimes (Catalano & Hawkins, 1992). When families, schools, and communities have clearly stated policies and expectations for young people's behavior, children are less likely to become involved in crime and delinquency. Healthy beliefs and clear standards, communicated consistently by the significant individuals and social groups to whom the child is bonded, build a web of protection for young people exposed to risk of delinquency and violence.

Smith et al. (1995) identified 12 school, family, peer, and individual protective factors that buffer the effects of risk factors. Their analysis focused on high-risk youth, those who had five or more risk factors for serious and violent delinquency who did not become serious delinquents. The risk factors, measured at early stages in the children's lives, were low parental education, parental unemployment, family receipt of welfare, teenage motherhood, frequent family moves, drug-problem parents, criminogenic parents, child maltreatment, and placement of the child outside the family. Family protective factors included in the analysis were high levels of parental supervision and attachment. Reading ability, mathematics skills, commitment to school, doing well in school, aspirations and expectations to go to college, and parents' expectation for the child to go to college were the educational factors included in the analysis. The peer factors consisted of association with conventional peers and peers who were approved by their parents. One individual characteristic, self-esteem, was included.

In the short run, even during the peak age of delinquency involvement, protective factors did a very good job of insulating high-risk youth—82% of the youth who had nine or more protective factors were resilient at ages 13-14. The more protective factors, the more resilience they exhibited. The most salient protective factors for delinquency were school factors, followed by family and peer factors. The positive effects, however, did not last long. By ages 15-17, high-risk youth with many protective factors were no more likely than youth with fewer protective factors to be resilient and avoid delinquency. Because all the protective factors in this study occurred naturally, it remains to be seen whether synthetically developed protective factors can be more effective in the long term. For interventions with high-risk youth to be effective, Smith and colleagues (1995) suggest that they should be broad-based and address several risk factors, placing priority on school-based interventions.

Risk- and Protective-Focused Prevention

Risk- and protective-focused prevention (Brewer et al., 1995, pp. 62-63) was pioneered by public health professionals (Mercy & O'Carroll, 1988; Rosenberg & Fenley, 1991), who successfully demonstrated that such conditions as cardiovascular disease and traffic-related injuries can be prevented (Institute of Medicine, 1994). The aim of risk-focused prevention is to interrupt the causal processes that lead to a problem (Coie et al., 1993; Hawkins & Catalano, 1992). Risk factors are conditions in the individual or environment that predict an increased likelihood of developing a problem such as violent behavior. Protective factors, on the other hand, are conditions in the individual or environment

that counter risk factors or increase resistance to them, thus inhibiting the development of problems even in the face of risk exposure. Risk and protective factors predict increased or decreased probability of developing problem behaviors but, just as actuarial tables do not predict an individual's life experience, they do not guarantee that an individual will develop or avoid delinquent and violent behavior problems.

Preventive efforts based on a risk-focused approach seek to reduce risk factors and promote protective factors as a means of averting problems. For example, risk-focused approaches to the prevention of cardiovascular disease seek to reduce identified risk factors such as smoking and enhance protective factors such as regular exercise. Risk-focused approaches to the prevention of delinquency and violence seek to reduce or eliminate factors that predict a greater probability of developing these problems during adolescence and young adulthood and to strengthen factors that mediate or moderate exposure to risk. Not all the known risk factors for violence and delinquency can be changed, but knowledge of these risk factors can help define populations that should receive preventive interventions that enhance protection in the face of risk exposure. To illustrate, a family history of heart disease is a risk factor for cardiovascular disease. Although this risk factor cannot be changed, protective measures including a low-fat diet, regular exercise, and routine medical checkups can reduce the likelihood of cardiovascular disease in individuals characterized by this risk factor.

Risk and protective factors stabilize as predictors of delinquency and violence at different points in human development. If risk and protective factors are addressed at or slightly before the developmental point that they begin to predict later delinquency and violence, it is more likely that risk reduction efforts will be effective.

No specific prevention program has been declared a panacea. LeBlanc (1993, pp. 279-280) classifies prevention programs into three options. The first is according to a classification scheme such as primary, secondary, and tertiary or in relation to institutions, such as the family or school. The second involves scientific identification of risk factors and the selection of programs that can reduce the impact of the most deleterious factors. The third is selection of programs according to a theoretical point of view. One approach, which appears to hold the most promise, is the combined approach pioneered by Hawkins and Catalano, based on the social development theory (Catalano & Hawkins, 1996; Weis & Hawkins, 1979).

What makes the Hawkins-Catalano model so promising and unique from others is that it incorporates all three strategies LeBlanc identifies. It encompasses the key institutions and domains that research has shown to be most directly correlated with delinquency and related problem behaviors: the family, peer group, school, community, and individual characteristics. Second, through the *Communities That Care* strategy, the Hawkins-Catalano model provides a systematic process for assessing risk factors in each of the above domains, as well as prioritizing them for intervention. Third, their theoretical framework provides not only an explanation of delinquency but also a theory-driven process for selecting program interventions that reduce the priority risk factors and increase protective factors, thereby increasing the likelihood of preventing delinquency.

Another advantage of the Hawkins-Catalano prevention theory and community strategy is that it encompasses adult and societal contributions that generate delinquency, which are virtually ignored in other theoretical formulations. The recent tendency is to place an inordinate amount of blame on children and adolescents, and to attempt to correct them through punishment and other coercive techniques. As we saw in Chapter 3, adults make enormous contributions to the delinquency of their offspring and also to children and adolescents they victimize. These adults are mainly those with whom children have no choice but to associate, including criminogenic parents. Ironically, a current trend is to punish parents for the misbehavior of their children. Many of these parents, however, cannot control their own behavior or do not have the resources to control their children.

The social system also contributes to the development of adolescent delinquency and violence through economic and community conditions, unhealthy societal norms, condoning violent means of resolving interpersonal conflict, and in its overly zealous social control strategies, such as the War on Crime, the War on Drugs, and "zero tolerance." Although the Hawkins-Catalano model is much better equipped to account for the immediate risks adults present than macrolevel factors, it is capable of encompassing a broad array of community and social system risk factors.

The Social Development Strategy

The Social Development Strategy is a prevention approach for reducing identified risk factors and enhancing known protective factors against health and behavior problems (Hawkins & Catalano, 1992). It is derived from major criminological theories including social learning theory, differential association theory, and social control theory (Catalano & Hawkins, 1996). This strategy specifies how protective factors can be introduced to work together to protect children exposed to risk. At the same time, risk factors must be reduced.

Catalano and Hawkins (1996) organize their developmental model in relation to four periods: preschool, elementary school, middle school, and high school. These are distinct developmental periods organized by different socialization environments and developmentally appropriate processes that may influence youth toward either prosocial or antisocial behavior. At each stage, the behavior of youth is determined largely by a preponderance of prosocial or antisocial influences. As the social development processes unfold in the preschool period, the family is of primary importance as a socializing unit. During the elementary school period, the school joins the family as an important socializing environment, with peer influences emerging toward the end. In the middle/junior high school period, peers increase in importance as a socializing force. Environmental constraints begin to come into play during this period, including school policies and legal codes. By the time youths enter high school, many of the risk and protective factors for drug use and delinquency have been established. During the high school period, their theory emphasizes factors related to the maintenance of prosocial or antisocial behaviors.

To build bonding to a social unit, three conditions must be met (Hawkins et al., 1995, p. 51). Children must be provided with meaningful, challenging *opportunities* to contribute to their family, school, peers, and community, opportunities that help them feel responsible and significant. Children also must be taught the *skills* needed to take advantage effectively of the opportunities they are provided. If children do not have the skills necessary to be successful, they experience frustration and/or failure. Finally, children must receive *recognition* for their efforts. Recognition and acknowledgment both give children the incentive to continue to contribute and reinforce their skillful performance. Individual protective factors affect one's ability to perceive opportunities, develop skills, and perceive recognition. For example, if a child has a positive social orientation, he or she is more likely to see a child care setting as an opportunity to make new friends. A child with high intelligence may have an easier time learning to read in the classroom of a mediocre teacher than do other children. These processes are illustrated in the Social Development Strategy.

Like other developmental models, Catalano and Hawkins' (1996) is recursive. They posit reciprocal relationships among hypothesized causal factors across developmental periods.

> If the four models are laid out end to end, prosocial and antisocial influences from one period affect variables at the beginning of the causal chain in the next. In this sense, each submodel is a phase or period, whose outcomes affect the levels of the beginning variables in the next phase or period. (p. 178)

For example, children who engage in aggressive behavior in the preschool period will be less likely to perceive new encounters in the elementary period as opportunities for prosocial bonding. Transitions from one developmental period to the next "present opportunities to change behavior as old conditions of social life are replaced by new ones. These are times when the new conditions, rules, and structures are not yet clear, and the applicability of the old conditions, rules and structures is diminished" (Catalano & Hawkins, 1996, p. 179).

Prevention Principles

Authorities are beginning to see the need to focus prevention and juvenile justice system resources on the serious, violent, and chronic juvenile offender. As Thornberry and colleagues (1995) have pointed out, if we want to reduce the overall level of violence in our society, we must intervene successfully in the lives of high-risk offenders because they commit about 75% of all violent juvenile offenses even though they

constitute only about 15% of high-risk youth. Their observation is sobering: "Even if we were 100 percent successful in preventing the non-chronic violent offenders from ever engaging in violence, we would only reduce the level of violent offending by 25 percent" (p. 17). The only way to realize a substantial reduction in serious and violent offending, therefore, is through prevention and early intervention with those who are on paths toward becoming serious, violent, and chronic offenders.

An understanding of the evidence on risk and protective factors for crime, violence, and substance abuse suggests a set of principles that should guide prevention programming (Hawkins, Catalano, & Brewer, 1995, pp. 51-52).

1. To be effective, prevention efforts must address known risk factors for crime, violence, and substance abuse.

2. Prevention efforts must make a clear connection between the program activities and the goal of risk reduction. To illustrate, family management problems have been identified as a risk factor for health and behavior problems in children. Family management problems may emerge from different sources. If, for example, family management problems are thought to occur because parents who work need more effective ways to monitor their children's behavior, child care centers, schools, and latchkey programs could supervise children's daily behavior so that parents can assist these institutions in monitoring their children's behavior when they are not present. Alternatively, family management problems may arise from a lack of knowledge of effective discipline techniques. In this case, providing parents with opportunities to learn and practice a variety of discipline techniques may be effective. The link between prevention activities and the risk-reduction objective should be specified clearly.

3. Prevention programs should seek to strengthen protective factors while reducing risk.

4. Risk-reduction activities should address risks at or before the time they become predictive of later problems. Intervening early to reduce risk is likely to minimize the effort needed and maximize the out-

come. For example, interventions to improve family management practices prenatally and in infancy are likely to be more effective than waiting to initiate the intervention until after a referral for abuse and neglect.

5. Interventions should target individuals and communities that are exposed to multiple risk factors. Because there is evidence that those exposed to multiple risks are at elevated risk, efforts to prevent chronic and serious problems of crime, violence, and substance abuse are most likely to be effective if focused on these populations. Working with high-risk communities has advantages in that individual children are not labeled at very early ages as potential problems. Families at risk include those headed by single, poor, and/or teenage mothers. Communities at risk include poor and disorganized neighborhoods with high levels of crime, violence, and substance abuse. A communitywide approach allows higher- and lower-risk families in a neighborhood to work and learn together, modeling, supporting, and reinforcing efforts to strengthen protective factors and processes.

6. Because multiple risks present in multiple domains predict serious crime, violence, and substance abuse, multistranded prevention approaches should be used that address key risk factors affecting a neighborhood or community.

7. Prevention programs must be designed and implemented to reach and be acceptable to the diverse racial, cultural, and socioeconomic groups to be included.

Summary

Developmental criminology holds a great deal of promise for providing critically needed information on adult career criminals. As we saw in Chapter 3, their total contribution to the total volume of violence in the United States is unknown, largely because much of their crime appears to be hidden. Until longitudinal studies collect self-reports of crime on their samples through adulthood, the presumed midlife disappearance of crime will remain an empirical question. Ignorance of actual adult offending leads to the erroneous conclusion that juveniles account for a larger proportion of total crime than is, in fact, the case. In the meantime, developmental criminology is making valuable contributions to our understanding of serious, violent, and chronic delinquency.

"Developmental prevention is the new frontier of crime prevention efforts" (Tonry & Farrington, 1995, p. 10; see also Farrington, 1994; Tremblay & Craig, 1995). Juvenile violence is rare and intermittent; thus, it is very difficult to predict. The prospects of success are greatly enhanced by merging developmental criminology with the public health model, hence developmental prevention. Among developmental prevention approaches, the Social Development Model and Communities That Care strategy hold the most promise for communitywide prevention.

Further advances in developmental criminology will add further improvements to successful intervention in serious, violent, and chronic juvenile careers. For example, the prospects appear quite good for merging information on the relative position of an adolescent in Loeber's developmental pathways with an offender career model that frames onset, persistence, and desistance. This would permit a comparison of offending career stages with pathway progression. It would be very useful to examine offender career progression in relation to juvenile justice system interventions, to see what offender career changes, if any, accompany treatment and control. Loeber and his colleagues (in press, p. 29) succinctly state the intervention implications: "Knowledge of individuals' position in pathways can inform . . . more specifically what to prevent. This is possible because individuals' position in pathways also specifies the problem behaviors that are developmentally next in line, and which can form suitable targets for preventive interventions."

Recent knowledge generated by developmental approaches brings us closer to specifying which interventions work best for offenders at particular developmental stages and at specific points in offender careers. The gap, however, remains very wide. Much more evaluation of interventions is needed to add significantly to the knowledge base. The new generation of longitudinal studies is amassing voluminous developmental knowledge of offenders and careers. We already have an effective strategy for mobilizing and empowering communities to prevent delinquency, in the Communities That Care process. Early intervention (with parent training combined with child care) has demonstrated effectiveness. Significant progress is being made in implementing effective graduated sanctions. The immediate challenge is to put all these components together in a comprehensive strategy. That is the subject of the final chapter.

9

A Comprehensive Strategy

The research and data presented in the preceding chapters support the following conclusions. First, most violent juvenile offending is not brought to the attention of juvenile justice authorities. The juvenile justice system does not have an opportunity to rehabilitate these offenders. Second, in most cases the juvenile justice system is intervening toward the end of self-reported offending careers, when the delinquency reduction potential is much lower. Third, scarce resources often are wasted on noncareer juvenile delinquents who are unlikely to commit further offenses because they are at the end of their short offending span. Fourth, prevention programs are much more likely to be successful than intervention programs that attempt to reduce and offset risk factors that, over time, multiply and become more interwoven. Fifth, intervention programs must target career offenders early. Persistent aggressive behavior in different settings predicts a high likelihood of later diversified and violent offending. Sixth, prevention and intervention programs must be comprehensive, addressing multiple risk factors. Seventh, a subset of serious, violent, and chronic juvenile offenders must be targeted for graduated sanctions and intensive treatment. To reduce significantly the overall level of violence in our society, we must intervene successfully in the careers of serious, violent, and chronic juvenile offenders because they constitute about 15% of high-risk populations but account for 75% of all juvenile violent offenses.

An earlier iteration of these conclusions supported development of the Comprehensive

Strategy for Serious, Violent, and Chronic Juvenile Offenders (Wilson & Howell, 1993). The reader is encouraged to review it (see the Appendix) before proceeding, because the aim of this chapter is to show how the Comprehensive Strategy can help prevent and reduce serious, violent, and chronic juvenile delinquency.

A Comprehensive Strategy

Since the 1970s, juvenile justice has been dominated by the popular but erroneous view that "nothing works." Lipsey (1992a) has conducted the most thorough review to date of juvenile delinquency treatment programs. He reviewed nearly 400 experimentally designed studies of delinquency treatment reported since 1950. Surprisingly, Lipsey found that juveniles in treatment groups have recidivism rates about 10% lower than untreated juveniles in control groups. The best intervention programs produced 20-30% reductions in recidivism rates and similar improvements in other outcomes. These treatment programs typically focused on changing overt behavior through structured training or behavior modification interventions designed to improve interpersonal relations, self-control, school achievement, and specific job skills. Treatment programs found to be most effective were characterized by multimodal services, more intensive services (contact hours, duration, and intensity), and services more closely monitored by research teams, which resulted in better implementation. After completing his review, Lipsey (1992b, p. 16) observed that

> It is no longer constructive for researchers, practitioners, and policymakers to argue about whether delinquency treatment and related rehabilitative approaches "work," as if that were a question that could be answered with a simple "yes" or "no." As a generality, treatment clearly works. We must get on with the business of developing and identifying the treatment models that will be most effective and providing them to the juveniles they will benefit.

Fourteen effective prevention and early interventions were identified, along with 18 other potentially promising interventions, in a national assessment of programs for serious, chronic, and violent offenders (Hawkins, Catalano, & Brewer, 1995; Brewer et al., 1995). The review of graduated sanctions (Krisberg et al., 1995) identified 14 effective programs and more than 100 promising graduated sanction programs. The National Center for Juvenile Justice (Montgomery et al., 1994) surveyed 3,000 juvenile justice professionals, including judges and probation officers, to identify programs that practitioners deemed effective. More than 1,000 were nominated. Among these, the researchers designated 425 as promising interventions. These include 80 programs for serious, chronic, and violent offenders.

The Comprehensive Strategy for the Serious, Violent, and Chronic Juvenile Offender is based on accumulated knowledge of causes and correlates of delinquency and on knowledge of effective programs. It incorporates use of the best tools for managing delinquency prevention and juvenile justice system interventions. It is "comprehensive" in five respects. First, it encompasses prevention, early intervention, and graduated sanctions—the entire juvenile justice apparatus. Second, while it provides a framework for dealing with all delinquent offenders, it targets serious, violent, and chronic juvenile offenders. Third, it calls for an integrated system response, bringing the juvenile justice system together with the mental health, child welfare, education, health, and law enforcement systems, and communities as well, to address multiple risk factors and co-occurring problem behaviors. Fourth, it assumes that more cost-effective juvenile justice system interventions will permit reallocation of mo-

nies saved in costly secure correction options for prevention programs. Fifth, in the long run, adult crime reduction is expected to be a benefit of the Comprehensive Strategy. Preventing and reducing juvenile crime decreases the likelihood of criminal persistence into adulthood.

A key assumption of the Comprehensive Strategy is that a combination of interventions can achieve a larger measure of overall juvenile crime reduction than is possible by means of incarceration. Both juvenile and adult crime policy tend to search for the "magic bullet," a single panacea. Boot camps were the fad a few years ago, and remain popular. The most recent panacea is severe punishment of juveniles, ultimately by transferring them to the criminal justice system and incarcerating them in adult prisons. Unfortunately, a magic bullet does not exist and never will. Several interventions are needed to counter multiple risk factors. Moreover, different kinds of interventions are required at various stages in the juvenile justice system.

A recent cost-benefit study of juvenile delinquency prevention and treatment programs illustrates the cumulative benefits of multiple program approaches. RAND researchers (Greenwood et al., 1996) found that a combination of only four delinquency prevention and treatment programs achieves the same level of serious crime (violent crimes plus burglary) reduction as California's "three strikes" law—at less than one-fifth the cost. The RAND study team said that "the policy implications of these findings are fairly clear: Based on current best estimates of program costs and benefits, investments in some interventions for high-risk youth may be several times more cost-effective in reducing serious crime than mandatory sentences for repeat offenders" (p. 40).

Because of the impending bankruptcy of state budgets that "three strikes" laws bring (Greenwood et al., 1994) and the fact that increased imprisonment resulting from these laws has not produced large crime reduction effects in the general population (Zimring & Hawkins, 1995), juvenile prevention and intervention holds the most promise for long-term crime reduction. The successful interventions Greenwood and his colleagues identified are parent training (reviewed below), graduation incentives (Taggart, 1995), and delinquent supervision (the 8% Early Intervention Program, reviewed below). Greenwood and his colleagues concluded that home visits combined with day care produce a much smaller crime prevention effect than incapacitation; however, their study may not have taken into full account the long-term benefits of these programs (see Yoshikawa, 1995).

A broader continuum of prevention and rehabilitation options, coupled with graduated sanctions, can be even more effective than the four programs the RAND researchers identified in preventing and reducing delinquency, including serious, violent, and chronic delinquent behavior. To achieve a high level of effectiveness, these must be integrated in a comprehensive framework. We illustrate this logical approach in this chapter with several of the most promising and effective prevention and graduated sanctions options.

Target Group

The Comprehensive Strategy target group is serious, violent, and chronic juvenile offenders (see the Appendix). Serious offenders are those who commit felonies. Violent offenders are those who commit FBI Violent Index Crimes. Chronic offenders are juveniles adjudicated delinquent for three or more offenses. In other words, the Comprehensive Strategy targets career serious or violent offenders.

Moffitt (1993) distinguishes two groups of offenders: those who begin early and continue to engage in antisocial behavior at every life stage, and those who are antisocial only during adolescence. She calls the first (smaller) group *life-course persistent* and the second group *adolescence-limited*. Empirical data clearly distinguish these two groups of offenders. In the New Zealand study (Moffitt, 1991), 5% of the boys exhibited stable and pervasive antisocial behavior beginning in preschool. These were joined by about one-third of the sample, who began delinquent lifestyles between ages 11 and 15. By the age of 15, the adolescent newcomers equaled the preschool-onset group in the variety of laws they had broken, the frequency with which they broke them, and the number of times they appeared in juvenile court (Moffitt, 1991). National Youth Survey data and longitudinal studies in Denver, Pittsburgh, and Rochester allow us to examine these two groups in more detail.

Life-course persistent offenders. In the National Youth Survey conducted by Elliott

(1994a) and his colleagues, the life-course persistent group represents only about 4% of male adolescents. These offenders self-report sustained careers of serious violence; that is, three or more violent offenses per year for five years (Elliott et al., 1986). The size of this group is comparable in urban samples. In the Rochester sample, 11% began violent offending at the age of 9 or younger (Thornberry et al., 1995). More than a third (39%) of these early starters went on to become chronic violent offenders in adolescence. Thus, the life-course persistent group in this sample represents nearly 4% of the sample. In the Denver sample, 62% of those who began committing violent offenses at the age of 9 or younger became chronic violent offenders in adolescence. Thus, the life-course persistent group in this sample appears to be larger than in Rochester.

Age of onset is significantly earlier for the life-course persistent group than for the adolescence-limited group. The average age of onset for violent offending among chronic violent offenders in the urban Denver sample is 11.5 years, compared to 14.0 years for nonchronic violent offenders (the adolescence-limited group). In Rochester, the age difference between these two groups is slightly smaller. In both samples, the life-course persistent group began general delinquency offending about a year before the adolescence-limited group (see Thornberry et al., 1995, p. 221).

Moffitt (1993, p. 679) describes the offending history of life-course persisters. This group exhibits changing manifestations of antisocial behavior across the life course: biting and hitting at the age of 4, shoplifting and truancy at the age of 10, selling drugs and stealing cars at the age of 16, robbery and rape at the age of 22, and fraud and child abuse at the age of 30. Several studies show that life-course persisters lie at home, steal from shops, cheat at school, fight in bars, and embezzle at work (see Moffitt, 1993, p. 679). The underlying antisocial disposition changes as age and circumstances alter crime opportunities (Moffitt, 1993, p. 679). Thus, the life-course persisters evidence multiple problem behaviors and engage in a wide variety of offenses, both violent and nonviolent (Thornberry et al., 1995).

Intervention with life-course persisters must occur early, before unconventional behavioral patterns are established. If the early onset child's parents are contributing to problem behavior, as generally is the case, then early intervention in the family is all the more important. Moffitt (1993) describes the difficulties these children experience as they progress into adolescence. Because of their poor self-control, aggressiveness, and unpredictability, they are rejected by peers and adults. They learn to expect rejection; thus, they are likely to withdraw from others or strike out preemptively when presented with opportunities to affiliate with prosocial peers and are thereby robbed of chances to develop prosocial skills. "Simply put, if social and academic skills are not mastered in childhood, it is very difficult to later recover lost opportunities" (p. 684).

Adolescence-limited offenders. The adolescence-limited group is much larger than the life-course persistent group. In Moffitt's sample, 12% were classified as new delinquents at the age of 13. By the age of 15, another 20% began offending (Moffitt, 1993). This group of adolescence-limited offenders is somewhat larger in the urban Rochester sample. In Rochester, 18% began violent offending between the ages of 10 and 12, and 71% at the age of 13 or older (Thornberry et al., 1995). In the National Youth Survey, more than half of all violent offenders initiated their violence between the ages of 14 and 17 (Elliott, 1994a). Onset of serious violent offending doubled between the ages of 13 and 14, continued to increase to a peak at ages 16-17, dropped by 50% by the age of 18, and continued to decrease through the age of 27 (Elliott, 1994a; Elliott et al., 1986).

The prevalence of serious violent offending is surprisingly high. Among the National Youth Survey sample, the overall annual rate was approximately 5% for all 12-17-year-olds, and 8% for males. Approximately 35% of the males and 11% of the females were classified as serious violent offenders for at least 1 year by the age of 21 (Elliott et al., 1986). The violence prevalence rate is somewhat higher in urban samples. In Denver, 47% of the adolescent population committed at least one violent offense between the ages of 12 and 17, and 34% committed a serious violent offense (see Thornberry et al., 1995, p. 224). About half of the latter group (16% of the total sample) committed only one serious violent offense.

Moffitt (1993, p. 686) describes the adolescence-limited group as having distinctive empirical characteristics: "modal onset in early adolescence, recovery by young adulthood, widespread prevalence, and lack of continuity." They have no prior antisocial history. Adolescence-limited offenders lack consistency in their antisocial behavior in different situations. They may shoplift while with a group of friends but obey school and family rules. The adolescence-limited delinquents "are likely to engage in antisocial behavior in situations where such responses seem profitable to them, but they also are able to abandon antisocial behavior when prosocial styles are more rewarding" (Moffitt, 1993, p. 686). The variety of offenses committed by nonchronic violent offenders is quite similar to that of chronic violent offenders; the main difference is that a smaller proportion of them engages in property crimes, drug sales, and minor offenses (Thornberry et al., 1995).

The main target group of the Comprehensive Strategy is the life-course persistent offenders that Moffitt (1993) identifies.

Comprehensive Strategy Components

The Comprehensive Strategy consists of two main components: prevention and graduated sanctions. The prevention component is based on a risk-focused approach. The Comprehensive Strategy's risk-focused approach to delinquency prevention intervenes according to the child's chronological and developmental stage, beginning with prenatal care. It calls on communities to systematically assess their delinquency problem, to identify local risk factors, and to implement programs to counteract them. Effective delinquency prevention efforts must be comprehensive, covering known risk factors, and correspond to the social development process. As shown in Chapter 1, the juvenile justice system was founded on the recognition that children and adolescents are not emotionally and socially well-developed, and that the juvenile justice system is the key mechanism in our society for promoting prosocial behavior among at-risk and delinquent children and adolescents.

The juvenile justice system has always had a rudimentary system of graduated sanctions, from police lecture and release, to arrest, court intake counseling, informal probation, detention, adjudication and formal probation, and secure confinement. In theory, these components match the developmental history of the delinquent career. Youths in more advanced stages of pathways to serious and violent delinquency receive more restrictive sanctions and more intensive treatment. When they fail to respond to previous treatments and sanctions, more restrictive and intensive ones are applied. The inability of the research community to describe delinquent careers empirically and developmentally in relation to juvenile justice system processes, as well as a lack of precision tools for identifying youths most likely to advance in pathways to chronic offending, has hampered the juvenile justice system in effectively employing more structured and precise graduated systems.

Where must we start in building a comprehensive approach to serious and violent juvenile delinquency? The Comprehensive Strategy calls for a series of social interventions that address delinquency in general, along with serious, violent, and chronic delinquency in particular. These interventions are comprehensive community programs, early intervention, immediate sanctions, intermediate sanctions, secure care, and aftercare. These gradations (and sublevels within them) are viewed as forming a continuum of intervention options (or graduated sanctions) that is paralleled by a continuum of treatment options. As offenders progress in the graduated sanctions system, treatments must become more structured and intensive, to deal effectively with the more intractable problems that more difficult and dangerous offenders present. How can these interventions be managed and coordinated?

The *Guide for Implementing the Comprehensive Strategy for Serious, Violent, and Chronic Juvenile Offenders* (Howell, 1995b) includes a "blueprint" for implementing the Comprehensive Strategy that any community can use. This blueprint details the steps involved in implementing both the prevention (community) and graduated sanctions (juvenile justice system) components. A summary of these steps follows after a brief introduction.

Community Delinquency Prevention

Community delinquency and crime prevention does not have an encouraging history (Hope, 1995). Early efforts to change the conditions in communities that are believed to contribute to delinquency and crime have em-

ployed a wide range of intervention techniques (see Bursik & Grasmick, 1993; Hope, 1995). Few have been based on social theories, excepting the Chicago Community Action Program (Shaw & McKay, 1942) and the New York City Mobilization for Youth program (see Bibb, 1967). Other strategies in a succession of policy paradigms (Hope, 1995) include community surveillance and other techniques (block watch and neighborhood watch) for reducing resident fear and victimization (see Skogan, 1990), environmental modification through "defensible space" (Newman, 1973), efforts to forestall or halt urban deterioration (see Hope, 1995), and counterurbanization (Champion, 1989). None of these has produced notable successes, mainly because of "insufficient understanding of the nature of social relations within residential areas and how community crime careers are shaped by the wider urban market" (Hope, 1995, p. 21). Community efforts to ameliorate juvenile delinquency and violence suffer less from a lack of community organization than from the lack of a network of services in economic areas where youth violence is more prevalent (Fagan, 1986). As Bursik and Grasmick (1993, pp. 176-177) note, "those communities most in need of effective crime control programs are often those characterized by a very segmented set of networks that may be difficult to unite in a collective effort."

Community reconstruction is said to be the ideal (Eisenhower Foundation, 1990). Empowerment Zones (revitalization of communities through economic and social services) and Enterprise Communities (promoting physical and human development) are large-scale programs supported through the federal Department of Housing and Urban Development (OJJDP, 1995b) that aim to reconstruct selected inner-city areas. Private foundations have pioneered efforts in response to the community rehabilitation challenge. In the adolescent arena, for example, the Annie E. Casey Foundation launched the New Futures Initiative in 1987, designed by the Center for the Study of Social Policy (1995). Ten mid-sized cities, all of which had high poverty levels, high dropout rates, and large minority populations, were awarded $5-$12.5 million over 5 years to improve the life chances of disadvantaged youths in their communities. Each was to restructure and realign existing institutions to be more responsive to the needs of at-risk youths and their families to accomplish four objectives: reduce the school dropout rate, improve students' academic performance, prevent teen pregnancies and births, and increase the number of college entrants. These were to be accomplished through the formation of new local governance bodies, called collaboratives, made up of representatives of local agencies, parents, community representatives, government officials, business representatives, and elected officials. New policies and practices for meeting the needs of at-risk youth would be devised, and accountability for positive outcomes would be required.

The results of an evaluation of the program by the Center for the Study of Social Policy (1995) were disappointing. None of the sites achieved the objectives of the program. On the positive side, one of the major accomplishments of the program was that it instigated cross-system solutions to youth problems. In some instances, comprehensive problem definitions led to innovative service delivery; however, "for the most part, the collaboratives were largely unable to define a comprehensive action plan that cut across multiple organizations. Instead, they reverted to what they knew best: funding discrete interventions" (p. xiii). The evaluators concluded that "our collective rhetoric about cross-system change is far ahead of any operational knowledge about how to get there from here" (p. xiii).

This is an important lesson that can be applied to the delinquency prevention arena. A recent review of comprehensive community interventions (Catalano, Arthur, Hawkins, & Olson, 1996) "suggests that multiple prevention strategies crossing multiple domains that are mutually reinforcing and that are maintained for several years produce the greatest impact" (p. 22). This means that community participation and participant ownership of prevention initiatives are essential. An example of an approach for community implementation of a risk-focused prevention strategy is the Communities That Care (CTC) strategy (Hawkins & Catalano, 1992). It is based on the Social Development Model pioneered by Weis and Hawkins (1979; Hawkins & Fraser, 1981; Hawkins & Weis, 1980, 1985; Weis & Sederstrom, 1981). The CTC strategy is a comprehensive, long-term, communitywide approach that allows communities to tailor early intervention efforts in response to epidemiological evidence on risk and protective in the community (Hawkins, Catalano, & Brewer, 1995). The strategy recognizes and builds on existing resources and programs in the community to develop a comprehensive system for risk reduction and enhancement of protective factors.

The Communities That Care strategy results from more than 16 years of research on delinquency and substance abuse prevention. It consists of a planning phase and an implementation phase. The planning phase, which spans 1 year, involves community mobilization, risk and resource assessment, and strategic planning. This phase begins by orienting key community leaders, including mayors, police chiefs, judges, school superintendents, and business, civic, and religious leaders, to the risk-focused prevention approach. The orientation assists key leaders in assessing their community's readiness for the approach. Involving key leaders in the process makes it more likely that they will commit resources to prevention once the community's strategic prevention plan is completed. After the orientation, the key leaders appoint or identify a community prevention board that is made up of diverse community members including key informal leaders, grassroots community leaders, and educational, law enforcement, and health and human service delivery personnel. The prevention board is established as a permanent institution of the community. Once established or identified, the community prevention board is trained to assess its community's risks and resources through collecting data on risk factor indicators and assessing existing programs. After assessment is completed, the community board prioritizes risk factors that are elevated or trending in unwanted directions, identifies programming gaps, and learns about effective approaches to address priority risk factors. The board then creates a strategic prevention plan that specifies prevention programs to address high-priority risk factors in the community. Existing programs that address high-priority risk factors in the community are included in the strategic plan. The plan includes a design for process and outcome evaluations of the strategy.

The implementation phase begins at this point. The board creates task forces for each program element in the action plan. These task forces oversee program planning and implementation in that area. The board then implements the identified programs. On an ongoing basis, the community board systematically evaluates the implementation and outcomes of the programs, completing a new risk and resource assessment at least every 2 years. As changes in risk and protective factors occur in the community, the community board can adjust its prevention plan to reflect these changes. This allows the prevention board to redesign its plan to meet changing conditions produced by either the preventive interventions' effectiveness or changing risk conditions. This strategic process activates both community leaders and grassroots sectors of the community to take ownership of the prevention planning process. As Catalano and his colleagues suggest (Catalano et al., 1996, p. 26), "recent advances in prevention science and health epidemiology are providing tools communities can use to plan an implement strategic, outcome-focused plans for reducing the prevalence of antisocial behavior among adolescents and young adults."

The CTC strategy initially was field tested in the states of Washington and Oregon, then implemented in a Six State Consortium Project (see Catalano et al., 1996, for results of these experiments). Altogether, CTC is being implemented in about 300 communities in the United States. Selected communities in 43 states and Puerto Rico have received training and technical assistance in risk-focused prevention using the CTC process under the Juvenile Justice and Delinquency Prevention Act Title V Delinquency Prevention Program since it began in 1994 (OJJDP, 1995f, 1996). A General Accounting Office (1996) review of the early implementation stages of the Title V Prevention Program found it to be successful. The OJJDP's (1996) report to Congress on the JJDP Act Title V Prevention Program concludes that it shows "every indication of promise as an effective community response to rising rates of juvenile delinquency, violence, and other problem behaviors" (p. 76). Baseline data can be used by states to hold prevention programs accountable for reducing risk these factors and increasing protective factors specified in the Social Development Model. The next logical step is the development of national indicators of risk and protective factors, for use in federal program planning and implementation, not only in delinquency and violence prevention but also in other adolescent problem behavior areas (school dropout, teenage pregnancy, and substance abuse).

Delinquency prevention is cost-effective. The total cost of a murder is more than $2.9 million (including $1 million in tangible costs to society; Miller et al., 1996). The annual cost of a prison cell is $15,000-$20,000 (Miller et al., 1996). Incarcerating a juvenile for 1 year costs approximately $34,000 (OJJDP, 1995a). Early intervention programs cost about $3,200 (OJJDP, 1995a). Conservatively, Lipsey (1984) estimates a direct saving of $1.40 for every $1.00 spent on prevention.

Early Intervention

The case for early intervention in delinquent careers is compelling. Programs are needed "that interrupt, at early stages, developmental pathways that lead to serious delinquency and violence before these behaviors have become a stable part of the persons's behavioral repertoire" (Thornberry et al., 1995, p. 233). Older offenders are likely to be involved in various forms of delinquency, to exhibit other problem behaviors, and to have multiple risk factors and social deficits. "Moreover, these problem behaviors and risk factors are likely to interact with one another and to be reciprocally interrelated with delinquency over time. The consequence is a spiraling behavioral trajectory that is exceedingly difficult for prosocial forces to penetrate" (Thornberry et al., 1995, p. 233). Early interventions, therefore, are more likely to be successful.

Knowing this and that severe antisocial behaviors in childhood are the strongest predictors of chronic delinquency is not a sufficient basis for designing successful early interventions. The task is complicated by knowledge that most juvenile delinquency and other problem behaviors develop from multiple risk factors across multiple settings: community, family, school, peer group, and individual characteristics. Knowing that problem behaviors occur developmentally and that the interplay of individual and family characteristics is most directly related to early onset, however, provides a much stronger basis for designing early interventions. But can they prevent serious, violent, and chronic delinquency?

In a detailed review of evaluations of 40 early intervention programs, Yoshikawa (1995) concluded that four programs demonstrated positive long-term effects on serious, violent, and chronic delinquency. All of them focused on improving individual capacity (cognitive ability) and family functioning through a combination of early childhood education and family support services. The programs offered both home visits (parent training) and center-based educational child care or preschool (aimed at improving cognitive skills). They are the High/Scope Perry Preschool Project (Schweinhart et al., 1993), the Syracuse University Family Development Research Program (Lally et al., 1988), the Yale Child Welfare Project (Seitz & Apfel, 1994), and the Houston Parent Child Development Center (Johnson & Walker, 1987). The High/Scope and Syracuse programs have been shown to be effective in reducing severe and chronic delinquency in long-term follow-ups.

High/Scope Perry Preschool was designed to prevent delinquency by targeting preschoolers. The most recent follow-up (Schweinhart et al., 1993) of High/Scope study groups showed that, at the age of 27, significantly fewer program group members than nonprogram group members were frequent offenders, that is, arrested five or more times in their lifetimes (7% vs. 35%) or as adults (7% vs. 31%). The program group also had noticeably fewer juvenile arrests and significantly fewer arrests for drug manufacturing or drug distribution offenses (7% vs. 25%). The Syracuse program also showed a decrease in the total number, severity, and chronicity of later involvement in officially recorded offenses. Yoshikawa (1995) concluded that it is primarily multicomponent programs (providing early education and family support) that produced long-term declines in antisocial behavior and delinquency. He attributes their success to obtaining effects on multiple risks for chronic delinquency. All four programs mainly targeted urban, low-income families.

Yoshikawa (1995, p. 70) issues a cautionary note concerning the future potential of these programs. Because they were carried out in the 1970s, "numerous demographic, social and economic changes have occurred since then which might affect the outcomes of early intervention," including the higher rate of employment among women (that might reduce the attractiveness of frequent home visiting) and increased involvement of youth in the drug trade and handguns. This "suggests that family-focused interventions alone, without broader efforts to attack these neighborhood-level causal factors, may not have their intended impact" (p. 70). Yoshikawa (1995, p. 71) nevertheless concludes that "as one element in a comprehensive plan to address poverty, drugs, guns, and other environmental causes of crime, early education and family support programs may lessen the current devastating impact of chronic delinquency on America's children and families." The implication of Yoshikawa's conclusion is that community-based prevention (CTC) and early intervention programs need to be combined in a comprehensive community approach.

The Seattle Social Development Project (see Hawkins et al., 1991; Hawkins, Catalano, Morrison, et al., 1992) has produced a major breakthrough in designing comprehensive delinquency prevention programs. It is a multicomponent intervention designed to prevent delinquency and other problem behaviors, employing a package of classroom management and instruction methods in the elementary grades, including cooperative learning, proactive classroom management, and interactive teaching (Hawkins, Catalano, & Miller, 1992; O'Donnell et al., 1995). Proactive classroom management consists of establishing expectations for classroom behavior; using methods of maintaining classroom order that minimized interruptions to instruction and learning; and giving frequent, specific, and contingent praise and encouragement for student effort and progress. Interactive teaching involves clear specification of learning objectives, continuous monitoring of students, and remediation, requiring students to master specific learning objectives before proceeding to more advanced work.

Structured cooperative learning groups were used in experimental classrooms from Grades 2 through 6. In the experimental intervention, teachers of the elementary grades were trained to use these three methods of instruction. These methods were tested in combination with a social competence curriculum and parent training over the 6 years of elementary school. The intervention was tested with a multiethnic urban sample.

By the end of Grade 2, boys in intervention classrooms were rated as significantly less aggressive than boys in control classrooms (Hawkins et al., 1991). By the beginning of Grade 5, experimental students were significantly less likely to have initiated delinquent behavior and alcohol use than controls (Hawkins, Catalano, Morrison, et al., 1992). By the end of Grade 6, intervention boys from low-income families had significantly greater academic achievement, better teacher-rated behavior, and lower rates of delinquency initiation than did control boys from low income families (O'Donnell et al., 1995). A 6-year follow-up at the age of 18 found significantly higher achievement and lower rates of lifetime violent delinquent behavior among children exposed to the full intervention compared with controls (Hawkins et al., 1996).

Graduated Sanctions

The first step a community must take to develop a risk-focused graduated sanctions system is to form a Graduated Sanctions Working Group (Howell, 1995b, pp. 35-36). It must include all key juvenile justice decision makers in the jurisdiction, including judges, prosecutors, police, and youth corrections managers. The Working Group is responsible for conducting an assessment of the juvenile justice system and its clientele and developing a continuum of graduated sanctions and treatment program options. Its assessment tools include risk, needs, and placement assessments. Before illustrating the juvenile justice system assessment process, a brief explanation of these tools is in order.

Risk Assessments

In the juvenile justice system, the focus of risk assessment shifts from the community, family, school, peer group, and individual factors to public safety and rehabilitation considerations. The success of risk assessments in the adult corrections arena in predicting in-custody treatment and reincarceration outcomes in a variety of correctional settings (see Andrews & Bonta, 1994; Bonta, 1996; Bonta & Motiuk, 1990; Jones, 1996) led to their adoption in the juvenile justice system. Risk assessment instruments sort offenders into groups with differing probabilities of reoffending (Wiebush, Baird, Krisberg, & Onek, 1995), using a predetermined set of scale items known to have a statistical relationship with recidivism. These actuarial devices, which have replaced clinical judgments, include "static" risk predictors (offense history, age of initial arrest or adjudication) and dynamic predictors, the major risk factors for delinquent behavior. These instruments are designed to estimate the likelihood of reoffending within a given time period (say, 18-24 months) and are based on the statistical relationship between youth characteristics and recidivism rates (see Wiebush et al., 1995, pp. 181-183 for a discussion of the essential properties of assessment and classification systems).

Because risk assessment instruments are based on group data, their effectiveness is limited to prediction of aggregate outcomes. These instruments cannot predict outcomes accurately for specific individuals, nor whether or not an individual will commit a violent offense. The main obstacle to development of instruments that can predict violent behavior is that the proportion in any given juvenile offender population who go on to commit a violent offense is quite low—usually less than 10%. This low base rate makes it difficult to identify with statistical confidence characteristics that discriminate between youth who do and do not subsequently commit violent offenses. General recidivism is easier to predict than violence because minor or moderately serious offenses occur more frequently, and a statistical prediction that a new offense of any type will be committed is easier than a prediction of future violent behavior. The ability to discriminate risk potential for different subgroups of offenders provides the basis for targeting interventions and resources on those at the highest level of risk, while using less costly and labor-intensive interventions for those at the lowest risk level.

A core set of variables has been identified in several validations as recidivism predictors for juvenile offenders (Wiebush et al., 1995). Their comparison of seven empirically based instruments validated (using juvenile court records) for use in probation/parole (see Baird, 1984) shows the consistency of certain predictors. These variables include offending career items (age at first court referral, number of prior offenses, severity of current offense, and number of prior out-of-home placements) and individual characteristics (school problems, drug/alcohol abuse, family problems/parent control, and peer relationships). Not surprisingly, the individual characteristics that predict recidivism are almost identical to the five major risk factors for delinquency: community, family, school, peer group, and individual characteristics (see Table 9.1). There is one exception. Community conditions generally are not included in risk assessment instruments.

It is encouraging to see the high level of congruence in these two risk factor compilations, which suggests that even greater recidivism prediction efficiency can be achieved using risk assessment instruments once information sources and accuracy are improved. The first column in Table 9.1 shows the items in the model risk assessment instrument developed

TABLE 9.1 Comparison of Risk Predictors in Eight Jurisdictions

Risk Item	Model Risk	County Systems				State Systems		
		Calhoun	Cobb	Cuyahoga	Lucas	Indiana	Michigan	Wisconsin
Age at first referral	X		X	X	X	X	X	X
Number of priors	X		X			X	X	X
Current offense		X		X	X		X	
Prior assault	X							X
Prior out-of-home placement	X					X	X	X
Drug/alcohol abuse	X		X	X	X	X	X	X
School problems	X	X	X	X	X	X	X	X
Special education					X			
Peers	X	X	X		X	X		X
Mental health stability								X
Family problems	X	X	X	X	X	X		
Runaway				X			X	X
Victim abuse/ neglect				X				X
Gender		X	X					
Prior supervision adjustment			X			X	X	
Other				X	X			

SOURCE: "Risk Assessment and Classification for Serious, Violent, and Chronic Juvenile Offenders" (p. 178), Wiebush, Baird, Krisberg, and Onek, in J. C. Howell, B. Krisberg, J. D. Hawkins, & J. J. Wilson (Eds.), *Sourcebook on Serious, Violent, and Chronic Juvenile Offenders*, ©copyright 1995 by Sage Publications, Inc.

by the NCCD. It can be refined using research results from longitudinal causes and correlates studies to improve prediction of chronic and serious offending. The prospects of predicting violent offending are not good, however, because the base rate is too low.

Successfully targeting violent juvenile offenders in the juvenile justice system has proved to be very difficult, because they represent such a small proportion of cases. Several large-scale programs have attempted to target this subgroup for priority arrest, prosecution, and treatment, with little success. The OJJDP VJO program initially defined target youth as chronic violent juvenile offenders (Fagan & Hartstone, 1984). Two court convictions were required for violent offenses (murder, rape, robbery, kidnapping, and arson of an occupied dwelling). After 4 months, only 12 youth were found to meet this criterion in five large urban sites. Intake criteria, therefore, had to be relaxed to allow in enough youths to operate the programs. After relaxing the criteria three times, the program targeted arrested youths with a prior adjudication for a felony offense.

The OJJDP Serious, Habitual Offender/Drug Involved Program, which operated in police departments in five medium-sized cities, wound up taking in mostly burglary and theft offenders. Only one in six offenses of the chronic juvenile offenders was a violent offense (Pindur & Wells, 1986). A similar program, the OJJDP Habitual, Serious, and Violent Juvenile Offender Program, operated in 13 medium-sized to very large cities, targeting juveniles with prior adjudications for robbery, burglary, rape, aggravated assault, homicide, or another crime against a person. Project sites wound up making exceptions (Cronin, Bourque, Mell, Gragg, & McGrady, 1988). Only 18% of juveniles brought into the program were charged with robbery, and only 12% with felony assault. Most were burglars (37%).

Successfully targeting the most dangerous, or potentially dangerous, juvenile offenders is not insurmountable. First, a comprehensive array of treatment options and sanctions must be developed. Second, the juvenile justice system must develop the capacity to assess and classify juvenile offenders accurately, in such a way that the impact of those interventions will be maximized while scarce resources are conserved. Well-designed assessment procedures improve the ability to accurately and consistently identify those who are, or may become, serious, violent, and chronic juvenile offenders. Carefully crafted classification systems ensure that the system's response is equitable and graduated. They also provide for a direct linking of the offender's need for control and services with the most appropriate intervention (Wiebush et al., 1995, p. 207).

Needs Assessments

Needs assessment instruments contain objective criteria for determining the presence and severity of problems that need to be addressed in major areas of a juvenile's life. Table 9.2 shows a comparison of needs assessment items in instruments used in seven jurisdictions (and the model instrument developed by the NCCD). Note that family relationships, school problems, peer relationships, mental stability, and substance abuse items are included in every instrument in the comparison. These and other items in the needs assessment instruments point to areas in offenders' lives in which risk reduction and protective factor enhancement is needed. Use of these instruments will help ensure that the full range of problem areas is taken into account when formulating a case plan, that a baseline for monitoring a juvenile's progress is established, that periodic assessments of treatment effectiveness are conducted, and that a system-wide database of treatment needs is used for the planning and evaluation of program, policies, and procedures. Use of needs assessments also will help to allocate scarce resources more effectively and efficiently (Wiebush et al., 1995, pp. 181-183).

Systematic use of risk and needs assessments will improve matching of offenders' needs to effective program placements that are also appropriate for the level of risk they present. Because serious, violent, and chronic offenders possess multiple risk factors, it is important that all these risk factors be addressed in program placements. Achieving the best match between risk-needs and a wide array of program options will result in higher rehabilitation success rates.

Placement or Custody Assessment

The third type of assessment tool frequently used in the juvenile justice system is called a "placement assessment" or "custody assessment" instrument (Wiebush et al., 1995, pp. 179-180). Although they may include predictive items, placement or custody assessment instruments generally are driven by policy considerations (public safety) rather than recidivism results. They may be used in several different ways: as a screening tool to determine whether a youth should be placed into detention pending an adjudication hearing, as a guide for corrections officials in determining the appropriate placement or level of security, or as a method for determining the custody needs of incarcerated youth. Because public safety is the main consideration, these instruments typically include measures of current and prior offense severity.

Juvenile Justice System Assessment

The Working Group decides which population to screen using the classification instruments. Ideally, the classification instrument would be applied to all youth in a juvenile justice system. In practice, because of budget and staffing limitations, many jurisdictions choose to focus initially on youth in secure care, which accounts for the bulk of juvenile justice expenditures. It is important, however, that assessments be conducted across the entire juvenile justice system population because juveniles' (actual) offense histories probably are much longer than their official record indicates and they are likely to have multiple problem behaviors and be experiencing multiple risk factors. Starting at the front end of the system would have greater payoff, by helping reduce later incarceration. Besides, early intervention strategies with younger offenders are more likely to be successful (Thornberry et al., 1995).

Once the Working Group decides which population to screen, it develops a risk assessment instrument. This can be done in two ways, using either the empirical model or the consensus model. A community using the empirical model conducts original research on the recidivism rates of its juvenile justice population to determine which items to include in its risk assessment instrument. Items are selected that correlate statistically with high recidivism rates. Under the consensus model, the working

TABLE 9.2 Comparison of Needs Assessment Items

Need Item	Model Instrument	County Systems			State Systems			
		Cuyahoga	Lucas	Orange	Delaware	Indiana	Michigan	Wisconsin
Substance abuse	x	x	x	x	x	x	x	x
Family relationships	x	x	x	x	x	x	x	x
Parent problems[a]			x		x		x	x
Parent skills			x	x	x		x	x
Mental health stability	x	x	x	x	x	x	x	x
Intellectual ability/ academic achievement	x	x		x	x	x	x	x
Special education	x	x		x	x	x		x
Employment/ vocational skills	x	x		x		x	x	x
School problems	x	x	x	x	x	x	x	x
Peer relationships	x	x	x	x	x	x	x	x
Health/hygiene	x	x	x	x			x	x
Sexual adjustment	x		x	x	x		x	x
Victimization					x	x	x	x
Housing/ finances		x			x		x	
Structured activities		x	x		x	x		
Independent living skills					x			x

SOURCE: "Risk Assessment and Classification for Serious, Violent, and Chronic Juvenile Offenders" (p. 183), Wiebush, Baird, Krisberg, and Onek, in J. C. Howell, B. Krisberg, J. D. Hawkins, & J. Wilson (Eds.), *Sourcebook on Serious, Violent, and Chronic Juvenile Offenders*, ©copyright 1995 by Sage Publications, Inc.

a. Includes substance abuse, criminality, and/or mental health.

group takes an instrument that has been validated elsewhere and modifies it to conform to its community norms. The working group must decide the cutoff points for classifying youth as high risk, medium risk, and low risk. These risk classifications usually will be one of two dimensions to be taken into account in selecting programs and placement levels for individual youth. Offense severity is the other.

The working group then develops a needs assessment instrument. Offenders' treatment needs are not considered until the level of security has been determined. Needs assessments ensure the selection of the most appropriate program for a youth within the security level already determined for that youth through the risk assessment process. Developing a program selection (or placement) matrix is the next task for the Working Group. This process is illustrated later in this chapter, in the use of the In-

tensive Supervision Program model. The classification determined by the program selection matrix leads directly to the level and type of placement for each youth. Using the program matrix, low-risk youth with limited offense histories are recommended for immediate sanctions; high-risk youth who are serious or violent offenders are recommended for secure incarceration; and youth who fall between these two categories are recommended for intermediate sanction programs.

The working group next applies the matrix to the selected population categories of youth. This step involves conducting an analysis of the offender population to develop groupings, first by offense severity, and second by risk level. A key step is to apply the program selection matrix to a large sample of youth. The results will show how many youth fall into each box on the program matrix grid, giving the jurisdiction a sense of what types of programs it needs and how many slots it needs in each program area. This step also involves assessing the adequacy of existing programs, identifying gaps, and specifying program development needs. The working group must make recommendations about what these programs should be. The completed matrix is a blueprint for a comprehensive, risk-focused continuum of care, including both graduated sanctions and treatment options that are tied integrally to the risk assessment and needs assessment process.

It is important to think of sanctions and treatment options as forming a continuum from least to most intrusive and from least intensive to most intensive, respectively. The most effective program managers creatively link services from the network of options to children and their families, rather than bouncing clients from one program location to another. Effective "case management" is essential to success (see Baird, 1984, for a Model Case Management system).

The remainder of this chapter illustrates the graduated sanctions component of the Comprehensive Strategy with sanctions and program options. These are chosen either because of their compatibility with the Comprehensive Strategy or because of evidence supporting their success. Most important, we aim to illustrate the types of sanctions and interventions that help form a comprehensive framework.

Consideration of program components should take into account their theoretical soundness. Because juvenile justice system interventions have the same general goal as prevention programs—healthy children and adolescents—the Social Development Model is applicable. Thus, *skills* development, provision of *opportunities* for effective use of new skills, and *recognition* for successful use of skills are requirements of any program.

Immediate Intervention

This is the first level of graduated sanctions. Unfortunately, it has been the weakest link in the graduated sanctions system. It is often assumed that adolescents reaching the juvenile court are new offenders, that aside from police contacts and perhaps an arrest or two, juvenile court officials have the first opportunity to correct a child's behavior. This is an erroneous perception. Stouthamer-Loeber, Loeber, Van Kammen, and Zhang (1995) investigated the problem be-

havior of boys who had been referred to the Pittsburgh juvenile court, the extent of their problems, and the timing of parental help-seeking. Their study had its foundation in research showing that youngsters appearing in juvenile court for the first time generally have engaged in problem behaviors for some time, usually starting with minor delinquent acts and progressing to more serious offenses (Loeber et al., 1993).

Stouthamer-Loeber and colleagues (1995) found that by the time these youngsters get to court, their parents may have coped for several years with the child's problem behavior. By the eighth grade (about age 14), 20% of the sample of boys who had committed delinquent acts had been referred to juvenile court. Only 41% of the boys' parents had ever sought help from anyone for the boys' problems. The average interval between the time of initial problem behaviors and court contact was 4 years. For youths who exhibited more serious problem behaviors, the average interval was 2 years. In 16% of the cases, the child's problems had been occurring for more than 10 years, and more than half had exhibited problem behaviors for 5 years or more. Thus, by the time the juvenile court has to deal with the deliquents, their parents may have struggled with their problem for years.

Comparison of the court versus no-court delinquents showed that the court delinquents were involved in significantly more serious covert behavior and authority avoidance, and slightly more overt behavior. They also had a later age of onset of serious disruptive behaviors, had reached higher steps in Loeber's three pathways to serious and violent offending, and were more likely to have reached the second or third steps in several pathways. There were no differences between the two groups in the percentage for whom any type of help had been sought (less than 45% of both groups). Professional help had been sought for less than 30% of both groups. The court delinquents, however, had received more intensive professional help than had the noncourt youths (much of which could have been court-initiated).

Comparison of help and no-help delinquents showed that the help group had earlier onset of general problem behaviors and serious disruptive problems. They also had reached higher steps in the pathways than the no-help group. The number of help attempts caretakers made was astonishing. Among the court group, by the time they reached juvenile court, these youngsters had received a mean number of 25 help contacts, 13 of which were from professional sources. In contrast, the no-court group had received 14 help contacts, half of which were from professional sources.

Two levels of immediate intervention are needed. The first of these is needed before problematic child and adolescent behavior is brought to the attention of the juvenile justice system. Unfortunately, only a limited number of models are available that intervene at this point, the preferred level of intervention. The Pittsburgh juvenile court study indicates that early intervention is needed for some families and their children long before court referral becomes necessary.

Level-one immediate intervention. To help families temporarily manage out-of-control adolescents involved in delinquency, a typical community might have a runaway shelter. Only a few communities have family crisis centers or stabilizing facilities; most have only a crisis hotline for adolescents—which provides little parental support. Many have shelter care facilities that serve as temporary alternatives to detention and are useful in helping resolve family conflicts. Several level-one immediate intervention models have been developed.

In 1983, New Jersey created Juvenile-Family Crisis Intervention Units (CIUs) to provide troubled juveniles and their families a noncoercive resource to help resolve conflicts and access needed services (Juvenile Delinquency Commission, 1991). Each county in the state has a 24-hour CIU, handling cases that otherwise, eventually, would likely be taken to juvenile court. Illinois has a similar program, called the 1500 system, that consists of crisis intervention units (Studzinski & Pierce, n.d.). Services are provided on a no-decline basis, including in-home if needed. The goals of the 1500 system are family preservation, family reunification, and adolescent independence where reunification is not possible.

An innovative program in Hennepin County, Minnesota, resulted from a study showing that problem children under 10 years of age referred to child welfare were not receiving services (Hennepin County Attorney's Office, 1995). A new program was created in the Child Welfare Department to provide services to these children and their families. Experiences to date of these types of crisis intervention show that the childhood and adolescent clients have multiple, co-occurring problems.

Lerman and Pottick's (1995) study of youths referred to Newark CIU (and community mental health centers) is illustrative. Psychological testing of the children and adolescents (average age, 14.5 years) using the Achenbach Child Behavior Checklist (Achenbach and Edelbrock, 1983) revealed coexistence of delinquency, aggression, and psychological problems among most of them. Boys were more likely than girls to be in the high delinquent/low aggression type. Conversely, girls were more likely than boys to be in the high aggression/low delinquent type. Parents reported that they were aware of the seriousness of their child's problems for about a year before referral. In 71% of the cases, they said that bringing the child to either of these centers was the idea of someone not related to them, generally after police or court contact. Coming to the centers thus appeared to be involuntary. Initial reliance on these sources is illustrated by findings regarding who first noticed the child's problems. Parents or other intimates (77%) were the largest category of noticers, followed by school personnel (26%).

Only 29% of the parents had ever brought their child to an agency before. Most (64%) had relied on their own efforts in working with their child, including behavior modification techniques, using rewards and punishments, but to no avail. More than a third had talked to counselors or taken the child to counseling, a hospital, a doctor, or a psychiatrist to get help, but again to no avail. The rank order of informal help-seeking contacts with formal sources was teachers (73%), police/court (59%), family crisis workers (44%), doctors or ministers (41%), and mental health or social service agencies (38% each). Talks with teachers were least likely to result in a specific agency suggestion. Talks with doctors, ministers, and even mental health workers were not likely to produce a suggestion of an agency where the parent and child might get help. Talks with police and court officials were most productive, followed by those with state youth workers and family workers.

These findings of Lerman and Pottick's (1995) study are very revealing of parent and child service needs. Parents of these urban youths, with the help of family intimates and friends, are most likely to notice child and adolescent problem behaviors. Parents, however, do not know where to turn for help, and the sources they initially rely on are not very helpful. Although teachers were the only professional group that noticed a substantial amount of problem behavior, they were the least likely to be able to suggest a specific agency where the family might get help. None of the sources appeared to understand the mental health problems experienced by the problem youth and often made inappropriate suggestions for help. Lerman and Pottick (1995) make several recommendations for improving individual-level services: improving the responsiveness of agency systems, improving the ability of parents to become effective help seekers, improving the utilization of services, providing multiple services for multiple problems, expanding sensitivity to gender differences, and encouraging youths to become their own help seekers. These recommendations and others Lerman and Pottick make (1995, pp. 216-236) can help inform the design of effective level-one immediate intervention programs.

LeBlanc and colleagues (1994) contend that it is easy to differentiate between children with early manifestations of problem behaviors and those without indicators. Childhood antecedents include frequent sanctions by school authorities and insufficient investment in school activities. Major family-related factors include inconsistent supervision and inappropriate sanctions. Aggressive acts are the dominant form of disorder at that age. These may be followed by vagrancy, frequenting arcades, and associating with deviant peers. Like LeBlanc and his colleagues, Loeber (1996) reports that early childhood problems in both the family and school domains most strongly predict persistent problems.

Level-one immediate intervention programs, therefore, should concentrate on the school and family domains to identify youth who could benefit from services. Although most childhood and adolescent problems are temporary and disappear without special intervention, many youngsters needing help do not receive it, help comes late in the development of problem behavior patterns, and the adequacy of help may be in question. "We are in sore need of more precise information concerning when to intervene and which behaviors to target" (Stouthamer-Loeber et al., 1995). Program development must respect families' right to privacy. Although programs that invade private family matters can alienate families from mainstream life (Dryfoos, 1990), to say that parents experiencing persistent problems with their children and adolescents would welcome

help is an understatement, based on the Pittsburgh study by Stouthamer-Loeber and her colleagues and the Lerman-Pottick Newark study. Much remains to be learned about help-seeking behavior (Lerman & Pottick, 1995; Stouthamer-Loeber et al., 1995).

Immediate intervention in criminogenic families is more problematic. Given the knowledge that adult criminals are likely to abuse or neglect infants and children in the family (Farrington, 1996, p. 32), it is possible to target these (typically disrupted) family environments, but how can they be identified with minimal false positives and offered help? The Children's Research Center (CRC, 1993) model is an innovative method of identifying the relative degree of risk for continued abuse or neglect among families that already have a substantiated abuse or neglect referral. Using Child Protective Services case records, CRC applies risk assessment instruments to classify cases according to risk levels. These instruments are based on an analysis of the relationship between family characteristics and case outcomes, using large samples of previously substantiated cases. The risk level is used to set a service level for opened cases, and in some states, as a key criterion in case-opening decisions. The risk assessment instruments have distinguished significant differences in the risk potential of the client population. Families classified as high risk had a recidivism rate 10 times as high as low-risk families (Wiebush et al., 1995). The results of these risk assessments can be linked with criminal justice system data to identify the common characteristics of criminal parents. In addition to abusive and neglectful behavior, problem parents and other adults can be targeted, based on patterns of violence in different settings (e.g., the workplace, community, and homes). Effectively intervening with problem parents appears necessary to break the cycle of violence.

Level-two immediate intervention. On December 22, 1995, Maggie and Cornelius Oberly of Montclair, Maryland, chained their 16-year-old son, Chris, inside his bedroom to a set of exercise weights (Smith, 1996). They did this not to abuse him but to protect him from criminal involvement and perhaps getting killed in youth gang activity. Their son was out of control and unmanageable. It was a sense of hopelessness that drove them to lock up their son during the day with an 8-foot chain around his waist, allowing plenty of mobility to go to the bathroom and take regular meals.

Until his freshman year in high school, Chris was an excellent student and typical child. Then, his parents said, he changed virtually overnight. He began failing his classes, snorting cocaine, smoking marijuana in the house, dealing drugs, bringing home expensive jewelry, and hanging out with known gang members. He came and went as he pleased, leaving the door wide open as he left. His parents could not stop him. In response to their efforts to control him, he ran away, slept in some bushes, and got friends to bring him food. He preferred not to come home because of his parents' attempts to restrict his behavior.

Police came to the Oberly house more than 20 times, either returning him home or looking for him. The Oberlys tried to get help many times from the police and the county's social services department. They were told that it was not the role of the police or county to play parent. Social service officials said they did not deal with delinquents, only abused and neglected children. His parents started the process to have him detained in a detention center but learned that this would take months and appeared to be only a temporary solution. They chained him for a few days to keep him out of trouble over the Christmas school break, until they could make arrangements to send him to family members in Liberia, where he will attend a strict boarding school. After interviewing the Oberlys, the county prosecutor refused to press charges. Agreeing with other authorities that Chris's parents showed poor judgment in their determination to protect their out-of-control son, the prosecutor decided that they lacked criminal intent.

What other alternatives did Chris's mother and father have? Not many. Parents typically have two options for dealing with out-of-control adolescents: confinement in a detention center or commitment to an adolescent psychiatric facility. Detention of such youths does not seem to be necessary to introduce sufficient control. More immediate intervention is needed before adolescent problem behaviors reach a crisis stage such as the Oberlys experienced. If a shelter care facility is not available (or is filled, as usually is the case), another alternative is needed.

The "8% Early Intervention Program" in Orange County, California, is an excellent exam-ple of a program that can be effective with offenders like Chris Oberly. This program is one of the initial experiments implementing the Comprehensive Strategy (see Kurz & Moore, 1994), and it is the effective "delinquent supervision" program identified in the RAND cost-benefits study (Greenwood et al., 1996). The program is based on an analysis of court referrals showing that 8% of referred adolescents account for more than half of all repeat offenses in the County (Kurz & Moore, 1994). These offenders typically have at least five prior arrests. The 8% program targets court referrals at risk of becoming chronic juvenile offenders. Risk indicators include gang involvement. Potential 8% cases are identified initially during probation intake and verified through a comprehensive assessment process.

Once youths are admitted to the 8% Early Intervention Program, the initial goal is to bring their behavior under control and in compliance with probation terms and conditions, while working to achieve stability in the adolescent's home (Orange County Probation Department, 1995). From that point, a broad range of sanctions options (from day reporting to community confinement) is used in conjunction with a continuum of program options for the juvenile and family members to achieve habilitation goals, while providing intensive case supervision. These options include individual incentives, family problem assessment and intervention services, family preservation and support services (including home-based intervention, respite care, and parent aids), individualized treatment for particular problem behaviors (e.g., mental health and abuse of drugs or alcohol), and a wide range of community service opportunities for the 8% minors.

A preliminary evaluation comparing a pilot group of program clients with the original study group shows about a 50% reduction in new offenses, court petitions, probation violations, and subsequent correctional commitments among the 8% program group in a 12-month follow-up (Orange County Probation Department, 1996). Greenwood and colleagues (1996, p. 38) estimate that the program costs about $14,000 per serious crime prevented (about 70 serious crimes per million dollars). The California legislature recently appropriated funds for replication and testing of the program in six other counties within the state.

Another mechanism designed to handle cases like that of the Oberlys is Florida's Juvenile Assessment Centers (Dembo & Brown, 1994; Dembo & Rivers, 1996). Sharing housing with a detention center, a truancy program, law enforcement booking functions, court intake, a psychologist, and a social worker, the centers perform a complete psychosocial assessment on youths police apprehend, ensure that their service needs are addressed in dispositional recommendations, refer at-risk youth and their families to needed services, and track outcomes of these problem-identification and program-linking activities. Preliminary screening is performed, using the Problem Oriented Screening Instrument for Teenagers (National Institute on Drug Abuse, 1991). Information is maintained in a comprehensive information system that helps facilitate interagency coordination and avoid duplication of effort.

The Juvenile Assessment Centers are structured to identify the problems of high-risk youth before they enter the juvenile justice system. Juveniles who are in early stages of pathways to delinquency (for example, truants) are targeted specifically for alternative services. In initial screening, youths identified for more in-depth assessment are administered the NYS self-report delinquency instrument and are referred elsewhere to receive needed intervention and treatment, following further assessment of their problems and needs, using the Personal Experience Inventory (Winters & Henley, 1989). The PEI assesses drug use patterns, personal risk factors, and health and maltreatment. A wide range of services is made available including substance abuse treatment, mental health services, retardation services, literacy training, and other educational services. Youths referred for services are tracked for the purpose of assessing services and program development.

The effectiveness of treatments and graduated sanctions can be increased significantly by collaborative treatment governed by a comprehensive plan, because of the coexistence of multiple risk factors for delinquency and other problem behaviors for which the respective agencies have responsibility. A wide array of promising programs is available that target the major risk and protective factors. It is important that mechanisms like the Florida Juvenile Assessment Centers be created at the entry level of immediate sanctions to integrate the juvenile justice, mental health, social services, child welfare, and education systems because they often have the same clients, even simultane-ously—both the children and their families—yet may be working at cross purposes or duplicating services.

"Agency labels and boundaries become meaningless when we realize that mental health agencies, substance abuse programs, the criminal justice system, and schools are all dealing with the same individuals" (Hawkins, 1985, p. 4). Because of the co-occurrence of adolescent problem behaviors with delinquency, mental health, juvenile justice, education, child welfare, and social services systems must be joined in collaborative efforts. Their history of coordination is not impressive. Actually, more advances have been made in this area by the mental health profession than by others (Lerman, 1995). Knitzer's (1982) landmark investigation of the lack of public responsibility for children in need of mental health services led to a federal program called the Child and Adolescent Service System Program (CASSP), funded in 1984 to improve the system of care available at the community level for children and their families (Duchnowski & Kutash, 1996). The CASSP philosophy (Stroul & Friedman, 1986) of child-centered and family-centered mental health services resulted in such innovations as "wraparound" services in North Carolina, a mechanism through which case managers can wrap services around the needs of children and families in a flexible and individualized manner (Duchnowski & Kutash, 1996). CASSP also spurred development of mental health system collaborations (see Lerman, 1995, pp. 362-384; Nelson, Rutherford, & Wolford, 1996).

Second-level immediate intervention programs target initial referrals to juvenile court. Restitution is a good example of a single sanction that can be linked with treatment program components. For juveniles referred to court for delinquency, restitution has proven somewhat successful (Schneider, 1986; Schneider et al., 1980; Schneider et al., 1982). When combined with community service or employment, restitution instills accountability in youths while they are earning money to repay their victims (Bazemore, 1991). Work has the added benefit of teaching youths skills, providing an opportunity to use the learned skills, and receiving recognition for successfully having done so. These are essential requirements of the Social Development Model. Graduated sanctions are incorporated by linking restitution with court-imposed sanctions, with which the model appears to work best (Bazemore, 1991; Hughes & Schneider, 1990). Bazemore (1991) calls the model "productive engagement" because of its combination of work experience with restitution. Several methods have been developed for linking the program with juvenile court services: subsidized individual placements (using public funds to pay offenders for work performed), private sector job banks, work crews supervised by project staff, and youth-managed enterprises supervised by restitution project staff.

Intermediate Sanctions

Intermediate sanctions programs are designed for juvenile offenders whose offenses are too serious for placement in immediate sanction programs but not serious enough for placement in secure corrections. For these offenders, intermediate sanctions can encompass a wide variety of programs including short-term detention, outdoor programs, electronic monitoring, and inpatient drug treatment.

The San Diego County Probation Department (1996) operates a Juvenile Correctional Intervention Program (JCIP) that incorporates five levels of sanction and treatment options, beginning at the point of delinquency adjudication. In the first level, the probationer is enrolled in a community program, REFLECTIONS (intensive in-home parent development and family support services). Home detention is required in the second level, along with a stayed commitment to a correctional facility. In the third level, the offender is placed in secure detention for a maximum of 30 days, then released to home confinement. The fourth level carries a commitment to a minimum-security facility (for boys) or a local correctional facility (for girls), followed by admission to an aftercare transition program. In the fifth level, the probationer is committed to either a boys' or girls' minimum security facility. An assessment team recommends a specific option level and a treatment plan, based on risk-needs assessment. The probation department's graduated sanctions plan also specifies intensity of supervision in each sanction level.

Intensive probation is a popular program model for mid-range to upper-range intermediate sanction candidates. Because intensive probation has been used mainly as a means of increasing surveillance but not treatment, evaluations have not shown appreciably better recidivism results than regular probation. An evaluation of the Wayne County Intensive Probation Program (Barton & Butts, 1990), which served as an alternative to incarceration, showed this particular model to hold promise for serious and violent juvenile offenders. Although the program was no more effective than incarceration for all offenders, it cost only a third as much and saved an estimated $8.8 million over a 3-year period. It appears that use of better risk and needs assessments to improve selection of candidates and to achieve a better match between supervision level and treatment needs might result in better treatment outcomes.

For youth at the highest level of intermediate sanctions, the most effective treatment program is the Multisystemic Therapy (MST) program (see Chapter 6). MST has been found to be effective in a number of clinical trials in treating multiple problems of serious and violent juvenile offenders in different settings (Family Services Research Center, 1995), including violent offending (Borduin et al., 1995). MST also has been shown to be more cost effective than incarceration. Its cost per client is about $3,500, compared to nearly $18,000 for institutional placements (Henggeler et al., 1992). One of the keys to MST's success is its emphasis on promoting behavior change in the youth's natural environment. MST "views individuals as being nested within a complex of interconnected systems that encompass individual, family, and extrafamilial (peer, school) factors; and intervention may be necessary in any one or a combination of these systems" (Family Services Research Center, 1995, p. 5). The treatment approach consists of family preservation services, directed toward the variety of psychological, social, educational, and material needs families face when their child is at imminent danger of out-of-home placement. "Most significantly, the conceptual framework of the multisystemic approach fits closely with the findings from multidimensional causal models of delinquency and substance abuse" (p. 5).

The previous section identified several mechanisms for coordinating immediate interventions. A different mechanism is needed to ensure interagency coordination and collaboration in the delivery of intermediate interventions. Virginia's Norfolk Interagency Consortium (Pratt, 1994) is an exemplary interagency collaboration model that grew out of the CASSP philosophy. It targets youths at risk of placement in residential facilities. A comprehensive assessment is made of individual youths and their families by an interagency team of juvenile justice, public health, mental health, social services, child welfare, education, parent, and private provider representatives (Community Assessment Team, CAT). CAT members bring to the comprehensive assessment (which is discussed with the child and parents) the history of their agency's work with the child and his family members, as well as their professional expertise in assessing problem behaviors and selecting the most appropriate combination of sanctions and treatment. The result is a long-term treatment plan (supported by nine combined funding streams) that is monitored by the CAT, with rotating lead responsibility among the six involved agencies. As an example of the success of the Norfolk model, in its first 3 years of operations, the number of youths in state psychiatric facilities was reduced from 70 to just 2 (Pratt, 1994). The remainder were provided family- and community-based mental health services combined with other treatment services. The NIC recently began screening youths earlier, at court intake, for mental health, delinquency, and other problem behaviors. An independent evaluation concluded that the NIC is effective in its collaboration and comprehensive, community-centered treatment (Wilt, 1996).

In September 1993, a group of professionals representing the five major human systems that serve troubled youth—education, mental health, social welfare, juvenile justice, and health—met to discuss the problems, strategies, and issues involved in serving troubled youth within these systems. Participants all had a key interest in developing collaborative systems. The Shakertown Symposium generated recommendations for developing a comprehensive system of integrated services for troubled youth that can serve as a resource and guide for jurisdictions interested in designing system collaborations (see Nelson et al., 1996).

Secure Care and Aftercare

As we saw in Chapter 4 (Figure 4.12), only 14% of 1992 admissions to state juvenile corrections facilities were committed for chronic serious or violent crimes. The largest category

(52%) of admissions was for property, drug, public order, or traffic offenses and consisted of first-time commitments. It appears that much more efficient use could be made of costly long-term correctional placements. In fact, application of risk assessment instruments to correctional populations in 14 states (Krisberg, Onek, Jones, & Schwartz, 1993) showed that an average of 31% of juveniles housed in these facilities could be placed in less secure settings at much less cost. Other risk assessment studies show that overincarceration of girls and minorities is a common problem (Butts, 1990; Butts & DeMuro, 1989; DeMuro & Butts, 1989; Van Vleet & Butts, 1990).

Community-based residential programs can handle about one-third of the juveniles currently confined in long-term correctional facilities. An excellent example is the Thomas O'Farrell Youth Center. It is a 38-bed, unlocked, staff-secure residential program for male youth committed to the Maryland Department of Juvenile Services. The typical O'Farrell juvenile has numerous prior court referrals, generally for property crimes and drug offenses. Graduated sanctions are built into the O'Farrell treatment program. The program begins with an orientation phase of about 1 month. In Phase I, about 60 days, youths acquire more knowledge about O'Farrell and its normative system. To move to Phase II, residents must demonstrate consistent and positive behavior in all aspects of O'Farrell life, including school attendance, work details, and group meetings. In Phase II, youths must demonstrate high levels of success in on-campus jobs and are encouraged to find part-time employment in the community. Aftercare (Phase III) lasts for 6 months and includes assistance in reentering school, vocational counseling, crisis intervention, family counseling, transportation, and mentoring.

Even confined violent juvenile offenders can be controlled and rehabilitated effectively in a secure correctional confinement. A national survey (A. R. Roberts, 1987) of correctional agencies identified secure treatment for violent offenders as one of their most effective programs. One secure treatment model is the OJJDP Violent Juvenile Offender (VJO) program that provided treatment for violent and property felony offenders, beginning with small secure facilities, followed by gradual reintegration into the community through community-based residential programs, then intensive neighborhood supervision. Evaluation of the program (Fagan, 1990) showed that in the two sites that best implemented the program design, VJO youths had significantly lower recidivism rates, with less serious offenses, and with recidivism occurring less quickly than in the control group.

The Florida Environmental Institute (FEI), also known as the "Last Chance Ranch," targets the state's most serious juvenile offenders, most of whom are referred back from the adult system for treatment under a special provision in Florida's law. Almost two-thirds of FEI youths are committed for crimes against person, the rest for chronic property or drug offenses (Krisberg et al., 1995). FEI, an environmentally secure program (located in a swamp in a remote area of the state), provides a highly structured program with a low staff-to-student ratio consisting of several phases. After about a year of therapeutic hard work, educational and vocational training, restitution, and reintegration programming, clients are assisted with community living in an extensive aftercare phase. Evaluation of the program has shown quite promising results (dampened only by small sample sizes and lack of an experimental design in the research). FEI has produced much lower recidivism rates than other Florida programs. The state of Florida is convinced of its effectiveness and is replicating it in other parts of the state.

Surprisingly, a Texas program has proven promising for rehabilitating juvenile murderers. The Capital Offender Program (COP), operated in a juvenile training school, is an intensive 16-week program for only eight juveniles. These are the worst juvenile offenders in the state. Group psychotherapy and role playing in crime reenactment are used in the treatment regimen. The COP program has been evaluated rigorously by the Texas Youth Commission (see Krisberg et al., 1995, pp. 165-166). After 1 year, program participants were significantly less likely than controls to be rearrested or reincarcerated. These differences disappeared, however, after 3 years. These later failures may have been associated with returning to their original communities without adequate aftercare support.

The Intensive Supervision Program (ISP) (Krisberg et al., 1994) is a constructed model for integrating secure care (confinement) in a graduated sanctions system. It incorporates incapacitation strategies, including small caseloads, frequent contacts, use of surveillance, preventive conditions, and the ability to impose swift and certain consequences for violation of program conditions. The ISP model has been implemented successfully in Arizona. It has all the features of the types of programs Lipsey (1992a) found to be most effective.

The primary ISP target population is adjudicated delinquents committed to state or local correctional institutions. Eligible clients are selected using risk assessment and needs assessment instruments, as well as a program selection matrix that includes options from probation to institutional placement (Figure 9.1). Low-risk youth with limited offense histories would be recommended for traditional probation. High-risk youth with multiple violent offenses would be recommended for incarceration. Youths in between these two subgroups would be recommended for ISP. The ISP model is a highly structured, continuously monitored, individualized plan that consists of five phases with decreasing levels of restrictiveness: (a) short-term placement in secure confinement, (b) day treatment, (c) outreach and tracking, (d) routine supervision, and (e) discharge and follow-up. The ISP model incorporates a wide range of program options in the first four stages.

Phases 2-5 of the ISP model constitute what traditionally has been called "reintegration," for which the terms "aftercare" or "stepdown services" are now more commonly used. Phase 2, the first step toward community reintegration, allows the youth to function in a highly controlled environment with assumption of greater self-responsibility for the first time, while remediation of skill deficits and development of a prosocial network begin. During Phase 3, the juvenile is expected to demonstrate that he can function productively and responsibly in a community setting. Programming focuses on the youth and his interactions with parents, peers, school or work, and the community persons and agencies involved with his reintegration. Phase 4 is a transition phase, preparing the juvenile for discharge from correctional supervision. He should have a stable living environment, be employed or completing job training/educational objectives, and be involved in prosocial networks. The youth is discharged (Phase 5) when a community-based support system is in place. Another aftercare model, the Intensive Juvenile Aftercare Program (Altschuler & Armstrong, 1994a) is being implemented and tested under an OJJDP program.

Committing Offense Offense History	Low	Moderate	High
Major Violent and Multiple Violent Offense[1]	Institutional Placement	Institutional Placement	Long-Term Institutional Placement
Violent Chronic Offense[2]	ISP/Institutional Placement	ISP/Institutional Placement	Institutional Placement
Violent Chronic Offense (single violent episode)[3]	ISP/Probation	ISP	ISP/Institutional Placement
Serious Chronic Offense[4]	ISP	ISP	ISP
Nonserious Chronic Offense[5]	Probation	Probation	ISP
Nonserious Nonchronic Offense[6]	Probation	Probation	Probation

1. Murder, rape, kidnapping, or history of violent offenses (e.g., two+ aggravated assault).
2. Instant offense is violent (robbery, aggravated assault); no other violent, but five or more delinquent offenses.
3. Instant offense is violent (robbery, aggravated assault); but fewer than five delinquent priors.
4. Instant offense is violent (burglary); and has five or more priors.
5. Instant offense is nonserious (theft); and has five or more priors.
6. Instant offense is a nonserious (theft); and has less than five years.

Figure 9.1. ISP selection matrix

SOURCE: *Juvenile Intensive Supervision Planning Guide*, Krisberg et al., 1994.

Massachusetts is the most exemplary illustration of statewide implementation of a community-based graduated sanctions system (see Loughran & Guarino-Ghezzi, 1995). Twenty-five years after closing its juvenile training schools, Massachusetts continues to operate an innovative correctional system similar to the ISP model. Keys to the state's success are case management, provision of a continuum of care, and a public-private partnership (National Governors' Association, 1991). Only 15% of all state correctional commitments are placed in secure care, facilities that are reserved exclusively for the most serious offenders. Thirteen small, secure facilities of 15-18 beds each provide secure care for them. The state's Department of Youth Services uses a classification grid to determine the need for secure confinement, select an appropriate facility given the offender's needs, and recommend a confinement term. Services are part of a comprehensive treatment plan, which is modified as the youngster progresses, so most youth experience a variety of programs during their state confinement. The most recent evaluation of Massachusetts' statewide program found it to be effective, even in rehabilitation of the most serious offenders,

and cost-effective, saving an estimated $11 million annually by relying on community-based care (Krisberg, Austin, & Steele, 1989).

RECLAIM Ohio is an innovative statewide model that provides financial incentives to juvenile courts to place juveniles in community-based alternatives in lieu of incarceration in state correctional facilities (Natalucci-Persichetti, 1996). Begun in 1994, RECLAIM Ohio aims to reduce the high rate of juvenile incarceration through the creation of an infrastructure of local sanctions and services for nonviolent juvenile offenders, reserving secure facilities for violent offenders. A growing number of community-based programs is being developed.

Connecticut is implementing the Comprehensive Strategy in statewide legislation (Public Act 95-225). This statutory model places responsibility for risk and needs assessments with the Judicial Branch of state government (Justice Education Center, 1996). A new Office of Alternative Sanctions is responsible for the development and evaluation of graduated sanctions. A coordinated statewide network of graduated sanctions is expected to increase accountability among serious and violent offenders while making greater use of community-based alternatives for other offenders. It is expected that the use of more structured decision making using risk and needs assessments will re-establish use of the state's juvenile training school as an institution for the most serious juvenile offenders. A significant proportion of funding for new programs is expected to come from savings derived from reducing the number of institution-based programs.

Meanwhile, a number of states' juvenile correctional systems are "battling for credibility." Many of them are experiencing conditions of confinement the courts have found unacceptable, including overcrowding and below-standard living conditions, lack of security and discipline, inadequate medical and psychological treatment, cruel use of isolation, inadequate programming and education, and inappropriate placements (Guarino-Ghezzi & Loughran, 1996, p. 51). Risk, needs, and placements instruments, as well as other tools, can help ameliorate the crowding problem.

Resolving juvenile correctional system problems will not be an easy task (Krisberg, 1996). Complex issues are involved in correctional administration. These reflect the underlying philosophies and practices of each state. In some states, juvenile court judges are battling correctional administrators over placement authority. In others, the main issue is release authority. In yet others, state correctional authorities are battling restrictive legislation such as mandatory sentences or court transfer policies. Many state correctional agencies' overcrowding problems are a result of not being in control of placement and length of stay. "In general, developing balanced systems of programs that match the supervision and programming needs of offenders is confounded by the irrationality of fluctuating resources, organizational interests, politics, and philosophies" (Guarino-Ghezzi & Loughran, 1996, p. 63).

A number of states have successfully countered the trend of excessive reliance on incarceration (Guarino-Ghezzi & Loughran, 1996; Krisberg & Austin, 1993; Lerner, 1990). "Instead of endlessly debating points of waiver and other fairly arbitrary strategies for removing youths from juvenile court jurisdiction, some jurisdictions have worked toward developing intensive, high quality services and programs in which youths and families are willing to participate" (Guarino-Ghezzi & Loughran, 1996, p. 113). These states are using confinement in secure facilities according to a systematic and objective process that protects public safety and increases the effectiveness of programs.

Summary

More than 20 years ago, Empey (1974) described delinquency prevention as the "fugitive utopia." Happily, the prospects now look much better. Because of the accumulation of a large body of research on risk factors for delinquency, the development of a risk- and protective-focused Social Development Model, and a strategic process (Communities That Care) for empowering communities to identify and address priority risk factors based on epidemiological evidence on local risk and protective factors, delinquency prevention has become a scientific process. States that are using the CTC risk- and protective-focused model in the OJJDP Title V Prevention Program are realizing its strengths. It is empirically grounded, systematically measures the major risk factor domains, produces measurable outcomes across these domains, and empowers communities to assume ownership of delinquency prevention.

Prevention programs can be combined with early interventions and graduated sanctions to prevent and reduce even serious, violent, and chronic delinquency. As the RAND cost-benefits study shows, only four program interventions are needed to achieve the crime reduction potential of "three strikes" incapacitation. A much greater reduction can be achieved by including other interventions in a continuum of program options and graduated sanctions. The prospects for rehabilitating serious, violent, and chronic juvenile offenders in the juvenile justice system are excellent, provided that treatment resources are made available and structured decision making replaces the imprecise methods currently being used. Clearly, the juvenile justice system is clogged with nonserious offenders. As much as a third of the juvenile offenders in long-term secure settings could be placed in community alternatives. Accomplishing this would permit allocation of limited correctional resources to the more difficult offenders and produce higher success rates.

Recent meta-analyses show convincingly that experimental juvenile justice programs are effective. The tools are available to achieve a better match than ever before between the risks and needs that juvenile offenders present and programs that address priority risk and protective factors. To experience continued success with them demands that juvenile justice officials take advantage of both the best available tools and knowledge of effective programs because of their growing multiple risk factors and multiple problem behaviors.

The graduated sanctions component of the Comprehensive Strategy for Serious, Violent, and Chronic Juvenile Offenders provides a framework that should help jurisdictions take a more systematic and cost-effective approach. Savings realized by reducing costly long-term incarceration must be invested in intensive treatment programs that are multimodal, highly structured, and of long duration. The serious, violent, and chronic juvenile offender problem can be managed in the juvenile justice system, provided that it is allocated the necessary resources and is integrated with the other human services systems in comprehensive treatment plans. Even greater effectiveness can be achieved by integrating delinquency prevention and graduated sanctions components in a coordinated community strategy.

Conclusion
Return to Rationality

The United States is experiencing a peculiar and unsettling period in its juvenile delinquency policy. Americans, especially politicians, are overreacting to a new generation of adolescents, one that presumably more than ever before resorts quickly to violent responses. "From antiquity every generation has entertained the opinion that many if not most of its youth are the most vicious in the history of the race . . . our ancestors also saw their world disintegrating under assaults from juvenile barbarians" (Hamparian, Schuster, Dinitz, & Conrad, 1978, p. 11). A measure of reality should be gained in recognizing that, in any generation, adolescents mirror the behavior of their adult role models—sometimes aggressive, violence-prone, or given to taking matters in their own hands. Violent adult responses in everyday life are growing: use of guns to gain the right-of-way on highways, running others off the road by aggressive driving, growing domestic violence, growing child abuse and infant homicides, and growing violence in the workplace. The adult murder happens 10 times more often than the juvenile murder.

Some observers argue that political leaders merely follow the public will; voters are outraged by crime and want tougher policies (DiIulio, 1992). "This is a half-truth that gets the causal order backwards" (Tonry, 1994b, p. 490). As Tonry explains, public opinion polls for many years have shown that the public expresses sentiments for both punishment and treatment. Frustrated about crime, citizens want offenders punished. At the same time, surveys show that the public wants government to rehabilitate offenders, especially juveniles, because citizens understand that crime has its main sources in troubled families, poverty, and social injustice. Conservative politicians stress public support of punishment and ignore public support of rehabilitation and the recognition that crime presents complex, not easy, challenges. "By presenting crime control issues only in emotional, stereotyped ways, conservative politicians have raised its salience as a political issue but made it impossible for their opponents to respond other than in the same stereotyped ways" (Tonry, 1994b, p. 491).

It seems that lawmakers hold views with respect to treatment of juveniles that are at odds not only with the public but also with juvenile justice professionals. The latter continue to exercise their belief that rehabilitation holds the most promise. "Anyone who has spent much time talking with judges or corrections officials knows that most, whatever their political affiliations, do not believe that harsher penalties significantly enhance public safety" (Tonry, 1994b, p. 477). In a recent survey of 540 police chiefs (Broder, 1996), only 14% of them favored trying more juveniles as adults and sentencing more of them to adult prisons. Ideologues, undaunted by overwhelming evidence of effective juvenile justice programs, persist in their claim that the juvenile justice system is not effective and continue to call for increased punishment of juveniles.

How can the extreme punitiveness of U.S. delinquency policy be explained? It is partly explained by the general philosophical shift in crime policy from treatment to punishment. Perhaps more important, the United States appears to be in a state of "moral panic" over juvenile violence. Cohen (1980, p. 9) described the stages of this extreme form of societal reaction:

Societies appear to be subject, every now and then, to periods of moral panic. A condition, episode, person or group of persons emerges to become defined as a threat to societal values and interests; its nature is presented in a stylized and stereotypical fashion by the mass media; the moral barricades are manned by editors, bishops, politicians and other right-thinking people; socially accredited experts pronounce their diagnoses and solutions; ways of coping are evolved or (more often) resorted to; the condition then disappears, submerges or deteriorates and becomes more visible.

Panics in relation to social issues can be understood in the context of a philosophical cyclical process, for example, what Bernard (1992) calls "the cycle of juvenile justice," which alternates between treatment-oriented and punishment-oriented policies and programs. In an analysis of Massachusetts' juvenile reforms, Miller and colleagues (1977a, 1977b) described this process. At the risk of oversimplifying their analysis, once policies move to the extreme in a given direction, the other side rises up in a state of "moral panic" and promotes a crisis, marshals its forces, and attempts to swing the pendulum in the opposite direction. If they are successful and go to the extreme in implementing their reforms, the losing side eventually will rise up and repeat the process.

A case in point of the extremes to which laws can go is "asset forfeiture" laws, an instrument of the War on Drugs. The Supreme Court recently upheld the constitutionality of these laws, which allow law enforcement agencies to seize cars, boats, homes, and other properties used in some connection with criminal drug trafficking—prior to conviction of the alleged offender (Biskupic, 1996). A defendant, Guy Jerome Ursery, was caught growing marijuana on his land. Law enforcement agencies seized his home. He argued double jeopardy, contending that he was punished twice for the same offense. The Supreme Court ruled against him, in an 8 to 1 vote. Speaking for the majority, Chief Justice William H. Rehnquist reasoned that the government did not violate Ursery's constitutional right against double jeopardy because the civil action was taken against his home, not him. His house was deemed guilty.

The current panic is the third in the child and adolescent area in the past 15 years. "Missing children" was the first one. In the early 1980s, a panic was created over stranger abductions of children. It was triggered by the mysterious abduction of Adam Walsh in Florida (which has not yet been solved). Astronomical estimates of the prevalence of this problem were fed to the media: Some 20,000-50,000 children were said to be abducted by strangers each year, whose cases remain unsolved by the end of the year (Jay Howell, quoted in Scardino, 1985). Among the stranger abductions, an estimated 2,000 unidentified dead children were said to be buried in unmarked graves each year in this country prior to 1982 (Walsh, 1984). These numbers led to the establishment of a National Center for Missing and Exploited Children (NCMEC). Public service announcements depicted children disappearing from playgrounds, presumably abducted by strangers in black luxury cars, clad in trenchcoats, and armed with pornographic pictures. Near national hysteria ensued (Treanor, 1986a). Photographs of missing children appeared everywhere—on television, on grocery bags, on milk cartons, and in public places. Children across the country were fingerprinted and otherwise provided permanent identification for fear of being abducted by strangers.

The extent of the "missing" children problem was challenged from many quarters (see Treanor, 1986b), including a Pulitzer Prize-winning expose (Griego & Klizer, 1985) of the "numbers gap," pointing out that the FBI investigated only 67 stranger abductions of children in 1984. The NCMEC lowered its estimate to 4,000 to 20,000 stranger abductions per year, "but the early estimates had a life of their own" (Best, 1988, p. 85). As it turns out, a National Incidence Study of Missing, Abducted, Runaway, and Thrownaway Children (Finkelhor et al., 1990) debunked all the unrealistic estimates, finding that 99% of an estimated 359,000 child abductions each year were family-related. In 81% of the cases, parents said they knew where their children were. An estimated 300-4,600 kidnappings and abductions each year were believed to involve nonfamily members. The study report and other data sources led to the conclusion that only 52-100 children were kidnapped and murdered by strangers each year (OJJDP, 1989). The "found facts" (Sweet, 1990) helped quell the panic. The National Center for Missing and Exploited Children still exists, providing information and technical assistance mainly on runaways, sexually exploited children, and family abductions.

Youth gangs were the target of the second moral panic. It began in the Southwest. In the late 1970s, Phoenix police estimated that the city's gangs grew from 50-60 to 100-120 inside of a 6-month period (Zatz, 1987). As shown in Chapter 6, in the mid-1980s youth gangs were depicted as the primary agents in the crack cocaine epidemic. They were believed to be spreading all over the country, setting up satellite operations. This perception led to panic. In Los Angeles, police launched an antigang sweep called Operation Hammer (see Klein, 1995), using more than a thousand police officers to round up nearly 1,500 apparent gang members, resulting in only 32 felony charges. When fires smoldered in riot-torn sections of Los Angeles in 1992, juvenile gangs were blamed for much of the violence (Hunzeker, 1993). Police in Nebraska, trained by California police, today talk of the spread of gangs from California to their state. Their perception is that whatever gang problems California has today, Nebraska will have in 5 years. The recent national gang migration study (Maxson et al., 1995) dispels these myths. As Klein (1995, p. 96) put it, gangs are "homegrown problems." How soon the empirical evidence will change erroneous perceptions about gangs remains to be seen.

The current panic is juvenile "superpredators," who "will be flooding the nation's streets" and "will come at us in waves over the next 20 years" (DiIulio, 1996, p. 25). They are "fatherless, Godless, and jobless juvenile superpredators" who have already begun to arrive on Florida's streets, and "the next crime storm will hit Florida many times harder than the crack epidemic did, and it will do more damage. The only real question is how the damage can be minimized. Time is running out" (DiIulio, 1996, p. 25). Others convey similar messages that stimulate panic. "Our nation faces a future juvenile violence problem that may make today's epidemic pale in comparison" (Fox, 1996,

p. 3). "There is, however, still time to stem the tide, and to avert the coming wave of teen violence. But time is of the essence" (p. i).

The current overreaction to juveniles is more complex than the previous moral panics. It is rooted in the "conflict cycle" described by Brendtro and Long (1994, p. 4). The public (adults), outraged by youth violence, becomes hooked into conflict cycles. In the first stage, *stress* evokes irrational beliefs such as the view that nothing can be done to influence youth violence. Adults fear adolescents because of a feeling that we cannot control them, thus feeling helpless and impotent. In the second stage, helplessness triggers distressed, furious *feelings*.

> The natural human response in such situations is to "down-shift" our brains from rational thought to lower brain survival mechanisms of fight/flight. If the adult cannot escape from the source of stress, the likely response is anger and rage. Rage is a primitive hostile feeling which drives adults to want to get even. The person in this state is a blink away from striking out at the slightest provocation. (p. 4)

Feelings drive *behavior* in the third stage. The behavioral response is "make the transgressor suffer." Righteous rage occurs when juveniles' offending behavior so violates adults' values of decency that we feel justified in punishing the offending adolescents. A primitive part of us even "enjoys" punishment. In the fourth stage, punishment provokes a *reaction*. Harsh punishment increases the likelihood of counteraggression, triggering more rage on the part of the juvenile. Feeling that he was treated unfairly, even though guilty, sets the stage for further aggression against society. "Violence begets violence," thus completing the cycle (p. 4).

Our society's punitive behavior in response to furious feelings toward juveniles, expressed in such mantras as "do adult crime; do adult time" and "treat them as adults" (Hunzeker, 1995), places growing numbers of juveniles at risk of harm in prisons. That juveniles in adult prisons suffer rape, aggravated assault, sexual assault, attacks with weapons, and beatings by staff at a far greater rate than juveniles who remain in the comparatively benign environment of a training school (Forst et al., 1989) appears to be ignored. Condoning such inhumane treatment of adolescents can be understood only in the context of the cycle of conflict that Brendtro and Long describe. Righteous rage blinds us to the consequences of our actions.

Outsiders have noticed that the U.S. public is engulfed in the cycle of conflict described by Brendtro and Long (1994). In an article in the London *Economist*, titled "Violent and Irrational—And That's Just the Policy" (1996), the editors view with incredulity the fact that the U.S. imprisonment rate is seven times as high as in the average European country. American policy, however, is not supported by evidence that imprisonment effectively reduces the level of crime or by cost-benefit arguments.

Practitioners and scholars have long known that manipulation of penalties has little, if any, effect on crime rates (Tonry, 1994b, pp. 476-477). Three expert advisory bodies in the United States have drawn this same conclusion, each little more than a decade apart, in the past 30 years, after reviewing the scientific evidence (President's Commission of Law Enforcement and Administration of Justice, 1967a; National Academy of Sciences Panel on Research on Deterrent and Incapacitative Effects, 1978; National Academy of Sciences Panel on the Understanding and Control of Violent Behavior—Reiss & Roth, 1993). A Canadian Sentencing Commission (1987) drew the same conclusion, that the empirical basis does not support using deterrence to guide the imposition of sanctions. Tonry (1994b, p. 479) concludes that "a fair-minded survey of existing knowledge provides no grounds for believing that the War on Drugs or the harsh policies exemplified by 'three strikes and you're out' laws and evidenced by a tripling in America's prison population since 1980 could achieve their ostensible purposes." Why then, do we persist? Caught up in the cycle of conflict, we are unable to see the faults in our crime and delinquency policies. Like the difficulty of seeing the long-term positive benefits of prevention and early intervention programs, the long-term negative benefits of punitive policies are not easily comprehended. These punitive policies may be the surest way to create a truly "dangerous class" (Sampson & Laub, 1993).

Before the current wave of tougher criminal court sanctions on juveniles could be played out, juvenile arrests for violent crimes dropped. The violent juvenile arrest rate declined 4% from 1994 to 1995 (FBI, 1996). The juvenile arrest rate for murder leveled off earlier, in 1991 (Snyder et al., 1996), before the spate of get-tough legislation began in 1992. The attorney general suggested that we may not have to face a juvenile crime wave after all (Johnson, 1996; Johnson & Fields, 1996; Suro, 1996). Fox allowed that his doomsday forecast (1996) might be wrong and admitted that part of what he was trying to do involved getting the public's attention (Johnson, 1996).

Unfortunately for juveniles, much damage already has been done. "Since 1992, 48 (90%) of the 51 state legislatures (including the District of Columbia) 'have made substantive changes to their laws targeting juveniles who commit violent or serious crimes" (Torbet et al., 1996, p. xv). The main thrust of these new laws is to increase juveniles' eligibility for criminal court processing and punishment in adult prisons (see Hurst, 1996; Potok & Sanchez, 1995). Nearly half (21) of the states expanded criminal court jurisdiction to include violent juvenile offenses, 22 toughened sentencing of violent juvenile offenders, 23 expanded the capacity of secure juvenile correctional facilities, and 10 expanded the number of beds for youthful offenders in prisons (Romero & Brown, 1995). Missouri lowered the age for transfer to criminal court to 12 for any felony (Torbet et al., 1996, p. 6). Shortly before he left Congress, Senator Robert Dole introduced a bill (S. 1854) in the U.S. Senate that would establish a nationwide system to prosecute juveniles 13 years of age and older for committing certain federal crimes. "More juveniles are being charged and tried in criminal court, detained longer, and incarcerated more frequently in the adult correctional system than ever before" (Torbet et al., 1996, p. 6).

Changes in the administration of juvenile justice in the 1990s can be characterized fairly as a War on Juveniles. Virginia's experiences, which appear to be typical of many states, illustrate the consequences of the new responses to juvenile delinquency. Because of a recent statutory change in the Commonwealth of Virginia that broadens the category of offenses that qualify a juvenile as a "major offender," as well as more severe sanctions for probation and parole violations, more juveniles are being incarcerated and for longer periods of time for less serious and violent offenses (Joint Legislative Audit and Review Commission, 1996). In 1995, only 20% of juveniles admitted to a Virginia corrections facility were admitted for a violent offense, and only 8% had a violent offense in their prior criminal record. This JLARC (1996) study shows that previous overcrowding of Virginia's state juvenile corrections facilities has been exacerbated by higher incarceration rates. Worse overcrowding is resulting in higher rates of institutional violence and more use of physical restraints, including "shackling," "maximum restraint posture," "four-point restraint," and use of long periods of confinement in isolation. It is not surprising that recidivism rates are high: 73% are rearrested within 3 years because of ineffective treatment programs. It also appears as if the average sentence juveniles convicted of murder receive is longer than recommended by Virginia Sentencing Guidelines (Criminal Justice Research Center, 1996). Juveniles convicted of murder in Virginia are now incarcerated for nearly 3 years longer than adults convicted of similar murders. Recidivism involving violent crimes among juveniles transferred to the state's criminal justice system has grown by 100% (JLARC, 1996).

It would be timely to pause and assess objectively our delinquency policies using a historical perspective. The current punitive U.S. juvenile crime policy, particularly the use of adult prisons to punish adolescents, previously has been tried, not even a century ago, and found to be ineffective, morally wrong, and unjust. Our predecessors put in place a more enlightened and effective apparatus, the juvenile court system, designed to steer children and adolescents away from crime and delinquency, correct those who erred by their own volition, and help those who fell victim to society's flaws. Now would be a good time to return to those more enlightened policies, else history will not be kind to us.

Epilogue

As we go to press, the Study Group on Serious and Violent Juvenile Offenders (chaired by Loeber and Farrington[1]) is completing its examination of offending careers, risk factors, and programs specifically for them. This 26-member group, which includes many renowned juvenile delinquency researchers, made a number of important discoveries of direct relevance to arguments advanced in this book. I cannot resist the temptation to note just two of its valuable findings.

First, the Study Group's examination of juvenile court data produced findings similar to Elliott's (1994b) observation that the increase in juvenile delinquency in the late 1980s and early 1990s amounts to about an 8%-10% increase in the number of adolescents who commit serious violent offenses, not an increase in the incidence of violent offending. Snyder's[2] analysis of court data in the Study Group, using 16 cohorts of referrals to the Phoenix juvenile court, shows that the main change in these cohorts' offending patterns from 1980 to 1995 is an increase of about 4% in the proportion of chronic offenders among all referrals, from 13% to about 17% over the 16 year period. However, on average, their offending careers (court referrals) did not include significantly more serious or violent offenses in the 1990s than in the 1980s; nor did they start offending younger. Thus no evidence of "superpredators" was found.

The second Study Group discovery concerns effective programs. Recall that Lipsey's 1992 meta-analysis of nearly 400 treatment programs for all types of juvenile offenders showed that experimental programs reduced recidivism on average about 10%, and that the better

interventions achieved a 20%-30% reduction in recidivism. A new meta-analysis in the Study Group (Lipsey and Derzon[3]) of 200 evaluations of treatment programs (that had at least a relatively high proportion of serious offenders) shows that the average experimental program reduces recidivism by about 12%, compared to traditional programs. But the best programs reduce recidivism rates by as much as 40%. Remarkably, *programs appear to be as effective with more serious offenders as with less serious offenders.* These results bring to mind Lipsey's observation following his first meta-analysis (1992b:16): "We must get on with the business of developing and identifying the treatment models that will be ostensible effective and providing them to the juveniles they will benefit."

NOTES

1. Loeber, R., & Farrington, D. P. (in press). *Serious and violent juvenile offenders: risk factors and successful interventions.* Thousand Oaks, CA: Sage.

2. Snyder, H. N. Serious, violent, and chronic juvenile offenders: An assessment of the extent of and trends in officially-recognized serious criminal behavior in a delinquent population. In R. Loeber & D. P. Farrington (in press). *Serious and violent juvenile offenders: risk factors and successful interventions.* Thousand Oaks, CA: Sage.

3. Lipsey, M. W., & Derzon, J. Effective interventions for serious juvenile offenders: A synthesis of research. In R. Loeber & D. P. Farrington (in press). *Serious and violent juvenile offenders: risk factors and successful interventions.* Thousand Oaks, CA: Sage.

Appendix
A Comprehensive Strategy for Serious, Violent, and Chronic Juvenile Offenders[1]

General Principles

The following general principles provide a framework to guide our efforts in the battle to prevent delinquent conduct and reduce juvenile involvement in serious, violent, and chronic delinquency:

- Strengthen the family in its primary responsibility to instill moral values and provide guidance and support to children. Where there is no functional family unit, a family surrogate should be established and assisted to guide and nurture the child.

- Support core social institutions—schools, religious institutions, and community organizations—in their roles of developing capable, mature, and responsible youth. A goal of each of these societal institutions should be to ensure that children have the opportunity and support to mature into productive, law-abiding citizens. A nurturing community environment requires that core social institutions be actively involved in the lives of youth. Community organizations include public and private youth-serving agencies; neighborhood groups; and business and commercial organizations providing employment, training, and other meaningful economic opportunities for youth.

- Promote delinquency prevention as the most cost-effective approach to dealing with juvenile delinquency. Families, schools, religious institutions, and community organizations, including citizen volunteers and the private sector, must be enlisted in the nation's delinquency prevention efforts. These core socializing institutions must be strengthened and assisted in their efforts to ensure that children have the opportunity to become capable and responsible citizens. When children engage in "acting out" behavior, such as status offenses, the family and community, in concert with child welfare agencies, must take primary responsibility for responding with appropriate treatment and support services. Communities must take the lead in designing and building comprehensive prevention approaches that address known risk factors and target other youth at risk of delinquency.

- Intervene immediately and effectively when delinquent behavior occurs to successfully prevent delinquent offenders from becoming chronic offenders or progressively committing more serious and

AUTHOR'S NOTE: This chapter originally was published in J. J. Wilson and J. C. Howell, *Comprehensive Strategy for Serious, Violent, and Chronic Juvenile Offenders* (1993).

violent crimes. Initial intervention efforts, under an umbrella of system authorities (police, intake, and probation), should be centered in the family and other core societal institutions. Juvenile justice system authorities should ensure that an appropriate response occurs and act quickly and firmly if the need for formal system adjudication and sanctions has been demonstrated.

■ Identify and control the small group of serious, violent, and chronic juvenile offenders who have committed felony offenses or have failed to respond to intervention and nonsecure community-based treatment and rehabilitation services offered by the juvenile justice system. Measures to address delinquent offenders who are a threat to community safety may include placements in secure community-based facilities or, when necessary, training schools and other secure juvenile facilities.

Under the OJJDP's comprehensive strategy, it is the family and community, supported by our core social institutions, that have primary responsibility for meeting the basic socializing needs of our nation's children. Socially harmful conduct, acting-out behavior, and delinquency may be signs of the family being unable to meet its responsibility. It is at these times that the community must support and assist the family in the socialization process, particularly for youth at the greatest risk of delinquency.

The proposed strategy incorporates two principal components: (a) preventing youth from becoming delinquent by focusing prevention programs on at-risk youth, and (b) improving the juvenile justice system response to delinquent offenders through a system of graduated sanctions and a continuum of treatment alternatives that include immediate intervention, intermediate sanctions, and community-based corrections sanctions, incorporating restitution and community service when appropriate.

Target Populations

The initial target population for prevention programs is juveniles at risk of involvement in delinquent activity. Although primary delin-

quency prevention programs provide services to all youth wishing to participate, maximum impact on future delinquent conduct can be achieved by seeking to identify and involve in prevention programs youth at greatest risk of involvement in delinquent activity. This includes youth who exhibit known risk factors for future delinquency or for drug and alcohol abuse, as well as youth who have had contact with the juvenile justice system as nonoffenders (neglected, abused, and dependent), status offenders (runaways, truants, alcohol offenders, and incorrigibles), or minor delinquent offenders.

The next target population is youth, both male and female, who have committed delinquent (criminal) acts, including juvenile offenders who evidence a high likelihood of becoming, or who already are, serious, violent, or chronic offenders.

Program Rationale

What can communities and the juvenile justice system do to prevent the development of and interrupt the progression of delinquent and criminal careers? Juvenile justice agencies and programs are one part of a larger picture that involves many other local agencies and programs that are responsible for working with at-risk youth and their families. It is important that juvenile delinquency prevention and intervention programs are integrated with local police, social service, child welfare, school, and family preservation programs and that these programs reflect local community determinations of the most pressing problems and program priorities. Establishing community planning teams that include a broad base of participants drawn from local government and the community (e.g., community-based youth development organizations, schools, law enforcement, social service agencies, civic organizations, religious groups, parents, and teens) will help create consensus on priorities and services to be provided as well as build support for a comprehensive program approach that draws on all sectors of the community for participation. Comprehensive approaches to delinquency prevention and intervention will require collaborative efforts between the juvenile justice system and other service provision systems, including mental health, health, child welfare, and education. Developing mecha-

nisms that effectively link these different service providers at the program level will need to
be an important component of every community's comprehensive plan.

Evidence suggests that a risk-reduction and
protective-factor-enhancement approach to
prevention is effective. Risk factors include the
family, the school, the peer group, the community, and characteristics of juveniles themselves. The more risk factors present in a community, the greater the likelihood of youth
problems in that community as children are exposed to those risk factors. Prevention strategies will need to be comprehensive, addressing
each of the risk factors as they relate to the
chronological development of children being
served.

Research and experience in intervention
and treatment programming suggest that a
highly structured system of graduated sanctions holds significant promise. The goal of
graduated sanctions is to increase the effectiveness of the juvenile justice system in responding to juveniles who have committed criminal
acts. The system's limited resources have diminished its ability to respond effectively to serious, violent, and chronic juvenile crime. This
trend must be reversed by empowering the juvenile justice system to provide accountability
and treatment resources to juveniles. This includes gender-specific programs for female offenders, whose rates of delinquency generally
have been increasing faster than those of males
in recent years, and who now account for 23%
of juvenile arrests. It will also require programs
for special needs populations such as sex offenders and mentally retarded, emotionally
disturbed, and learning disabled delinquents.

The graduated sanctions approach is designed to provide immediate intervention at the
first offense to ensure that the juvenile's misbehavior is addressed by the family and community or through formal adjudication and
sanctions by the juvenile justice system, as appropriate. Graduated sanctions include a range
of intermediate sanctions and secure corrections options to provide intensive treatment
that serves the juvenile's needs, provides accountability, and protects the public. They offer
an array of referral and dispositional resources
for law enforcement, juvenile courts, and juvenile corrections officials. The graduated sanctions component requires that the juvenile justice system's capacity to identify, process,
evaluate, refer, and track delinquent offenders
be enhanced.

The Juvenile Justice System

The juvenile justice system plays a key role in
protecting and guiding juveniles, including responding to juvenile delinquency. Law enforcement plays a key role by conducting investigations, making custody and arrest determinations,
or exercising discretionary release authority.
Police should be trained in community-based
policing techniques and provided with program resources that focus on community
youth, such as Police Athletic Leagues.

The traditional role of the juvenile and family court is to treat and rehabilitate the dependent or wayward minor, using an individualized
approach and tailoring its response to the particular needs of the child and family, with goals
of (a) responding to the needs of troubled youth
and their families, (b) providing due process
while recognizing the rights of the victim, (c)
rehabilitating the juvenile offender, and (d) protecting both the juvenile and the public. Although juvenile and family courts have been
successful in responding to the bulk of youth
problems to meet these goals, new ways of organizing and focusing the resources of the juvenile justice system are required to effectively
address serious, violent, and chronic juvenile
crime. These methods might include the establishment of unified family courts with jurisdiction over all civil and criminal matters affecting
the family.

A recent statement by the National Council
of Juvenile and Family Court Judges (NCJFCJ)
succinctly describes the critical role of the
court:

> The Courts must protect children and
> families when private and other public
> institutions are unable or fail to meet their
> obligations. The protection of society by
> correcting children who break the law, the
> preservation and reformation of families,
> and the protection of children from abuse
> and neglect are missions of the Court.
> When the family falters, when the basic
> needs of children go unmet, when the be-
> havior of children is destructive and goes
> unchecked, juvenile and family courts
> must respond. The Court is society's offi-

cial means of holding itself accountable for the well-being of its children and family unit. (National Council of Juvenile and Family Court Judges, 1993)

Earlier, the NCJFCJ developed 38 recommendations regarding serious juvenile offenders and related issues facing the juvenile court system. These issues included confidentiality of the juvenile offender and his or her family, transfer of a juvenile offender to adult court, and effective treatment of the serious juvenile offender (NCJFCJ, 1984).

Finally, juvenile corrections has the responsibility to provide treatment services that will rehabilitate the juvenile and minimize his or her chances of reoffending. Juvenile courts and corrections will benefit from a system that makes a continuum of services available that respond to each juvenile's needs.

The juvenile justice system, armed with resources and knowledge that permit matching juveniles with appropriate treatment programs while holding them accountable, can have a positive and lasting impact on the reduction of delinquency. Developing effective case management and management information systems (MIS) will be integral to this effort. The OJJDP will provide leadership in building system capacity at the state and local levels to take maximum advantage of available knowledge and resources.

Delinquency Prevention

Most juvenile delinquency efforts have been unsuccessful because of their negative approach—attempting to keep juveniles from misbehaving. Positive approaches that emphasize opportunities for healthy social, physical, and mental development have a much greater likelihood of success. Another weakness of past delinquency prevention efforts is their narrow scope, focusing on only one or two of society's institutions that have responsibility for the social development of children. Most programs have targeted either the school arena or the family. Communities are an often neglected area. Successful delinquency prevention strategies must be positive in their orientation and comprehensive in their scope.

The prevention component of the OJJDP's comprehensive strategy is based on a risk-focused delinquency prevention approach (Hawkins & Catalano, 1992). This approach states that to prevent a problem from occurring, the factors contributing to the development of that problem must be identified, and then ways must be found (protective factors) to address and ameliorate those factors.

Research conducted over the past half century has clearly documented five categories of causes and correlates of juvenile delinquency: (a) individual characteristics such as alienation, rebelliousness, and lack of bonding to society; (b) family influences such as parental conflict, child abuse, and family history of problem behavior (substance abuse, criminality, teen pregnancy, and school dropouts); (c) school experiences such as early academic failure and lack of commitment to school; (d) peer group influences such as friends who engage in problem behavior (minor criminality, gangs, and violence); and (e) neighborhood and community factors such as economic deprivation, high rates of substance abuse and crime, and low neighborhood attachment. These categories can also be thought of as risk factors.

To counter these causes and risk factors, protective factors must be introduced. Protective factors are qualities or conditions that moderate a juvenile's exposure to risk. Research indicates that protective factors fall into three basic categories: (a) individual characteristics such as a resilient temperament and a positive social orientation; (b) bonding with prosocial family members, teachers, and friends; and (c) healthy beliefs and clear standards for behavior. Although individual characteristics are inherent and difficult to change, bonding and clear standards for behavior work together and can be changed. To increase bonding, children must be provided with opportunities to contribute to their families, schools, peer groups, and communities; skills to take advantage of opportunities; and recognition for their efforts to contribute. Simultaneously, parents, teachers, and communities need to set clear standards that endorse prosocial behavior.

The risk-focused delinquency prevention approach calls on communities to identify and understand what risk factors their children are exposed to and to implement programs that counter these risk factors. Communities must enhance protective factors that promote positive behavior, health, well-being, and personal success. Effective delinquency prevention efforts must be comprehensive, covering the five causes or risk factors described below, and correspond to the social development process.

Individual Characteristics

Our children must be taught moral, spiritual, and civic values. The decline in inculcating these values has contributed significantly to increases in delinquent behavior; therefore, opportunities for teaching positive values must be increased.

Youth Leadership and Service Programs can provide such opportunities and can reinforce and help internalize in children such positive individual traits as discipline, character, self-respect, responsibility, teamwork, healthy lifestyles, and good citizenship. They also can provide opportunities for personal growth, active involvement in education and vocational training, and life skills development.

A Youth Leadership and Service Program could consist of a variety of components targeted to the needs of grade school, junior high, and high school youth. Elementary and junior high school children could be assisted in achieving healthy social development through instillation in them of basic values. Youth of high school age could be supported in the development of leadership skills and community service in preparation for adulthood. The components of a Youth Leadership and Service Program may include the following types of program activities:

- Youth Service Corps
- Adventure Training (leadership, endurance, and team building);
- mentoring;
- recreational;
- summer camp;
- literacy and learning disability; and
- law-related education.

A variety of prevention programs address individual growth and development, including:

- Head Start;
- Boys and Girls Clubs;
- Scouting;
- 4-H Clubs;
- recreational activities;

- leadership and personal development;
- health and mental health; and
- career-oriented youth development.

Family Influences

The family is the most important influence in the lives of children and the first line of defense against delinquency. Programs that strengthen the family and foster healthy growth and development of children from prenatal care through adolescence should be widely available. These programs should encourage the maintenance of a viable family unit and bonding between parent and child, and they should provide support for families in crisis. Such programs should involve other major spheres of influence such as religious institutions, schools, and community-based organizations. By working together, these organizations will have a pronounced impact on preserving the family and preventing delinquency.

To have the greatest impact, assistance must reach families before significant problems develop. The concept of earliest point of impact therefore should guide the development and implementation of prevention programs involving the family. Researchers in the area of juvenile delinquency and the family have found that the following negative family involvement factors are predictors of delinquency:

- inadequate prenatal care;
- parental rejection;
- inadequate supervision and inconsistent discipline by parents;
- family conflict, marital discord, and physical violence; and
- child abuse.

The following programs directly address negative family involvement factors and how to establish protective factors:

- teen abstinence and pregnancy prevention;
- parent effectiveness and family skills training;
- parent support groups;
- home instruction program for preschool youngsters;

- family crisis intervention services;
- court appointed special advocates;
- surrogate families and respite care for families in crisis;
- permanency planning for foster children;
- family life education for teens and parents; and
- runaway and homeless youth services.

School Experiences

Outside the family, the school has the greatest influence in the lives of children and adolescents. The school profoundly influences the hopes and dreams of youth.

Many of America's children bring one or more of the aforementioned risk factors to school with them, and these factors may hinder the development of their academic and social potential. School prevention programs, including traditional delinquency prevention programs not related to the school's educational mission, can assist the family and the community by identifying at-risk youth, monitoring their progress, and intervening with effective programs at critical times during a youth's development.

School-based prevention programs may include:

- drug and alcohol prevention and education;
- bullying prevention;
- violence prevention;
- alternative schools;
- truancy reduction;
- school discipline and safety improvement;
- targeted literacy programs in the primary grades;
- law-related education;
- after school programs for latchkey children;
- teen abstinence and pregnancy prevention;
- values development; and
- vocational training.

Providing youth with structured opportunities to develop skills and contribute to the community in nonschool hours is particularly important for at-risk youth who have lower levels of personal and social support. Communities need to develop strategies and programs, such as those recommended by the Carnegie Council on Adolescent Development, to address this need.

Peer Group Influences

Research on the causes and correlates of delinquency confirms that associating with delinquent, drug-using peers is strongly correlated with delinquency and drug use. These relationships are mutually reinforcing. Membership in a gang is strongly related to delinquency and drug use. Those who remain in gangs over long periods of time have high rates of delinquency, particularly during active gang membership.

Peer leadership groups offer an effective means of encouraging leaders of delinquency-prone groups to establish friendships with more conventional peers. These groups have been established in schools, at all levels, across the country. As noted above, school-based after school programs for latchkey children also provide the same function for children at high risk for negative influences. Crime prevention programs that educate youth on how to prevent juvenile violence and crime and provide opportunities for youth to actually work on solving specific community delinquency problems are another effective way of encouraging peer leadership.

Promising approaches have been identified for combating juvenile gangs. "Community mobilization" appears to be effective in cities with chronic gang problems and in cities where the gang problem is just beginning. Other promising preventive options include efforts to dissolve associations with delinquent peers and develop alternative behaviors that promote moral development and reject violence as a means of resolving interpersonal disputes. Opportunities to achieve success in conventional, nondelinquent activities are also imperative.

The following programs reflect these principles:

- gang prevention and intervention;
- conflict resolution-peer mediation;
- peer counseling and tutoring;
- self-help fellowship for peer groups;
- individual responsibility training;
- community volunteer service;

- competitive athletic team participation; and
- teens, crime, and the community.

Neighborhood and Community

Children do not choose where they live. Children who live in fear of drug dealers, street violence, and gang shootings cannot enjoy childhood. Children are dependent on parents, neighbors, and police to provide a safe and secure environment in which to play, go to school, and work. Community policing can play an important role in creating a safer environment. Community police officers not only help to reduce criminal activity but also become positive role models and establish caring relationships with the youth and families in a community. On-site neighborhood resource teams, composed of community police officers, social workers, health care workers, housing experts, and school personnel, can ensure that a wide range of problems are responded to in a timely and coordinated manner.

Also required are innovative and committed individuals, groups, and community organizations to work together to improve the quality of life in their communities and, if necessary, to reclaim the communities from gangs and other criminal elements. Such groups include youth development organizations, churches, tenant organizations, and civic groups. The private sector business community can make a major contribution through Private Industry Councils and other partnerships by providing job training, apprenticeships, and other meaningful economic opportunities for youth.

Neighborhood and community programs include:

- community policing;
- safe havens for youth;
- neighborhood mobilization for community safety;
- drug-free school zones;
- after school programs, sponsored by community organizations, in tutoring, recreation, mentoring, and cultural activities;
- community and business partnerships;
- foster grandparents;
- job training and apprenticeships for youth;

- neighborhood watch; and
- victim programs.

The Carnegie Council on Adolescent Development (1992), following an extensive study of adolescent development, concluded that community-based youth programs, offered by more than 17,000 organizations nationwide, can provide the critical community support necessary to prevent delinquency. This can be done, the council concluded, through community organizations' contributions to youth development in conjunction with family- and school-focused efforts. Communities must be created that support families, educate adolescents for a global economy, and provide opportunities to develop skills during nonschool hours. The council found that many adolescents are adrift during nonschool hours and can be actively involved in community-based programs that provide opportunities to develop a sense of importance, well-being, belonging, and active community participation. Through such programs, risks can be transformed into opportunities.

Graduated Sanctions

An effective juvenile justice system program model for the treatment and rehabilitation of delinquent offenders is one that combines accountability and sanctions with increasingly intensive treatment and rehabilitation services. These graduated sanctions must be wide-ranging to fit the offense and include both intervention and secure corrections components. The intervention component includes the use of immediate intervention and intermediate sanctions, and the secure corrections component includes the use of community confinement and incarceration in training schools, camps, and ranches.

Each of these graduated sanctions components should consist of sublevels, or gradations, that together with appropriate services constitute an integrated approach. The purpose of this approach is to stop the juvenile's further penetration into the system by inducing law-abiding behavior as early as possible through the combination of appropriate intervention and treatment sanctions. The juvenile justice system must work with law enforcement, courts, and corrections to develop reasonable, fair, and humane sanctions.

At each level in the continuum, the family must continue to be integrally involved in treatment and rehabilitation efforts. Aftercare must be a formal component of all residential placements, actively involving the family and the community in supporting and reintegrating the juvenile into the community.

Programs will need to use risk and needs assessments to determine the appropriate placement for the offender. Risk assessments should be based on clearly defined objective criteria that focus on (a) the seriousness of the delinquent act; (b) the potential risk for reoffending, based on the presence of risk factors; and (c) the risk to the public safety. Effective risk assessment at intake, for example, can be used to identify those juveniles who require the use of detention as well as those who can be released to parental custody or diverted to nonsecure community-based programs. Needs assessments will help ensure that (a) different types of problems are taken into account when formulating a case plan, (b) a baseline for monitoring a juvenile's progress is established, (c) periodic reassessments of treatment effectiveness are conducted, and (d) a systemwide database of treatment needs can be used for the planning and evaluation of programs, policies, and procedures. Together, risk and needs assessments will help to allocate scarce resources more efficiently and effectively. A system of graduated sanctions requires a broad continuum of options.

Intervention

For intervention efforts to be most effective, they must be swift, certain, and consistent, and they must incorporate increasing sanctions, including the possible loss of freedom. As the severity of sanctions increases, so must the intensity of treatment. At each level, offenders must be aware that, should they continue to violate the law, they will be subject to more severe sanctions and ultimately could be confined in a secure setting, ranging from a secure community-based juvenile facility to a training school, camp, or ranch.

The juvenile court plays an important role in the provision of treatment and sanctions. Probation traditionally has been viewed as the court's main vehicle for delivery of treatment services and community supervision. Traditional probation services and sanctions, however, have not had the resources to effectively target delinquent offenders, particularly serious, violent, and chronic offenders.

The Balanced Approach to juvenile probation is a promising approach that specifies a clear and coherent framework. The Balanced Approach consists of three practical objectives: (a) accountability, (b) competency development, and (c) community protection. Accountability refers to the requirement that offenders make amends to the victims and the community for harm caused. Competency development requires that youth who enter the juvenile justice system should exit the system more capable of being productive and responsible citizens. Community protection requires that the juvenile justice system ensure public safety.

The following graduated sanctions are proposed within the intervention component.

Immediate intervention. First-time delinquent offenders (misdemeanors and nonviolent felonies) and nonserious repeat offenders (generally misdemeanor repeat offenses) must be targeted for system intervention based on their probability of becoming more serious or chronic in their delinquent activities. Nonresidential community-based programs, including prevention programs for at-risk youth, may be appropriate for many of these offenders. Such programs are small and open, located in or near the juvenile's home, and maintain community participation in program planning, operation, and evaluation. Community police officers, working as part of neighborhood resource teams, can help monitor the juvenile's progress. Other offenders may require sanctions tailored to their offense(s) and their needs to deter them from committing additional crimes. The following programs apply to these offenders:

- neighborhood resource teams;
- diversion;
- informal probation;
- school counselors serving as probation officers;
- home on probation;
- mediation (victims);
- community service;
- restitution;
- day-treatment programs;

- alcohol and drug abuse treatment (outpatient); and
- peer juries.

Intermediate sanctions. Offenders who are inappropriate for immediate intervention (first-time serious or violent offenders) or who fail to respond successfully to immediate intervention as evidenced by reoffending (such as repeat property offenders or drug-involved juveniles) would begin with or be subject to intermediate sanctions. These sanctions may be nonresidential or residential.

Many of the serious and violent offenders at this stage may be appropriate for placement in an Intensive Supervision Program as an alternative to secure incarceration. The OJJDP's Intensive Supervision of Probationers Program Model is a highly structured, continuously monitored individualized plan that consists of five phases with decreasing levels of restrictiveness: (a) short-term placement in community confinement, (b) day treatment, (c) outreach and tracking, (d) routine supervision, and (e) discharge and follow-up. Other appropriate programs include:

- drug testing;
- weekend detention;
- alcohol and drug abuse treatment (inpatient);
- Challenge Outdoor Programs;
- community-based residential programs;
- electronic monitoring; and
- boot camp facilities and programs.

Secure Corrections

The criminal behavior of many serious, violent, and chronic juvenile offenders requires the application of secure sanctions to hold these offenders accountable for their delinquent acts and to provide a structured treatment environment. Large congregate-care juvenile facilities (training schools, camps, and ranches) have not proven to be particularly effective in rehabilitating juvenile offenders. Although some continued use of these types of facilities will remain a necessary alternative for those juveniles who require enhanced security to protect the public, the establishment of small community-based facilities to provide intensive services in a secure environment offers the best hope for successful treatment of those juveniles who require a structured setting. Secure sanctions are most effective in changing future conduct when they are coupled with comprehensive treatment and rehabilitation services.

Standard parole practices, particularly those that have a primary focus on social control, have not been effective in normalizing the behavior of high-risk juvenile parolees over the long term; consequently, growing interest has developed in intensive aftercare programs that provide high levels of social control and treatment services. The OJJDP's Intensive Community-Based Aftercare for High-Risk Juvenile Parolees Program provides an effective aftercare model.

The Intensive Aftercare Program incorporates five programmatic principles: (a) preparing youth for progressive responsibility and freedom in the community, (b) facilitating youth-community interaction and involvement, (c) working with both the offender and targeted community support systems (e.g., families, peers, schools, and employers) to facilitate constructive interaction and gradual community adjustment, (d) developing needed resources and community support, and (e) monitoring and ensuring the youth's successful reintegration into the community.

The following graduated sanctions strategies are proposed within the Secure Corrections component:

Community confinement. Offenders whose presenting offense is sufficiently serious (such as a violent felony) or who fail to respond to intermediate sanctions as evidenced by continued reoffending may be appropriate for community confinement. Offenders at this level represent the more serious (such as repeat felony drug trafficking or property offenders) and violent offenders among the juvenile justice system correctional population.

The concept of community confinement provides secure confinement in small community-based facilities that offer intensive treatment and rehabilitation services. These services include individual and group counseling, educational programs, medical services, and intensive staff supervision. Proximity to the community enables direct and regular family involvement with the treatment process as well as a phased reentry into the community that draws upon community resources and services.

Incarceration in training schools, camps, and ranches. Juveniles whose confinement in the community would constitute an ongoing threat to community safety or who have failed to respond to community-based corrections may require an extended correctional placement in training schools, camps, ranches, or other secure options that are not community-based. These facilities should offer comprehensive treatment programs for these youth with a focus on education, skills development, and vocational or employment training and experience. These juveniles may include those convicted in the criminal justice system prior to their reaching the age at which they are no longer subject to the original or extended jurisdiction of the juvenile justice system.

Expected Benefits

The proposed strategy provides for a comprehensive approach in responding to delinquent conduct and serious, violent, and chronic criminal behavior, consisting of (a) community protection and public safety, (b) accountability, (c) competency development, (d) individualization, and (e) balanced representation of the interests of the community, victim, and juvenile. By taking these factors into account in each program component, a new direction in the administration of juvenile justice is fostered.

Delinquency Prevention

This major component of the comprehensive strategy involves implementation of delinquency prevention technology that has been demonstrated to be effective. Prevention strategies within the major areas that influence the behavior of youth (individual development, family, school, peer group, and community) parallel the chronological development of children. Because addressing these five areas has been found to be effective in reducing future delinquency among high-risk youth, it should result in fewer children entering the juvenile justice system in demonstration sites. This would, in turn, permit concentration of system resources on fewer delinquents, thereby increasing the effectiveness of the graduated sanctions component and improving the operation of the juvenile justice system.

Graduated Sanctions

This major component of the comprehensive strategy is premised on a firm belief that the juvenile justice system can effectively handle delinquent juvenile behavior through the judicious application of a range of graduated sanctions and a full continuum of treatment and rehabilitation services. Expected benefits of this approach include

- increased juvenile justice system responsiveness. This program will provide additional referral and dispositional resources for law enforcement, juvenile courts, and juvenile corrections. It will also require these system components to increase their ability to identify, process, evaluate, refer, and track juvenile offenders.

- increased juvenile accountability. Juvenile offenders will be held accountable for their behavior, decreasing the likelihood of their development into serious, violent, or chronic offenders and tomorrow's adult criminals. The juvenile justice system will be held accountable for controlling chronic and serious delinquency while also protecting society. Communities will be held accountable for providing community-based prevention and treatment resources for juveniles.

- decreased costs of juvenile corrections. Applying the appropriate graduated sanctions and developing the required community-based resources should reduce significantly the need for high-cost beds in training schools. Savings from the high costs of operating these facilities could be used to provide treatment in community-based programs and facilities.

- increased responsibility of the juvenile justice system. Many juvenile offenders currently waived or transferred to the criminal justice system could be provided opportunities for intensive services in secure community-based settings or in long-term treatment in juvenile training schools, camps, and ranches.

- increased program effectiveness. As the statistical information presented herein indicates, credible knowledge exists about the characteristics of chronic, serious, and violent offenders. Some knowledge also exists about what can effectively be done regarding their treatment and re-habilitation. More must be learned, how-ever, about what works best for whom un-der what circumstances to intervene successfully in the potential criminal ca-reers of serious, violent, and chronic ju-venile offenders. Follow-up research and rigorous evaluation of programs imple-mented as part of this strategy should pro-duce valuable information.

Crime Reduction

The combined effects of delinquency preven-tion and increased juvenile justice system ef-fectiveness in intervening immediately and ef-fectively in the lives of delinquent offenders should result in measurable decreases in delin-quency in sites where the above concepts are demonstrated. In addition, long-term reduction in crime should result from fewer serious, vio-lent, and chronic delinquents becoming adult criminal offenders.

NOTE

1. Which juveniles are determined to be serious, violent, or chronic offenders is an important matter. The consequences of being placed in one of these categories are critical to the allocation of scarce treat-ment resources. In some jurisdictions, identification of a juvenile as a serious, violent, or chronic offender determines how a juvenile is "handled" in the system, for example, whether a juvenile is subject to estab-lished minimum periods of secure confinement or subject to criminal court jurisdiction. Generally, such determinations are made at the state and local levels.

The OJJDP has developed the following defini-tions of serious, violent, and chronic juvenile offend-ers for purposes of this program. Definitions used in various research and statistics-gathering efforts often vary.

Juvenile refers to a person under the age estab-lished by a state to determine when an individual is no longer subject to original juvenile court jurisdic-tion for (any) criminal misconduct. Although this age is 18 in a majority of jurisdictions, it ranges from 16 to 19 years of age. *Serious juvenile offenders* are those adjudicated delinquent for committing any felony of-fense, including larceny or theft, burglary or breaking and entering, extortion, arson, and drug trafficking or other controlled dangerous substance violations. *Violent juvenile offenders* are those serious juvenile offenders adjudicated delinquent for one of the fol-lowing felony offenses: homicide, rape or other fel-ony sex offenses, mayhem, kidnapping, robbery, or aggravated assault. *Chronic juvenile offenders* are ju-veniles adjudicated delinquent for committing three or more delinquent offenses. These definitions in-clude juveniles convicted in criminal court for par-ticular offense types.

An informative discussion of the research and is-sues involved in formulating a working definition of these and related terms is found in Fagan and Hart-stone (1984).

References

Abbott, E. (1916). *The one hundred and one county jails of Illinois and why they should be abolished.* Chicago: Juvenile Protective Association.

Abbott, J., Johnson, R., Koziol-McLain, J., & Lowenstein, S. R. (1995). Domestic violence against women: Incidence and prevalence in an emergency department population. *The Journal of the American Medical Association, 273,* 1763-1767.

Achenbach, T. M., & Edelbrock, C. (1983). *Manual for the Child Behavior Checklist and Revised Child Behavior Profile.* Burlington: University of Vermont, Department of Psychiatry.

Adler, W. (1995). *Land of opportunity.* New York: Atlantic Monthly.

Adult treatment of juvenile offenders may aggravate recidivism. (1996, May 15). *Law Enforcement News,* p. 8.

Aichorn, A. (1939). *Wayward youth.* New York: Viking.

Alinsky, S. D. (1946). *Reveille for radicals.* Chicago: University of Chicago Press.

Allen, F. (1981). *The decline of the rehabilitative ideal: Penal policy and social purpose.* New Haven, CT: Yale University Press.

Allen-Hagen, B. (1993). *Conditions of confinement in juvenile detention and correctional facilities* (Fact Sheet #1). Washington, DC: Office of Juvenile Justice and Delinquency Prevention.

Allen-Hagen, B., & Howell, J. C. (1982, June). A closer look at juvenile justice standards. *Corrections Today,* pp. 28-34.

Altschuler, D. M., & Armstrong, T. L. (1994a). *Intensive aftercare for high-risk juveniles: A community care model.* Washington, DC: U.S. Justice Department, Office of Juvenile Justice and Delinquency Prevention.

Altschuler, D. M., & Armstrong, T. L. (1994b). *Intensive aftercare for high-risk juveniles: An assessment.* Washington, DC: U.S. Department of Justice, Office of Juvenile Justice and Delinquency Prevention.

Altschuler, D. M., & Armstrong, T. L. (1994c). *Intensive aftercare for high-risk juveniles: Policies and procedures.* Washington, DC: U.S. Department of Justice, Office of Juvenile Justice and Delinquency Prevention.

Altschuler, D. M., & Armstrong, T. L. (1995). Managing aftercare services for delinquents. In B. Glick & A. P. Goldstein (Eds.), *Managing delinquency programs that work* (pp. 137-170). Laurel, MD: American Correctional Association.

Altschuler, D. M., & Brounstein, P. J. (1991). Patterns of drug use, drug trafficking, and other delinquency among inner-city adolescent males in Washington, D.C. *Criminology, 29,* 589-621.

Altschuler, D. M., & Luneburg, W. V. (1992). The Juvenile Justice and Delinquency Prevention Formula Grant Program: Federal-state relationships in a quasi-regulatory context. *Criminal Justice Policy Review, 6,* 136-158.

American Academy of Child and Adolescent Psychiatry. (1990). *Prevention in child and adolescent psychiatry: The reduction of risk for mental disorders.* Washington, DC: Author.

American Academy of Pediatrics, Committee on Adolescence. (1992). Firearms and adolescents. *Pediatrics, 89,* 784-787.

American Bar Association. (1980). *Juvenile justice standards.* Cambridge, MA: Ballinger.

American Bar Association. (1993). *America's children at risk: A national agenda for legal action* (Report of the ABA Presidential Working Group on the Unmet Legal Needs of Children and Their Families). Washington, DC: Author.

American Correctional Association. (1977). *Manual of standards for adult local detention facilities* (Standard 5338). Laurel, MD: Author.

American Friends Service Committee. (1971). *Struggle for justice: A report on crime and punishment in America.* New York: Hill and Wang.

American Medical Association. (1995). *Report card: Violence in America*. Chicago: Author.

American Psychological Association. (1993). *Violence and youth: Report of the APA Commission on Violence and Youth*. Washington, DC: Author.

American Youth Work Center. (1993, May/June). Giving at-risk youth the business: How does it work? *Youth Today*, pp. 16-17.

Anderson, N., & Rodriguez, O. (1984). Conceptual issues in the study of Hispanic delinquency. *Research Bulletin, 7*, 2-5.

Andrews, D. A., & Bonta, J. (1994). *The psychology of criminal conduct*. Cincinnati, OH: Anderson.

Andrews, D. A., Zinger, I., Hodge, R. D., Bonta, J., Gendreau, P., & Cullen, F. T. (1990). Does correctional treatment work? *Criminology, 28*, 369-404.

Annie E. Casey Foundation. (1994). *Kids count*. Baltimore, MD: Author.

Aries, P. (1962). *Centuries of childhood* (R. Baldick, Trans.). New York: Alfred A. Knopf.

Arnaud, J. A., & Mack, T. C. (1982). The deinstitutionalization of status offenders in Massachusetts: The role of the private sector. In J. F. Handler & J. Zatz (Eds.), *Neither angels nor thieves: Studies in deinstitutionalization of status offenders* (pp. 335-371). Washington, DC: National Academy Press.

August, R. (1981). *Study of juveniles transferred for prosecution to the criminal justice system*. Miami: Criminal Justice Council.

Auletta, K. (1982). *The underclass*. New York: Random House.

Austin, J., Dimas, J., & Steinhart, D. (1992). *The overrepresentation of minority youth in the California juvenile justice system*. San Francisco: National Council on Crime and Delinquency.

Austin, J., Elms, W., Krisberg, B., & Steele, P. (1991). *Unlocking juvenile corrections: Evaluating the Massachusetts Department of Youth Services*. San Francisco: National Council on Crime and Delinquency.

Austin, J., Krisberg, B., DeComo, R., Rudenstine, S., & Del Rosario, D. (1994). *Juveniles taken into custody research program: FY 1993 annual report*. Washington, DC: U.S. Department of Justice, Office of Juvenile Justice and Delinquency Prevention.

Austin, J., & McVey, A. D. (1989, December). *The 1989 NCCD prison population forecast: The impact of the War on Drugs* (Focus). San Francisco: National Council on Crime and Delinquency.

Baird, S. C. (1984). *Classification of juveniles in corrections: A model systems approach*. Madison, WI: National Council on Crime and Delinquency.

Baird, S. C., & Neuenfeldt, D. (1988, July). *Assessing potential for abuse and neglect* (NCCD Focus). San Francisco: National Council on Crime and Delinquency.

Bakal, Y. (1973). *Closing correctional institutions*. Lexington, MA: D. C. Heath.

Baker, H. (1910). Procedure of the Boston juvenile court. *Survey, 23*, 643-652.

Barnes, C. W., & Franz, R. S. (1989). Questionably adult: Determinants and effects of the juvenile waiver decision. *Justice Quarterly, 6*, 117-135.

Barton, W. H., & Butts, J. A. (1990). Viable options: Intensive supervision programs for juvenile delinquents. *Crime and Delinquency, 36*, 238-256.

Bastian, L. D., & Taylor, B. M. (1991). *School crime: A National crime victimization report*. Washington, DC: U.S. Department of Justice, Bureau of Justice Statistics.

Battin, S. R., Hill, K. G., Abbott, R. D., Catalano, R. F., & Hawkins, J. D. (1996, November). *The contribution of gang membership to deliquency beyond delinquent friends*. Paper presented at the annual meeting of the American Society of Criminology, Chicago.

Baumeister, R. F., Smart, L., & Boden, J. W. (1996). Relation of threatened egotism to violence and aggression: The dark side of high self-esteem. *Psychological Review, 103*, 5-33.

Bayh, B. (1974a, July 18). *Congressional Record*, pp. S13487-S13488.

Bayh, B. (1974b, August 19). *Congressional Record*, p. S15263.

Bazemore, G. (1991). Work experience and employment programming for serious juvenile offenders: Prospects for a "productive engagement" model of intensive supervision. In T. L. Armstrong (Ed.), *Intensive interventions with high-risk youths* (pp. 123-152). Monsey, NY: Criminal Justice.

Bazemore, G., & Umbreit, M. S. (1994). *Balanced and restorative justice*. Washington, DC: U.S. Department of Justice, Office of Juvenile Justice and Delinquency Prevention.

Beccaria, C. (1963). *On crimes and punishments* (H. Paolucci, Trans.). Indianapolis, IN: Bobbs-Merrill.

Beck, A. J., & Shipley, B. E. (1987, May). *Recidivism of young parolees* (Special Report). U.S. Department of Justice, Bureau of Justice Statistics.

Beck, A. J., & Shipley, B. E. (1989, April). *Recidivism of prisoners released in 1983* (Special Report). U.S. Department of Justice, Bureau of Justice Statistics.

Becker, H. S. (1963). *Outsiders: Studies in the sociology of deviance*. New York: Free Press.

Bentham, J. (1948). *An introduction to the principles of morals and legislation* (L. J. Lafleur, Ed.). New York: Hafner.

Bernard, T. (1992). *The cycle of juvenile justice*. New York: Oxford University Press.

Best, J. (1988). Missing children, misleading statistics. *The Public Interest, 92*, 84-92.

Bibb, M. (1967). Gang-related services of Mobilization for Youth. In M. Klein & B. G. Myerhoff (Eds.), *Juvenile gangs in context* (pp. 175-182). Englewood Cliffs, NJ: Prentice Hall.

Bishop, D. M., & Frazier, C. E. (1988). The influence of race in juvenile justice processing. *Journal of Research in Crime and Delinquency, 25*, 242-263.

Bishop, D. M., & Frazier, C. E. (1990). *A study of race and juvenile processing in Florida*. Gainesville:

Center for Studies in Criminology and Law, University of Florida.

Bishop, D. M., & Frazier, C. E. (1991). Transfer of juveniles to criminal court: A case study and analysis of prosecutorial waiver. *Notre Dame Journal of Law, Ethics and Public Policy, 5*, 281-302.

Bishop, D. M., & Frazier, C. E. (1992). Gender bias in juvenile justice processing: Implications of the JJDP Act. *Journal of Criminal Law and Criminology, 82*, 1162-1186.

Bishop, D. M., Frazier, C. E., & Henretta, J. C. (1989). Prosecutorial waiver: Case study of a questionable reform. *Crime & Delinquency, 35*, 179-201.

Bishop, D. M., Frazier, C. E., Lanza-Kaduce, L., & Winner, L. (1996). The transfer of juveniles to criminal court: Does it make a difference? *Crime and Delinquency, 42*, 171-191.

Biskupic, J. (1996, June 25). Civil forfeiture in drug cases upheld, 8 to 1. *The Washington Post*, pp. A1, A3.

Bittner, E. (1970). *The functions of the police in modern society* (Publication No. 2059). Washington, DC: Government Printing Office.

Bjerregaard, B., & Lizotte, A. J. (1995). Gun ownership and gang membership. *The Journal of Criminal Law and Criminology, 86*, 37-58.

Bjerregaard, B., & Smith, C. (1993). Gender differences in gang participation, delinquency, and substance use. *Journal of Quantitative Criminology, 9*, 329-355.

Blackman, P. H. (1992, November). *Children and firearms: Lies the CDC loves*. Paper presented at the annual meeting of the American Society of Criminology, New Orleans, LA.

Block, C. R. (1985a). *Lethal violence in Chicago over seventeen years*. Chicago: Illinois Criminal Justice Information Authority.

Block, C. R. (1985b). Specification of patterns over time in Chicago homicide: Increases and decreases, 1965-1981. Chicago: Illinois Criminal Justice Information Authority.

Block, C. R. (1986). *Homicide in Chicago*. Chicago: Center for Urban Policy, Loyola University of Chicago.

Block, C. R. (1993). Lethal violence in the Chicago Latino community. In A. V. Wilson (Ed.), *Homicide: The victim/offender connection* (pp. 267-342). Cincinnati, OH: Anderson.

Block, C. R., & Block, R. (1991). Beginning with Wolfgang: An agenda for homicide research. *Journal of Crime and Justice, 14*, 31-70.

Block, C. R., & Christakos, A. (1995). *Major trends in Chicago homicide: 1965-1994*. Chicago: Illinois Criminal Justice Information Authority.

Block, C. R., Christakos, A., Jacob, A., & Przybylski, R. (1996). *Street gangs and crime: Patterns and trends in Chicago* (Research Bulletin). Chicago: Illinois Criminal Justice Information Authority.

Block, R., & Block, C. R. (1992). Homicide syndromes and vulnerability: Violence in Chicago community areas over 25 years. *Studies on Crime and Prevention, 1*, 61-87.

Block, R., & Block, C. R. (1993). *Street gang crime in Chicago* (Research in Brief). Washington, DC: U.S. Department of Justice, National Institute of Justice.

Bloom, B., Chesney-Lind, M., & Owen, B. (1994). *Women in California prisons: Hidden victims of the war on drugs*. San Francisco: Center on Juvenile and Criminal Justice.

Blumstein, A. (1993). Making rationality relevant—the American Society of Criminology 1992 presidential address. *Criminology, 31*, 1-16.

Blumstein, A. (1995a, August). Violence by young people: Why the deadly nexus? *National Institute of Justice Journal*, pp. 1-9.

Blumstein, A. (1995b). Youth violence, guns, and the illicit-drug industry. *Journal of Criminal Law and Criminology, 86*, 10-36.

Blumstein, A. (1996, June). *Youth violence, guns, and illicit drug markets* (Research Preview). Washington, DC: U.S. Department of Justice, National Institute of Justice.

Blumstein, A., & Cohen, J. (1987). Characterizing criminal careers. *Science, 237*, 985-991.

Blumstein, A., Cohen, J., & Nagin, D. (Eds.). (1978). *Deterrence and incapacitation: Estimating the effects of criminal sanctions on crime rates*. Washington, DC: National Academy of Sciences.

Blumstein, A., Cohen, J., Roth, J. A., & Visher, C. A. (1986). *Criminal careers and "career criminals"*. Washington, DC: National Academy Press.

Bonta, J. (1996). Risk-needs assessment and treatment. In A. T. Harland (Ed.), *Choosing correctional options that work* (pp. 18-32). Thousand Oaks, CA: Sage.

Bonta, J., & Motiuk, L. L. (1990). Classification to halfway houses: A quasi-experimental evaluation. *Criminology, 28*, 497-506.

Borduin, C. M., Mann, B. J., Cone, L. T., Henggeler, S. W., Fucci, B. R., Blaske, D. M., & Williams, R. A. (1995). Multisystemic treatment of serious juvenile offenders: Long-term prevention of criminality and violence. *Journal of Consulting and Clinical Psychology, 63*, 569-587.

Bortner, M. A. (1986). Traditional rhetoric, organizational realities: Remand of juveniles to adult court. *Crime and Delinquency, 32*, 53-73.

Bortner, M. A. (1992). *Transfer of juveniles to adult court. Maricopa and Pima Counties, 1990*. Unpublished report, Arizona State University.

Bowker, L. H. (1983). *Beating wife-beating*. Lexington, MA: Lexington Books.

Bowlby, J. (1951). *Maternal care and mental health*. Geneva: World Health Organization.

Brace, C. (1967). *The dangerous classes of New York, and twenty years work among them*. Montclair, NJ: Patterson Smith. (Original work published 1872)

Breed, A. (1953). California Youth Authority Forestry Camp Program. *Federal Probation, 17*, 37-43.

Bremner, R. (Ed.). (1970). *Children and youth in America: A documentary history* (3 vols.). Cambridge, MA: Harvard University Press.

Brendtro, L. K., & Long, N. J. (1994). Violence begets violence: Breaking conflict cycles. *Journal of Emotional and Behavioral Problems: Reclaiming Children and Youth, 3*, 2-7.

Brennan, P., Mednick, S., & Kandel, E. (1991). Congenital determinants of violent and property offending. In D. J. Pepler & K. H. Rubin (Eds.), *The development and treatment of childhood aggression* (pp. 81-92). Hillsdale, NJ: Erlbaum.

Brewer, D. D., Hawkins, J. D., Catalano, R. F., & Neckerman, H. J. (1995). Preventing serious, violent, and chronic offending: A review of evaluations of selected strategies in childhood, adolescence, and the community. In J. C. Howell, B. Krisberg, J. D. Hawkins, & J. Wilson (Eds.), *Sourcebook on serious, violent, and chronic juvenile offenders* (pp. 61-141). Thousand Oaks, CA: Sage.

Bridges, G. S., & Weis, J. G. (1989). Measuring violent behavior: Effects of study design on reported correlates of violence. In N. A. Weiner & M. E. Wolfgang (Eds.), *Violent crime, violent criminals* (pp. 14-34). Newbury Park, CA: Sage.

Brien, P. M., & Beck, A. J. (1996, March). *HIV in prisons 1994* (Bureau of Justice Statistics Bulletin). Washington, DC: U.S. Department of Justice, Bureau of Justice Statistics.

Broder, D. S. (1996, July 28). Before the crimes begin. *The Washington Post*, p. C7.

Broder, P. K. (1980). *Further observations on the link between learning disabilities and juvenile delinquency*. Williamsburg, VA: National Center for State Courts.

Brodt, S. J., & Smith, J. S. (1988). Part I: public policy and the serious juvenile offender. *Criminal Justice Policy Review, 2*, 70-85.

Brown, J. (1995). Beyond the mandates. *Juvenile Justice, 2*, 22-24.

Bryant, D. (1989, September). *Communitywide responses crucial for dealing with youth gangs* (Juvenile Justice Bulletin). Washington, DC: U.S. Department of Justice, Office of Juvenile Justice and Delinquency Prevention.

Bullis, M., & Walker, H. M. (1996). Characteristics and causal factors of troubled youth. In C. M. Nelson, R. B. Rutherford, & B. I. Wolford (Eds.), *Comprehensive and collaborative systems that work for troubled youth: A national agenda* (pp. 15-28). Richmond: Eastern Kentucky University.

Bureau of Justice Statistics. (1988). *Census of local jails, 1983*. Washington, DC: U.S. Department of Justice, Bureau of Justice Statistics.

Bursik, R. J., Jr., & Grasmick, H. G. (1993). *Neighborhoods and crime: The dimension of effective community control*. New York: Lexington Books.

Burt, S. C. (1925). *The young delinquent*. London: St. Paul's House.

Butterfield, F. (1995, May 23). Serious crimes fall for third year, but experts warn against seeing trend. *The New York Times*, p. A14.

Butts, J. A. (1990). *Juvenile corrections risk assessment: Recent state-based studies*. Ann Arbor: University of Michigan, Center for the Study of Youth Policy.

Butts, J. A. (1996). *Offenders in juvenile court, 1994* (Juvenile Justice Bulletin). Washington, DC: U.S. Department of Justice, Office of Juvenile Justice and Delinquency Prevention.

Butts, J. A., & Connors-Beatty, D. J. (1992). *A comparison of juvenile court's and criminal court's response to violent offenders: 1985-1989*. Pittsburgh: National Center for Juvenile Justice.

Butts, J. A., & DeMuro, P. (1989). *Risk assessment of adjudicated delinquents: Division for Children and Youth Services, Department of Health and Human Services, State of New Hampshire*. Ann Arbor: University of Michigan, Center for the Study of Youth Policy.

Butts, J. A., Snyder, H. N., Aughenbaugh, A. L., & Poole, R. S. (1995). *Juvenile court statistics 1993*. Washington, DC: U.S. Department of Justice, Office of Juvenile Justice and Delinquency Prevention.

Butts, J. A., Snyder, H. N., Finnegan, T. A., Aughenbaugh, A. L., Tierney, N. J., Sullivan, D. P., & Poole, R. S. (1995). *Juvenile court statistics 1992*. Washington, DC: U.S. Department of Justice, Office of Juvenile Justice and Delinquency Prevention.

Cairns, R. B., & Cairns, B. D. (1991). Social cognition and social networks: A developmental perspective. In D. J. Pepler & K. H. Rubin (Eds.), *The development and treatment of childhood aggression* (pp. 249-278). Hillsdale, NJ: Erlbaum.

Cairns, R. B., Cairns, B. D., & Neckerman, H. J. (1989). Early school dropout: Configurations and determinants. *Child Development, 60*, 1437-1452.

Cairns, R. B., Cairns, B. D., Neckerman, H. J., Ferguson, L. L., & Gariepy, J.-L. (1989). Growth and aggression: I. Childhood to early adolescence. *Developmental Psychology, 25*, 320-330.

California Council on Criminal Justice. (1989). *Task force report on gangs and drugs*. Sacramento, CA: Author.

Callahan, C. M., & Rivara, F. P. (1992). Urban high school youth and handguns: A school-based survey. *Journal of the American Medical Association, 267*, 3038-3042.

Campbell, J. C. (1921). *The Southern Highlander and his homeland*. Lexington: University of Kentucky Press.

Canadian Sentencing Commission. (1987). *Sentencing reform: A Canadian approach*. Ottawa: Canadian Government Publishing Centre.

Capaldi, D. M., & Patterson, G. R. (1989). *Psychometric properties of fourteen latent constructs from the Oregon Youth Study*. New York: Springer-Verlag.

Capizzi, M., Cook, J. I., & Schumacher, M. (1995, Fall). The TARGET model: A new approach to the prosecution of gang cases. *The Prosecutor*, pp. 18-21.

Caplan, G. (1976). Criminology, criminal justice, and the war on crime. *Criminology, 14*, 3-16.

Carnegie Council on Adolescent Development. (1989). *Turning points: Preparing American youth for the 21st century.* Washington, DC: Carnegie Corporation of New York.

Carnegie Council on Adolescent Development. (1992). *A matter of time: Risk and opportunity in the nonschool hours.* New York: Carnegie Corporation of New York.

Carnegie Council on Adolescent Development. (1995). *Great transitions: Preparing adolescents for a new century.* Washington, DC: Carnegie Corporation of New York.

Cartwright, D. S., Howard, K. I., & Reuterman, N. J. (1970). Multivariate analysis of gang delinquency: II. Structural and dynamic properties of gangs. *Multivariate Behavioral Research, 5*, 303-324.

Catalano, R. F., Arthur, M. W., Hawkins, D. F., & Olson, J. J. (1996). Community interventions to prevent antisocial behavior. University of Washington, School of Social Development Research Group.

Catalano, R. F., & Hawkins, J. D. (1996). The social development model: A theory of antisocial behavior. In J. D. Hawkins (Ed.), *Delinquency and crime: Current theories* (pp. 149-197). New York: Cambridge University Press.

Catalano, R. F., Morrison, D. M., Wells, E. A., Gillmore, M. R., Iritani, B., & Hawkins, J. D. (1992). Ethnic differences in family factors related to early drug initiation. *Journal of Studies of Alcohol, 53*, 208-217.

Cederblom, J. B., & Blizek, W. L. (1977). *Justice and punishment.* Cambridge, MA: Ballinger.

Center for Successful Child Development. (1993). *Beethoven's Fifth: The first five years of the Center for Successful Child Development* (Executive Summary). Chicago: Ounce of Prevention Fund.

Center for the Study of Social Policy. (1995). *Building new futures for at-risk youth: Findings from a five-year, multi-site evaluation.* Washington, DC: Author.

Centers for Disease Control and Prevention. (1990). Forum on youth violence in minority communities: Setting the agenda for prevention. Atlanta, GA, December 10-12. *Public Health Report, 106*, 225-279.

Centers for Disease Control and Prevention. (1993). Violence-related attitudes and behaviors of high school students—New York City, 1992. *Morbidity and Mortality Weekly Report, 42*, 40-45.

Centers for Disease Control and Prevention. (1994). Homicides among 15-19-year-old males. *Morbidity and Mortality Weekly Report, 43*, 725-727.

Centers for Disease Control and Prevention. (1996). *Spotlight on Health—U.S., 1995.* Atlanta, GA: Centers for Disease Control and Prevention.

Chaiken, M. R., & Chaiken, J. M. (1991, March). *Priority prosecution of high-rate dangerous offenders* (Research in Action). Washington, DC: U.S. Department of Justice, National Institute of Justice.

Champion, A. G. (Ed.). (1989). *Counterurbanisation: The changing pace and nature of population deconcentration.* London: Edward Arnold.

Champion, D. J. (1989). Teenage felons and waiver hearings: Some recent trends, 1980-88. *Crime and Delinquency, 35*, 577-588.

Chein, I., Gerard, D. L., Lee, R. S., & Rosenfeld, E. (1964). *The road to H: Narcotics, delinquency, and social policy.* New York: Basic Books.

Chelimsky, E., & Dahman, J. (1981). Career criminal program national evaluation: Final report. Washington, DC: National Institute of Justice.

Chesney-Lind, M. (1993). Girls, gangs and violence: Anatomy of a backlash. *Humanity & Society, 17*, 321-344.

Children's Defense Fund. (1976). *Children in adult jails.* Washington, DC: Author.

Children's Defense Fund. (1991). *The state of America's children, 1991.* Washington, DC: Author.

Children's Research Center. (1993). *A new approach to child protection: The CRC model.* Madison, WI: National Council on Crime and Delinquency.

Chin, K.-L. (1989). *Triad subculture and criminality: A study of triads, tongs, and Chinese gangs.* Report to the New York City Criminal Justice Department.

Chin, K.-L. (1990a). Chinese gangs and extortion. In C. R. Huff (Ed.), *Gangs in America* (pp. 129-145). Newbury Park, CA: Sage.

Chin, K.-L. (1990b). *Chinese subculture and criminality: Non-traditional crime groups in America.* Westport, CT: Greenwood.

Chin, K.-L., & Fagan, J. A. (1990, November). *The impact of crack on drug and crime involvement.* Paper presented at the Annual Meeting of the American Society of Criminology, New Orleans, LA.

Clark, C. S. (1991). Youth gangs. *Congressional Quarterly Research, 22*, 755-771.

Clarke, E. E. (1994). *Treatment of juveniles as adults: A report on trends in automatic transfer to criminal court in Cook County, Illinois.* Chicago: Children and Family Center of the Northwestern University Legal Clinic.

Cloward, R. A., & Ohlin, L. (1960). *Delinquency and opportunity.* New York: Free Press.

Coalition for Juvenile Justice. (1989). *A report on the delicate balance.* Washington, DC: Author.

Coalition for Juvenile Justice. (1993). *Pursuing the promise: Equal justice for all juveniles.* Washington, DC: Author.

Coalition for Juvenile Justice. (1994). *No easy answers: Juvenile justice in a climate of fear.* Washington, DC: Author.

Coates, R., & Miller, A. (1973). Neutralization of community resistance to group homes. In Y. Bakal (Ed.), *Closing correctional institutions* (pp. 67-84). Lexington, MA: D. C. Heath.

Coates, R., Miller, A., & Ohlin, L. (1973). A strategic innovation in the process of deinstitutionalization: The University of Massachusetts Conference. In Y. Bakal (Ed.), *Closing correctional institutions* (pp. 127-148). Lexington, MA: D. C. Heath.

Coates, R., Miller, A., & Ohlin, L. (1978). *Diversity in a youth correctional system.* Cambridge, MA: Ballinger.

Cocozza, J. J. (1992). *Responding to the mental health needs of youth in the juvenile justice system.* Seattle, WA: The National Coalition for the Mentally Ill in the Criminal Justice System.

Cohen, A. K. (1960). *Delinquent boys: The culture of the gang.* Glencoe, IL: Free Press.

Cohen, R., Parmalee, D. X., Irwin, L., Weisz, J. R., Howard, P., Purcell, P., & Best, A. M. (1990). Characteristics of children and adolescents in a psychiatric hospital and a correction facility. *Journal of the American Academy of Child and Adolescent Psychiatry, 29,* 909-913.

Cohen, S. (1980). *Folk devils and moral panics: The creation of the mods and rockers.* New York: Basil Blackwell.

Coie, J. D., Dodge, K., & Kupersmidt, J. B. (1990). Peer group behavior and social status. In S. R. Asher & J. D. Coie (Eds.), *Peer rejection in childhood* (pp. 17-59). Cambridge, UK: Cambridge University Press.

Coie, J. D., Watt, N. F., West, S. G., Hawkins, J. D., Asarnow, J. R., Markman, H. J., Ramey, S. L., Shure, M. B., & Long, B. (1993). The science of prevention: A conceptual framework and some directions for a national research program. *American Psychologist, 48,* 1013-1022.

Committee on Education and Labor, U.S. House of Representatives (1974, June 21). *Report on the Juvenile Justice and Delinquency Prevention Act of 1974* (Report No. 93-1135, 93rd Cong., 2nd Sess.). Washington, DC: Government Printing Office.

Committee on the Judiciary, U.S. Senate. (1974, July 16). *Report on the Juvenile Justice and Delinquency Prevention Act of 1974* (Report No. 93-1101, 93rd Cong., 2nd Sess.). Washington, DC: Government Printing Office.

Community Research Center. (1980). *Juvenile suicides in adult jails* (Juvenile Justice Transfer Series). Washington, DC: U.S. Department of Justice, Office of Juvenile Justice and Delinquency Prevention.

Cook, P. J. (Ed.). (1981a). Gun control. *Annals of the American Academy of Political and Social Science, 455,* 1-167.

Cook, P. J. (1981b). The "Saturday night special": An assessment of alternative definitions from a policy perspective. *Journal of Criminal Law and Criminology, 72,* 1735-1745.

Cook, P. J. (1991). The technology of personal violence. In M. Tonry (Ed.), *Crime and justice: An annual review of research* (Vol. 14, pp. 1-71). Chicago: University of Chicago Press.

Cook, P. J., & Nagin, D. (1979). *Does the weapon matter?* Washington, DC: INSLAW.

Corsica, J. Y. (1993). Employment training interventions. In A. Goldstein & C. R. Huff (Eds.), *The gang intervention handbook* (pp. 301-317). Champaign, IL: Research Press.

Cressey, D. R. (1973). Adult felons in prison. In L. E. Ohlin (Ed.), *Prisoners in America* (pp. 117-150). Englewood Cliffs, NJ: Prentice Hall.

Criminal Justice Research Center. (1996). *Juvenile murder in Virginia: A study of arrests and convictions.* Richmond, VA: Department of Criminal Justice Services.

Cristoffel, K. K. (1991). Toward reducing pediatric injuries from firearms: Charting a legislative and regulatory course. *Pediatrics, 88,* 294-305.

Cronin, R. (1994). *Innovative community partnerships: Working together for change.* Washington, DC: U.S. Department of Justice, Office of Juvenile Justice and Delinquency Prevention.

Cronin, R. C., Bourque, B. B., Mell, J. M., Gragg, F. E., & McGrady, A. A. (1988). *Evaluation of the Habitual Serious and Violent Juvenile Offender Program* (Executive summary). Washington, DC: U.S. Department of Justice, Office of Juvenile Justice and Delinquency Prevention.

Cullen, R. (1995, October 22). Kids shouldn't be getting away with murder. *The Washington Post,* p. A12.

Curry, G. D., Ball, R. A., & Decker, S. H. (1995). *Developing national estimates of gang-related crime: Report to the National Institute of Justice.* Unpublished manuscript, Department of Criminology and Criminal Justice, University of Missouri-St. Louis.

Curry, G. D., Ball, R. A., & Decker, S. H. (1996). *Estimating the national scope of gang crime from law enforcement data* (Research in Brief). Washington, DC: U.S. Department of Justice, National Institute of Justice.

Curry, G. D., & Spergel, I. A. (1988). Gang homicide, delinquency, and community. *Criminology, 26,* 381-405.

Curry, G. D., & Spergel, I. A. (1992). Gang involvement and delinquency among Hispanic and African-American adolescent males. *Journal of Research in Crime and Delinquency, 29,* 273-291.

Dade County Grand Jury. (1985, May 14). *Dade youth gangs* (Final report of the Grand Jury, Miami). Miami, FL: Dade County District Attorney.

Dade County Grand Jury. (1988, May 11). *Dade County gangs—1988* (Final report of the Grand Jury, Miami). Miami, FL: Dade County District Attorney.

Danser, K. R., & Laub, J. H. (1981). *Juvenile criminal behavior and its relation to economic conditions* (Monograph 4, Analysis of National Crime Victimization Survey data to study serious delinquent behavior). Washington, DC: U.S. Department of Justice, Office of Juvenile Justice and Delinquency Prevention.

Datesman, S. K., & Aickin, M. (1985). Offense specialization and escalation among status offenders. *Journal of Criminal Law and Criminology, 75,* 246-275.

Davis, K. (1979). Demographic changes and the future of childhood. In L. T. Empey (Ed.), *The future of childhood and juvenile justice* (pp. 75-89). Charlottesville: University Press of Virginia.

Dean, C. W., & Reppucci, N. D. (1974). Juvenile correctional institutions. In D. Glaser (Ed.), *Handbook of criminology* (pp. 865-894). Chicago: Rand McNally.

Decker, S., & Pennell, S. (1995, September). *Arrestees and guns: Monitoring the illegal firearms market* (Research Preview). Washington, DC: U.S. Department of Justice, National Institute of Justice.

Decker, S. H., & Van Winkle, B. (1994). Slinging dope: The role of gangs and gang members in drug sales. *Justice Quarterly, 11,* 583-604.

Decker, S. H., & Van Winkle, B. (1996). *Life in the gang: Family, friends, and violence.* New York: Cambridge University Press.

DeComo, R. (1993, September). *The juveniles taken into custody research program: Estimating the prevalence of juvenile custody by race and gender* (Focus). San Francisco: National Council on Crime and Delinquency.

DeComo, R., Krisberg, B., Rudenstine, S., & Del Rosario, D. (1995). *Juveniles taken into custody research program: FY 1994 annual report.* Washington, DC: U.S. Department of Justice, Office of Juvenile Justice and Delinquency Prevention.

DeComo, R., Tunis, S., Krisberg, B., & Herrera, N. (1994). *Juveniles taken into custody research program: FY 1992 annual report.* Washington, DC: U.S. Department of Justice, Office of Juvenile Justice and Delinquency Prevention.

DeMause, L. (Ed.). (1974). *The history of childhood.* New York: Psychohistory.

Dembo, R., & Brown, R. (1994). The Hillsborough County Juvenile Assessment Center. *Journal of Child & Adolescent Substance Abuse, 3,* 25-43.

Dembo, R., Hughes, P., & Jackson, L. (1993). Crack cocaine dealing by adolescents in two public housing projects: A pilot study. *Human Organization, 52,* 89-96.

Dembo, R., & Rivers, J. E. (1996, December). *Juvenile assessment centers: The Florida experience.* Paper presented at the Office of Juvenile Justice and Delinquency Prevention National Conference. Baltimore, MD.

DeMuro, P., & Butts, J. A. (1989). *At the crossroads: A population profile of youths committed to the Alabama Department of Youth Services.* Ann Arbor: University of Michigan, Center for the Study of Youth Policy.

Devoe, E. (1848). *The refuge system, or prison discipline applied to delinquency.* Cambridge, MA: Harvard Divinity School, Sprague Pamphlet Collection.

DiIulio, J. J., Jr. (1992). *Rethinking the criminal justice system: Toward a new paradigm.* Princeton, NJ: Princeton University Press.

DiIulio, J. J., Jr. (1996, Spring). They're coming: Florida's youth crime bomb. *Impact,* pp. 25-27.

Dodge, K. A., Bates, J. E., & Pettit, G. S. (1990). Mechanisms in the cycle of violence. *Science, 250,* 1678-1683.

Dolan, E. F., & Finney, S. (1984). *Youth gangs.* New York: Julian Messner.

Doleschal, E. (1970). Hidden crime. *Crime and Delinquency Literature, 2,* 546-572.

Downey, J. J. (1970). *State responsibility for juvenile detention care.* Washington, DC: Government Printing Office.

Drug Enforcement Administration. (1988). *Crack cocaine availability and trafficking in the United States.* Washington, DC: U.S. Department of Justice, Drug Enforcement Administration.

Dryfoos, J. (1990). *Adolescents at risk: Prevalence and prevention.* New York: Oxford University Press.

Duchnowski, A. J., & Kutash, K. (1996). A mental health perspective. In C. M. Nelson, R. B. Rutherford, & B. I. Wolford (Eds.), *Comprehensive and collaborative systems that work for troubled youth: A national agenda* (pp. 90-110). Richmond: Eastern Kentucky University.

Duke, S. B., & Gross, A. C. (1993). *America's longest war: Rethinking our tragic crusade against drugs.* New York: Putnam.

Dunford, F. W., Osgood, D. W., & Weichselbaum, H. F. (1982). *National evaluation of diversion projects* (Executive Summary). Washington, DC: U.S. National Institute for Juvenile Justice and Delinquency Prevention, Office of Juvenile Justice and Delinquency Prevention.

Dunston, L. G. (1990). *Reaffirming prevention: Report of the Task Force on Juvenile Gangs.* Albany, NY: New York State Division for Youth.

Dykatra, L. (1980). *Cost analysis of juvenile jailing and detention alternative.* Champaign, IL: Community Research Forum.

Easterlin, R. A. (1978). What will 1984 be like? Socioeconomic implications of recent twists in age structure. *Demography, 15,* 397-432.

Edwards, L. P. (1992). The juvenile court and the role of the juvenile court judge. *Juvenile and Family Court Journal, 43,* 1-45.

Eigen, J. P. (1981). The determinants and impact of jurisdictional transfer in Philadelphia. In J. C. Hall, D. M. Hamparian, J. M. Pettibone, & J. L. White (Eds.), *Major issues in juvenile justice information and training: Readings in public policy* (pp. 333-350). Columbus, OH: Academy for Contemporary Problems.

Eisenhower Foundation. (1990). *Youth investment and community reconstruction: Street lessons and drugs and crime for the nineties.* Washington, DC: Author.

Elias, M. (1996, July 8). Epidemic of violence on the job at an all-time high. *USA Today,* p. A1.

Elliott, D. S. (1994a). Serious violent offenders: Onset, developmental course, and termination. The

American Society of Criminology 1993 Presidential Address. *Criminology, 32*, 1-21.

Elliott, D. S. (1994b). Youth violence: An overview. Boulder, CO: University of Colorado, Center for the Study and Prevention of Violence.

Elliott, D. S. (1995, November). *Lies, damn lies and arrest statistics.* Paper presented at the annual meeting of the American Society of Criminology, Boston.

Elliott, D. S., Ageton, S. S., Huizinga, D., Knowles, B. A., & Canter, R. J. (1983). *The prevalence and incidence of delinquent behavior: 1976-1980* (National Youth Survey Report No. 26). Boulder, CO: Behavioral Research Institute.

Elliott, D. S., Huizinga, D., & Ageton, S. S. (1985). *Explaining delinquency and drug use.* Newbury Park, CA: Sage.

Elliott, D. S., Huizinga, D., & Menard, S. (1989). *Multiple problem youth: Delinquency, substance use and mental health problems.* New York: Springer-Verlag.

Elliott, D. S., Huizinga, D., & Morse, B. (1986). Self-reported violent offending. *Journal of Interpersonal Violence, 1*, 472-514.

Elliott, D. S., & Menard, S. (1996). Delinquent friends and delinquent behavior: Temporal and developmental patterns. In J. D. Hawkins (Ed.), *Delinquency and crime: Current theories* (pp. 28-67). New York: Cambridge University Press.

Elliott, D. S., & Voss, H. L. (1974). *Delinquency and dropout.* Lexington, MA: D. C. Heath.

Empey, L. T. (1967). *Alternatives to incarceration.* Washington, DC: Government Printing Office.

Empey, L. T. (1974). Crime prevention: The fugitive utopia. In D. Glaser (Ed.), *Handbook of criminology* (pp. 1095-1123). Chicago: Rand McNally.

Empey, L. T. (1978). *American delinquency: Its meaning and construction.* Homewood, IL: Dorsey.

Empey, L. T. (1985). The family and delinquency. *Today's Delinquent, 4*, 5-46.

Empey, L. T., & Stafford, M. C. (1991). *American delinquency: Its meaning and construction* (3rd ed.). Belmont, CA: Wadsworth.

Erikson, K. T. (1966). *Wayward puritans.* New York: John Wiley and Sons.

Erlanger, H. S. (1979). Estrangement, machismo and gang violence. *Social Science Quarterly, 60*, 235-248.

Eron, L. D. (1987). The development of aggressive behavior from the perspective of a developing behaviorist. *American Psychologist, 42*, 435-442.

Eron, L. D., & Slaby, R. G. (1994). Introduction. In L. D. Eron, J. H. Gentry, & P. Schlegel (Eds.), *Reason to hope: A psychosocial perspective on violence and youth* (pp. 1-22). Washington, DC: American Psychological Association.

Esbensen, F.-A., & Huizinga, D. (1993). Gangs, drugs, and delinquency in a survey of urban youth. *Criminology, 31*, 565-589.

Esbensen, F.-A., Huizinga, D., & Weiher, A. W. (1993). Gang and non-gang youth: Differences in explanatory variables. *Journal of Contemporary Criminal Justice, 9*, 94-116.

Esbensen, F.-A., & Osgood, D. W. (1997). *National evaluation of G.R.E.A.T.* (Research in Brief). Washington, DC: U.S. Department of Justice, National Institute of Justice.

Fagan, J. A. (1986). Gangs, drugs, and neighborhood change. In C. R. Huff (Ed.), *Gangs in America* (pp. 39-74). Thousand Oaks, CA: Sage.

Fagan, J. A. (1989). The social organization of drug use and drug dealing among urban gangs. *Criminology, 27*, 633-669.

Fagan, J. A. (1990). Treatment and reintegration of violent juvenile offenders: Experimental results. *Justice Quarterly, 7*, 233-263.

Fagan, J. A. (1995). Separating the men from the boys: The comparative advantage of juvenile versus criminal court sanctions on recidivism among adolescent felony offenders. In J. C. Howell, B. Krisberg, J. D. Hawkins, & J. J. Wilson (Eds.), *Sourcebook on serious, violent, and chronic juvenile offenders* (pp. 238-274). Thousand Oaks, CA: Sage.

Fagan, J. A., & Deschenes, E. P. (1990). Determinants of judicial waiver decisions for violent juvenile offenders. *Journal of Criminal Law and Criminology, 81*, 314-347.

Fagan, J. A., Forst, M., & Vivona, T. S. (1987). Racial determinants of the judicial transfer decision: Prosecuting violent youth in criminal court. *Crime and Delinquency, 33*, 259-286.

Fagan, J. A., & Hartstone, E. (1984). Strategic planning in juvenile justice: Defining the toughest kids. In R. A. Mathias (Ed.), *Violent juvenile offenders: An anthology* (pp. 31-51). San Francisco: National Council on Crime and Delinquency.

Fagan, J. A., Hartstone, E., Rudman, G. J., & Hansen, K. V. (1984). System processing of violent juvenile offenders. In R. A. Mathias (Ed.), *Violent juvenile Offenders: An anthology* (pp. 117-136). San Francisco: National Council on Crime and Delinquency.

Fagan, J. A., Rudman, C. J., & Hartstone, E. (1984). Intervening with violent juvenile offenders: A community reintegration model. In R. A. Mathias (Ed.), *Violent juvenile offenders: An anthology* (pp. 207-229). San Francisco: National Council on Crime and Delinquency.

Family Services Research Center. (1995, October). *Multisystemic therapy using home-based services: A clinically effective and cost effective strategy for treating serious clinical problems in youth.* Medical University of South Carolina, Department of Psychiatry and Behavioral Sciences, Charleston.

Farrington, D. P. (1973). Self-reports of deviant behavior: Predictive and stable? *British Journal of Criminal Law & Criminology, 64*, 99-110.

Farrington, D. P. (1979). Environmental stress, delinquent behavior, and convictions. In I. G. Sarason

& C. D. Spielberger (Eds.), *Stress and anxiety* (Vol. 6, pp. 93-107). Washington, DC: Hemisphere.

Farrington, D. P. (1986a). Age and crime. In M. Tonry & N. Morris (Eds.), *Crime and justice: An annual review of research* (Vol. 7, pp. 189-250). Chicago: University of Chicago Press.

Farrington, D. P. (1986b). Stepping stones to adult criminal careers. In D. Olweus, J. Block, & M. R. Yarrow (Eds.), *Development of antisocial and prosocial behavior* (pp. 359-384). New York: Academic Press.

Farrington, D. P. (1989a). Early predictors of adolescent aggression and adult violence. *Violence and Victims, 4*, 79-100.

Farrington, D. P. (1989b). Later adult life outcomes of offenders and non-offenders. In M. Brambring, F. Losel, & H. Skowronek (Eds.), *Children at risk: Assessment, longitudinal research, and intervention* (pp. 220-224). Berlin: De Gruyter.

Farrington, D. P. (1990). Age, period, cohort, and offending. In D. M. Gottfredson & R. V. Clarke (Eds.), *Policy and theory in criminal justice: Contributions in honor of Leslie T. Wilkins* (pp. 51-75). Aldershot, UK: Avebury.

Farrington, D. P. (1991). Childhood aggression and adult violence: Early precursors and later life outcomes. In D. J. Pepler & K. H. Rubin (Eds.), *The development and treatment of childhood aggression* (pp. 5-29). Hillsdale, NJ: Erlbaum.

Farrington, D. P. (1992). Explaining the beginning, progress and ending of antisocial behaviour from birth to adulthood. In J. McCord (Ed.), *Facts, frameworks and forecasts: Advances in criminological theory* (Vol. 3, pp. 253-286). New Brunswick, NJ: Transaction.

Farrington, D. P. (1993). Have any individual, family or neighbourhood influences on offending been demonstrated conclusively? In D. P. Farrington, R. J. Sampson, & P.-O. H. Wikstrom (Eds.), *Integrating individual and ecological aspects of crime* (pp. 7-37). Stockholm: National Council for Crime Prevention.

Farrington, D. P. (1994). Early developmental prevention of juvenile delinquency. *Criminal Behavior and Mental Health, 4*, 209-227.

Farrington, D. P. (1995). The development of offending and antisocial behaviour from childhood: Key findings from the Cambridge Study in Delinquent Development. *Journal of Child Psychology and Psychiatry, 360*, 929-964.

Farrington, D. P. (1996). The explanation and prevention of youthful offending. In J. D. Hawkins (Ed.), *Delinquency and crime: Current theories* (pp. 68-148). New York: Cambridge University Press.

Farrington, D. P., & West, D. J. (1990). The Cambridge Study in delinquent development: A long-term follow-up of 411 London males. In H.-J. Kerner & G. Kaiser (Eds.), *Criminality: Personality, behaviour and life history* (pp. 115-138). Berlin: Springer-Verlag.

Farrington, D. P., & West, D. J. (1993). Criminal, penal and life histories of chronic offenders: Risk and protective factors and early identification. *Criminal Behavior and Mental Health, 3*, 492-523.

Federal Bureau of Investigation. (1993a). *Age-specific arrest rates and race-specific arrest rates for selected offenses 1965-1992.* Washington, DC: U.S. Department of Justice, Federal Bureau of Investigation.

Federal Bureau of Investigation. (1993b). *Crime in the United States, 1992.* Washington, DC: U.S. Department of Justice, Federal Bureau of Investigation.

Federal Bureau of Investigation. (1994). *Uniform crime reports 1993.* Washington, DC: U.S. Department of Justice, Federal Bureau of Investigation.

Federal Bureau of Investigation. (1995). *Crime in the United States, 1994.* Washington, DC: U.S. Department of Justice, Federal Bureau of Investigation.

Federal Bureau of Investigation. (1996). *Crime in the United States, 1995.* Washington, DC: U.S. Department of Justice, Federal Bureau of Investigation.

Federation for Community Planning. (1983). *Juveniles transferred to adult court: Recent Ohio experience.* Columbus, OH: Federation for Community Planning.

Feld, B. C. (1983). Delinquent careers and criminal policy: Just deserts and the waiver decision. *Criminology, 2*, 195-212.

Feld, B. C. (1984). Criminalizing juvenile justice: Rules of procedure for juvenile court. *Minnesota Law Review, 69*, 141-276.

Feld, B. C. (1987). The juvenile court meets the principle of the offense: Legislative changes in juvenile waiver statutes. *The Journal of Criminal Law and Criminology, 78*, 471-533.

Feld, B. C. (1988). Juvenile court meets the principle of offense: Punishment, treatment, and the difference it makes. *Boston University Law Review, 68*, 821-915.

Feld, B. C. (1993). Criminalizing the American juvenile court. In M. Tonry (Ed.), *Crime and justice: An annual review of research* (Vol. 7, pp. 197-280). Chicago: University of Chicago Press.

Feld, S. L., & Straus, M. A. (1989). Escalation and desistance of wife assault in marriage. *Criminology, 27*, 141-161.

Feldman, D. (1969). Psychoanalysis and crime. In D. R. Cressey & D. A. Ward (Eds.), *Delinquency, crime, and social process* (pp. 433-442). New York: Harper and Row.

Ferster, E. Z., Snethen, E. N., & Courtless, T. F. (1969). Juvenile detention: Protection, prevention or punishment? *Fordham Law Review, 38*, 161-196.

Ferster, E. Z., Snethen, E. N., & Courtless, T. F. (1970). Separating official and unofficial delinquents: Juvenile court intake. *Iowa Law Review, 55*, 864-893.

Feyerherm, W., Pope, C, & Lovell, R. (1992). *Youth gang prevention and early intervention programs: Report to the U.S. Department of Justice, Office of Juvenile Justice and Delinquency Prevention.* Washington, DC: U.S. Department of Justice, Office of Juvenile Justice and Delinquency Prevention.

Finestone, H. (1976). *Victims of change*. Westport, CT: Greenwood.

Fingerhut, L. A., Jones, C., & Makuc, D. M. (1994). *Firearm and motor vehicle injury mortality: Variations by state, race, and ethnicity: United States, 1990-1991* (Advance Data No. 242). Hyattsville, MD: National Center for Health Statistics.

Finkelhor, D., & Dziuba-Leatherman, J. (1994a). Children as victims of violence: A national survey. *Pediatrics, 94*, 413-420.

Finkelhor, D., & Dziuba-Leatherman, J. (1994b). Victimization of children. *American Psychologist, 49*, 173-183.

Finkelhor, D., Hotaling, G. T., & Sedlak, A. (1990). *Missing, abducted, runaway, and thrownaway children in America*. Washington, DC: U.S. Department of Justice, Office of Juvenile Justice and Delinquency Prevention.

Fishman, J. (1923). *Crucibles of crime*. New York: Cosmopolis.

Flaherty, M. (1980). *An assessment of the incidence of juvenile suicide in adult jails, lock-ups, and juvenile detention centers*. Champaign, IL: Community Research Forum.

Florida Governor's Task Force on Juvenile and Adult Criminal Dispositions and Coordination. (1984). *Final report*. Report submitted to the governor of the state of Florida.

Florida Youth Services Program Office. (1980). *Analysis of the penetration of children into the adult criminal justice system in Florida*. Tallahassee: Florida Youth Services Program Office.

Fogel, D. (1979). *We are the living proof: The justice model for corrections*. Cincinnati, OH: Anderson.

Fogel, D., & Hudson, J. (Eds.). (1981). *Justice as fairness: Perspectives on the justice model*. Cincinnati, OH: Anderson.

Fontana, V. J. (1983). *Somewhere a child is crying: Maltreatment causes and prevention*. New York: New American Library.

Fontanarosa, P. B. (1995). The unrelenting epidemic of violence in America: Truths and consequences. *Journal of the American Medical Association, 273*, 1792-1793.

Forst, M. L. (Ed.). (1995). *The new juvenile justice*. Chicago: Nelson-Hall.

Forst, M. L., Fagan, J., & Vivona, T. S. (1989). Youth in prisons and state training schools. *Juvenile and Family Court Journal, 39*, 1-14.

Fox, J. A. (1996). *Trends in juvenile violence: A report to the United States Attorney General on current and future rates of juvenile offending*. Boston, MA: Northeastern University Press.

Fox, S. J. (1970). Juvenile justice reform: An historical perspective. *Stanford Law Review, 22*, 1187-1239.

Fox, S. J. (1972). *Cases and materials on modern juvenile justice*. St. Paul, MN: West.

Fox, S. J. (1974). The reform of juvenile justice: The child's right to punishment. *Juvenile Justice, 25*, 2-9.

Frazier, C. E. (1991). *Deep end juvenile justice placements or transfer to adult court by direct file?* Report prepared for the Florida Legislature Commission on Juvenile Justice.

Fritsch, E., & Hemmens, C. (1995). Juvenile transfer in the United States 1979-1995: A comparison of state waiver statutes. *Juvenile and Family Court Journal, 17*, 105-123.

Gardiner, G. S., & McKinney, R. N. (1991). The great American war on drugs: Another failure of tough-guy management. *Journal of Drug Issues, 21*, 605-616.

Gardner, M. (1987). Punitive juvenile justice: Some observations on a recent trend. *International Journal of Law and Psychiatry, 10*, 129-151.

Garmezy, N. (1985). Stress-resistant children: The search for protective factors. *Journal of Child Psychology and Psychiatry, 4*(Book Suppl.), 213-233.

Garofalo, J., Siegel, L., & Laub, J. (1987). School-related victimizations among adolescents: An analysis of National Crime Survey (NCS) narratives. *Journal of Quantitative Criminology, 3*, 321-338.

Gaylin, W., & Rothman, D. J. (1976). Introduction. In A. Von Hirsch, *Doing justice: The choice of punishments* (pp. xxi-xxii). New York: Hill and Wang.

Geerken, M. (1994). Rap sheets in criminological research. *Journal of Quantitative Criminology, 10*, 3-21.

Genelin, M. (1993). Gang prosecution: The hardest game in town. In A. P. Goldstein & C. R. Huff (Eds.), *The gang intervention handbook* (pp. 417-426). Champaign, IL: Research Press.

General Accounting Office. (1989). *Nontraditional organized crime*. Washington, DC: Government Printing Office.

General Accounting Office. (1991). *The war on drugs: Arrests burdening local criminal justice systems*. Washington, DC: Author.

General Accounting Office. (1995). *Juvenile justice: Juveniles processed in criminal court and case dispositions*. Washington, DC: Author.

General Accounting Office. (1996). *Status of delinquency prevention program and description of local projects*. Washington, DC: Author.

Gibbs, J. C., Potter, G., & Goldstein, A. P. (in press). *EQUIP: Equipping youth to help one another*. Champaign, IL: Research Press.

Gillespie, L. K., & Norman, M. D. (1984). Does certification mean prison: Some preliminary findings from Utah. *Juvenile and Family Court Journal, 35*, 23-35.

Gilliard, D. K. (1992). *National corrections reporting program, 1990*. Washington, DC: U.S. Department of Justice, Bureau of Justice Statistics.

Gilliard, D. K., & Beck, A. J. (1996). *Prison and jail inmates, 1995*. Washington, DC: U.S. Department of Justice, Bureau of Justice Statistics.

Gillis, J. R. (1974). *Youth and history*. New York: Academic Press.

Glasgow. D. G. (1980). *The Black underclass: Poverty, unemployment and entrapment of ghetto youth*. San Francisco: Jossey-Bass.

Glueck, S., & Glueck, E. (1968). *Delinquents and nondelinquents in perspective*. Cambridge, MA: Harvard University Press.

Gold, M., & Osgood, D. W. (1992). *Personality and peer influence in juvenile corrections*. Westport, CT: Greenwood.

Gold, M., & Reimer, D. J. (1975). Changing patterns of delinquent behavior among Americans 13-16 years old: 1967-1972. *Crime and Delinquency Literature, 7*, 483-517.

Goldstein, A. P. (1993). Interpersonal skills training interventions. In A. P. Goldstein & C. R. Huff (Eds.), *The gang intervention handbook* (pp. 87-157). Champaign, IL: Research Press.

Goldstein, A. P., & Glick, B. (1994). *The prosocial gang: Implementing aggression replacement training*. Thousand Oaks, CA: Sage.

Goldstein, A. P., & Soriano, F. I. (1994). Juvenile gangs. In L. D. Eron, J. H. Gentry, & P. Schlegel (Eds.), *Reason to hope: A psychosocial perspective on violence and youth* (pp. 1-22). Washington, DC: American Psychological Association.

Goldstein, P. J. (1985). The drugs/violence nexus: A tripartite conceptual framework. *Journal of Drug Issues, 15*, 493-506.

Gorman-Smith, D., Tolan, P. H., Zelli, A., & Huesmann, L. R. (1996). The relation of family functioning to violence among inner-city minority youths. *Journal of Family Psychology, 10*, 115-129.

Gottfredson, D. C. (1987). Examining the potential of delinquency prevention through alternative education. *Today's Delinquent, 6*, 87-100.

Gottfredson, G. D. (1981). Schooling and delinquency. In S. E. Martin, L. B. Sechrest, & R. Redner (Eds.), *New directions in the rehabilitation of criminal offenders* (pp. 424-469). Washington, DC: National Academy Press.

Gottfredson, M., & Hirschi, T. (1986). The value of lambda would appear to be zero: An essay on career criminals, criminal careers, selective incapacitation, cohort studies and related topics. *Criminology, 24*, 213-234.

Gottfredson, S. D., & Taylor, R. B. (1986). Person-environment interactions in the prediction of recidivism. In J. M. Byrne & R. J. Sampson (Eds.), *The social ecology of crime* (pp. 133-155). New York: Springer-Verlag.

Gragg, F. (1986). *Juveniles in adult court: A review of transfers at the habitual serious and violent juvenile offender program sites* (Report to the Office of Juvenile Justice and Delinquency Prevention). Washington, DC: American Institutes for Research.

Graham, F. (1970). *The self-inflicted wound*. New York: Free Press.

Grant, J., & Capell, F. J. (1983). *Reducing school crime: A report on the school team approach*. Berkeley, CA: Social Action Research Center.

Greenberg, D. F. (Ed.). (1977). *Corrections and punishment*. Beverly Hills, CA: Sage.

Greenfeld, L. A. (1992). *Prisons and prisoners in the United States*. Washington, DC: U.S. Department of Justice, Bureau of Justice Statistics.

Greenfeld, L. A. (1996). *Child victimizers: Violent offenders and their victims*. Washington, DC: U.S. Department of Justice, Bureau of Justice Statistics and the Office of Juvenile Justice and Delinquency Prevention.

Greenfeld, L. A., & Zawitz, M. W. (1995, November). *Weapons offenses and offenders* (Selected Findings). Washington, DC: U.S. Department of Justice, Bureau of Justice Statistics.

Greenwood, P. W. (1986). Differences in criminal behavior and court responses among juvenile and young adult defendants. In M. Tonry & N. Morris (Eds.), *Crime and justice: An annual review of research* (Vol. 7, pp. 151-187). Chicago: University of Chicago Press.

Greenwood, P. W., Abrahamse, A., & Zimring, F. E. (1984). *Factors affecting offense severity for young adult offenders*. Santa Monica, CA: RAND.

Greenwood, P. W., Lipson, A. J., Abrahamse, A., & Zimring, F. E. (1983). *Youth crime and juvenile justice in California: A report to the legislature*. Santa Monica, CA: RAND.

Greenwood, P. W., Model, K. E., Rydell, C. P., & Chiesa, J. (1996). *Diverting children from a life of crime: Measuring costs and benefits*. Santa Monica, CA: RAND.

Greenwood, P. W., Petersilia, J., & Zimring, F. E. (1980). *Age, crime and sanctions: The transition from juvenile to adult court*. Santa Monica, CA: RAND.

Greenwood, P. W., Rydell, C. P., Abrahamse, A. F., Caulkins, J. P., Chiesa, J., Model, K. E., & Klein, S. P. (1994). *Three strikes and you're out: Estimated benefits and costs of California's new mandatory-sentencing law*. Santa Monica, CA: RAND.

Griego, D., & Klizer, L. (1985, May 12). Exaggerated statistics stir national paranoia. *The Denver Post*, pp. A1, A12.

Grisso, T. (1980). Juveniles' capacities to waive Miranda rights: An empirical analysis. *California Law Review, 68*, 1134-1166.

Groves, B. M., Zuckerman, B., Marans, S., & Cohen, D. J. (1993). Silent victims: Children who witness violence. *Journal of the American Medical Association, 269*, 262-264.

Guarino-Ghezzi, S., & Loughran, E. J. (1996). *Balancing juvenile justice*. New Brunswick, NJ: Transaction.

Guest, T., & Pope, V. (1996, March 25). Crime time bomb. *U.S. News & World Report*, pp. 29-36.

Hagan, J., & Leon, J. (1977). Rediscovering delinquency: Social history, political ideology and the sociology of law. *American Sociological Review, 42*, 587-598.

Hagedorn, J. M. (1988). *People and folks: Gangs, crime and the underclass in a rustbelt city.* Chicago: Lakeview Press.

Hagedorn, J. M. (1994). Neighborhoods, markets, and gang drug organization. *Journal of Research in Crime and Delinquency, 31,* 264-294.

Hairston, G. E. (1981). Black crime and the New York State Juvenile Offender Law: A consideration of the effects of lowering the age of criminal responsibility. In J. C. Hall, D. M. Hamparian, J. M. Pettibone, & J. L. White (Eds.), *Major issues in juvenile justice information and training* (pp. 295-308). Columbus, OH: Academy for Contemporary Problems.

Hall, J. C., Barker, B. S., Parkhill, M. A., Pilotta, J. L., & White, J. L. (1982). *The out-of-state placement of children.* Columbus, OH: Academy for Contemporary Problems.

Hall, J. C., Hamparian, D. M., Pettibone, J. M., & White, J. L. (1981). *Major issues in juvenile justice information and training.* Columbus, OH: Academy for Contemporary Problems.

Hamburg, B. A., Kraemer, H. C., & Jahnke, W. (1975). Behavioral and attitudinal correlates of substantial drug use. *American Journal of Psychiatry, 132,* 627-647.

Hamburg, D. A. (1992). *Today's children.* New York: Random House.

Hamparian, D. M., Estep, L., Muntean, S., Priestino, R., Swisher, R., Wallace, P., & White, J. L. (1982). *Youth in adult courts: Between two worlds.* Washington, DC: U.S. Department of Justice, Office of Juvenile Justice and Delinquency Prevention.

Hamparian, D. M., Schuster, R., Dinitz, S., & Conrad, J. P. (1978). *The violent few.* Lexington, MA: D. C. Heath.

Handler, J. F., & Zatz, J. (1982). *Neither angels nor thieves: Studies in deinstitutionalization of status offenders.* Washington, DC: National Academy Press.

Harden, B. (1996, May 29). Criminal justice failing, Dole says, eying Clinton. *The Washington Post,* p. A8.

Harris, R. (1972, March 25). The new justice. *The New Yorker,* pp. 44-105.

Hawes, J. (1971). *Children in urban society: Juvenile delinquency in nineteenth-century America.* New York: Oxford University Press.

Hawkins, J. D. (1985). *Executive summary. Drug abuse, mental health and delinquency.* Washington, DC: Office of Juvenile Justice and Delinquency Prevention.

Hawkins, J. D., Arthur, M. W., & Catalano, R. F. (1995). Preventing substance abuse. In M. Tonry & D. P. Farrington (Eds.), *Building a safer society: Strategic approaches to crime prevention* (pp. 343-428). Chicago: University of Chicago Press.

Hawkins, J. D., & Catalano, R. F. (1992). *Communities that care.* San Francisco: Jossey-Bass.

Hawkins, J. D., & Catalano, R. F. (1993). *Risk-focused prevention using the social development strategy.* Seattle, WA: Developmental Research and Programs.

Hawkins, J. D., Catalano, R. F., & Brewer, D. D. (1995). Preventing serious, violent, and chronic offending: Effective strategies from conception to age 6. In J. C. Howell, B. Krisberg, J. D. Hawkins, & J. Wilson (Eds.), *Sourcebook on serious, violent, and chronic juvenile offenders* (pp. 36-60). Thousand Oaks, CA: Sage.

Hawkins, J. D., Catalano, R. F., Kosterman, R., Abbott, R. D., Hill, K. G., & Janosz, M. (1996, October). *Promoting academic success and preventing adolescent health risk behaviors: Six year follow-up of the Seattle Social Development Project.* Paper presented at the meeting of the Life History Research Society, London.

Hawkins, J. D., Catalano, R. F., & Miller, J. Y. (1992). Risk and protective factors for alcohol and other drugs problems in adolescence and early adulthood: Implications for substance abuse prevention. *Psychological Bulletin, 112,* 64-105.

Hawkins, J. D., Catalano, R. F., Morrison, D. M., O'Donnell, J., Abbott, R. D., & Day, L. E. (1992). The Seattle Social Development Project: Effects of the first four years on protective factors and problem behavior. In J. McCord & R. Tremblay (Eds.), *The prevention of antisocial behavior in children* (pp. 139-161). New York: Guilford.

Hawkins, J. D., Doueck, H. J., & Lishner, D. M. (1988). Changing teaching practices in mainstream classrooms to improve bonding and behavior in low achievers. *American Educational Research Journal, 25,* 31-50.

Hawkins, J. D., Farrington, D. P., & Catalano, R. F. (in press). Reducing violence through the schools. In D. Elliott & B. Hamburg (Eds.) *Schools and violence.*

Hawkins, J. D., & Fraser, M. W. (1981). Theory and practice in delinquency prevention. *Social Work Research and Abstracts, 17,* 3-13.

Hawkins, J. D., & Lishner, D. M. (1987). Schooling and delinquency. In E. H. Johnson (Ed.), *Handbook on crime and delinquency prevention* (pp. 179-221). New York: Greenwood.

Hawkins, J. D., Von Cleve, E., & Catalano, R. F. (1991). Reducing early childhood aggression: Results of a primary prevention program. *Journal of the American Academy of Child & Adolescent Psychiatry, 30,* 208-217.

Hawkins, J. D., & Weis, J. G. (1980). *The social development model: An integrated approach to delinquency prevention.* Washington, DC: U.S. Department of Justice, Office of Juvenile Justice and Delinquency Prevention.

Hawkins, J. D., & Weis, J. G. (1985). The social development model: An integrated approach to delinquency prevention. *Journal of Primary Prevention, 6,* 73-97.

Hayeslip, D. W., Jr. (1989). *Local-level drug enforce-ment: New strategies* (Research in Action No. 213). Washington, DC: U.S. Department of Justice, National Institute of Justice.

Hearings Before the Subcommittee on Equal Opportunity, Committee on Education and Labor, U.S. House of Representatives. (1974). The Juvenile Justice and Delinquency Prevention Act—H.R. 6265, H.R. 13737, and H.R. 9298.

Hearings Before the Subcommittee to Investigate Juvenile Delinquency, Committee on the Judiciary, U.S. Senate. (1972-1973). The Juvenile Justice and Delinquency Prevention Act—S. 3148 and S. 821.

Hearings Before the Subcommittee to Investigate Juvenile Delinquency, Committee on the Judiciary, U.S. Senate. (1973). Investigative hearings on the detention and jailing of juveniles.

Henggeler, S. W., & Borduin, C. M. (1990). *Family therapy and beyond: A multisystemic approach to treating the behavior problems of children and adolescents.* Pacific Grove, CA: Brooks/Cole.

Henggeler, S. W., Cunningham, P. B., Pickrel, S. G., Schoenwald, S. K., & Brondino, M. J. (1996). Multisystemic therapy: An effective violence prevention approach for serious juvenile offenders. *Journal of Adolescence, 19,* 47-61.

Henggeler, S. W., Melton, G. B., & Smith, L. A. (1992). Family preservation using multisystem therapy: An effective alternative to incarcerating serious juvenile offenders. *Journal of Consulting and Clinical Psychology, 60,* 953-961.

Henggeler, S. W., Melton, G. B., Smith, L. A., Schoenwald, S. K., & Hanley, J. H. (1993). Family preservation using multisystem treatment: Long-term follow-up to a clinical trial with serious juvenile offenders. *Journal of Child and Family Studies, 2,* 283-293.

Hennepin County Attorney's Office. (1995). *Delinquents under 10 in Hennepin County: A statistical analysis and practices and experiences of police jurisdiction.* Minneapolis, MN: Author.

Heuser, J. P. (1985). *Juveniles arrested for serious felony crimes in Oregon and "remanded" to adult criminal courts: A statistical study.* Salem: Oregon Department of Justice Crime Analysis Center.

Hill, K. G., Hawkins, J. D., Catalano, R. F., Kosterman, R., Abbott, R., & Edwards, T. (1996, November). *The longitudinal dynamics of gang membership and problem behavior: A replication and extension of the Denver and Rochester gang studies in Seattle.* Paper presented at the annual meeting of the American Society of Criminology, Chicago.

Hill, K. G., Hawkins, J. D., Catalano, R. F., Maguin, E., & Kosterman, R. (1995, November). *The role of gang membership in delinquency, substance use, and violent offending.* Paper presented at the annual meeting of the American Society of Criminology, Boston.

Hindelang, M. J., & McDermott, M. J. (1981). *Juvenile criminal behavior: An analysis of rates and victim characteristics.* Washington, DC: U.S. Department of Justice, Office of Juvenile Justice and Delinquency Prevention.

Hirschi, T. (1969). *Causes of delinquency.* Berkeley: University of California Press.

Hofford, M. (Ed.). (1989). *Families in court.* Reno, NV: National Council of Juvenile and Family Court Judges.

Holden, G. A., & Kapler, R. A. (1995). Deinstitutionalizing status offenders: A record of progress. *Juvenile Justice, 2*(Fall/Winter), 3-10.

Holl, J. (1971). *Juvenile reform in the Progressive era.* Ithaca, NY: Cornell University Press.

Holtz, L. E. (1987). *Miranda* in a juvenile setting: A child's right to silence. *The Journal of Criminal Law and Criminology, 78,* 534-556.

Hope, T. (1995). Community crime prevention. In M. Tonry & D. P. Farrington (Eds.), *Building a safer society: Strategic approaches to crime prevention* (Vol. 19, pp. 21-89). Chicago: University of Chicago Press.

Horne, A. M. (1993). Family-based interventions. In A. P. Goldstein & C. R. Huff (Eds.), *The gang intervention handbook* (pp. 189-218). Champaign, IL: Research Press.

Horowitz, R. (1983). *Honor and the American Dream: Culture and identity in a Chicano community.* New Brunswick, NJ: Rutgers University Press.

Horowitz, R., & Schwartz, G. (1974). Honor, normative ambiguity and gang violence. *American Sociological Review, 39,* 238-251.

Houghtalin, M., & Mays, G. L. (1991). Criminal dispositions of New Mexico juveniles transferred to adult court. *Crime & Delinquency, 37,* 393-407.

Howard, B. (1995). A "Cadillac" job-training program delivers for disadvantaged youth. *Youth Today, 1*(January/February), 28-30.

Howell, J. C. (1995a). Gangs and youth violence: Recent research. In J. C. Howell, B. Krisberg, J. D. Hawkins, & J. J. Wilson (Eds.), *Sourcebook on serious, violent and chronic juvenile offenders* (pp. 261-274). Newbury Park, CA: Sage.

Howell, J. C. (Ed.). (1995b). *Guide for implementing the comprehensive strategy for serious, violent, and chronic juvenile offenders.* Washington, DC: U.S. Department of Justice, Office of Juvenile Justice and Delinquency Prevention.

Howell, J. C. (1995c). A national perspective. In B. Glick & A. P. Goldstein (Eds.), *Managing delinquency programs that work* (pp. 11-23). Laurel, MD: American Correctional Association.

Howell, J. C. (1997a). *Youth gang homicides and drug trafficking* (Report prepared for the U.S. Department of Justice, Office of Juvenile Justice and Delinquency Prevention). Tallahassee, FL: National Youth Gang Center.

Howell, J. C. (1997b). *Youth gang violence prevention and intervention: What works* (Report prepared for the U.S. Department of Justice, Office of Juvenile

Justice and Delinquency Prevention). Tallahassee, FL: National Youth Gang Center.

Howell, J. C. (1997c). *Youth gangs in the United States: An overview* (Report prepared for the U.S. Department of Justice, Office of Juvenile Justice and Delinquency Prevention). Tallahassee, FL: National Youth Gang Center.

Howell, J. C., Hill, K. G., Battin, S. R., & Hawkins, J. D. (1996, November). *Youth gang involvement in drug trafficking and violent crime in Seattle*. Paper presented at the annual meeting of the American Society of Criminology, Chicago.

Howell, J. C., Krisberg, B., Hawkins, J. D., & Wilson, J. J. (Eds.). (1995). *Sourcebook on serious, violent, and chronic juvenile offenders*. Thousand Oaks, CA: Sage.

Hruska, R. (1974, July 18). *Congressional Record*, p. S12834.

Huff, C. R. (1993). Gangs in the United States. In A. Goldstein & C. R. Huff (Eds.), *The gang intervention handbook* (pp. 3-20). Champaign, IL: Research Press.

Hughes, S. P., & Schneider, A. L. (1990). *Victim-offender mediation in the juvenile justice system*. Washington, DC: U.S. Department of Justice, Office of Juvenile Justice and Delinquency Prevention.

Huizinga, D. (1979, April). *Dynamic typologies*. Paper presented at the annual meeting of the Classification Society, Gainesville, FL.

Huizinga, D. (1995). Developmental sequences in delinquency. In L. Crockett & N. Crowder (Eds.), *Pathways through adolescence: Individual development in context* (pp. 15-34). New York: Lawrence Erlbaum.

Huizinga, D. (1996). *The influence of delinquent peers, gangs, and co-offending on violence*. Fact sheet prepared for the Office of Juvenile Justice and Delinquency Prevention.

Huizinga, D., Esbensen, F.-A., & Weiher, A. W. (1991). Are there multiple paths to delinquency? *Journal of Criminal Law and Criminology, 82*, 83-118.

Huizinga, D., Esbensen, F.-A., & Weiher, A. W. (1994). Examining developmental trajectories in delinquency using accelerated longitudinal designs. In E. G. M. Weitekamp & H.-J. Kerner (Eds.), *Cross-national longitudinal research on human development and criminal behavior* (pp. 203-216). The Netherlands: Kluwer.

Huizinga, D., Loeber, R., & Thornberry, T. (1994). *Urban delinquency and substance abuse: Initial findings*. Washington, DC: U.S. Department of Justice, Office of Juvenile Justice and Delinquency Prevention.

Huizinga, D., Loeber, R., & Thornberry, T. P. (1995). *Recent findings from the Program of Research on Causes and Correlates of Delinquency* (Report to the Office of Juvenile Justice and Delinquency Prevention). Washington, DC: Office of Juvenile Justice and Delinquency Prevention.

Huizinga, D., Menard, S., & Elliott, D. S. (1989). Delinquency and drug use: Temporal and developmental patterns. *Justice Quarterly, 6*, 419-455.

Hunsaker, A. (1981). The behavioral-ecological model of intervention with Chicano gang delinquents. *Hispanic Journal of Behavioral Sciences, 3*, 225-239.

Hunzeker, D. (1993, May). Ganging up against violence. *State Legislatures*, pp. 28-31.

Hunzeker, D. (1995, May). Juvenile crime, grown up time. *State Legislatures*, pp. 15-19.

Hurst, H. H., III. (1990, Winter). Juvenile probation in retrospect. *Perspectives*, pp. 16-19.

Hurst, H. H., III. (1996, Summer). Juvenile justice and democracy. *Juvenile and Family Justice Today*, p. 23.

Hutson, H. R., Anglin, D., Kyriacou, D. N., Hart, J., & Spears, K. (1995). The epidemic of gang-related homicides in Los Angeles County from 1979 through 1994. *The Journal of the American Medical Association, 274*, 1031-1036.

Hutson, H. R., Anglin, D., & Mallon, W. (1992a). Injuries and deaths from gang violence: They are preventable. *Annals of Emergency Medicine, 21*, 1234-1236.

Hutson, H. R., Anglin, D., & Mallon, W. (1992b). Minimizing gang violence in the emergency department. *Annals of Emergency Medicine, 21*, 1291-1293.

Hutson, H. R., Anglin, D., Mallon, W., & Pratts, M. J. (1994). Caught in the crossfire of gang violence: Small children as innocent victims of drive-by shootings. *Journal of Emergency Medicine, 12*, 385-388.

Hutson, H. R., Anglin, D., & Pratts, M. J. (1994). Adolescents and children injured or killed in drive-by shootings in Los Angeles. *New England Journal of Medicine, 330*, 324-327.

Hutzler, J. (1982). Cannon to the left, canon to the right: Can the juvenile court survive? *Today's Delinquent, 1*, 25-38.

Hyman, A., Schillinger, D., & Lo, B. (1995). Laws mandating reporting of domestic violence. *Journal of the American Medical Association, 273*, 1781-1787.

Hymel, S., Wagner, E., & Butler, L. J. (1990). Reputational bias: View from the peer group. In S. R. Asher & J. D. Coie (Eds.), *Peer rejection in childhood* (pp. 156-188). Cambridge, UK: Cambridge University Press.

Illick, J. E. (1974). Child-rearing in seventeenth century England and America. In L. DeMause (Ed.), *The history of childhood*. New York: Psychohistory.

Institute of Judicial Administration, and the American Bar Association. (1980). *Juvenile justice standards*. Cambridge, MA: Ballinger.

Institute of Medicine. (1994). *Reducing risks for mental disorders: Frontiers for preventive intervention research*. Washington, DC: National Academy Press.

Jackson, P. I. (1991). Crime, youth gangs, and urban transition: The social dislocations of postindustrial economic development. *Justice Quarterly, 8,* 379-397.

Jacob, H. (Ed.). (1974). *The potential for reform of criminals.* Beverly Hills, CA: Sage.

James, H. (1967). *Crisis in the courts.* New York: David McKay.

Janson, C. G. (1977). *The handling of juvenile delinquency cases* (Project Metropolitan Research Report No. 7). Stockholm: Department of Sociology, Stockholm University.

Janson, C. G. (1982). *Delinquency among metropolitan boys* (Project Metropolitan Research Report No. 17). Stockholm: Department of Sociology, Stockholm University.

Jennings, W. S., Kilkenny, R., & Kohlberg, L. (1983). Moral-development theory and practice for youthful and adult offenders. In W. S. Laufer & J. M. Day (Eds.), *Personality theory, moral development, and criminal behavior* (pp. 281-356). Lexington, MA: Lexington Books.

Jensen, E. L, & Metsger, L. K. (1994). A test of the deterrent effect of legislative waiver on violent juvenile crime. *Crime and Delinquency, 40,* 96-104.

Jessor, R. (1987). Problem-behavior theory, psychosocial development, and adolescent problem drinking. *British Journal of Addiction, 82,* 331-342.

Jessor, R., & Jessor, S. L. (1977). *Problem behavior and psychological Development: A longitudinal study of youth.* San Diego, CA: Academic Press.

Johns, C. J. (1992). *Power, ideology, and the war on drugs: Nothing succeeds like failure.* Westport, CT: Praeger.

Johnson, D. L., & Walker, T. (1987). Primary prevention of behavior problems in Mexican-American children. *American Journal of Community Psychology, 15,* 375-385.

Johnson, K. (1996, December 13). Study eases fear of teen crime wave. *USA Today,* p. A1.

Johnson, K., & Fields, G. (1996, December 13). Juvenile crime "wave" may be just a ripple. *USA Today,* p. A4.

Johnston, L. D., O'Malley, P. M., & Bachman, J. G. (1995). *Selected outcome measures from the monitoring the future study* (Special report to the National Education Goals Panel). Ann Arbor, MI: Institute for Social Research, University of Michigan.

Joint Legislative Audit and Review Commission. (1996). *The operation and impact of juvenile corrections services in Virginia.* Richmond: Virginia General Assembly.

Jones, P. R. (1996). Risk prediction in criminal justice. In A. T. Harland (Ed.), *Choosing correctional options that work* (pp. 33-68). Thousand Oaks, CA: Sage.

Jordan, D. C., & Dye, L. (1970). *Delinquency: An assessment of the Juvenile Delinquency Prevention and Control Act of 1968.* Amherst: University of Massachusetts Press.

Justice Education Center. (1996). *Juvenile alternative sanctions plan.* Hartford, CT: Author.

Juvenile Delinquency Commission. (1991). *Juvenile-family crisis intervention moves ahead* (Report of the Juvenile Delinquency Commission Clearinghouse). Trenton, NJ: Author.

Kandel, D. B. (1980). Developmental stages in adolescent drug involvement. In D. J. Lettieri, M. Sayers, & H. W. Pearson (Eds.), *Theories on drug abuse: Selected contemporary perspectives* (Research Monograph 30). Washington, DC: National Institute on Drug Abuse.

Kandel, D. B., & Faust, R. (1975). Sequence and stages in patterns of adolescent drug use. *Archives in General Psychiatry, 32,* 923-932.

Kaplan, S. L., & Busner, J. (1992). A note on racial bias in the admission of children and adolescents to state mental health facilities versus correctional facilities in New York. *American Journal of Psychiatry, 149,* 768-772.

Kazdin, A. E. (1987). *Conduct disorder in childhood and adolescence.* Newbury Park, CA: Sage.

Kazdin, A. E. (1996). Interventions for aggressive and adolescent children. In L. D. Eron, J. H. Gentry, & P. Schlegel (Eds.), *Reason to hope: A psychosocial perspective on violence and youth* (pp. 341-382). Washington, DC: American Psychological Association.

Keenan, K., Loeber, R., Zhang, Q., Stouthamer-Loeber, M., & Van Kammen, W. (1995). The influence of deviant peers on the development of boys' disruptive behavior: A temporal analysis. *Development and Psychopathology, 7,* 715-726.

Keiter, R. B. (1973). Criminal or delinquent: A study of juvenile cases transferred to the criminal court. *Crime and Delinquency, 19,* 528-538.

Keller, O., & Alper, B. (1970). *Halfway houses: Community-centered correction and treatment.* Lexington, MA: D. C. Heath.

Kellerman, A. L., Lee, R. K., Mercy, J. A., & Banton, J. (1991). The epidemiologic basis for the prevention of firearm injuries. *Annual Review of Public Health, 12,* 17-40.

Kellerman, A. L., & Reay, D. T. (1986). Protection or peril?: An analysis of firearm-related deaths in the home. *New England Journal of Medicine, 314,* 1557-1560.

Kelly, D. G., & Balch, R. W. (1971). Social origins and school failure: A re-examination of Cohen's theory of working class delinquency. *Pacific Sociological Review, 14,* 413-430.

Kempf, K. L. (1992). *The role of race in juvenile justice processing in Pennsylvania.* Shippensburg, PA: Center for Juvenile Justice Training and Research, Shippensburg University.

Kempf, K. L., Decker, S., & Bing, R. L. (1990). *An analysis of apparent disparities in the handling of black youth within Missouri's juvenile justice systems.* St. Louis: University of Missouri Press.

Kennedy, D. M., Piehl, A. M., & Braga, A. A. (1996). *Juvenile gun violence in Boston: Gun markets, serious juvenile offenders, and a use reduction strategy.* Unpublished manuscript, John F. Kennedy School of Government, Harvard University.

Ketcham, O. W. (1961). The unfilled promise of the juvenile court. *Crime and Delinquency, 7,* 97-103.

Ketcham, O. W., & Paulsen, M. G. (Eds.). (1967). *Cases and materials relating to juvenile courts.* Brooklyn, NY: The Foundation Press.

Kinder, K., Veneziano, C., Fichter, M., & Azuma, H. (1995). A comparison of the dispositions of juvenile offenders certified as adults with juvenile offenders not certified. *Juvenile and Family Court Journal, 37,* 124-129.

Klein, M. W. (1968). *The Ladino Hills project: Final report.* Los Angeles: University of Southern California, Youth Studies Center.

Klein, M. W. (1971). *Street gangs and street workers.* Englewood Cliffs, NJ: Prentice Hall.

Klein, M. W. (1979). Deinstitutionalization and diversion of juvenile offenders: A litany of impediments. In N. Morris & M. Tonry (Eds.), *Crime and justice: An annual review of research* (Vol. 1, pp. 145-202). Chicago: University of Chicago Press.

Klein, M. W. (1984). Offence specialization and versatility among juveniles. *British Journal of Criminology, 24,* 185-194.

Klein, M. W. (1993). Attempting gang control by suppression: The misuse of deterrence principles. *Studies on Crime and Prevention* (pp. 88-111). Stockholm: Scandinavian University Press.

Klein, M. W. (1995). *The American street gang.* New York: Oxford University Press.

Klein, M. W., & Maxson, C. L. (1989). Street gang violence. In M. E. Wolfgang & N. A. Weiner (Eds.), *Violent crime, violent criminals* (pp. 198-234). Newbury Park, CA: Sage.

Klein, M. W., Maxson, C. L., & Cunningham, L. C. (1988). *Gang involvement in cocaine rock trafficking in Los Angeles.* Los Angeles: Social Science Research Institute, University of California.

Klein, M. W., Maxson, C. L., & Cunningham, L. C. (1991). Crack, street gangs, and violence. *Criminology, 29,* 623-650.

Klepinger, D., & Weis, J. G. (1981). *Projecting arrest trends: An age, period, and cohort model.* Unpublished manuscript, University of Washington, Seattle.

Knitzer, J. (1982). *Unclaimed children: The failure of public responsibility to children and adolescents in need of mental health services.* Washington, DC: The Children's Defense Fund.

Kobetz, R. W. (1971). *The police role and juvenile delinquency.* Gaithersburg, MD: International Association of Chiefs of Police.

Kobrin, S., & Klein, M. W. (1983). *Community treatment of juvenile offenders: The DSO experiments.* Beverly Hills, CA: Sage.

Kodluboy, D. W., & Evenrud, L. A. (1993). School-based interventions: Best practices and critical issues. In A. Goldstein & C. R. Huff (Eds.), *The gang intervention handbook* (pp. 257-299). Champaign, IL: Research Press.

Kohn, G., & Shelly, C. (1991, August). *Juveniles and gangs.* Paper presented at the annual convention of the American Psychological Association.

Kolvin, I., Miller, F. J. W., Fleeting, M., & Kolvin, P. A. (1988). Social and parenting factors affecting criminal-offense rates. *British Journal of Psychiatry, 152,* 80-90.

Kolvin, I., Miller, F. J. W., Scott, D. M., Gatzanis, S. R. M., & Fleeting, M. (1990). *Continuities of deprivation?* Aldershot, UK: Avebury.

Kosterman, R., Hawkins, J. D., Hill, K. G., Abbott, R. D., Catalano, R. F., & Guo, J. (1996, November). *The developmental dynamics of gang initiation: When and why young people join gangs.* Paper presented at the annual meeting of the American Society of Criminology, Chicago.

Krisberg, B. (1981). *National evaluation of prevention: Final report.* San Francisco: National Council on Crime and Delinquency.

Krisberg, B. (1996). The historical legacy of juvenile corrections. In American Correctional Association (Ed.), *Correctional issues: Juvenile justice programs and trends* (pp. 45-50). Upper Marlboro, MD: Graphic Communications.

Krisberg, B., & Austin, J. F. (1993). *Reinventing juvenile justice.* Newbury Park, CA: Sage.

Krisberg, B., Austin, J. F., & Steele, P. A. (1989). *Unlocking juvenile corrections.* San Francisco: National Council on Crime and Delinquency.

Krisberg, B., Currie, E., Onek, D., & Wiebush, R. G. (1995). Graduated sanctions for serious, violent, and chronic juvenile offenders. In J. C. Howell, B. Krisberg, J. D. Hawkins, & J. J. Wilson (Eds.), *Sourcebook on serious, violent, and chronic juvenile offenders* (pp. 142-170). Thousand Oaks, CA: Sage.

Krisberg, B., DeComo, R., Rudenstine, S., & Del Rosario, D. (1996). *Juveniles taken into custody research program: FY 1994 annual report.* Washington, DC: U.S. Department of Justice, Office of Juvenile Justice and Delinquency Prevention.

Krisberg, B., Neuenfeldt, D., Wiebush, R. G., & Rodriguez, O. (1994). *Juvenile intensive supervision: Planning guide.* Washington, DC: U.S. Department of Justice, Office of Juvenile Justice and Delinquency Prevention.

Krisberg, B., Onek, D., Jones, M., & Schwartz, I. (1993). *Juveniles in state custody: Prospects for community-based care of troubled adolescents* (Focus). San Francisco: National Council on Crime and Delinquency.

Kurz, G. A., & Moore, L. E. (1994). *The "8% problem": Chronic juvenile offender recidivism*. Santa Ana, CA: Orange County Probation Department.

Lab, S. P., & Clark, R. D. (1996). *Discipline, control, and school crime: Identifying effective intervention strategies*. Paper prepared for the U.S. Department of Justice, National Institute of Justice.

Lally, J. R., Mangione, P. L., & Honig, A. S. (1988). The Syracuse University Family Development Research Project: Long-range impact of an early intervention with low-income children and their families. In D. R. Powell (Ed.), *Annual advances in applied developmental psychology* (Vol. 3, pp. 79-104). Norwood, NJ: Ablex.

Langan, P. A. (1985). Racism on trial: New evidence to explain the racial composition of prisons in the United States. *Journal of Criminal Law and Criminology, 76*, 666-683.

Langan, P. A. (1991). America's soaring prison population. *Science, 251*, 1568-1573.

Langan, P. A., & Greenfeld, L. A. (1983, June). *Career patterns in crime* (Special Report). Washington, DC: U.S. Department of Justice, Bureau of Justice Statistics.

Langsam, M. (1964). *Children west*. Madison: University of Wisconsin Press.

Lanning, K. (1984, October 1-4). Testimony presented at the National Symposium on Child Molestation. *Proceedings of the National Symposium on Child Molestation*. Washington, DC: U.S. Department of Justice.

Laub, J. H., & Hindelang, M. J. (1981). *Juvenile criminal behavior in urban, suburban, and rural areas* (Monograph Three, Analysis of National Crime Victimization Survey data to study serious delinquent behavior). Washington, DC: U.S. Department of Justice, Office of Juvenile Justice and Delinquency Prevention.

Laub, J. H., & Lauritsen, J. L. (1993). Violent criminal behavior over the life course: A review of the longitudinal and comparative research. *Violence and Victims, 8*, 235-252.

Law Enforcement Assistance Administration. (1971). *Survey of inmates in local jails, 1970*. Washington, DC: U.S. Department of Justice, Law Enforcement Assistance Administration.

Law Enforcement Assistance Administration. (1974). *Survey of inmates in local jails, 1972*. Washington, DC: U.S. Department of Justice, Law Enforcement Assistance Administration.

Lawrence, J. (1996, December 16). Wanted: Good citizens, close communities. *USA Today*, pp. A1-A2.

LeBlanc, M. (1993). Prevention of adolescent delinquency, an integrative multilayered control theory based perspective. In D. P. Farrington, R. J. Sampson, & P-O. H. Wikstrom (Eds.), *Integrating individual and ecological aspects of crime* (pp. 279-322). Stockholm: National Council for Crime Prevention.

LeBlanc, M., & Frechette, M. (1989). *Male criminal activity from childhood through youth*. New York: Springer-Verlag.

LeBlanc, M., & Loeber, R. (1993). Precursors, causes and the development of criminal offending. In D. F. Hay & A. Angold (Eds.), *Precursors and causes in development and psychopathology* (pp. 233-263). New York: John Wiley & Son.

LeBlanc, M., McDuff, P., & Tremblay, R. E. (1994). The emergence of behavior disorders and the consequences for the course of latency. *Canadian Journal of Criminology, 36*, 103-136.

Lee, L. (1994). Factors determining waiver in a juvenile court. *Journal of Criminal Justice, 22*, 329-339.

Leeman, L. W., Gibbs, J. C., & Fuller, D. (in press). Evaluation of a multi-component treatment program for juvenile delinquents. *Aggressive Behavior*.

Leffert, N., & Petersen, A. C. (1995). Patterns of development during adolescence. In M. Rutter & D. Smith (Eds.), *Psychosocial disorders in young people: Time trends and their causes* (pp. 67-103). New York: Wiley.

Lemert, E. M. (1951). *Social pathology*. New York: McGraw-Hill.

Lemert, E. M. (1967). The juvenile court—Quest and realities. In Crime Commission on Law Enforcement and Administration of Justice (Ed.), *Task force report: Juvenile delinquency and youth crime* (pp. 91-106). Washington, DC: Government Printing Office.

Lemmon, J. H., Sontheimer, H., & Saylor, K. (1991). *A study of Pennsylvania juveniles transferred to criminal court*. Harrisburg: The Pennsylvania Juvenile Court Judges' Commission.

Lerman, P. (1970a). *Delinquency and social policy*. New York: Praeger.

Lerman, P. (1970b). Evaluative studies of institutions for delinquents. In P. Lerman (Ed.), *Delinquency and social policy* (pp. 317-328). New York: Praeger.

Lerman, P. (1971). Child convicts. *Trans-Action, 8*, 35-44.

Lerman, P. (1995). Child protection and out-of-home care: System reforms and regulating placements. In G. B. Melton & F. D. Barry (Eds.), *Protecting children from abuse and neglect* (pp. 353-437). New York: Guilford.

Lerman, P., & Pottick, K. J. (1995). *The parents' perspective: Delinquency, aggression, and mental health*. Chur, Switzerland: Harwood Academic.

Lerner, S. (1990). *The good news about juvenile justice*. Bolinas, CA: Common Knowledge Press.

Lesce, T. (1993). Gang resistance education and training (GREAT). *Law and Order, 41*, 47-50.

Lewis, D. O. (1980). Race bias in the diagnosis and disposition of violent adolescents. *American Journal of Psychiatry, 137*, 1211-1216.

Lindsay, B., & McGillis, D. (1986). Citywide community crime prevention: An assessment of the Seattle program. In D. P. Rosenbaum (Ed.), *Commu-

nity crime prevention: Does it work? (pp. 46-67). Beverly Hills, CA: Sage.

Linebaugh, P. (1984). Testimony. Child molestation: The public's concern. In U.S. Department of Justice, *National symposium on child molestation*. Washington, DC: U.S. Department of Justice.

Lipsey, M. W. (1984). Is delinquency prevention a cost-effective strategy? A California perspective. *Journal of Research in Crime and Delinquency, 21*, 279-302.

Lipsey, M. W. (1992a). Juvenile delinquency treatment: A meta-analytic inquiry into the variability of effects. In T. D. Cook, H. Cooper, D. S. Cordray, H. Hartman, L. V. Hedges, R. J. Knight, T. A. Louis, & F. Mosteller (Eds.), *Meta-analysis for explanation* (pp. 83-127). New York: Russell Sage Foundation.

Lipsey, M. W. (1992b, September). *What do we learn from 400 research studies on the effectiveness of treatment with juvenile delinquents?* Paper presented at the "What Works" Conference, University of Salford, UK.

Lipsey, M. W., & Derzon, J. H. (in press). *Predictors of serious delinquency in adolescence and early adulthood*. In R. Loeber & D. P. Farrington (Eds.) *Serious and violent juvenile offenders: Risk factors & successful interventions*. Thousand Oaks, CA: Sage.

Lipton, D., Martinson, R., & Wilks, J. (1975). *The effectiveness of correctional treatment: A survey of treatment evaluation studies*. New York: Praeger.

Lizotte, A. J., Tesoriero, J. M., Thornberry, T. P., & Krohn, M. D. (1994). Patterns of adolescent firearms ownership and use. *Justice Quarterly, 11*, 51-73.

Lockhart, L. L., Kurtz, P. D., & Sutphen, R. (1991). *Georgia's juvenile justice system: A retrospective investigation of racial disparity*. Athens: University of Georgia, School of Social Work.

Loeber, R. (1982). The stability of antisocial and delinquent child behavior: A review. *Child Development, 53*, 1431-1446.

Loeber, R. (1988). Natural histories of juvenile conduct problems, delinquency, and associated substance use: Evidence for developmental progressions. In B. B. Lahey & A. E. Kazdin (Eds.), *Advances in clinical child psychology* (Vol. 11, pp. 73-124). New York: Plenum.

Loeber, R. (1990). Development and risk factors of juvenile antisocial behavior and delinquency. *Clinical Psychology Review, 10*, 1-41.

Loeber, R. (1996). Developmental continuity, change, and pathways in male juvenile problem behaviors and delinquency. In J. D. Hawkins (Ed.), *Delinquency and crime: Current theories* (pp. 1-27). New York: Cambridge University Press.

Loeber, R., & Dishion, T. (1983). Early predictors of male delinquency: A review. *Psychological Bulletin, 94*, 68-99.

Loeber, R., Farrington, D. P., Stouthamer-Loeber, M., & Van Kammen, W. B. (1994). *Delinquency, sub-*

stance use, and mental health problems during childhood and adolescence. Unpublished manuscript, University of Pittsburgh.

Loeber, R., Green, S. M., Keenan, K., & Lahey, B. B. (1995). Which boys will fare worse? Early predictors of the onset of conduct disorder in a six-year longitudinal study. *Journal of the American Academy of Child and Adolescent Psychiatry, 34*, 499-509.

Loeber, R., & Hay, D. F. (1994). Developmental approaches to aggression and conduct problems. In M. Rutter & D. F. Hay (Eds.), *Development through life: A handbook for clinicians* (pp. 488-516). Oxford, UK: Blackwell Scientific.

Loeber, R., Keenan, K., & Zhang, Q. (in press). Boys' experimentation and persistence in developmental pathways toward serious delinquency. *Journal of Child and Family Studies*.

Loeber, R., & LeBlanc, M. (1990). Toward a developmental criminology. In M. Tonry & N. Morris (Eds.), *Crime and justice: An annual review of research* (Vol. 12, pp. 375-473). Chicago: University of Chicago Press.

Loeber, R., & Stouthamer-Loeber, M. (1986). Family factors as correlates and predictors of juvenile conduct problems and delinquency. In M. Tonry & N. Morris (Eds.), *Crime and justice: An annual review of research* (Vol. 7, pp. 29-149). Chicago: University of Chicago Press.

Loeber, R., & Stouthamer-Loeber, M. (1987). Prediction. In H. C. Quay (Ed.), *Handbook of juvenile delinquency* (pp. 325-382). New York: Wiley.

Loeber, R., Stouthamer-Loeber, M., Van Kammen, W. B., & Farrington, D. P. (1991). Initiation, escalation and desistance in juvenile offending and their correlates. *Journal of Criminal Law and Criminology, 82*, 36-82.

Loeber, R., & Wikstrom, P.-O. H. (1993). Individual pathways to crime in different types of neighborhood. In D. P. Farrington, R. J. Sampson, & P.-O. H. Wikstrom (Eds.), *Integrating individual and ecological aspects of crime* (pp. 169-204). Stockholm: National Council for Crime Prevention.

Loeber, R., Wung, P., Keenan, K., Giroux, B., Stouthamer-Loeber, M., Van Kammen, W. B., & Maughan, B. (1993). Developmental pathways in disruptive child behavior. *Development and Psychopathology, 5*, 103-133.

Loftin, C. (1986). Assaultive violence as a contagious social process. *Bulletin of the New York Academy of Medicine, 62*, 550-555.

Loughran, E. J. (Ed.). (1986). *Reinvesting youth corrections resources: A tale of three states*. Minneapolis: Center for the Study of Youth Policy, Hubert H. Humphrey Institute of Public Affairs, University of Minnesota.

Loughran, E. J., & Guarino-Ghezzi, S. (1995). A state perspective. In B. Glick & A. P. Goldstein (Eds.), *Managing delinquency programs that work* (pp.

25-51). Laurel, MD: American Correctional Association.

Lusane, C., & Desmond, D. (1991). *Pipe dream blues: Racism and the war on drugs*. Boston: South End Press.

Maguin, E., & Loeber, R. (1996). Academic performance and delinquency. *Crime and Justice, 20*, 145-264.

Maguire, K., & Pastore, A. L. (Eds.). (1995). *Bureau of Justice Statistics sourcebook of criminal justice statistics—1994*. Washington, DC: U.S. Department of Justice, Bureau of Justice Statistics.

Maloney, D., Romig, D., & Armstrong, T. (1988). Juvenile probation: The balanced approach. *Juvenile and Family Court Journal, 39*, 1-63.

Mann, C. R. (1993). *Unequal justice: A question of color*. Bloomington: Indiana University Press.

Martinson, R. (1974). What works? Questions and answers about prison reform. *Public Interest, 35*, 22-54.

Massachusetts Governor's Juvenile Justice Advisory Committee. (1981). *The violent juvenile offender in Massachusetts: A policy analysis*. Boston: Massachusetts Committee on Criminal Justice.

Mattick, H. (1974). The contemporary jails of the United States: An unknown and neglected area of justice. In D. Glaser (Ed.), *Handbook of criminology* (pp. 777-848). Chicago: Rand McNally.

Mattick, H., & Sweet, R. (1969). *Illinois jails, challenge and opportunity for the 70s*. Chicago: University of Chicago Law School.

Mauer, M. (1990). *Young black men and the criminal justice system: A growing national problem*. Washington, DC: Sentencing Project.

Maxson, C. L. (1995, September). *Street gangs and drug sales in two suburban cities* (Research in Brief). Washington, DC: U.S. Department of Justice, National Institute of Justice.

Maxson, C. L., Gordon, M. A., & Klein, M. W. (1985). Differences between gang and nongang homicides. *Criminology, 23*, 209-222.

Maxson, C. L., & Klein, M. W. (1990). Street gang violence: Twice as great, or half as great? In C. R. Huff (Ed.), *Gangs in America* (pp. 71-100). Newbury Park, CA: Sage.

Maxson, C. L., Woods, K., & Klein, M. W. (1995). *Street gang migration in the United States*. Report to the U.S. Department of Justice, National Institute of Justice.

McCart, L. (Ed.). (1994). *Kids and violence*. Washington, DC: National Governors' Association.

McCord, J. (1979). Some child-rearing antecedents of criminal behavior in adult men. *Journal of Personality and Social Psychology, 37*, 1477-1486.

McCord, J. (1980). Patterns of deviance. In S. B. Sells, R. Crandall, M. Roff, J. S. Strauss, & W. Pollin (Eds.), *Human functioning in longitudinal perspective* (pp. 157-167). Baltimore: Williams and Wilkins.

McCord, J. (1982). A longitudinal view of the relationship between paternal absence and crime. In J. Gunn & D. P. Farrington (Eds.), *Abnormal offenders, delinquency, and the criminal justice system* (pp. 113-128). Chichester, UK: Wiley.

McCorkle, L. (1952). Group therapy in the treatment of offenders. *Federal Probation, 16*, 28-32.

McDermott, M. J., & Hindelang, M. J. (1981). *Juvenile criminal behavior in the United States: Its trends and patterns*. Washington, DC: U.S. Department of Justice, Office of Juvenile Justice and Delinquency Prevention.

McDowall, D., & Loftin, C. (1983). Collective security and the demand for legal handguns. *American Journal of Sociology, 88*, 1146-1161.

McEwen, C. A. (1978). *Designing correctional organizations for youths: Dilemmas of subcultural development*. Cambridge, MA: Ballinger.

McKelvey, B. (1968). *American prisons*. Montclair, NJ: Patterson-Smith.

McKinney, K. C. (1988, September). *Juvenile gangs: Crime and drug trafficking* (Juvenile Justice Bulletin). Washington, DC: U.S. Department of Justice, Office of Juvenile Justice and Delinquency Prevention.

McManus, M. (1984). Psychiatric disturbance in serious delinquents. *Journal of the American Academy of Child Psychiatry, 23*, 602-615.

McNulty, E. W. (1995, November). *The transfer of juvenile offenders to adult court: Panacea or problem?* Paper presented at the annual meeting of the American Society of Criminology, Boston.

Meddis, S. V. (1993a, July 23). Is the drug war racist? *USA Today*, p. A1.

Meddis, S. V. (1993b, October 29). Poll: Treat juveniles the same as adult offenders. *USA Today*, pp. A1, A11.

Meehan, P. J., & O'Carroll, P. W. (1992). Gangs, drugs, and homicide in Los Angeles. *American Journal of the Disabled Child, 146*, 683-687.

Menard, S. (1987). Short-term trends in crime and delinquency: A comparison of UCR, NCS, and self-report data. *Justice Quarterly, 4*, 455-474.

Mennel, R. (1973). *Thorns and thistles: Juvenile delinquents in the United States, 1825-1940*. Hanover, NH: University Press of New England.

Mercy, J. A., & O'Carroll, P. W. (1988). New directions in violence prediction: The public health arena. *Violence and Victims, 3*, 285-301.

Merola, M. (1975). The major offense bureau: A blueprint for effective prosecution of career criminals. *Prosecutor, 11*, 8-15.

Michaels, D., & Levine, C. (1992). Estimates of the number of motherless youth orphaned by AIDS in the United States. *Journal of the American Medical Association, 268*, 3456-3461.

Milakovich, M. E., & Weis, K. (1975). Politics and measures of success in the war on crime. *Crime and Delinquency, 21*, 10-20.

Miller, A., & Ohlin, L. (1985). *Delinquency and Community*. Beverly Hills, CA: Sage.

Miller, A., Ohlin, L., & Coates, R. (1977a). The aftermath of extreme tactics in juvenile justice reform: A crisis four years later. In D. Greenberg (Ed.), *Corrections and punishment* (pp. 227-246). Beverly Hills, CA: Sage.

Miller, A., Ohlin, L., & Coates, R. (1977b). *A theory of social reform: Correctional changes processes in two states*. Cambridge, MA: Ballinger.

Miller, J. (1973). The politics of change: Correctional reform. In Y. Bakal (Ed.), *Closing correctional institutions* (pp. 3-8). Lexington, MA: D. C. Heath.

Miller, T. R., Cohen, M. A., & Wiersema, B. (1996). *Victim costs and consequences: A new look*. Washington, DC: U.S. Department of Justice, National Institute of Justice.

Miller, W. B. (1958). Lower class culture as a generating milieu of gang delinquency. *Journal of Social Issues, 14*, 5-19.

Miller, W. B. (1966). Violent crimes in city gangs. *Annals of the American Academy of Political and Social Science, 364*, 96-112.

Miller, W. B. (1974). American youth gangs: Past and present. In A. Blumberg (Ed.), *Current perspectives on criminal behavior* (pp. 410-420). New York: Knopf.

Miller, W. B. (1980). Gangs, groups, and serious youth crime. In D. Shicker & D. H. Kelly (Eds.), *Critical issues in juvenile delinquency* (pp. 186-197). Lexington, MA: Lexington Books.

Miller, W. B. (1982). *Crime by youth gangs and groups in the United States*. Washington, DC: U.S. Department of Justice, Office of Juvenile Justice and Delinquency Prevention.

Miller, W. B. (1985). Historical review of programs and theories of work with youth gangs. In D. Ingemunsen & G. Johnson (Eds.), *Report on the Illinois Symposium on Gangs* (pp. 1-22). Springfield: Illinois Department of Children and Family Services.

Miller, W. B. (1990). Why the United States has failed to solve its youth gang problem. In C. R. Huff (Ed.), *Gangs in America* (pp. 263-287). Newbury Park, CA: Sage.

Miller, W. B. (1993). *Critique of "Weed and Seed" project with a proposal for a new prevention initiative*. (Report to the Office of Juvenile Justice and Delinquency Prevention). Washington, DC: Office of Juvenile Justice and Delinquency Prevention.

Miller, W. B. (1994). *Boston assaultive crime*. (Memorandum available from James C. Howell, 2795 Mansway Drive, Herndon, VA 22071)

Moffitt, T. E. (1990a). Juvenile delinquency and attention deficit disorder: Boys' developmental trajectories from age 3 to age 15. *Child Development, 61*, 893-910.

Moffitt, T. E. (1990b). The neuropsychology of juvenile delinquency: A critical review. In M. Tonry & N. Morris (Eds.), *Crime and justice: An annual review of research* (Vol. 12, pp. 99-169). Chicago: University of Chicago Press.

Moffitt, T. E. (1991, September). *Juvenile delinquency: Seed of a career in violent crime, just sowing wild oats—or both?* Paper presented at the Science and Public Policy Seminars of the Federation of Behavioral, Psychological, and Cognitive Sciences, Washington, DC.

Moffitt, T. E. (1993). Adolescence-limited and life-course-persistent antisocial behaviour: A developmental taxonomy. *Psychological Review, 100*, 674-701.

Moffitt, T. E., Mednick, S. A., & Gabrielli, W. F., Jr. (1989). Predicting careers of criminal violence: Descriptive data and predispositional factors. In D. A. Brizer & M. L. Crowner (Eds.), *Current approaches to the prediction of violence* (pp. 13-34). Washington, DC: American Psychiatric Press.

Moffitt, T. E., & Silva, P. A. (1988a). IQ and delinquency: A direct test of the differential detection hypothesis. *Journal of Abnormal Psychology, 97*, 330-333.

Moffitt, T. E., & Silva, P. A. (1988b). Self-reported delinquency: Results from an instrument for New Zealand. *Australian and New Zealand Journal of Criminology, 21*, 227-240.

Montgomery, I. M., Torbet, P. M., Malloy, D. A., Adamcik, L. P., Toner, M. J., & Andrews, J. (1994). *What works: Promising interventions in juvenile justice*. Washington, DC: U.S. Department of Justice, Office of Juvenile Justice and Delinquency Prevention.

Mooar, B., & Perez-Rivas, M. (1996, July 4). Drug policy ignites debate in Montgomery. *The Washington Post*, pp. A1, A13.

Moone, J. (1994). *Juvenile victimization: 1987-1992* (Fact Sheet #17). Washington, DC: Office of Juvenile Justice and Delinquency Prevention.

Moore, J. W. (1978). *Homeboys*. Philadelphia: Temple University Press.

Moore, J. W. (1985). Isolation and stigmatization in the development of an underclass: The case of Chicano gangs in East Los Angeles. *Social Problems, 33*, 1-13.

Moore, J. W. (1988). Introduction: Gangs and the underclass: A comparative perspective. In J. M. Hagedorn, *People and folks: Gangs, crime and the underclass in a rustbelt city* (pp. 3-17). Chicago: Lakeview Press.

Moore, J. W. (1990). Gangs, drugs, and violence. In M. De La Rosa, E. Y. Lambert, & B. Gropper (Eds.), *Drugs and violence: Causes, correlates, and consequences* (Research Monograph No. 103, pp. 160-176). Rockville, MD: National Institute for Drug Abuse.

Moore, J. W. (1991). *Going down to the barrio: Homeboys and homegirls in change*. Philadelphia: Temple University Press.

Moore, J. W., Garcia, R., Cerda, L., & Valencia, F. (1978). *Homeboys: Gangs, drugs and prison in the barrios of Los Angeles.* Philadelphia: Temple University Press.

Moos, R. H. (1975). *Evaluating correctional and community settings.* New York: John Wiley.

Morales, A. (1992). A clinical model for the prevention of gang violence and homicide. In R. C. Cervantes (Ed.), *Substance abuse and gang violence* (pp. 105-118). Newbury Park, CA: Sage.

Morash, M. (1983). Gangs, groups, and delinquency. *British Journal of Criminology, 23,* 309-331.

Moreland, D. W. (1941). History and prophecy: John Augustus and his successors. *National Probation Association Yearbook: 1941.* Washington, DC: National Probation Association.

Mulvihill, D. J., & Tumin, M. M. (1969). *Crimes of violence* (Staff report submitted to the National Commission on the Causes and Prevention of Violence, Vol. 11). Washington, DC: Government Printing Office.

Murphy, P. (1972). Social change and the police. *Police, 16,* 63-66.

Murray, C. A. (1977). *The link between learning disabilities and juvenile delinquency: Current theory and knowledge.* Washington, DC: Government Printing Office.

Murray, C. A. (1984). *Losing ground: American social policy.* New York: Basic Books.

Nagin, D. S., & Farrington, D. P. (1992a). The onset and persistence of offending. *Criminology, 30,* 501-523.

Nagin, D. S., & Farrington, D. P. (1992b). The stability of criminal potential from childhood to adulthood. *Criminology, 30,* 235-260.

Nagin, D. S., Farrington, D. P., & Moffitt, T. E. (1995). Life-course trajectories of different types of offenders. *Criminology, 33,* 111-139.

Nagin, D. S., & Land, K. C. (1993). Age, criminal careers, and population heterogeneity: Specification and estimation of a nonparametric, mixed Poisson model. *Criminology, 31,* 327-362.

Nagin, D. S., & Paternoster, R. (1991). On the relationship of past to future delinquency. *Criminology, 29,* 163-189.

Natalucci-Persichetti, G. (1996). Youth violence: A learned behavior? In American Correctional Association (Ed.), *Correctional issues: Juvenile justice programs and trends* (pp. 51-62). Upper Marlboro, MD: Graphic Communications.

National Advisory Commission on Criminal Justice Standards and Goals. (1973). *A national strategy to reduce crime* (with companion volumes, *Criminal Justice System, Police, Courts, Corrections,* and *Community Crime Prevention*). Washington, DC: Government Printing Office.

National Advisory Commission on Criminal Justice Standards and Goals. (1973). *Task force report on corrections.* (Standard 22.3). Washington, DC: Government Printing Office.

National Advisory Committee. (1980). *Standards for the administration of juvenile justice and delinquency prevention.* Washington, DC: Government Printing Office.

National Center for Education Statistics. (1995). *Gangs and victimization at school. Education policy issues: Statistical perspective.* Washington, DC: U.S. Department of Education.

National Center for Health Statistics. (1994). *Monthly vital statistics report, 43*(Suppl. 6). Hyattsville, MD: Public Health Service.

National Center for Juvenile Justice. (1991). *Desktop guide to good juvenile probation practice.* Washington, DC: U.S. Department of Justice, Office of Juvenile Justice and Delinquency Prevention.

National Center for Child Abuse and Neglect. (1995). *Child maltreatment 1993: Reports from the states to the National Center on Child Abuse and Neglect.* Washington, DC: U.S. Department of Health and Human Services.

National Center on Child Abuse and Neglect. (1996a). *Child maltreatment 1994: Reports from the states to the National Center on Child Abuse and Neglect.* Washington, DC: U.S. Department of Health and Human Services.

National Center on Child Abuse and Neglect. (1996b). *National incidence studies 1993.* Washington, DC: U.S. Department of Health and Human Services.

National Coalition for Jail Reform. (1980). *Proceedings of the National Symposium on Children in Jail.* Washington, DC: National Coalition for Jail Reform.

National Coalition of State Juvenile Justice Advisory Groups. (1993). *Myths and realities: Meeting the challenge of serious, violent and chronic juvenile offenders—1992 annual report.* Washington, DC: Author.

National Commission on Children. (1991). *Beyond rhetoric: A new American agenda for children and families.* Washington, DC: Author.

National Conference of State Legislatures. (1996). *A legislator's guide to comprehensive juvenile justice.* Denver, CO: Author.

National Council of Juvenile and Family Court Judges. (1984). *The juvenile court and serious offenders: 38 recommendations.* Reno, NV: Author.

National Council of Juvenile and Family Court Judges. (1993). *Children and families first: A mandate for change.* Reno, NV: Author.

National Council on Crime and Delinquency. (1961). *Standards and guides for the detention of children.* New York: Author.

National Council on Crime and Delinquency. (1967). Correction in the United States: Data summary. In the Crime Commission on Law Enforcement and Administration of Justice, *Task force report: Corrections* (pp. 115-213). Washington, DC: Government Printing Office.

National Council on Crime and Delinquency. (1993). *Reducing crime in America: A pragmatic approach.* San Francisco: Author.

National Drug Intelligence Center. (1995). *NDIC street gang symposium. Johnstown, Pennsylvania, November 2-3*. Washington, DC: Author.

National Governors' Association. (1991). *Kids in trouble: Coordinating social and correctional service systems for youth*. Washington, DC: Author.

National Institute of Justice. (1995, December). *Youth violence, guns, and illicit drug markets* (Research in Brief). Washington, DC: U.S. Department of Justice, National Institute of Justice.

National Institute on Drug Abuse. (1991). *The adolescent assessment/referral system manual*. Rockville, MD: U.S. Department of Health and Human Services, Alcohol, Drug Abuse, and Mental Health Administration.

National Research Council. (1978). *Panel on research on deterrent and incapacitative effects*. Washington, DC: National Academy of Sciences.

National Research Council. (1993). *Losing generations: Adolescents in high risk settings*. Washington, DC: National Academy Press.

National Sheriff's Association (1974). *Jail security, classification, and discipline*. Washington, DC: Author.

National Youth Gang Center. (in press). *1995 Youth Gang Survey*. Washington, DC: U.S. Department of Justice, Office of Juvenile Justice and Delinquency Prevention.

Nelson, C. M., Rutherford, R. B., & Wolford, B. I. (1996). *Comprehensive and collaborative systems that work for troubled youth: A national agenda*. Richmond: Eastern Kentucky University Press.

New York City Youth Board. (1960). *Reaching the fighting gang*. New York: City of New York.

Newman, O. (1973). *Defensible space*. London: Architectural Press.

Newton, G. D., & Zimring, F. E. (1969). *Firearms and violence in American life: A staff report to the National Commission on the Causes and Prevention of Violence*. Washington, DC: Government Printing Office.

Nimick, E. H., Szymanski, L., & Snyder, H. N. (1986). *Juvenile court waiver: A study of juvenile court cases transferred to criminal court*. Pittsburgh: National Center for Juvenile Justice.

O'Donnell, J., Hawkins, J. D., Catalano, R. F., Abbott, R. D., & Day, L. E. (1995). Preventing school failure, drug use, and delinquency among low-income children: Effects of a long-term prevention project in elementary schools. *American Journal of Orthopsychiatry, 65*, 87-100.

Office of Justice Programs, Working Group on Gangs. (1996). *A report to the Assistant Attorney General, Office of Justice Programs, U.S. Department of Justice*.

Office of Juvenile Justice and Delinquency Prevention. (1989). *Preliminary estimates developed on stranger abduction homicides of children* (Juvenile Justice Bulletin). Washington, DC: U.S. Department of Justice, Office of Juvenile Justice and Delinquency Prevention.

Office of Juvenile Justice and Delinquency Prevention. (1994). Disproportionate minority representation. *Juvenile Justice, 2*, 21-23.

Office of Juvenile Justice and Delinquency Prevention. (1995a). *Delinquency prevention works*. Washington, DC: U.S. Department of Justice, Office of Juvenile Justice and Delinquency Prevention.

Office of Juvenile Justice and Delinquency Prevention. (1995b). *Matrix of community-based initiatives*. Washington, DC: Office of Juvenile Justice and Delinquency Prevention.

Office of Juvenile Justice and Delinquency Prevention. (1995c). Meeting the mandates. *Juvenile Justice, 2*, 25-28.

Office of Juvenile Justice and Delinquency Prevention. (1995d). 1993 monitoring compliance report summary (Unpublished report prepared by the OJJDP State Relations and Assistance Division). Washington, DC: Author.

Office of Juvenile Justice and Delinquency Prevention. (1995e). *Reducing youth gun violence: A summary of programs and initiatives*. Washington, DC: Author.

Office of Juvenile Justice and Delinquency Prevention. (1995f). *Title V incentive grants for local delinquency prevention programs—1995 report to Congress*. Washington, DC: Author.

Office of Juvenile Justice and Delinquency Prevention. (1996). *Title V incentive grants for local delinquency prevention programs—1996 report to Congress*. Washington, DC: Author.

Office of Technology Assessment. (1991). *Adolescent health. Vol. II: Background and the Effectiveness of Selected Prevention and Treatment Services*. Washington, DC: Government Printing Office.

Ohio Department of Youth Services. (1993). *Juveniles transferred to adult court in Ohio: Fiscal year 1992*. Columbus: Ohio Department of Youth Services.

Ohlin, L., Coates, R., & Miller, A. (1978). *Reforming juvenile corrections: The Massachusetts experience*. Cambridge, MA: Ballinger.

Olds, D. L., Henderson, C. R., Tatelbaum, R., & Chamberlin, R. (1988). Improving the life-course development of socially disadvantaged mothers: A randomized trial of nurse home visitation. *American Journal of Public Health, 78*, 1436-1445.

Olweus, D. (1978). *Aggression in the schools*. Washington, DC: Hemisphere.

Olweus, D. (1979). Stability of aggressive reaction patterns in males: A review. *Psychological Bulletin, 86*, 852-857.

Olweus, D. (1980). Familial and temperamental determinants of aggressive behavior in adolescent boys: A causal analysis. *Developmental Psychology, 16*, 644-660.

Olweus, D. (1992). Bullying among school children: Intervention and prevention. In R. D. Peters, R. J.

McMahon, & V. L. Qinsey (Eds.), *Aggression and violence throughout the life span* (pp. 100-125). Newbury Park, CA: Sage.

Olweus, D. (1994). Bullying at school: Basic facts and defects of a school based intervention programme. *Journal of Child Psychology and Psychiatry, 35,* 1171-1190.

Orange County Probation Department. (1995). *8% Early Intervention Program: Program design and preliminary field test results.* Santa Ana, CA: Author.

Orange County Probation Department. (1996). *8% Early Intervention Program field test results (12 months).* Santa Ana, CA: Author.

Osbun, L. A., & Rode, P. A. (1984) Prosecution of juveniles as adults: The quest for "objective" decisions. *Criminology, 22,* 187-202.

Osgood, D. W. (1983). Offense history and juvenile diversion. *Evaluation Review, 7,* 793-806.

Osgood, D. W. (1989). Time trends and age trends in arrests and self-reported illegal behavior. *Criminology, 27,* 389-415.

Osgood, D. W., Gruber, E., Archer, M. A., & Newcomb, T. M. (1985). Autonomy for inmates: Counterculture or cooptation? *Criminal Justice and Behavior, 12,* 71-89.

Osofsky, J. D., & Fenichel, E. (Eds.). (1994). *Caring for infants and toddlers in violent environments.* Arlington, VA: Zero to Three/National Center for Clinical Infant Programs.

Padilla, F. M. (1992). *The gang as an American enterprise: Puerto Rican youth and the American dream.* New Brunswick, NJ: Rutgers University Press.

Palmer, T. (1978). *Correctional intervention and research: Current issues and future prospects.* Lexington, MA: Lexington Books.

Pappenfort, D. M., & Kilpatrick, D. M. (1970). *A census of children's residential institutions in the United States, Puerto Rico, and the Virgin Islands: 1966: Vol. 7. Detention facilities.* Chicago: University of Chicago Press.

Parent, D., Leiter, V., Livens, L., Wentworth, D., & Stephen, K. (1994). *Conditions of confinement: Juvenile detention and corrections facilities.* Washington, DC: U.S. Department of Justice, Office of Juvenile Justice and Delinquency Prevention.

Patterson, G. R. (1982). *Coercive family process.* Eugene, OR: Castalia.

Patterson, G. R., & Dishon, T. J. (1988). Multilevel family process models: Traits, interactions and relationships. In R. Hinde & J. Stevenson-Hinde (Eds.), *Relationships within families: Mutual influences* (pp. 283-310). Oxford, UK: Clarendon.

Patterson, G. R., Reid, J. B., & Dishon, T. J. (1990). *Antisocial boys.* Eugene, OR: Castalia.

Peeples, F., & Loeber, R. (1994). Do individual factors and neighborhood context explain ethnic differences in juvenile delinquency? *Journal of Quantitative Criminology, 10,* 141-157.

Pennell, S., Evans, E., Melton, R., & Hinson, S. (1994). *Down for the set: Describing and defining gangs in San Diego.* San Diego, CA: Criminal Justice Research Division, Association of Governments.

Pennsylvania Joint Council on the Criminal Justice System. (1978). *The transfer of juveniles to the adult court in Pennsylvania.* Harrisburg, PA: Author.

Pepler, D. J., & Slaby, R. G. (1994). Theoretical and developmental perspectives on youth and violence. In L. D. Eron, J. H. Gentry, & P. Schlegel (Eds.), *Reason to hope: A psychosocial perspective on violence and youth* (pp. 27-58). Washington, DC: American Psychological Association.

Perales, D. P. (1989). *Patterns of homicide: Houston, Texas, 1987.* Unpublished doctoral dissertation, University of Texas School of Public Health.

Perez, J. (1991). *Tracking offenders, 1988* (Bureau of Justice Statistics Bulletin). Washington, DC: U.S. Department of Justice, Bureau of Justice Statistics.

Perkins, C. (1992). *National corrections reporting program, 1989.* Washington, DC: U.S. Department of Justice, Bureau of Justice Statistics.

Perkins, C. (1993). *National corrections reporting program, 1990.* Washington, DC: U.S. Department of Justice, Bureau of Justice Statistics.

Perkins, C. (1994). *National corrections reporting program, 1992.* Washington, DC: U.S. Department of Justice, Bureau of Justice Statistics.

Perkins, C., & Gilliard, D. K. (1992). *National corrections reporting program, 1988.* Washington, DC: U.S. Department of Justice, Bureau of Justice Statistics.

Perkins, C., & Klaus, P. (1996, April). *Criminal victimization 1994* (Bureau of Justice Statistics Bulletin). Washington, DC: U.S. Department of Justice, Bureau of Justice Statistics.

Petersen, A. C., & Chalk, R. (Eds.). (1993). *Understanding child abuse and neglect.* Washington, DC: National Academy Press.

Philibosian, R. H. (1989). *Report of the state task force on gangs and drugs* (Report to the California Department of Justice). Sacramento: California Department of Criminal Justice.

Phillips, M. R. (1994). *Some observations regarding the certification and direct filing of juveniles to be tried in Utah's adult court system.* Unpublished manuscript, Utah State Juvenile Court, Salt Lake City.

Pickett, R. (1969). *House of refuge: Origins of juvenile reform in New York State, 1815-1857.* Syracuse, NY: Syracuse University Press.

Pindur, W., & Wells, D. K. (1986). *Final report: The serious habitual offender/drug involved program.* Report to the U.S. Department of Justice, Office of Juvenile Justice and Delinquency Prevention.

Platt, A. M. (1969). *The child savers.* Chicago: University of Chicago Press.

Platt, A. M. (1970). Saving and controlling delinquent youth: A critique. *Issues in Criminology, 5,* 1-24.

Platt, A. M. (1977). *The child savers: The invention of delinquency* (Rev. ed.). Chicago: University of Chicago Press.

Podkopacz, M. R., & Feld, B. C. (1995). Judicial waiver policy and practice: Persistence, seriousness, and race. *Law and Inequality, 14,* 101-207.

Podkopacz, M. R., & Feld, B. C. (1996). The end of the line: An empirical study of judicial waiver. *The Journal of Criminal Law and Criminology, 86,* 449-492.

Polier, J. W. (1973). *Prepared statement of Hon. Justine Wise Polier.* Hearings before the Subcommittee to Investigate Juvenile Delinquency, Committee on the Judiciary, U.S. Senate, pp. 495-499.

Polk, K. (1975). Schools and the delinquency experience. *Criminal Justice and Behavior, 2,* 315-338.

Polk, K., & Halferty, D. S. (1966). Adolescence, commitment and delinquency. *Journal of Research in Crime and Delinquency, 3,* 82-96.

Pope, C. E., & Feyerherm, W. (1990). Minority status and juvenile justice processing. *Criminal Justice Abstracts, 22,* 327-336 and 527-542.

Pope, C. E., & Feyerherm, W. (1993). *Minorities and the juvenile justice system.* Washington, DC: U.S. Department of Justice, Office of Juvenile Justice and Delinquency Prevention.

Potok, M., & Sanchez, S. (1995, October 27). States toughen penalties for young, violent offenders. *USA Today,* p. A2.

Poulos, T. M., & Orchowsky, S. (1994). Serious juvenile offenders: Predicting the probability of transfer to criminal court. *Crime and Delinquency, 40,* 3-17.

Pratt, G. (1994, December). *Community based comprehensive wrap-around treatment strategies.* Paper presented at the Juvenile Justice Research Symposium, Phoenix, AZ.

President's Commission on Law Enforcement and Administration of Justice. (1967a). *The challenge of crime in a free society.* Washington, DC: Government Printing Office.

President's Commission on Law Enforcement and Administration of Justice. (1967b). *Task force report: Juvenile delinquency and youth crime.* Washington, DC: Government Printing Office.

Proceedings of the White House Conference on Children and Youth. (1960). Washington, DC: Government Printing Office.

Pynoos, R. S., & Nader, K. (1988). Psychological first aid and treatment approach to children exposed to community violence: Research implications. *Journal of Traumatic Stress, 1,* 445-473.

Quie, R. (1974, August 21). *Congressional Record,* pp. H8794-8795.

Raley, G. A. (1995). The JJDP Act: A second look. *Juvenile Justice, 2,* 11-18.

Rausch, S. (1983). Court processing versus diversion of status offenders: A test of deterrence and labeling theories. *Journal of Research in Crime and Delinquency, 20,* 39-54.

Regnery, A. S. (1985). Getting away with murder: Why the juvenile justice system needs an overhaul. *Policy Review, 34,* 65-68.

Regnery, A. S. (1986). A federal perspective on juvenile justice reform. *Crime and Delinquency, 32,* 39-51.

Reiman, J. H. (1979). *The rich get richer and the poor get prison.* New York: Wiley.

Reinarman, C., & Levine, H. G. (1989). Crack in context: Politics and media in the making of a drug scare. *Contemporary Drug Problems, 16,* 535-543.

Reiner, I. (1992). *Gangs, crime and violence in Los Angeles.* Unpublished manuscript, Office of the District Attorney of the County of Los Angeles.

Reiss, A. J. (1988). Co-offending and criminal careers. In M. Tonry & N. Morris (Eds.), *Crime and justice: An annual review of research* (Vol. 10, pp. 117-170). Chicago: University of Chicago Press.

Reiss, A. J., & Roth, J. A. (1993). *Understanding and preventing violence* (Report of the Panel on the Understanding and Control of Violent Behavior, National Academy of Sciences). Washington, DC: National Academy of Sciences.

Research and Action. (1981). *Increasing the capacity of voluntary organizations for the prevention and treatment of delinquency among girls.* New York: Author.

Rhoden, E. (1994). Disproportionate minority representation: First steps to a solution. *Juvenile Justice, 2,* 9-14.

Ribisl, K. M., & Davidson, W. S., II. (1993). Community change interventions. In A. Goldstein & C. R. Huff (Eds.), *The gang intervention handbook* (pp. 333-355). Champaign, IL: Research Press.

Ridge, T. (1995, May 1). News release. Harrisburg, PA: Office of the Governor.

Rivara, F. P., & Farrington, D. P. (in press). Head injury and criminal behavior. In D. Johnson, B. Pentland, & E. Glasgow (Eds.), *Head injury and litigation.* London: Sweet & Maxwell.

Rivers, J., & Trotti, T. (1995). *South Carolina delinquent males: An 11-year follow-up into adult probation and prisons.* Report prepared for the Office of Juvenile Justice and Delinquency Prevention, U.S. Department of Justice.

Roberts, A. R. (1987). National survey and assessment of 66 treatment programs for juvenile offenders. *Juvenile and Family Court Journal, 38,* 39-45.

Roberts, J. (1987). *Child sexual abuse: An analysis of case processing* (Report to the National Institute of Justice). Washington, DC: American Bar Association.

Robin, G. D. (1967). Gang member delinquency in Philadelphia. In M. W. Klein & B. G. Myerhoff (Eds.), *Juvenile gangs in context* (pp. 15-24). Englewood Cliffs, NJ: Prentice Hall.

Robins, L. N. (1966). *Deviant children grown up: A sociological and psychiatric study of sociopathic personality.* Baltimore: Williams & Wilkins.

Robins, L. N. (1979). Sturdy childhood predictors of adult outcomes: Replications from longitudinal studies. In J. M. Barrett, R. M. Rose, & G. L. Klerman (Eds.), *Stress and mental disorder* (pp. 219-235). New York: Raven.

Robins, L. N., West, P. J., & Herjanic, B. L. (1975). Arrests and delinquency in two generations: A study of black urban families and their children. *Journal of Child Psychology and Psychiatry, 16*, 125-140.

Romero, G., & Brown, D. E. (1995). *State progress in addressing youth violence.* Washington, DC: National Governor's Association.

Roscoe, M., & Morton, R. (1994). *Disproportionate minority confinement* (Fact Sheet #11). Washington, DC: Office of Juvenile Justice and Delinquency Prevention.

Rosenbaum, D. P., Lewis, D. A., & Grant, J. A. (1986). Neighborhood-based crime prevention: Assessing the efficacy of community organizing in Chicago. In D. P. Rosenbaum (Ed.), *Community crime prevention: Does it work?* (pp. 109-133). Beverly Hills, CA: Sage.

Rosenberg, M. L., & Fenley, M. A. (Eds.). (1991). *Violence in America: A public health approach.* New York: Oxford University Press.

Rosenberg, M. L., & Mercy, J. A. (1986). Homicide epidemiologic analysis at the national level. *Bulletin of the New York Academy of Medicine, 62*, 382-390.

Rosenheim, M. K. (1973). Detention facilities and temporary shelters. In D. Pappenfort (Ed.), *Child caring: Social policy and the institution* (pp. 253-299). Chicago: Aldine.

Rosenheim, M. K. (Ed.). (1976). *Pursuing justice for the child.* Chicago: University of Chicago Press.

Rothman, D. J. (1971). *The discovery of the asylum: Social order and disorder in the new republic.* Boston: Little, Brown.

Rothman, D. J. (1980). *Conscience and convenience: The asylum and its alternatives in progressive America.* Boston: Little, Brown.

Roush, D. W. (1996a). *Desktop guide to good detention practice.* Washington, DC: U.S. Department of Justice, Office of Juvenile Justice and Delinquency Prevention.

Roush, D. W. (1996b). *Juvenile detention training needs assessment: Research report.* Washington, DC: U.S. Department of Justice, Office of Juvenile Justice and Delinquency Prevention.

Roy, M. B., & Sagan, R. (1980). *Juvenile bindovers in Massachusetts—1979.* Unpublished paper, Massachusetts Commissioner of Probation, Boston.

Roysher, M., & Edelman, P. (1981). Treating juveniles as adults in New York: What does it mean and how is it working? In J. C. Hall, D. M. Hamparian, J. M. Pettibone, & J. L. White (Eds.), *Major issues in juvenile justice information and training* (pp. 265-293). Columbus, OH: Academy for Contemporary Problems.

Rubin, S. (1961). *Crime and juvenile delinquency—A rational approach to penal problems* (2nd ed.). New York: Oceana.

Rudenstine, S. (1995). *Juvenile admissions to state custody, 1993* (Fact Sheet #27). Washington, DC: Office of Juvenile Justice and Delinquency Prevention.

Rudenstine, S., & Moone, J. (1995). *Juvenile admissions to state custody, 1992* (Fact Sheet #23). Washington, DC: Office of Juvenile Justice and Delinquency Prevention.

Rudman, C., Hartstone, E., Fagan, J., & Moore, M. (1986). Violent youth in adult court: Process and punishment. *Crime and Delinquency, 32*, 75-96.

Rutter, M. (1980). *Changing youth in a changing society.* Cambridge, MA: Harvard University Press.

Rutter, M. (1985). Resilience in the face of adversity: Protective factors and resistance to psychiatric disorder. *British Journal of Psychiatry, 147*, 598-611.

Rutter, M. (1986). The developmental psychopathology of depression: Issues and perspectives. In M. Rutter, C. Izard, & P. B. Read (Eds.), *Depression in young people: Developmental and clinical perspectives.* New York: Guilford.

Rutter, M., Maughan, B., Mortimore, P., Ouston, J., & Smith, A. (1979). *Fifteen thousand hours: Secondary schools and their effects on children.* Cambridge, MA: Harvard University Press.

Sagatun, I., McCollum, L. L., & Edwards, L. P. (1985). The effect of transfers from juvenile to criminal court: A loglinear analysis. *Crime and Justice, 7*, 65-92.

Sampson, R. (1992). Family management and child development: Insights from social disorganization theory. In J. McCord (Ed.), *Advances in criminological theory* (Vol. 3, pp. 63-94). New Brunswick, NJ: Transaction.

Sampson, R. J. (1993). Family and community-level influences on crime: A contextual theory and strategies for research testing. In D. P. Farrington, R. J. Sampson, & P-O. H. Wikstrom (Eds.), *Integrating individual and ecological aspects of crime* (pp. 153-168). Stockholm: National Council for Crime Prevention.

Sampson, R. J., Castellano, T. C., & Laub, J. H. (1981). *Juvenile criminal behavior and its relation to neighborhood characteristics.* Washington, DC: U.S. Department of Justice, Office of Juvenile Justice and Delinquency Prevention.

Sampson, R. J., & Groves, W. B. (1989). Community structure and crime: Testing social disorganization theory. *American Journal of Sociology, 94*, 774-802.

Sampson, R. J., & Laub, J. H. (1990). Crime and deviance over the life course: The salience of adult social bonds. *American Sociological Review, 55*, 609-627.

Sampson, R. J., & Laub, J. H. (1993). *Crime in the making: Pathways and turning points through life.* Cambridge, MA: Harvard University Press.

Sampson, R. J., & Laub, J. H. (1994). Urban poverty and the family context of delinquency: A new look at structure and process in a classic study. *Child Development, 65,* 523-540.

Sanchez-Jankowski, M. S. (1991). *Islands in the street: Gangs and American urban society.* Berkeley: University of California Press.

Sanders, W. (1994). *Gangbangs and drive-bys: Grounded culture and juvenile gang violence.* New York: Aldine de Gruyter.

San Diego County Probation Department. (1996). *Juvenile correctional intervention program.* San Diego, CA: Author.

Santayana, G. (1948). *The life of reason.* New York: Charles Scribner's Sons.

Sarri, R. (1973). The detention of youth in jails and juvenile detention facilities. *Juvenile Justice, 24,* 2-18.

Sarri, R. (1974). *Under lock and key: Juveniles in jail and detention.* Ann Arbor: University of Michigan, National Assessment of Juvenile Corrections Project.

Sarri, R. (1981). The effectiveness paradox: Institutional vs. community placement of offenders. *Journal of Social Issues, 37,* 34-50.

Sarri, R., & Hasenfeld, Y. (1976). *Brought to justice? Juveniles, the courts, and the law.* Ann Arbor: University of Michigan, National Assessment of Juvenile Corrections Project.

Scardino, A. (1985, August 26). Experts question data on missing children. *Daily Journal* (Los Angeles), p. A1.

Schlossman, S. L. (1977). *Love and the American delinquent: The theory and practice of "progressive" juvenile justice.* Chicago: University of Chicago Press.

Schneider, A. (Ed.). (1985a). *Guide to juvenile restitution.* Washington, DC: Office of Juvenile Justice and Delinquency Prevention.

Schneider, A. (1985b). *The impact of deinstitutionalization on recidivism and secure confinement of status offenders.* Washington, DC: Office of Juvenile Justice and Delinquency Prevention.

Schneider, A. (1986). Restitution and recidivism rates of juvenile offenders: Results from four experimental studies. *Criminology, 24,* 533-552.

Schneider, A., & Schneider, P. (1980). Overview of restitution program models in the juvenile justice system. *Juvenile and Family Court Journal, 31,* 3-22.

Schneider, A., & Warner, J. (1989). *National trends in juvenile restitution programming.* Washington, DC: Office of Juvenile Justice and Delinquency Prevention.

Schneider, P., Griffith, W., & Schneider, A. (1980). *Juvenile restitution as a sole sanction or condition of probation—An empirical analysis.* Washington,

DC: Office of Juvenile Justice and Delinquency Prevention.

Schneider, P., & Schneider, A. (1977). Restitution requirements for juvenile offenders: A survey of practices in American juvenile courts. *Juvenile Justice Journal, 18,* 43-56.

Schneider, P., Schneider, A., Griffith, W., & Wilson, M. (1982). *A two-year report on the national evaluation of the juvenile restitution initiative: An overview of program performance* (Report to the U.S. Department of Justice, Office of Juvenile Justice and Delinquency Prevention). Washington, DC: U.S. Department of Justice, Office of Juvenile Justice and Delinquency Prevention.

Schorr, L. B. (1988). *Within our reach: Breaking the cycle of disadvantage.* New York: Doubleday.

Schur, E. (1971). *Labeling deviant behavior: Its sociological implications.* New York: Harper and Row.

Schur, E. (1973). *Radical non-intervention: Rethinking the delinquency problem.* Englewood Cliffs, NJ: Prentice Hall.

Schweinhart, L. J., Barnes, H. V., & Weikart, D. P. (1993). *Significant benefits: The High/Scope Perry Preschool Study through age 27.* Ypsilanti, MI: High/Scope Press.

Sechrest, L., White, S. O., & Brown, E. D. (1979). *The rehabilitation of criminal offenders: Problems and prospects.* Washington, DC: National Academy of Sciences.

Sedlak, A. (1990). Technical amendment to the study findings—National incidence and prevalence of child abuse and neglect: 1988. Rockville, MD: Westat.

Seitz, V., & Apfel, N. (1994). Parent-focused intervention: Diffusion effects on siblings. *Child Development, 65,* 667-683.

Shannon, L. W. (1988). *Criminal career continuity.* New York: Human Sciences Press.

Shannon, L. W. (1991). *Changing patterns of delinquency and crime: A longitudinal study in Racine.* Boulder, CO: Westview.

Shanok, S. S. (1983). A comparison of delinquent and nondelinquent adolescent psychiatric inpatients. *American Journal of Psychiatry, 140,* 582-585.

Shaw, C. R., & McKay, H. D. (1931). *Social factors in juvenile delinquency: Report on the causes of crime* (Vol. II). Washington, DC: Government Printing Office.

Shaw, C. R., & McKay, H. D. (1942). *Juvenile delinquency and urban areas.* Chicago: University of Chicago Press.

Sheley, J. F., & Wright, J. D. (1993). *Gun acquisition and possession in selected juvenile samples* (Research in Brief). Washington, DC: National Institute of Justice and Office of Juvenile Justice and Delinquency Prevention.

Sheley, J. F., & Wright, J. D. (1995). *In the line of fire: Youth, guns and violence in urban America.* Hawthorne, NY: Aldine de Gruyter.

Sherman, L. W. (1993). Defiance, deterrence, and irrelevance: A theory of the criminal sanction. *Journal of Research in Crime and Delinquency, 30,* 445-473.

Sherman, L. W., Shaw, J. W., & Rogan, D. P. (1995, January). *The Kansas City gun experiment* (Research in Brief). Washington, DC: U.S. Department of Justice, National Institute of Justice.

Shin, Y. (1981). Differentials in homicide in the United States, 1930-1975: A demographic study. Unpublished doctoral dissertation, University of Georgia, Athens.

Short, J. F., Jr. (1996). *Gangs and adolescent violence.* Boulder, CO: University of Colorado, Center for the Study and Prevention of Violence.

Short, J. F., Jr., & Strodtbeck, F. L. (1965). *Group process and gang delinquency.* Chicago: University of Chicago Press.

Silberberg, N. E., & Silberberg, M. C. (1971). School achievement and delinquency. *Journal of Educational Research, 41,* 17-33.

Singer, S. I. (1986). Victims of serious violence and their criminal behavior: Subcultural theory and beyond. *Violence and Victims, 1,* 61-70.

Singer, S. I. (1993). The automatic waiver of juveniles and substantive justice. *Crime and Delinquency, 39,* 253-261.

Singer, S. I. (1994). *The case processing of juvenile offenders in criminal court and legislative waiver in New York State* (Report to the U.S. Department of Justice, Office of Juvenile Justice and Delinquency Prevention). Washington, DC: U.S. Department of Justice, Office of Juvenile Justice and Delinquency Prevention.

Singer, S. I. (1996). *Recriminalizing delinquency: Violent juvenile crime and juvenile justice reform.* New York: Cambridge University Press.

Singer, S. I., & Ewing, C. E. (1986). Juvenile justice reform in New York State: The Juvenile Offender Law. *Law and Policy, 8,* 457-483.

Singer, S. I., & McDowall, D. (1988). Criminalizing delinquency: The deterrent effects of the juvenile offender law. *Law and Society Review, 22,* 521-535.

Skogan, W. G. (1990). *Disorder and decline: Crime and the spiral of decay in American neighborhoods.* New York: Free Press.

Skolnick, J. H. (1989). *Gang organization and migration—Drugs, gangs, and law enforcement.* Unpublished manuscript, University of California, Berkeley.

Skolnick, J. H., Correl, T., Navarro, E., & Rabb, R. (1990). The social structure of street drug dealing. *American Journal of Police, 9,* 1-41.

Slaby, R. G., & Roedell, W. C. (1982). Development and regulation of aggression in young children. In J. Worrell (Ed.), *Psychological development in the elementary years* (pp. 97-149). San Diego, CA: Academic Press.

Slott, I. (1991, November). *Lasting effects of the Office of Juvenile Justice and Delinquency Prevention.* Paper presented at the annual meeting of the American Society of Criminology, San Francisco.

Smith, C., Lizotte, A. J., Thornberry, T. P., & Krohn, M. D. (1995). Resilient youth: Identifying factors that prevent high-risk youth from engaging in delinquency and drug use. In J. Hagan (Ed.), *Delinquency in the life course* (pp. 217-247). Greenwich, CT: JAI.

Smith, C., & Thornberry, T. P. (1995). The relationship between childhood maltreatment and adolescent involvement in delinquency. *Criminology, 33,* 451-477.

Smith, D. J. (1995). Youth crime and conduct disorders: Trends, patterns, and causal explanations. In M. Rutter & D. Smith (Eds.), *Psychosocial disorders in young people: Time trends and their causes* (pp. 389-489). New York: Wiley.

Smith, L. (1996, March 30). Discipline out of desperation. *The Washington Post,* pp. H1, H11.

Smith, M. D. (1986). The era of increased violence in the United States: Age, period, or cohort effect? *Sociological Quarterly, 27,* 239-251.

Snyder, H. N. (1988). *Court careers of juvenile offenders.* Washington, DC: U.S. Department of Justice, Office of Juvenile Justice and Delinquency Prevention.

Snyder, H. N. (1994). *The criminal victimization of young children.* Pittsburgh, PA: National Center for Juvenile Justice.

Snyder, H. N., & Hutzler, J. L. (1981). *The serious juvenile offender: The scope of the problem and the response of juvenile courts.* Pittsburgh, PA: National Center for Juvenile Justice.

Snyder, H. N., & Sickmund, M. (1995). *Juvenile offenders and victims: A national report.* Washington, DC: U.S. Department of Justice, Office of Juvenile Justice and Delinquency Prevention.

Snyder, H. N., Sickmund, M., & Poe-Yamagata, E. (1996). *Juvenile offenders and victims: 1996 update on violence.* Washington, DC: U.S. Department of Justice, Office of Juvenile Justice and Delinquency Prevention.

Snyder, J., & Patterson, G. R. (1987). Family interaction and delinquent behavior. In H. C. Quay (Ed.), *Handbook of juvenile delinquency* (pp. 216-243). New York: Wiley.

Sobie, M. (1981). *The Juvenile Offender Act: A study of the act's effectiveness and impact on the New York juvenile justice system.* New York: Foundation for Child Development.

Soler, M. (1988). Litigation on behalf of children in adult jails. *Crime and Delinquency, 34,* 190-208.

Soriano, F. I. (1993). Cultural sensitivity and gang intervention. In A. Goldstein & C. R. Huff (Eds.), *The gang intervention handbook* (pp. 441-461). Champaign, IL: Research Press.

Sosin, D. M., Sniezek, J. E., & Waxweiler, R. J. (1995). Trends in death associated with traumatic brain injury, 1979 through 1992. *Journal of the American Medical Association, 273,* 1778-1780.

Spergel, I. A. (1984). Violent gangs in Chicago: In search of social policy. *Social Service Review, 58,* 199-226.

Spergel, I. A. (1991). *Youth gangs: Problem and response* (Report to the U.S. Department of Justice, Office of Juvenile Justice and Delinquency Prevention). Washington, DC: U.S. Department of Justice, Office of Juvenile Justice and Delinquency Prevention.

Spergel, I. A. (1995). *The youth gang problem.* New York: Oxford University Press.

Spergel, I. A., Chance, R. L., Ehrensaft, K., Regulus, T., Kane, C., & Alexander, A. (1992). *Prototype/models for gang intervention and suppression* (Report to the U.S. Department of Justice, Office of Juvenile Justice and Delinquency Prevention). Washington, DC: U.S. Department of Justice, Office of Juvenile Justice and Delinquency Prevention.

Spergel, I. A., Chance, L. R., Ehrensaft, K., Regulus, T., Kane, C., & Laseter, R. (1992). *Technical assistance manuals: National youth gang suppression and intervention program* (Report to the U.S. Department of Justice, Office of Juvenile Justice and Delinquency Prevention). Washington, DC: U.S. Department of Justice, Office of Juvenile Justice and Delinquency Prevention.

Spergel, I. A., Chance, L. R., Ehrensaft, K., Regulus, T., Kane, C., Laseter, R., Alexander, A., & Oh, S. (1994). *Gang suppression and intervention: Community models.* Washington, DC: U.S. Department of Justice, Office of Juvenile Justice and Delinquency Prevention.

Spergel, I. A., & Curry, G. D. (1993). The National Youth Gang Survey: A research and development process. In A. Goldstein & C. R. Huff (Eds.), *The gang intervention handbook* (pp. 359-400). Champaign, IL: Research Press.

Spergel, I. A., Curry, G. D., Chance, R., Kane, C., Ross, R., Alexander, A., Simmons, E., & Oh, S. (1994). *Gang suppression and intervention: Problem and response.* Washington, DC: U.S. Department of Justice, Office of Juvenile Justice and Delinquency Prevention.

Spergel, I. A., & Grossman, S. F. (1994, November). *Gang violence and crime theory: Gang violence reduction project.* Paper presented at the annual meeting of the American Society of Criminology, Miami.

Spergel, I. A., & Grossman, S. F. (1995, July). *Little Village gang violence reduction program.* Paper presented at the Annual Conference on Criminal Justice Research and Evaluation, Washington, DC.

Starkley, M. L. (1949). *The devil in Massachusetts.* New York: Knopf.

Stattin, H., & Magnusson, D. (1991). Stability and change in criminal behavior up to age 30. *British Journal of Criminology, 31,* 327-346.

Stattin, H., Magnusson, D., & Reichel, H. (1989). Criminal activity at different ages: A study based on a Swedish longitudinal research population. *British Journal of Criminology, 29,* 368-385.

Stephan, J. (1990). *Census of local jails, 1988.* Washington, DC: U.S. Department of Justice, Bureau of Justice Statistics.

Stephens, R. D. (1994). The taming of the crew. *School Safety, 2*(Fall), 1-2.

Stouthamer-Loeber, M., Loeber, R., Van Kammen, W. B., & Zhang, Q. (1995). Uninterrupted delinquent careers: The timing of parental help-seeking and juvenile court contact. *Studies on Crime & Crime Prevention: Biannual Review, 4,* 236-251.

Straus, M. A. (1995). Trends in cultural norms and rates of partner violence: An update to 1992. In S. M. Stith & M. A. Straus (Eds.), *Understanding partner violence: Prevalence, causes, consequences, and solutions* (pp. 30-33). Minneapolis, MN: National Council on Family Relations.

Straus, M. A., & Gelles, R. J. (1990). *Physical violence in American families: Risk factors and adaptations to violence in 8,145 families.* New Brunswick, NJ: Transaction.

Straus, M. A., Gelles, R., & Steinmetz, S. K. (1980). *Behind closed doors: Violence in the American family.* New York: Doubleday.

Street, D., Vinter, R., & Perrow, C. (1966). *Organization for treatment: A comparative study of institutions for delinquents.* New York: Macmillan.

Strodtbeck, F. L., & Short, J. F., Jr. (1964). Aleatory risks versus short-run hedonism in explanation of gang action. *Social Problems, 12,* 127-140.

Stroul, B., & Friedman, R. (1986). *A system of care for severely emotionally disturbed youth.* Washington, DC: Georgetown University, Child and Adolescent Service System Program Technical Assistance Center.

Studzinski, A., & Pierce, S. (n.d.). *How Illinois deals with status offenders.* Chicago: Illinois Department of Juvenile and Family Services.

Subcommittee on Human Resources, Committee on Education and Labor, U.S. House of Representatives. (1980). *Juvenile Justice Amendments of 1980.*

Substance Abuse and Mental Health Services Administration. (1994, November). *1994 preliminary estimates of drug-related emergency department episodes* (Advance Report Number 11). Rockville, MD: U.S. Department of Health and Human Services.

Substance Abuse and Mental Health Services Administration. (1995, September). *Preliminary estimates from the 1994 National Household Survey on Drug Abuse* (Advance Report No. 10). Rockville, MD: U.S. Department of Health and Human Services.

Sullivan, C. E., Grant, M. Q., & Grant, J. D. (1957). The development of interpersonal maturity: Applications to delinquency. *Psychiatry, 20*, 272-283.

Sullivan, M. L. (1989). *Getting paid: Youth crime and work in the inner city*. Ithaca, NY: Cornell University Press.

Sumner, H. (1971). Locking them up. *Crime and Delinquency, 17*, 168-179.

Suro, R. (1996, December 13). Violent crime drops among young teens. *The Washington Post*, pp. A1, A19.

Sussman, F., & Baum, F. (1969). *Law of juvenile delinquency* (3rd ed.). New York: Oceana.

Sweet, R. W. (1990, December). "Missing children": Found facts. *NIJ Reports*, pp. 15-16.

Taggart, R. (1995). *Quantum Opportunity Program*. Philadelphia, PA: Opportunities Industrialization Centers of America.

Tannenbaum, F. (1938). *Crime and the community*. New York: Columbia University Press.

Task Force on Juvenile Delinquency. (1967). *Task force report: Juvenile delinquency and youth crime*. Washington, DC: Government Printing Office.

Taylor, C. S. (1990a). *Dangerous society*. East Lansing: Michigan State University Press.

Taylor, C. S. (1990b). Gang imperialism. In C. R. Huff (Ed.), *Gangs in America* (pp. 103-115). Newbury Park, CA: Sage.

Teilmann, K. S., & Klein, M. W. (1979). *Summary of interim findings of the assessment of the impact of California's 1977 juvenile legislation*. Los Angeles: University of Southern California.

Teret, S. P., Wintemute, G. J., & Beilenson, P. L. (1992). The firearm fatality reporting system: A proposal. *Journal of the American Medical Association, 267*, 3073-3074.

Thomas, C. R. (1996, June). *The Second Chance Program*. Paper presented at the National Youth Gang Symposium, Dallas, TX.

Thomas, C. W. (1976). Are status offenders really so different?: A comparative and longitudinal assessment. *Crime and Delinquency, 22*, 438-455.

Thomas, C. W., & Bilchik, S. (1985). Prosecuting juveniles in criminal courts: A legal and empirical analysis. *The Journal of Criminal Law and Criminology, 76*, 439-479.

Thompson, D. W., & Jason, L. A. (1988). Street gangs and preventive interventions. *Criminal Justice Behavior, 15*, 323-333.

Thompson, D., & McAnany, P. D. (1984). Punishment and responsibility in juvenile court: Desert-based probation for delinquents. In P. D. McAnany, D. Thompson, & D. Fogel (Eds.), *Probation and justice: Reconsideration of a mission* (pp. 137-172). Cambridge, MA: Oelgeschlager Gunn & Hain.

Thornberry, T. P. (1987). Toward an interactional theory of delinquency. *Criminology, 25*, 863-891.

Thornberry, T. P. (1993). *Urban delinquency and substance abuse: Technical report*. Unpublished manuscript, The University at Albany, Albany, NY.

Thornberry, T. P. (1994). *Violent families and youth violence* (Fact Sheet #21). Washington, DC: Office of Juvenile Justice and Delinquency Prevention.

Thornberry, T. P. (1996). Empirical support for interactional theory: A review of the literature. In J. D. Hawkins (Ed.), *Delinquency and crime: Current theories* (pp. 198-235). New York: Cambridge University Press.

Thornberry, T. P. (in press). Gangs and serious, violent, and chronic offenders. In R. Loeber & D. P. Farrington (Eds.), *Serious and violent juvenile offenders: Risk factors and successful interventions*. Thousand Oaks, CA: Sage.

Thornberry, T. P., Huizinga, D., & Loeber, R. (1995). The prevention of serious delinquency and violence: Implications from the Program of Research on the Causes and Correlates of Delinquency. In J. C. Howell, B. Krisberg, J. D. Hawkins, & J. J. Wilson (Eds.), *Sourcebook on serious, violent, and chronic juvenile offenders* (pp. 213-237). Thousand Oaks, CA: Sage.

Thornberry, T. P., Krohn, M. D., Lizotte, A. J., & Chard-Wierschem, D. (1993). The role of juvenile gangs in facilitating delinquent behavior. *Journal of Research in Crime and Delinquency, 30*, 55-87.

Thornberry, T. P., Lizotte, A. J., Krohn, M. D., Farnworth, M., & Jang, S. J. (1991). Testing interactional theory: An examination of reciprocal causal relationships among family, school, and delinquency. *The Journal of Criminal Law and Criminology, 82*, 3-35.

Thornberry, T. P., Lizotte, A. J., Krohn, M. D., Farnworth, M., & Jang, S. J. (1994). Delinquent peers, beliefs, and delinquent behavior: A longitudinal test of interactional theory. *Criminology, 32*, 601-637.

Thurman, Q. C., Giacomazzi, A. L., Reisig, M. D., & Mueller, D. G. (1996). Community-based gang prevention and intervention: An evaluation of the Neutral Zone. *Crime and Delinquency, 42*, 279-295.

Tolan, P. H. (1990). *Pathways of adolescent antisocial behavior* (National Institute of Mental Health Grant Proposal ROI 48248, available from National Institute of Mental Health, 5600 Fishers Lane, Rockville, MD 20857).

Tolan, P. H., Guerra, N. G., & Kendall, P. C. (1995). A developmental-ecological perspective on antisocial behavior in children and adolescents: Toward a unified risk and intervention framework. *Journal of Consulting and Clinical Psychology, 63*, 579-584.

Tonry, M. J. (1994a). *Malign neglect: Race, crime, and punishment in America*. New York: Oxford University Press.

Tonry, M. (1994b). Racial politics, racial disparities, and the war on crime. *Crime and Delinquency, 40*, 475-494.

Tonry, M., & Farrington, D. P. (1995). Strategic approaches to crime prevention. In M. Tonry & D. P.

Farrington (Eds.), *Building a safer society: Strategic approaches to crime prevention* (Vol. 19, pp. 1-20). Chicago: University of Chicago Press.

Tonry, M., Ohlin, L. E., & Farrington, D. P. (1991). *Human development and criminal behavior: New ways of advancing knowledge* (Research in Criminology series). New York: Springer-Verlag.

Torbet, P., Gable, R., Hurst, H., Montgomery, I., Szymanski, L., & Thomas, D. (1996). *State responses to serious and violent juvenile crime*. Washington, DC: U.S. Department of Justice, Office of Juvenile Justice and Delinquency Prevention.

Tracy, P. E. (1979). *Subcultural delinquency: A comparison of the incidence and seriousness of gang and nongang member offensivity*. Unpublished manuscript, University of Pennsylvania, Center for Studies in Criminology and Criminal Law, Philadelphia.

Tracy, P. E., Wolfgang, M. E., & Figlio, R. M. (1990). *Delinquency careers in two birth cohorts*. New York: Plenum.

Treanor, W. (1986a, April 10). Feeding the hysteria that masks the truth. *USA Today*, pp. A1-A2.

Treanor, W. (1986b, August 4). Testimony before the Subcommittee on Human Resources, House Committee on Education and Labor. (Testimony and Index to Testimony available from American Youth Work Center, 1200 17th St., N.W., Washington, DC 20036)

Tremblay, R. E., & Craig, W. M. (1995). Developmental crime prevention. In M. Tonry & D. P. Farrington (Eds.), *Building a safer society: Strategic approaches to crime prevention* (Vol. 19, pp. 151-236). Chicago: University of Chicago Press.

Tremblay, R. E., Vitaro, F., Bertrand, L., LeBlanc, M., Beauchesne, H., Boileau, H., & David, L. (1992). Parent and child training to prevent early onset of delinquency: The Montreal longitudinal experimental study. In J. McCord & R. Tremblay (Eds.), *Preventing antisocial behavior* (pp. 117-138). New York: Guilford.

Twentieth Century Fund Task Force on Sentencing Policy Toward Young Offenders. (1978). *Confronting youth crime*. New York: Holmes & Meier.

Twig, B. (1996, April 19). New danger—anger—hogging the road. *USA Today*, p. A3.

U.S. Department of Health and Human Services. (1995, December 15). *National survey results on drug use from the Monitoring the Future Study* (press release). Washington, DC: Author.

U.S. Department of Justice. (1996, June 20). *New survey finds 25,000 youth gangs with more than 650,000 members* (press release). Washington, DC: Author.

United States Children's Bureau. (1964). *Delinquent children in penal institutions* (Pub. No. 45). Washington, DC: U.S. Department of Health, Education, and Welfare.

United States Children's Bureau. (1968). *Uniform Juvenile Court Act*. Washington, DC: Department of Health, Education, and Welfare. (Also in *Uniform laws annotated*, Vol. 9-A, sec. 34)

United States Children's Bureau. (1969). *Legislative guide for drafting family and juvenile court acts*. Washington, DC: Department of Health, Education, and Welfare.

Uting, D., Bright, J., & Henrickson, C. (1993). *Crime and the family*. London: Family Policy Studies Centre.

Van den Haag, E. (1975). *Punishing criminals: Concerning a very old and painful question*. New York: Basic Books.

Van Dusen, K. T. (1981). *Adult court transfer: A move toward tougher handling?* Report submitted to the U.S. Department of Justice, Office of Juvenile Justice and Delinquency Prevention.

Van Kammen, W. B., & Loeber, R. (1994a). Are fluctuations in delinquent activities related to the onset and offset in juvenile illegal drug use and drug dealing? *Journal of Drug Issues, 24*, 9-24.

Van Kammen, W. B., & Loeber, R. (1994b, November). *Delinquency, drug use and the onset of adolescent drug dealing*. Paper presented at the annual meeting of the American Society of Criminology, Miami.

Van Kammen, W. B., Maguin, E., & Loeber, R. (1994). Initiation of drug selling and its relationship with illicit drug use and serious delinquency in adolescent boys. In E. G. M. Weitekamp & H.-J. Kerner (Eds.), *Cross-national longitudinal research on human development and criminal behavior* (pp. 229-241). Netherlands: Kluwer.

Van Vleet, R., & Butts, J. A. (1990). *Risk assessment of committed delinquents: Nebraska Youth Development Center*. Ann Arbor: University of Michigan, Center for the Study of Youth Policy.

Vigil, J. D. (1988). *Barrio gangs: Street life and identity in Southern California*. Austin: University of Texas Press.

Vigil, J. D., & Yun, S. C. (1990). Vietnamese youth gangs in Southern California. In C. R. Huff (Ed.), *Gangs in America* (pp. 146-162). Newbury Park, CA: Sage.

Vinter, R. (Ed.) (1976). *Time out: A national study of juvenile correctional programs*. Ann Arbor: University of Michigan, National Assessment of Juvenile Corrections Project.

Vinter, R., Downs, G., & Hall, J. (1975). *Juvenile corrections in the states: Residential programs and deinstitutionalization*. Ann Arbor: University of Michigan, National Assessment of Juvenile Corrections Project.

Violent and irrational—And that's just the policy. (1996, June 8-14). *The Economist*, p. 23.

Virginia Commission on Youth. (1994). *The study of serious juvenile offenders* (General Assembly of Virginia, House Document No. 81). Richmond: General Assembly of Virginia.

Von Hirsch, A. (1976). *Doing justice: The choice of punishments*. New York: Hill and Wang.

Vorenberg, J. (1972, May). The war on crime: The first five years. *The Atlantic*, pp. 63-69.

Wagner, M., D'Amico, R., Marder, C., Newman, L., & Blackorby, J. (1992). *What happens next? Trends in postschool outcomes of youth with disabilities*. Menlo Park, CA: SRI International.

Waldorf, D. (1993). Don't be your own best customer—Drug use of San Francisco gang drug sellers. *Crime, Law and Social Change, 19*, 1-15.

Walsh, J. (1984, April 18). Statement made on the MacNeil/Lehrer NewsHour. Chevy Chase, MD: Radio TV Reports, Inc.

Wang, Z. (1995). Gang affiliation among Asian-American high school students: A path analysis of a social developmental model. *Journal of Gang Research, 2*, 1-13.

Warr, M. (1996). Organization and instigation in delinquent groups. *Criminology, 34*, 11-37.

Watts, R. J. (1991, June). *Manhood development for African-American boys: Program and organization development*. Paper presented at the American Society for Community Research and Action, Tempe, AZ.

Weeks, H. (1958). *Youthful offenders at Highfields*. Ann Arbor: University of Michigan Press.

Weiner, N. A. (1989). Violent criminal careers and "violent career criminals." In N. A. Weiner & M. E. Wolfgang (Eds.), *Violent crime, violent criminals* (pp. 35-138). Newbury Park, CA: Sage.

Weis, J. G. (1979). *Jurisdiction and the elusive status offender: A comparison of involvement in delinquent behavior and status offenses*. Washington, DC: National Institute for Juvenile Justice and Delinquency Prevention.

Weis, J. G., & Hawkins, J. D. (1979). *Preventing delinquency*. Washington, DC: U.S. Department of Justice, Office of Juvenile Justice and Delinquency Prevention.

Weis, J. G., & Sederstrom, J. (1981). *The prevention of serious delinquency: What to do?* Washington, DC: U.S. Department of Justice, Office of Juvenile Justice and Delinquency Prevention.

Weitekamp, E. G. M., Kerner, H.-J., Schindler, V., & Schubert, A. (1995). On the "dangerousness" of chronic/habitual offenders: A re-analysis of the 1945 Philadelphia birth cohort data. *Studies on Crime and Prevention, 42*, 159-175.

Werner, E. E., & Smith, R. S. (1982). *Vulnerable but invincible*. New York: McGraw-Hill.

Werner, E. E., & Smith, R. S. (1992). *Overcoming the odds*. Ithaca, NY: Cornell University Press.

West, D. J., & Farrington, D. P. (1973). *Who becomes delinquent?*. London: Heinemann.

West, D. J., & Farrington, D. P. (1977). *The delinquent way of life*. London: Heinemann.

Weston, J. (1993). Community policing: An approach to youth gangs in a medium-sized city. *The Police Chief, 60*, 80-84.

Whitaker, C. J., & Bastian, L. D. (1991). *Teenage victims: A national crime survey report*. Washington,

DC: U.S. Department of Justice, Bureau of Justice Statistics.

White, J. (1985). *The comparative dispositions study* (Report to the U.S. Department of Justice, Office of Juvenile Justice and Delinquency Prevention). Washington, DC: U.S. Department of Justice, Office of Juvenile Justice and Delinquency Prevention.

Whitebread, C. H., & Batey, R. (1981). The role of waiver in the juvenile court: Questions of philosophy and function. In J. C. Hall, D. M. Hamparian, J. M. Pettibone, & J. L. White (Eds.), *Major issues in juvenile justice information and training* (pp. 207-226). Columbus, OH: Academy for Contemporary Problems.

Whitlatch, W. G. (1987). A brief history of the National Council. *Juvenile and Family Court Journal, 38*, 1-13.

Widom, C. S. (1989a). The cycle of violence. *Science, 244*, 160-166.

Widom, C. S. (1989b). Does violence beget violence? A critical examination of the literature. *Psychological Bulletin, 106*, 3-28.

Widom, C. S. (1992). *The cycle of violence* (Research in Brief). Washington, DC: U.S. Department of Justice, National Institute of Justice.

Wiebush, R. G., Baird, C., Krisberg, B., & Onek, D. (1995). Risk assessment and classification for serious, violent, and chronic juvenile offenders. In J. C. Howell, B. Krisberg, J. D. Hawkins, & J. Wilson (Eds.), *Sourcebook on serious, violent, and chronic juvenile offenders* (pp. 171-212). Thousand Oaks, CA: Sage.

Williams, T. (1989). *The cocaine kids: The inside story of a teenage drug ring*. Reading, MA: Addison-Wesley.

Wilson, H. (1987). Parental supervision re-examined. *British Journal of Criminology, 27*, 275-301.

Wilson, J. J., & Howell, J. C. (1993). *A comprehensive strategy for serious, violent, and chronic juvenile offenders*. Washington, DC: U.S. Department of Justice, Office of Juvenile Justice and Delinquency Prevention.

Wilson, J. Q. (1983a). Crime and American culture. *Public Interest, 70*, 22-48.

Wilson, J. Q. (1983b). *Thinking about crime* (rev. ed.). New York: Basic Books.

Wilson, W. J. (1987). *The truly disadvantaged: The inner city, the underclass, and public policy*. Chicago: University of Chicago Press.

Wilt, M. B. (1996). *Evaluation report to the Norfolk Interagency Consortium*. Unpublished manuscript, Virginia Commonwealth University, Department of Psychology.

Wines, E. C. (1970). *The state of prisons and child-saving institutions in the civilized world*. Carbondale: Southern Illinois University, Center for the Study of Crime, Delinquency, and Correction. (Original work published 1880)

Winters, K. C., & Henley, G. A. (1989). *Personal Experience Inventory Manual*. Los Angeles: Western Psychological Services.

Wisotsky, S. (1986). *Breaking the impasse in the war on drugs*. Westport, CT: Greenwood.

Wizner, S. (1984). Discretionary waiver of juvenile court jurisdiction: An invitation to procedural arbitrariness. *Criminal Justice Ethics*, *3*, 41-50.

Wolfgang, M. E. (1982). Abolish the juvenile court system. *California Lawyer*, *2*, 12-13.

Wolfgang, M. E., Figlio, R. M., & Sellin, T. (1972). *Delinquency in a birth cohort*. Chicago: University of Chicago Press.

Wolfgang, M. E., Thornberry, T. P., & Figlio, R. M. (1987). *From boy to man, from delinquency to crime*. Chicago: University of Chicago Press.

Wood, D. (1980, March 19). Position paper—Amending section 223(a)(13) to require removal of children from adult jails and institutions. In *Hearing before the Subcommittee on Human Resources* (pp. 267-278). Washington, DC: Committee on Education and Labor, U.S. House of Representatives.

Woodson, R. L. (Ed.). (1977). *Black perspectives on crime and the criminal justice system*. Boston: G. K. Hall.

Woodson, R. L. (1981). *A summons to life: Mediating structures and the prevention of youth crime*. Cambridge, MA: Ballinger.

Woodson, R. L. (1986). *Gang mother: The story of Sister Falaka Fattah*. Elmsford, NY: Pergamon.

Wright, J. D. (1995, March/April). Ten essential observations on guns in America. *Society*, pp. 63-68.

Yoshikawa, H. (1994). Prevention as cumulative protection: Effects of early family support and education on chronic delinquency and its risks. *Psychological Bulletin*, *115*, 1-27.

Yoshikawa, H. (1995). Long-term effects of early childhood programs on social outcomes and delinquency. *The Future of Children*, *5*, 51-75.

Young, M. (1981). Waiver from a judge's standpoint. In J. C. Hall, D. M. Hamparian, J. M. Pettibone, & J. L. White (Eds.), *Major issues in juvenile justice information and training* (pp. 309-320). Columbus, OH: Academy for Contemporary Problems.

Young, T. M., & Pappenfort, D. M. (1977). *Secure detention and alternatives to its use*. Washington, DC: U.S. Department of Justice, Law Enforcement Assistance Administration.

Zatz, M. S. (1987). Chicano youth gangs and crime: The creation of moral panic. *Contemporary Crises*, *11*, 129-158.

Zawitz, M. W. (1996, April). *Firearm injury from crime* (Selected Findings). Washington, DC: U.S. Department of Justice, Bureau of Justice Statistics.

Zimmerman, J., & Broder, P. K. (1980). A comparison of different delinquency measures derived from self-report data. *Journal of Criminal Justice*, *8*, 147-162.

Zimmerman, J., Rich, W., Keilitz, I., & Broder, P. (1981). Some observations on the link between learning disabilities and juvenile delinquency. *Journal of Criminal Justice*, *9*, 1-17.

Zimring, F. E. (1976). Street crime and new guns: Some implications for firearms control. *Journal of Criminal Justice*, *4*, 95-107.

Zimring, F. E. (1977). Determinants of the death rate from robbery: A Detroit time study. *Journal of Legal Studies*, *6*, 317-332.

Zimring, F. E. (1978). Background paper. In Twentieth Century Fund Task Force on Sentencing Policy Toward Young Offenders, *Confronting youth crime* (pp. 3-20). New York: Holmes & Meier.

Zimring, F. E. (1981a). Kids, groups and crime: Some implications of a well-known secret. *The Journal of Criminal Law & Criminology*, *72*, 867-885.

Zimring, F. (1981b). Notes toward a jurisprudence of waiver. In J. C. Hall, D. M. Hamparian, J. M. Pettibone, & J. L. White (Eds.), *Major issues in juvenile justice information and training* (pp. 193-205). Columbus, OH: Academy for Contemporary Problems.

Zimring, F. E. (1985). Violence and firearms policy. In L. A. Curtis (Ed.), *American violence and public policy* (pp. 133-152). New Haven, CT: Yale University Press.

Zimring, F. E. (1993). Policy research on firearms and violence. *Health Affairs*, *12*, 109-121.

Zimring, F. E., & Hawkins, G. J. (1973). *Deterrence*. Chicago: University of Chicago Press.

Zimring, F. E., & Hawkins, G. J. (1987). *The citizen's guide to gun control*. New York: Macmillan.

Zimring, F. E., & Hawkins, G. J. (1992). *The search for rational drug control*. New York: Cambridge University Press.

Zimring, F. E., & Hawkins, G. J. (1995). *Incapacitation: Penal confinement and the restraint of crime*. New York: Oxford University Press.

Index

About the Author

James C. (Buddy) Howell is a graduate of East Texas Baptist College (B.A., sociology). He received his Master's degree in sociology from Stephen F. Austin State University and his doctorate from the University of Colorado, where he specialized in crime and delinquency research. He is former Director of Research and Program Development at the Office of Juvenile Justice and Delinquency Prevention (OJJDP) in the U.S. Department of Justice. He held various positions in the OJJDP from its establishment in 1975 to 1995. These include Director, National Institute on Juvenile Justice and Delinquency Prevention, and Deputy Administrator, Office of Juvenile Justice and Delinquency Prevention. He also served as a member of the National Advisory Board of the National Institute of Corrections, U.S. Department of Justice; the National Advisory Committee for Juvenile Justice and Delinquency Prevention; and the federal Coordinating Council for Juvenile Justice and Delinquency Prevention. Dr. Howell is currently an Adjunct Researcher at the National Youth Gang Center in Tallahasse, FL. In addition to this work, he is conducting research on youth gangs and assisting juridictions across the country on research and program development dealing with serious, violent, and chronic offenders.